THE NOVELS
AND RELATED WORKS OF

CHARLES BROCKDEN BROWN

BICENTENNIAL EDITION

VOLUME V

CLARA HOWARD

and

JANE TALBOT

Volumes in the
Bicentennial Edition

CHARLES BROCKDEN BROWN

CLARA HOWARD

in

A SERIES OF LETTERS

JANE TALBOT

A NOVEL

Bicentennial Edition

KENT STATE UNIVERSITY PRESS

The preparation of this volume was made possible (in part) by grants from the Program for Editions, and its publication was assisted by a grant from the Publications Program, of the National Endowment for the Humanities, an independent Federal agency.

CENTER FOR
SCHOLARLY EDITIONS
AN APPROVED EDITION
MODERN LANGUAGE
ASSOCIATION OF AMERICA

Library of Congress Cataloging in Publication Data

Brown, Charles Brockden, 1771–1810.
   Clara Howard : in a series of letters ; Jane Talbot.

   (The novels and related works of Charles Brockden
Brown : v. 5)
   1. Brown, Charles Brockden, 1771–1810. Clara Howard—
Addresses, essays, lectures. 2. Brown, Charles Brockden,
1771–1810. Jane Talbot—Addresses, essays, lectures.
I. Brown, Charles Brockden, 1771–1810. Jane Talbot.
1986. II. Title. III. Title: Jane Talbot. IV. Series:
Brown, Charles Brockden, 1771–1810. Novels ; v. 5.
PZ73.B814 Nr 5, vol. 5   [PS1132]   813'.2 s [813'.2] 85-8102
ISBN 0-87338-320-6

Copyright© 1986 by the Kent State University Press
All rights reserved
ISBN 0-87338-320-6
Library of Congress Catalog Card Number: 85-8102
Manufactured in the United States of America
Designed by Harold Stevens

EDITORS

FOREWORD

This volume contains critical texts of Charles Brockden Brown's *Clara Howard* and *Jane Talbot,* the last two of his major fictional works, both in the epistolary form and both published in Philadelphia in 1801. In each case the basis of the text is the 1801 edition. The Historical Essay, which follows the text, covers matters of background, composition, publication, reception, and evaluation, whereas the Textual Essay discusses the transmission of the text, choice of copy-text, and editorial policy. A general textual statement for the entire Bicentennial Edition appears in Volume I of the series.

It is a pleasure again to acknowledge the gracious assistance of institutions and individuals who have allowed us to make use of first editions and other materials. For the loan of early editions and other copies used for collation, we wish to thank the following:

William H. Loos, *Buffalo and Erie County Public Library;* Sharon Brown and Jean W. Burnham, *The New York Society Library;* Donald Anderle and Francis O. Mattson, *The New York Public Library;* Larry E. Sullivan, *The New York Historical Society;* John A. Tedeschi and Anthony J. Amodeo, *The Newberry Library;* Robert A. Tibbetts, *The Ohio State University Library;* Laura V. Monti, *Boston Public Library;* Peter VanWingen, *Library of Congress;* Julius C. Barclay and Joan St. C. Crane, *The University of Virginia Library.*

In appreciation of their continued support and aid in facilitating the work of the Bibliographical and Textual Center, we would like to thank the following members of the Kent State University Administration, Library, and English Department:

Michael Schwartz, Terry P. Roark, Rudolph O. Buttlar, Robert Bamberg, Eugene Wenninger, Carol Toncar, Hyman Kritzer, Dean Keller, Nancy Birk, Michael R. Cole, Linda Neloms, Bruce Harkness, Bobby L. Smith, and Lee Stockdale.

We wish also to express our thanks to our graduate research assistants, Lorie Roth, Jack Lent, Laura Davis-Clapper, Ramona Stamm, and our student assistants, J. C. Givens, Donna Griffith, Diane Suchetka, Jo-May Souders, John Bezpiaty, Kathy Murnane, Diane Kushnar, Bridget Cunningham, and Jo Zuppan.

Special thanks goes to Professors Peter L. Shillingsburg and Peter L. White.

Finally, Donald A. Ringe expresses his special gratitude to his late wife, Lucy B. Ringe, for her expert research assistance while he was working on the Historical Essay to this volume.

Kent, Ohio S.J.K.
April 1984 S.W.R.

Contents

Jane Talbot's Visit to the Watchmaker's Shop

Designed by John James Barralet and
engraved by Joseph H. Seymour for
Volume IV of Conrad's Select Novels, 1801.

Courtesy of The University of Virginia

CLARA HOWARD;

in

A SERIES OF LETTERS

INTRODUCTION

TO ＿＿＿ ＿＿＿

W HAT could excite in you any curiosity as to my affairs? You once knew me a simple lad, plying the file and tweezers at the bench of a watchmaker, with no prospect before me but of labouring, for a few years, at least, as a petty and obscure journeyman, at the same bench where I worked five years as an apprentice. I was sprung from obscurity, destitute of property, of parents, of patenal friends; was full of that rustic diffidence, that inveterate humility, which are alone sufficient to divert from us the stream of fortune's favours.

Such was I three years ago! Now am I rich, happy, crowned with every terrestrial felicity, in possession of that most exquisite of all blessings, a wife, endowed with youth, grace, dignity, discretion.

I do not, on second thoughts, wonder at your curiosity. It was impossible for me to have foreseen, absurd to have hoped for such a destiny. All that has happened, was equally beyond my expectations and deservings.

You ask me how all these surprising things came about? The inclosed letters, which I have put into a regular series, contain all the information you wish. The pacquet is a precious one; you will find in it, a more lively and exact picture of my life, than it is possible, by any other means, to communicate. Preserve it, therefore, with care, and return it safely and entire, as soon as you have read it.

CLARA HOWARD

LETTER I

TO CLARA HOWARD
New-York, March 7.

WHY do I write? For whose use do I pass my time thus? There is no one living who cares a jot for me. There was a time, when a throbbing heart, a trembling hand, and eager eyes were always prepared to read, and ruminate on the scantiest and poorest scribble that dropped from my pen, but she has disappeared. The veil between us is like death.

Yet why should I so utterly despair of finding her? What all my toils may not accomplish, may be effected at a moment the least expected, and in a manner the least probable. I may travel a thousand miles, north and south, and not find her. I may lingeringly and reluctantly give up the fruitless search, and return home. A few hours after, I may stroll, in melancholy, hopeless mood, into the next street . . . and meet her. By such invisible threads is the unwitting man led through this maze of life.

But how will she be met? Perhaps . . . horrid thought! . . . she may have become vile, polluted; and how shall I endure to meet her in that condition. One so delicate, carrying dignity to the verge . . . beyond the verge of pride; preferring to starve rather than incur contempt. But that degradation is impossible.

Yet, if she dreaded not my censure, if she despaired not of my acquiescence in her schemes, why conceal from me her flight? Why not leave behind her a cold farewel. Could she be insensible to the torments and inquietudes which her silence would entail upon me. Could she question the continuance and fervency of my zeal for her welfare? What have I done to estrange her heart, to awaken her resentment?

She does not live with Sedley. That question Mr. Phillips's report has decided. At least she does not live with him as *his wife*. Impossible that Mary Wilmot should be allied to any man by a different tie. It is sacrilege so much as to whisper to one's heart the surmise. Yet have I not written it? Have I not several times pondered on it? What has so often suggested these frightful images?

This mysterious, this impenetrable silence it is, that astounds and perplexes me. This evident desire, which her conduct betrayed, to be not sought after by me, and this departure in company with Sedley; the man whom so long a devotion, so many services had not induced her to suffer his visits. To sever herself thus abruptly and forever from *me,* to whom she had given all her tenderness, with whom she had divided all her cares, during years; to whom the marriage promise had been solemnly pledged, and trust herself, on some long and incomprehensible journey with one, whom she had thought it her duty to shun; to exclude, on all occasions, from her company; is beyond my comprehension.

But I am tired of the pen already; of myself; of the world.

* * *

Ah, Clara! can so groundless a punctilio govern thee? The settled gloom of thy aspect; thy agitation, when too tenderly urged by me; thy tears, that, in spite of heroic resolutions, will sometimes find way, prove thy heart to be still mine.

But I will urge thee, I will distress thee no more. Thy last words have put an end to my importunity. Can I ever forget them, or the looks and gestures with which they were spoken?

"I never will be yours! Have I not heard all your pleas;

6

all your reasonings? And am I not now furnished with all the means of a right judgment. I have listened to you twenty times upon this topic, and always patiently. Now listen to me.

"I never will be yours, while Mary's condition is unknown. I never will be yours while she is single; unmarried to another and unhappy. I will have no intercourse with you. I will not grant you even my esteem, unless you search for her; find her; and oblige her to accept your vows.

"There is now no obstacle on account of fortune. *I* have enough for several, and will give you half. All that my parents have, and you know they are rich, they will either divide between you and me, or will give entirely to me. In either case, competence, and even abundance shall be hers and yours."

* * *

'Tis nine months since I first entered this house: not on the footing of a stranger or a guest; but of a child. Yet my claims upon my revered friend are not filial. He loves me, because all the virtues I possess are of his own planting and rearing. He that was once the pupil has now become the son.

How painful and how sweet is the review of the past year. How benign were the auspices under which I entered this house. Commended to the confidence and love of their daughter, treated with complacency, at first; then with confidence by that daughter; and, finally, honoured with her love. And yet, a single conversation; the mention of one unhappy name, has reversed totally my condition. I am still beloved by Clara; but that passion produces nothing but her misery and mine.

I must go, she tells me; and duty tells me that I must go in search of the fugitive. I will not rest till I have ascertained her destiny. Yet I can forbode nothing but evil. The truth, whatever it be, will avail me nothing.

I set out to-morrow; meanwhile Clara shall have this scribble: perhaps, she will not spurn it. Wilt thou, Clara?

7

Thou once lovedst me: perhaps, dost love me still: Yet of that I must entertain some doubts. I part with thee to-morrow, perhaps, forever. This I will put into thy hands at parting.

LETTER II

TO CLARA HOWARD
Hatfield, March 20.

YOU knew my intention to stop, a few days, at this place, to see my sisters and my old friend. I promised to write to you, and inform you of my welfare. I gave the promise with coldness and reluctance, because I predicted that no benefit would flow to either from our correspondence. Will you believe that I was a little sullen at our parting; that your seeming cheerfulness was construed by my perverse heart, into something very odious? The words *inhuman* and *insensible* girl rose to my lips, and had like to have been uttered aloud.

I did not reflect, that, since you have resolved to pursue a certain path, my regard for you, if unmixed with selfishness, should prompt me to wish, that you may encounter as few asperities as possible, and to rejoice at the easiness of a sacrifice, which, whether difficult or easy, *must* be made.

I had not left you a day, before my inconstant disposition restored me to my virtuous feelings. I repented of the coldness with which I had consented to your scheme of correspondence, and tormented myself with imagining those pangs which my injustice must have given you. I determined to repair my fault as quickly as possible; to write to you often, and in the strain worthy of one who can enter into your feelings, and estimate, at its true value, the motive which governs your actions.

I have, indeed, new and more urgent motives for writing. I arrived, at this hospitable mansion, late in the evening.

9

I have retired, for the first time, to my chamber, and have instantly taken up my pen. The nature of the tidings I send, will justify my haste. I will relate what has happened, without further preface.

I approached my friend's door, and lifted the latch without giving any signal of my approach. I found the old gentleman, seated with his pipe, near the fire, and looking placidly on the two girls, who were busy at draughts, for which they had made squares on the pine table, with chalk, and employed yellow and red grains of corn in place of *pawns*.

They started at my entrance, and, seeing who it was, threw themselves into my arms, in a transport of surprise and delight. After the first raptures of our meeting had passed, Mr. Hickman said to me; Well, my boy, thou hast come just in time. Godfry Cartwright has just carried away letters for thee. He goes to town to-morrow, and I gave him a pacquet that has lain here for some time, to put into the office for thee.

A pacquet? For me? From whom?

When thou knowest the truth, thou wilt be apt to blame us a little, for our negligence; but I will tell thee the whole affair, and thou shalt judge how far we are culpable. A week ago, I was searching the drawers in my cherry-tree desk, for the copy of a bond which old Duckworth had placed in my hands for safe-keeping, when I lighted on a bulky pacquet, sealed up, and inscribed with thy name. I thought it strange, that a paper of that kind should be found in my possession, and looked at it again and again before I could comprehend the mystery. At last I noticed, in the corner, the words "By Mr. Cartwright." Cartwright, thou knowest is the man we employ to take and bring letters to and from the city. Hence, I supposed it to be a pacquet brought by him on some occasion, and left here for thee; but by whom it was received, when it was brought, and how it should chance to repose in this drawer, I could not guess. I mentioned the affair to my sister, but she had no knowledge of the matter. At length, after examining the pacquet and

10

comparing circumstances, she gradually recollected its history.

Alack-a-day! cried she, I do remember something of it now. Cartwright brought it here, just the same evening of the very day that poor Edward left here and went to town. I remember I put it into that drawer, supposing that to be as good a place as any to keep it safe in, till we should hear from the lad, and so have some inkling whereabouts to send it to him; but, as I am a living soul, I forgot all about it from that day to this.

Such is the history of your pacquet, which, you see, was mislaid through accident and my sister's bad memory.

This pacquet instantly connected itself, in my fancy, with the destiny of poor Mary. It came hither nearly at the time of her flight from Abingdon. It, no doubt, came from her, and contained information of unspeakable moment to our mutual happiness. When I reflected on the consequences of this negligence, I could scarely restrain my impatience. I eagerly inquired for the pacquet.

Not an half-hour ago, said Hickman, I delivered it to Cartwright, with directions to put it into the post-office for New-York. He sets out early in the morning, so that thou wilt receive it on thy return to New-York.

Cartwright lives five miles from this house. The least delay was intolerable; and, my horse not being yet unsaddled, I mounted him immediately, and set out, in spite of expostulation and intreaty. The night was remarkably gloomy and tempestuous, and I was already thoroughly fatigued; but these considerations were forgotten.

I arrived at Cartwright's hovel, in less than an hour, and having gotten the pacquet, I returned with equal dispatch. Immediately after, I retired to my chamber and opened the pacquet, on which I instantly recognised the well-known hand of Miss Wilmot. I will wave all comments, and send you the letter.

TO EDWARD HARTLEY

Abingdon, Nov. 11.

I need not tell you, my friend, what I have felt, in consequence of your silence. The short note which I received, a fortnight after you had left me, roused my curiosity and my fears, instead of allaying them. You promised me a longer account of some mysterious changes that had taken place in your condition. This I was to receive in a few days. At the end of a week I was impatient. The promised letter did not arrive. Four weeks passed away, and nothing came from you.

Your pacquet has at last put an end to suspense: But why did you not send it sooner? Why not send me your story piece-meal; or, at least, tell me, in half a line, how you were employed, and what occasioned your delay? Why did you not come yourself? Edward, I am *displeased;* I was going to say, *angry* with you. You have sported with my feelings. I ought to lay down my pen while I am in this humour. The pangs your negligence has given me, have not yet been soothed to rest, and when I find that so much unhappiness has been given through mere heedlessness, I can scarely keep my patience.

I was sitting on a bench in the garden, when a country lad entered the enclosure. As soon as I caught a glimpse of him, and observed that his attention was fixed upon me, and his right hand already in his pocket, my heart whispered that this was the bearer of tidings from you. I attempted to rise and meet him, but my knees trembled so much, that I was obliged to give up my design. He drew forth his pacquet and threw it into my lap, answering, at the same time, my inquiries, respecting you, by telling me that you were well, and that you had been busy, for a long time, night and day, in writing that *there* letter to me. He had stopt a moment to give it, and could not stay, but merely to receive three lines from me, informing you of my health.

You do not deserve the favour. Besides, my fingers partake the flutterings of my heart. A tumult of joy and vexation, overpowers me. But, though you do not merit it, you shall have a few lines. This paper was spread upon my lap, and I had taken the pen to write to my aunt Bowles, but I will devote it to you, though my tremors, you see, will scarcely permit me to write legibly.

Your messenger chides my lingering; and I will let him go with nothing but a verbal message, for on second thoughts, I will defer writing till I have read your long letter.

Nov. 15.

Yes; the narrative of Morton is true. The simple recital which you give, leaves me no doubt. The money is his, and shall be restored the moment he demands it. For what I have spent, I must a little while be his debtor. This he must consent to lose, for I never can repay it. Indeed, it is not much. Since my change of fortune, I have not been extravagant. An hundred dollars is the most that I have laid out, and some of this has been in furniture which I shall resign to him.

Be under no concern, my friend, on my account. Think not how I shall endure the evils of my former condition, for I never shall return to it. Thy Mary is hastening to the grave, with a very quick pace. That is her only refuge from humiliation and calamity, and to that she looks forward with more confidence than ever.

I was not fashioned of stubborn materials. Poverty, contempt, and labour, are a burden too great for me. I know, that for these only, am I reserved, and this interval of better prospects was no comfort to me. I always told you my brother had no just claim to this money, and that the rightful claimant would sooner or later appear. You were more sanguine, and were willing to incur, even on grounds so imperfect, the irrevocable obligations of marriage. See into what a gulf your rashness would have hurried you, and rejoice that my obstinacy insisted on a delay of half a year.

You know my motives for accepting, and on what

13

conditions I accepted your proffered vows. I have never concealed from you my love. What my penetration easily perceived, your candour never strove to conceal. Your indifference, your freedom from every thing like passion, was not only to be seen in your conduct, but was avowed by your lips. I was not so base as to accept your hand, without your heart. You talked of gratitude, and duty, and perfect esteem. I obtained, you told me, your entire reverence, and there was no female in the world whom you loved *so much*. It was true that you did not love *me*, but you *preferred* me to all other women. Union with me was your supreme desire. Your reason discerned and adored my merits, and the concurrence of the heart could not but follow.

Fondly devoted to you as I was, and urged as these arguments were, with pathetic eloquence, I could not be deceived for more than a moment. My heart was filled with contradictory emotions. I secretly upbraided you for obduracy in withholding your love, while I, at the same time, admired and loved you the more for your generosity. Your conduct rendered the sacrifice of my happiness to yours the more difficult, while it increased the necessity, and inforced the justice of that sacrifice. I could not discover the probability, that marriage would give birth to that love which previous tenderness and kindness had been unable to produce. I doubted not your fidelity, and that the consciousness of conferring happiness would secure your contentment; but I felt that this was insufficient for my pride, if not for my love.

I sought your happiness. To be the author of it was the object of inexpressible longings. To be happy without you was impossible, but the misery of loneliness, however great, was less than that of being the spectator of your misery, or even that of defrauding you of the felicity, attending marriage with a woman whom you could truly love. Meanwhile, our mutual poverty was itself an insurmountable bar to marriage.

My brother's death put me in seeming possession of competence. Circumstances were now somewhat changed. If no claimant appeared, I should be able, by giving myself to you, to bestow upon the object of my love that good, the want of which nothing can compensate. There were no other means of rescuing your sisters and yourself from indigence and dependence. What I was willing to share with you, you would not share with me on any terms but those of wedlock.

Too well did I see on what weak foundations was built this scheme of happiness. This property was never gained by my brother's own industry, and how could I apply to my own use what I could not doubt belonged to another, though that other should never appear to claim it at my hands.

My reluctance was partly subdued by your urgency. I consented, waveringly, and with a thousand misgivings, to be yours at the end of six months, if no one should appear, meantime, to make out a good title to this money. I listened to your arguments and suppositions, by which you would fain account for my brother's acquisition of so large a sum consistently with honesty, and for his silence as to his possession of it. I was willing to be convinced, and consented to sacrifice my peace by marrying the man I loved, because this marriage would secure to him the competence, which I could not enjoy alone.

This end cannot now be effected. New reasons have sprung up for foregoing your affection, even had Morton perished at sea. A friend has returned to you, who is far more able to relieve your poverty than I should be. It is easy to see on what conditions this relief is intended to be given. He has a daughter, whom he deems worthy of his adopted son. He knows your merit, and cannot fail of perceiving that it places you on a level with the most lovely and accomplished of human beings.

I see how it is. This Clara will be yours. That intelligence, that mien, that gracefulness, which rustic obscurity cannot hide, which the garb of a clown could never disguise, accompanied with the ardent commendations of her father, will fascinate her in a moment. I cannot hesitate what to wish, or how to act. That passion which a form, homely and uncouth like mine, tarnished and withered by drudgery and sorrow, and by comparative old age, for I am nine years older than you; which a mind, void of education, and the refinements of learned and polished intercourse was incapable of wakening, cannot fail to be excited by the youth and beauty, the varied accomplishments and ineffable graces of this stranger. She will offer you happiness, and wealth, and honour, and you will accept them at her hands.

As for me, I cannot be yours, because I am not my own. My resolution to be severed from you is unalterable; but this is not necessary to insure our separation. It cannot take place, even if all my wishes were in favour of it. Long before the expiration of the half year, I shall be removed beyond your reach. This is not the illusion of despair. I feel in my deepest vitals, the progress of death. Nature languishes within me, and every hour accelerates my decay.

My friend, thou must not parley with me; thou must not afflict me with arguments or intreaties, by letters or visits. I must see thee, and hear from thee no more: but I know thy character too well to expect this from thee. As soon as thou receivest this letter, thou wilt hasten hither, and endeavour to shake my purpose.

I am not doubtful of my own constancy, but I would save myself and thee from a trial that will answer no end. I shall leave this place early to-morrow. Whither I am going must never be told to thee. Thy pursuit and thy inquiries will be incessant and anxious, but the measures I have taken for eluding thy search, will defeat all thy efforts. I know that these assurances will not dissuade thee from making them, and I sorrow to reflect on the labours and anxieties to which thou wilt subject thyself for my sake; but I shall derive consolation from the belief, that my retreat will *never be discovered.*

I enclose an order on the bank for the money that remains in it, drawn in favour of Morton, and an assignment to him of the few tables and chairs that furnish my

16

lodgings here. These thou wilt faithfully deliver into his hands. I likewise return you your papers and letters.

And now . . . Edward . . . best and most beloved of men! . . . and is it come to this? Must I bid thee farewel forever?

Do not, I beseech thee, think hardly of me for what I have done. Nothing but a sense of duty, nothing but a supreme regard to thy happiness, could suggest my design. I cannot faulter in the execution, since I could not waver in the sense of my duty. I am ashamed of my weakness, that hinders me from pronouncing my last farewel.

Make haste to forget the unhappy Mary; make haste to the feet of your new friend, and to secure that felicity which an untoward fate denied me the power of bestowing.

My friend, my benefactor, farewel.

Mary.

LETTER III

TO CLARA HOWARD
Philadelphia, March 24.

I WRITE to you in a mood not very well suited to the business. I am weary and impatient. The company which surrounds me is alien to my temper and my habits. I want to shut out the tokens of their existence; to forget where I am, and restore myself to those rapturous scenes and that blissful period which preceded my last inauspicious meeting with Morton.

I write to you, and yet I have nothing to say that will please you. My heart overflows with bitterness. I would pour it out upon *you,* and yet my equity will only add new keenness to my compunction, when I come to review what I have written. I am disposed to complain. I want an object to whom to impute my disasters, and to gratify my malice by upbraiding. There is a kind of satisfaction in revenge that I want to taste. I want to shift my anxieties from my own shoulders to those of another, who deserves the burden more than I.

Your decision has made me unhappy. I believe your decision absurd, yet I know your motives are disinterested and heroic. I know the misery which adherence to your scheme costs you. It is only less than my own. Why then should I aggravate that misery? It is the system of nature that deserves my hatred and my curses: that system which makes our very virtues instrumental to our misery.

But chiefly my own folly have I to deplore: that folly which made me intrust to you the story of Miss Wilmot, before the bonds had been formed which no after-repentance could break. I ought to have forgotten her existence. I ought to have claimed your love and your hand. You would have bestowed them upon me, and my happiness would have been placed beyond the reach of caprice.

What has wrought this change in my thoughts? I set out from Hatfield with an heart glowing with zeal for the poor Mary. I burnt with impatience to throw myself at her feet, and tender her my vows. This zeal time has extinguished. I call to mind the perfections of another. I compare them with those of the fugitive. My soul droops at the comparison, and my tongue would find it impossible to utter the vows, which my untoward fate may exact from me.

Yet there is no alternative. I must finish the course that I have begun. I must conjure up impetuosity and zeal in this new cause. I must act and speak with the earnestness of sincerity and the pathos of hope. Otherwise I shall betray my cause and violate my duty. Alas! it is vain to deny it, my powers are not equal to this task.

I have inquired at the house where Mrs. Valentine formerly lived. A new family are there, and no intelligence of the former tenant can be gained from them. This lady has friends, no doubt, in the city; but I know them not. It is chance alone that can give me their company.

My efforts are lanquid and my prospects dim. I shall stay here for as short a time as possible, and then proceed to Virginia. I will not rest till I have restored to Mary her own. This money shall be faithfully delivered. To add my heart to the gift is impossible. With less than my affections she will never be satisfied, and they are no longer mine to bestow.

Having performed this duty, what will remain for me. My future destiny it will be your province to prescribe. I shall cease, however, to reason with you, or to persuade. Decide agreeably to your own conceptions of right, and secure to yourself happiness, even by allotting misery, banishment, or death, to

E. H.

LETTER V

TO E. HARTLEY
New-York, March 26.

I F I thought the temper which dictated your last letter would continue beyond the hour or the night, I should indeed be unhappy. My life has known much sorrow, but the sharpest pangs will be those arising from the sense of your unworthiness.

In my eyes marriage is no sensual or selfish bargain. I will never *vow to honour* the man who deserves only my contempt; and my esteem can be secured only by a just and disinterested conduct. Perhaps esteem is not the only requisite to marriage. Of that I am not certain; but I know that it is an indispensible requisite to love. I cannot love any thing in you but excellence. Infatuation will render you hateful or pitiable in my eyes. I shall hasten to forget you, and for that end shall estrange myself from your society, and drop your correspondence.

You know what it is that reason prescribes to you with regard to Miss Wilmot. If you cannot ardently and sincerely seek her presence, and find in the happiness which she will derive from union with you, sufficient motives to make you zealously solicit that union, you are unworthy not merely of my love, but of my esteem. Henceforth I will know you not.

Let me not have reason to charge you with hypocrisy, or to consider your love for me as the mere child of sensuality and selfishness. You have often told me that you desire my happiness above all things. That you love me for my own sake. Your sincerity and rectitude are now put to the test. Do not belie your professions, by a blind and unjust decision. Allow me to judge in what it is that my happiness consists, and prove your attachment to me by promoting my happiness.

Misguided friend! What is it you want? To gain your end by exciting my pity? Suppose the end should be thus accomplished; suppose I should become your wife merely to save your life, to prevent hazards and temptations to which my rejection might expose you. Mournful, indeed, full of anguish and of tears, would be the day which should make me your bride. My act would be a mere submission to humiliating and painful necessity. I should look to reap from such an alliance, nothing but repinings and sorrow. By soliciting my hand, by consenting to ratify a contract made on such principles, you would irretrievably forfeit my esteem. My condition would be the most disastrous that can betide a human being. I should be bound, beyond the power of loosening my bonds, to one whom I *despised*.

I am, indeed, in no danger of acting upon these principles. I shall never so little consult my own dignity and yours, as to accept your hand *through compassion*. I am not unacquainted with the schemes which your foolish despondency has suggested to you. I know very well what alternatives you have sometimes resolved to offer me; of compliance with your wishes, or of banishing you to the desert, and dissolving that connection between my father and you, which is so advantageous to yourself and your sisters. Fie upon you! Even to have entertained such thoughts fixes a stain upon your character not easily effaced. Nothing but the hope that the illusion is transitory, and that sober reflection will, in a short time, relieve you from the yoke of such cowardly and ignoble designs, prevents this from being the last token of friendship you will ever receive from

C. H.

21

LETTER V

Philadelphia, March 28.

CLARA, thou hast conquered me. I see the folly of my last letter, and deplore it. It, indeed, merited the indignation and the scorn which it has received. Never shall you again be grieved and provoked by the like folly. I am now master of my actions and my thoughts, and will steadily direct them to a single purpose, the pursuit of the poor Mary, and the promotion of her happiness.

How inconsistent and capricious is man. To-day, his resolution and motives are as adverse to those of yesterday, as those of one man, can be, at any time and in any situation, to those of another. Yesterday! Heaven preserve me from a repetition of the same thoughts! I shudder on looking back upon the gulf on the brink of which I was tottering. How could I so utterly forget my own interest; the regard due to the woman who truly loves me; to my sisters and my noble friend?

But the humiliation is now past. I think it is: I am sure it is. I am serene, resolute, and happy. The remorse my errors have produced is now at an end. Better thoughts, resolutions worthy of your pupil and your *friend* have succeeded. Not that my past feelings have been, perhaps, quite as culpable as you describe them. My repinings were drawn from fallacious sources, but they were not wholly selfish. I imagined you loved me; that my alliance with another, however sanctioned by your judgment, would produce some regret. Believing your judgment misinformed; believ-

22

ing these regrets to be needless, I was not willing to create them. I need not say that this was *all* my reluctance. That would be false; but, as they partly originated hence, my feelings were not wholly selfish, and if I may judge of my own emotions, surely you wrong me in calling my passion by the odious name of sensual.

But these things are past. You have not done me justice; and in return, I have imputed to you, feelings of which you knew nothing. Henceforth, my conduct shall convince you that I cannot stoop to solicit that boon from your pity, which is refused by your love. Conjugal claims and enjoyments are mutual. The happiness received is always proportioned to that conferred. A wretch, worthy of eternal abhorrence, must *he* be, and endowed with tyger-like ferocity, who seeks and is contented with the *person,* while the heart is averse or indifferent. Such an one, believe me, Clara, am not I.

On Tuesday, I expect to dispatch all my concerns in this city, and to proceed southward.

Adieu.
E. H.

LETTER VI

TO E. HARTLEY

New-York, April 1.

THERE is an obscurity in your letter, my friend, that I cannot dispel. The first part afforded me much pleasure, but the sequel disappointed me. You seem to have strangely misconstrued my meaning. Whether this misconstruction be real or pretended, it does not become me to enter into any explanation. If it be real, it affords a proof of a narrow and ungenerous heart, an heart incapable of perceiving the possibility of sacrificing my own personal gratification to that of another, and of deriving, from that very sacrifice, a purer and more lasting felicity. It shews you unable to comprehend that the welfare of another may demand self-denial from us, and that in bestowing benefits on others, there is a purer delight than in gratifications merely selfish and exclusive.

You question my love, because I exhort you to do your duty, and to make another happy that is worthier than I. Why am I anxious for that other and for you? Why should I rejoice in your integrity, and mourn for your degradation? Why should I harbour such glowing images of the bliss which your Mary should derive from union with you? Would not my indifference and negligence on these heads, would not my ardour to appropriate your affections to myself, prove me to be . . . there is no name sufficiently abhorrent and contemptuous for such an heart.

And yet, such is the deportment you expect from me! Any thing but this will prove me to be indifferent, or averse to you! Desist, I beseech you, in time. If you proceed

24

thus, quickly will you lose what remains of that esteem which I once felt for you. Instead of earnestly promoting your alliance with Miss Wilmot, I shall anxiously obstruct it, on account of your unworthiness.

If this misconstruction be *pretended* only, if you mean to assail, by this new expedient, my imaginary weakness; if you imagine, that in order to remove an unjust imputation from my character, I will do what will make me really culpable; if you imagine that I shall degrade myself in my own estimation, merely for the purpose of raising myself in yours, you have grossly deceived yourself.

Formerly you talked, with much self-complacency, of the trials to which I had subjected my fortitude, and *consoled* yourself with thinking that adhering to my new scheme, was productive of misery. I say, that you *consoled* yourself with this reflection. In your eyes, my character was estimable in proportion to the reluctance with which I performed what was just. Your devotion to me was fervent in proportion as the performance of my duty was attended with *anguish* and *suffering!*

Edward! are you, indeed, so sordid as to reason in this manner? Are you so blind as to account this the surest road to my esteem? Are you not ashamed of your infatuation and absurdity?

I need not disguise or deny my unhappiness from any pity to you, or through the value which I set on your esteem. You exult in proportion to my misery. You revere me in proportion as my sentiments are mean and selfish! I am to be upbraided and despised, in proportion to the fulness of that enjoyment, which, the approbation of my conscience, the sense of doing right myself, and of conferring good on others, has given me!

Let me constantly hear from you, respecting your movements. I am in hopes that time and reflection will instil into you better principles. Till then, I shall not be displeased, if your letters be confined to a mere narrative of your journey.

Adieu.
C. H.

LETTER VII

TO E. HARTLEY
New-York, April 5.

YOU were to leave Philadelphia on Tuesday, you told me. I imagined the interval would be engrossed with business, and, therefore, expected not to hear from you, till after that day; but that day, and the whole week is past, and no tidings.

This silence does not proceed from sullenness. I hope, I persuade myself, it does not. Whatever anger you have conceived against me, let not that, I intreat you, make you ungrateful to my father, cruel to your sisters, unjust to yourself.

Letters have been hourly expected from you, relative to concerns which you had in charge. Have you neglected them? Have you betrayed your trust? Have you suffered an unmanly dejection to unfit you for this charge? Have you committed any rashness?

Heaven forbid! Yet, what but some fatal event has occasioned this delay? Perhaps, while I thus write to you, you are . . .

Let me not think of it. I shiver with a deadly cold at the thought. Thou art fiery and impetuous, my friend. Thy spirit is not curbed by reason. There is no outrage on discretion; no crime against thyself, into which thy headlong spirit may not hurry thee.

Perhaps, my last letter was harsh, unjust. My censures were too bitter. I made not suitable allowances for your youth; the force of that attachment which you own for me. Knew I so little of my own nature, and the illusions of

26

passion, as to expect you to act and speak with perfect wisdom.

Would to heaven, I had not written that letter, or that I had sufficiently considered its contents before I sent it. It was scribbled hastily, in a moment of resentment. Of that, which I so acrimoniously censured in you, I was guilty myself. I ought to have staid till cool reflection had succeeded.

But, perhaps, we torment ourselves needlessly. It is said, that the late storms have overflowed the rivers, swept away the bridges, and flooded the roads. Perhaps, your letters are delayed from this cause. Perhaps, the ways have been impassable.

Mr. Talbot has been abroad during the morning. We expect him to return presently. He may bring us letters.

* * *

No intelligence yet received! I am excessively uneasy. Your friend is displeased. He is almost ready to repent the confidence he has placed in you. Nothing can justify your silence. Your sickness should not hinder you from inform- ing him of certain transactions. Their importance required you to give him early notice of any disaster that might befal you, and common prudence would enjoin you to take measures for conveying this intelligence by the hands of others, in case of your incapacity. . . .

The coming of the post has been interrupted only for one day. The reason why we have not heard from you, can only be your not having written. My thoughts are too much disturbed to permit me to write any more. I will lay down the pen, and dispatch this: perhaps, it may find you, and produce some effect.

C. H.

LETTER VIII

TO MISS HOWARD
Schuylkill, April 10.

I WRITE to you by the hand of another. Be not greatly surprised or alarmed. Perhaps, my strength is equal to the performance of this duty for myself, but my good friend and affectionate nurse, Mrs. Aston, insists upon guiding the pen for me. She sits by my side, and promises to write whatever I dictate.

My theme is of an interesting and affecting nature. Perhaps, it might appear to you improper to employ any hand but my own. Circumstances must apologize for me. I cannot hold the pen; the friend, whose hand I employ, deserves my affection and gratitude. On her discretion I can rely. Besides, I am now approaching a bourne, where our scruples and reserves usually disappear. The suggestions of self-interest, and the calculations of the future, are sure to vanish at the approach of death.

When I wrote you last, I told you my intention to leave the city on Tuesday. I afterwards received your letter. Your censure was far more severe than my conscience told me I deserved. But my own heart did not secure me from regret. I was highly culpable to allow my peace to be molested by the tenor of your letter. In different circumstances, I should certainly conceal from you, its effect upon my feelings. I intended to have concealed them from you. I perceived that, with respect to you, I was thenceforth to regard myself as a stranger and an out-cast; and resolved that you should see me and hear from me no more.

28

In embracing this scheme, I found no tranquillity. Clara, I loved you, and that love led me to place my supreme happiness in the possession of your heart. For this you call me sensual and selfish. This, at least, convinced me of one thing; that the happiness which I formed to myself, is beyond my reach! It behoved me, doubtless, to dismiss all fruitless repinings, as well as to forbear all unprofitable efforts. My courage was equal to the last, but not to the first. Though the confession will degrade me still lower in your opinion, it is now no time to prevaricate or counterfeit; and I will not hide from you my anguish, and dejection. These did not unfit me for performing my duty to your father, but they banished health and repose from my pillow.

I set out, on Tuesday morning, for Baltimore. The usual floods of this season having carried away the bridge on Schuylkill, we prepared to pass it in a boat. The horses which drew the stage, being unaccustomed to this mode of conveyance, and being startled by the whirlpools and eddies, took fright, when the boat had gained the middle of the river, and suddenly rushed out, at the further end, into the stream.

All the passengers, except two females, had dismounted from the carriage before it entered the boat. The air was extremely cold, and a drizzling shower was falling. These circumstances induced the father of the two girls, who was one of our company, to dissuade them from alighting, as he imagined no danger would arise, during the passage. Happily the passengers and boatmen were behind the carriage, so that, in rushing forward, the horses drew after them nothing but the coach and those in it.

The coach and horses instantly sunk. The curtains, on all sides, had been lowered and fastened; but the rushing waters burst the fastenings, and by a miraculous chance, the two females, who sat on one seat behind, were extricated in a moment from the poles and curtains. The coach sunk to the bottom, but the girls presently rose to the surface.

I threw off my upper and under coat in a moment, and watching the place of their reappearance, plunged into the

water, and by the assistance of others, lifted one breath-
less corpse into the boat. Meanwhile, the father, more
terrified, and less prudent, threw himself, cloaked and en-
cumbered as he was, into the water, to save his children.
Instead of effecting this, he was unable to save himself. No
one followed my example in plunging into the river, and
the father and one of his children perished together.

The immediate consequence of this exposure, in a fever-
ish state of my frame, was a violent ague, which gave place
to an high fever and delirium. I stopt at the inn on the
opposite bank, to change my wet clothes for dry; but, having done this, was unable to proceed, and betook myself
to my bed. I suspected nothing more than an intermittent,
which, however violent, during its prevalence, would pass
away in less than an hour. In this I was mistaken.

My understanding was greatly disturbed. I had no remembrance of the past, or foresight of the future. All was
painful confusion, which has but lately disappeared. Clear
conceptions have returned to me, but my strength is gone,
and I feel the cold of death gradually gaining on my heart.
My force of mind is not lessened. I can talk and reason
as coherently as ever; and my conclusions are far more wise
than while in perfect health.

The family of Mr. Aston, residing in this neighbourhood,
hearing of my condition, have afforded me every succour
and comfort I needed. It was not till this moment that I
have been able to employ the suitable means of conveying
to you tidings of these events. Your letter has just been
brought me from the post-office, and my good friend, who
now holds the pen, and who has watched by my pillow
during my sickness, was good enough to read it to me.

What shall I say? To one regarding me as selfish and
unjust; as even capable of villainy and foul ingratitude;
who, among so many conjectures, as to the cause of my
silence, was ready to suspect me of breach of faith, the low
guilt of embezzlement! What shall I say?

Nothing: I can say nothing. The prayers of a dying man
for thy felicity, Clara, will, at least, be accepted as sincere.

There is no personal motive to vitiate this prayer. Thy happiness must, henceforth, be independent of mine. I can neither be the author nor partaker of it. Be thou, lovely and excellent woman! *be happy!*

I break off here, to write to your father. I have much to say to him, which another day, perhaps, another hour, may forever prevent me from saying.

E. H.

LETTER IX

TO E. HARTLEY
New-York, April 26.

MY father carries you this. The merciful God grant that he may find you alive! Edward, is it possible for you to forgive me. . . . But I deserve it not. I have lost you forever! My wickedness and folly merited no less.

My father smiles and says there is hope. He vows to find you out; to restore you to health, to bring you back to us alive and happy.

Good God! what horrible infatuation was it that made me write as I did! If thou diest, just . . . just will be my punishment. Never more will I open my eyes to the light.

My father, my mother, will not suffer me to go to thee. To see thee once more; to receive thy last sigh; to clasp thy cold remains; to find my everlasting peace in the same grave. They will not hearken to me; they will not suffer me to go!

In my frantic thoughts, I ran to the water's edge. I was stepping into the boat to cross the river, determined to see thee ere a new day returned, but I was pursued. I am detained by force; by intreaties more powerful than bonds and fetters.

I need not go. Thou art gone forever. My prayer for forgiveness thou canst not hear. Heaven has denied me the power to repair the wrongs that I have done thee. To expiate my folly, to call thee back to my bosom; and to give my stubborn heart to thy possession, cannot be.

C. H.

LETTER X

TO MRS. HOWARD
Philadelphia, April 14.

I HAVE been here thirty hours, and have not written to you. I know your impatience, and that of your girl; but, till this hour I was unable to give you information that would relieve your fears. Edward was, indeed, ill. I found him in a state wholly desperate. He had not strength to lift his eye-lids at my approach, or to articulate a welcome.

I found in his chamber his nurse and his physician. The former is a young lady, newly married, who resides in this neighbourhood, and a sister of the person whom our pupil saved from drowning. She has paid him the kindest and most anxious attention.

Let me hasten to tell you that the crisis has passed, and terminated favourably. A profound sleep of ten hours, has left him free from pain and fever, though in a state of weakness which could not be carried beyond its present degree, without death.

Set your hearts at rest. The lad is safe. I promised to bring him back alive and well, and will certainly fulfil my promise; but some weeks must elapse before he will be fit for the journey. You must wait with patience till then. Farewel.

E. Howard.

33

LETTER XI

New-York, April 15.

TO describe the agony which my father's silence produced, both to my mother and myself, would be useless. Thanks to my God, you are out of danger. I can now breathe with freedom.

Tell me, beloved Edward, by your own hand, or, if your weakness will not suffer it, by that of your friend, that you forgive me. O! that I were not at this unfriendly distance from you! That I could pour out the tears of my remorse, of my gratitude, of my love, upon your hand. I am jealous of your lovely nurse. She is performing those functions which belong to me.

You are grateful for her services, are you not? Not more so than I am. Give her my fervent thanks . . . but stay, I will give them myself. I will write to her immediately, tell her of the obligations she has laid upon me, and solicit her friendship. She is an angel, I am sure.

Prithee, my friend, make haste and be well; and fly to us. The arms of thy Clara are open to receive thee. She is ready to kneel to thee for pardon; to expiate her former obduracy by years of gratitude and tenderness. Lay on my past offences what penalty thou wilt. The heavier it be the more cheerfully shall I sustain it; the more adequate it will be to my fault.

Mary. . . . My heart droops when I think of her. How imperfect are the schemes of human felicity. May Heaven assist me in driving from my mind the secret conviction, that her claim to your affection is still valid.

Alas! how fleeting is our confidence. Come to me my friend. Exert all thy persuasive eloquence. Convince me that I have erred in resigning thy heart and hand to another, in imagining the claim of Mary better than mine.

I call upon thy efforts to rescue me from self-condemnation; but I call on thee without hope. My reason cannot be deceived. The sense of the injustice I have done her, will poison every enjoyment which union with thee can afford me.

Yet come. I repent not of my invitation. I retract not my promise. Make me irrevocably thine. I shall at least be happy while I forget her, and I will labour to forget her.

Adieu.
C. H.

LETTER XII

TO MISS HOWARD
Philadelphia, April 23.

WHEN you know my reason for not accompanying your father, you will approve of my conduct. I am once more in health, but could not, at this season, perform the journey without hazard. Meanwhile, some affairs remain to be transacted in this city, to which my strength is fully equal; and the assurance of your love, has lulled all my cares to repose.

In less than a week I will be with you. Rely upon my power to convince you that your present decision is just. If I had doubts of its rectitude, your offer, transporting as it is, would never be accepted.

How little did you comprehend my character, in believing me capable of urging you to the commission of what I deemed wrong! And think you that even now I will accept your hand, unattended with the fullest concurrence of your reason? No: but I doubt not to obtain that concurrence. I will fly to you on the wings of transport, and armed with reasons which shall fully remove your scruples.

These reasons, as well as a thousand affecting incidents which have lately befallen me, I will reserve for our meeting. Meanwhile, place the inclosed portrait in your bosom. It is that of my *nurse,* Mrs. Aston. She sends it to you, and desires me to tell you that she has received your letter, and will answer it very shortly. Adieu.

E. H.

P.S. I stay at No. ____ north Eighth-street.

LETTER XIII

TO FRANCIS HARRIS
Philadelphia, April 23.

DO you wish for some account of my present situation? I will readily comply with your request. I am, indeed, in a mood, just now, extremely favourable to the telling of a long story. I have no companions in this city, and various circumstances, while they give me a few days solitude and leisure, strongly incline me likewise to ruminate and moralize on past adventures.

When I last wrote to you, I told you my destiny had undergone surprising changes since we parted. I had then no leisure to enter into minute particulars. Alas! my friend, changes still more surprising have since occurred, but changes very different from those to which I then alluded. Then they were all benign and joyous: since, they have been only gloomy and disastrous.

But how far must I go back to render my narrative intelligible? You went your voyage, if I mistake not, just after I was settled with my uncle and sisters, in the neighbourhood of Hatfield. I believe you were acquainted with the beginnings, at least, of my intercourse with Mr. Howard. I described to you, I believe, the dignified, grave and secluded deportment of that man; the little relish he appeared to have for the society around him, and the flattering regards he bestowed on me.

I was a mere country lad, with little education but what was gained by myself; diffident and bashful as the rawest inexperience could make me. He was a man of elevated and sedate demeanour; living, if not with splendour, yet with elegance; withdrawing in a great degree from the society of his neighbours; immersed in books and papers, and wholly given to study and contemplation.

I shall never forget the occasion on which he first honoured me with his notice; the unspeakable delight which his increasing familiarity and confidence; my admission to his house, and my partaking of his conversation and instructions afforded me. I recollect the gradual disappearance, in his intercourse with me, of that reserve and austerity which he still maintained to the rest of mankind, with emotions of gratitude and pleasure unutterable.

He had reason to regard me, indeed, somewhat like his own son. I had no father; I had no property: there was no one among my own relations, who had any particular claim upon my reverence or affection. A thousand tokens in my demeanour, must have manifested a veneration for him next to idolatry. My temper was artless and impetuous, and several little incidents occurred, during the many years that I frequented his house, that brought forth striking proofs of my attachment to him. I greedily swallowed his lessons, and remember how often his eyes sparkled, his countenance brightened into smiles, and his tongue lavished applause on my wonderful docility and rapid progress. He shewed his affection for me, by giving his instructions, inquiring into my situation, and directing me in every case of difficulty that occurred; but he never offered to become my real father; to be at the expense of my subsistence, or my education to any liberal profession. Indeed, he was anxious to persuade me that the farmer's life was the life of true dignity, and that, however desirable to me property might be, I ought to entertain no wish to change my mode of life. That was a lesson which he was extremely assiduous to teach.

He never gave me money, nor ever suffered the slightest hint to escape him that he designed to carry his munificence any farther than to lend me his company, his conversation and his books. Indeed, in my attachment to him, there was nothing sordid or mercenary. It never occurred to me to reflect on this frugality; this limitation of his bounty. What he gave was, in my own eyes, infinitely beyond my merits, and instead of panting after more, I was only astonished that he gave me so much. Indeed, had I had wisdom enough to judge of appearances, I should have naturally supposed that there existed many others who had stronger claims upon his fortune than I had, and might actually enjoy his bounty.

His family and situation were, indeed, wholly unknown to me and his neighbours. He was a native of Britain; had not been long in America; lived alone and in affluence; was a man past the middle of life; enjoyed a calm, studious and contemplative existence. This was the sum of all the knowledge I ever obtained of him. Indeed, my curiosity never carried me into stratagems or guesses, in order to discover what he did not voluntarily disclose, or what he was desirous to conceal.

The mournful day of his departure from Hatfield, and from America, at last arrived. I never was taught to believe that he designed to pass his life in America. I naturally regarded him as merely a sojourner, but never inquired how long he meant to stay among us. When he told me, therefore, that he should embark in a week, I felt no surprise, though it was impossible to conceal my impatience and regret. I never felt a keener pang than his last embrace gave me.

He parted with me with every mark of paternal tenderness. Yet he left nothing behind him, as a memorial of his affection. Even the books that I had often read under his roof, some of which were my chief favourites, and would have been prized, for the donor's sake, beyond their weight in rubies, he carried away with him. Neither did he explain the causes of his voyage, or give me any expectation of seeing him again.

My obligations to Mr. Howard cannot be measured. To him am I indebted for whatever distinguishes me from the stone which I turned up with my plough, or the stock which I dissevered with my axe. My understanding was awakened, disciplined, informed; my affections were cherished, exercised, and regulated by him. My heart was penetrated with a sentiment, in regard to him . . . perhaps, it would be impious to call it devotion. The divinity only can claim that; yet this man was a sort of divinity to me: the substitute and representative of heaven, in my eyes, and for my good.

I besought him to let me accompany him. I anxiously inquired whether I might cherish the hope of ever seeing him again. The first request he made me ashamed of having urged, by shewing me that I had sisters who needed my protection, and for whose sake I ought to labour to attain independence. His own destiny would be regulated by future events, but he deemed it most probable that we should never see each other more.

The melancholy inspired by this separation from one who was not only my best, but my sole friend, was not dissipated, like the other afflictions of youth, by the lapse of a few months. Being accompanied with absolute uncertainty as to his condition and place of residence, it produced the same effect that his death would have done. This melancholy, though no variety of scene could have effaced it, was, no doubt, aggravated by the cheerless solitude in which I was placed. The rustic life was wholly unsuitable to my temper and taste. My active mind panted for a nobler and wider sphere of action; and after enduring the inconveniences of my sequestered situation, for some time, I, at length, bound myself apprentice to a watch-maker in the city. My genius was always turned towards mechanics, and I could imagine no art more respectable or profitable than this.

Shortly after my removal to the city, I became acquainted with a young man by the name of Wilmot. There were many points of resemblance between us. We were equally fond of study and reflection, and the same literary pursuits happened to engage our passions. Hence a cordial and incessant intercourse took place between us.

I suppose you know nothing of Wilmot. Yet possibly you

40

have heard something of the family. They were of no small note in Delaware. Not natives of the country. The father was an emigrant, who brought a daughter and this son with him, when children, from Europe. He purchased a delightful place on *Brandywine,* built an house, laid out gardens, and passed a merry life among horses, dogs, and boon companions. He died, at length, by a fall from his horse, when his daughter Mary was sixteen years of age, and the son four or five years younger.

These children had been trained up in the most luxurious manner. The girl had been her own mistress, and the mistress of her father's purse from a very early age. All the prejudices and expectations of an heiress were early and deeply imbibed by her; and her father's character had hindered her from forming any affectionate or useful friends of her own sex, while those who called themselves *his* friends were either merely jovial companions or cunning creditors. It very soon appeared that Wilmot's fortune had lasted just as long as his life. House, and land, and stock were sold by auction, to discharge his numerous debts, and nothing but a surplus on the sale of the furniture, remained to the heirs.

Mary, after a recluse and affluent education, was thus left, at the inexperienced age of sixteen, friendless and forlorn, to find the means of subsistence for herself and her brother, in her own ingenuity and industry. It cannot be supposed that she escaped all the obvious and enervating effects of such an education. Her pride was sorely wounded by this reverse, but nature had furnished her with a vigorous mind, which made it impossible for her to sink, either into meanness or despair. She was not wise enough to endure poverty and straitened accommodations, and a toilsome calling, with serenity; but she was strenuous enough to adopt the best means for repairing the ills that oppressed her.

She retired, with the wreck of her father's property, from the scene in which she had been accustomed to appear with a splendour no longer hers. Her sensibility found consolation in living obscure and unknown. For this end, she removed to the city, took cheap lodgings in the suburbs, and reduced all her expences to the most frugal standard. With the money she brought with her, she placed her brother at a reputable grammar school, and her acquaintance, by very slow degrees, extending beyond her own roof among the good and considerate part of the community, she acquired, by the exercise of the needle, a slender provision for herself and her brother.

The boy was a noble and generous spirit, and endowed with ardent thirst of knowledge. He made a rapid progress in his learning, and at the age of sixteen, became usher in the school in which he had been trained. He was smitten with the charms of literature; and greatly to his sister's disappointment and vexation, refused to engage in any of those professions which lead to riches and honour. He adopted certain antiquated and unfashionable notions about the "grandeur of retreat," "honourable poverty," a studious life, and the dignity of imparting knowledge to others. The desk, bar, and pulpit, had no attractions for him. This, no doubt, partly arose from youthful timidity and self-diffidence, and age might have insensibly changed his views.

My intercouse with Wilmot, introduced me, of course, to the knowledge of his sister. I usually met him at her lodgings. Sundays and all our evenings were spent together, and as Mary had few or no visitants, on her own account, she was nearly on the same footing of domestic familiarity with me, as with her brother.

She was much older than I. Humiliation and anxiety had deeply preyed on her constitution, which had never been florid or robust, and made still less that small portion of external grace or beauty, which nature had conferred upon her. Dignity, however, was conspicuous in her deportment, and intelligence glowed in her delicate and pliant features. Her manners were extremely mild, her voice soft and musical, and her conversation full of originality and wisdom. The high place to which she admitted me in her esteem, and the pleasure she took in my company, demanded my esteem and gratitude in return. In a short time, she took place of her brother in my confidence and veneration.

I never loved Mary Wilmot. Disparity of age, the dignity and sedateness of her carriage, and perhaps the want of personal attractions, inspired me with a sentiment, very different from love. Yet there was no sacrifice of inclination which I would not cheerfully have made, in the cause of her happiness. Though union with her could not give me the raptures, that fortunate love is said to produce, it was impossible to find them with another while she was miserable.

I had no experience of the passions. I knew, and conversed with no woman but Mary, and imagined that no human being possessed equal excellences. I had no counter-longing to contend with; and, to say truth, did not suspect that my regard, for any woman, could possibly be carried further than what I felt for her.

Mary's knowledge of the heart, the persuasion of her own defects, or her refined conception of the passions, made her less sanguine and impetuous. Her love was to be indisputably requited by a love as fervent, before she would permit herself to indulge in hopes of felicity, or allow me to esteem, in her, my future wife: Our mutual situation, by no means justified marriage. Secure and regular means of subsistence were wanting, as I had, somewhat indiscreetly, bound myself to serve a parsimonious master, for a much longer period than was requisite to make me a proficient in my art. Meanwhile, there subsisted between us, the most affectionate and cordial intercourse, such as was worthy of her love, and my boundless esteem.

As long as the possibility of marriage was distant, this discord of feelings was of less moment. A very great misfortune, however, seemed to have brought it, for a time, very near. Wilmot embarked on the river, in an evil hour, and the boat being upset by a gust of wind, was drowned. The brother and sister tenderly loved each other, and this calamity was long and deeply deplored by the survivor. One unexpected good, however, grew out of this event. Wilmot was found to be credited in the bank of P. for so large a sum as five thousand dollars.

You will judge of the surprise produced by such a discovery, when I tell you that this credit appeared to have been given, above two years before Wilmot's death: that we, his constant and intimate associates, had never heard the slightest intimation of his possessing any thing beyond the scanty income of his school: that his expences, continued, till the day of his death, perfectly conformable to the known amount of this wretched income, and that no documents could be found among his papers, throwing any light on the mystery.

I shall not recount the ten thousand fruitless conjectures, that were formed to account for this circumstance. None was more probable, than that Wilmot held this money for another. Mary was particularly confident of the truth of this conclusion, though, to me, it was not unembarrassed with difficulties, for why was no written evidence; no memorandum or letter to be found respecting the trust; and why did he maintain so obstinate a silence on the subject, to us, to whom he was accustomed to communicate every action and every thought?

We endeavoured to recollect Wilmot's conversation and deportment, at the time this money was deposited, by him, in his own name, in bank. This clue seemed to lead to some discovery. I well remembered a thoughtfulness, at that period, not usual in my friend, and a certain conversation, that took place, between us, on the propriety of living on the bounty of others, when able to maintain ourselves by our own industry. In short, I was extremely willing to conclude that this money had been a present to Wilmot, from some paternal friend of his family, or, perhaps, some kinsman from a distance. At all events, as this sum had lain undisturbed in bank for two years, I saw no reason why it should not be applied to the purpose of subsistence, by his sister, to whom it now fully belonged.

It was difficult to overcome her scruples. At length she

determined to use as small a part as her necessities could dispense with, and to leave the rest untouched for half a year longer, when, if no claimant appeared, she might use it with less scruple. This half year of precaution expired, and nobody appeared to dispute her right.

She now became extremely anxious to divide this sum, gratuitously, with me. To me, the only obstacle to marriage was, the want of property. This obstacle, if Mary Wilmot consented to bestow her hand, where her heart had long reposed, would be removed. It was difficult, however, to persuade her to accept a man on whom she doated; but who, though urgent in his proffers, was not as deeply in love as herself. At length, she consented to be mine, provided, at the end of another half year, I should continue equally desirous of the gift.

At this time, I was become my own master, and having placed Mary in a safe and rural asylum at Abingdon, I paid a visit of a few weeks to my uncle near Hatfield. I had been here scarcely a fortnight, when, one evening, a stranger whom I had formerly known in my boyish days, as the son of a neighbouring farmer, paid me a visit. This person had been abroad, for several years, on mercantile adventures, in Europe and the West-Indies. He had just returned, and after various ineffectual inquiries after Wilmot, with whom he had been formerly in habits of confidence, he had come to me, in the prosecution of the same search.

After various preliminaries, he made me acquainted with the purpose of his search. The substance of his story was this: After toiling for wealth, during several years, in different ports of the Mediterranean, he at length acquired what he deemed sufficient for frugal subsistence in America. His property he partly invested in a ship and her cargo, and partly in a bill of exchange for *five thousand dollars*. This bill he transmitted to his friend Wilmot, with directions to reserve the proceeds till his arrival. He embarked, meanwhile, in his own vessel, sending, at the same time, directions to his wife, who was then at Glasgow, to meet him in America.

Unfortunately the ship was wrecked on the coast of Africa; the cargo was plundered or destroyed by the savage natives, and he, and a few survivors, were subjected to innumerable hardships, and the danger of perpetual servitude. From this he was delivered by the agents of the United States, in consequence of a treaty being ratified between *us* and the government of Algiers. Morton was among the miserable wretches whose chains were broken on that occasion, and he had just touched the shore of his native country.

His attention was naturally directed, in the first place, to the fate of the property transmitted to Wilmot. Wilmot, he heard, died suddenly. Wilmot's sister, his only known relation, was gone nobody could tell whither. The merchant, on whom his bills had been drawn, was partner in an Hamburg house, to which he had lately returned. The ships in which he sent his letters, had safely arrived. His bills had never been protested at any of the notaries, but all the written evidences of this transaction, that had remained in his own hands, had been buried, with his other property, in the waves.

After some suspense, and much inquiry, he was directed to me, as the dearest friend of Wilmot, and the intended husband of his sister.

You will see, my friend, that the mystery which perplexed us so long, was now at an end. The coincidence between the sum remitted, and that in our possession, and between the time of the probable receipt of the bills, and that of the deposit made by Wilmot at the bank, left me in no doubt as to the true owner of the money.

I explained to Morton, with the utmost clearness and simplicity, every particular relative to this affair. I acknowledged the plausibility of his claim; assured him of Miss Wilmot's readiness, and even eagerness, to do him justice, and promised to furnish him, on his return to Philadelphia, with a letter, introducing him to my friend. We parted.

This was a most heavy and unlooked-for disappointment

46

of all our schemes of happiness. My heart bled with compassion for the forlorn and destitute Mary. To be thus rescued from obscurity and penury, merely, to have these evils augmented by the bitterness of disappointment, was an hard lot.

I was just emancipated from my servitude. I was perfectly skilled in my art, but mere skill might supply myself with scanty bread, without enabling me to support a family. For that end, credit to procure an house, and the means of purchasing tools and materials, were necessary; but I knew not which way to look for them.

My nearest relation was my uncle Walter, who had taken me and my sisters, in our infancy, into his protection, and had maintained the girls, ever since. His whole property, however, was a small farm, whose profits were barely sufficient to defray the current expences of his family. At his death, this asylum would be lost to us, as his son, who would then become the occupant, had always avowed the most malignant envy and rancorous aversion to us. As my uncle was old, and of a feeble constitution, and as the girls were still young, and helpless, I had abundant theme on my own account, for uneasy meditation. To these reflections were added the miseries, which this reverse of fortune, would bring down upon the woman whom I prized beyond all the world.

One day, while deeply immersed in such contemplations as these, and musefully and mournfully pacing up and down the piazza of the inn at Hatfield, a chaise came briskly up to the door and stopped. I lifted my eyes, and beheld, alighting from it, a venerable figure, in whom I instantly recognized my friend and benefactor, Mr. Howard. The recognition was not more sudden on my side than on his, though a few years, at my age, were sufficient to produce great changes in personal appearance. Surprise and joy nearly deprived me of my senses, when he took me in his arms and saluted me in the most paternal manner. We entered the house, and as soon as I regained my breath, I gave utterance to my transports, in the most extravagant terms.

After the first emotion had subsided, he informed me that the sole object of his present journey to Hatfield, was a meeting with me. He had just arrived, with a wife and daughter, in America, where he designed to pass the rest of his days. It was his anxious hope to find me well and in my former situation, as he was now able to take the care of providing for me into his own hands. He inquired minutely into my history since we parted. I could not immediately conquer my reserve, on that subject, that was nearest my heart; but in other respects, I was perfectly explicit.

My narrative seemed not to displease him, and he condescended in his turn, to give me some insight into his own condition. I now discovered that he was sprung from the younger branch of a family, at once, ancient and noble. He received an education, more befitting his birth than his fortune; and had, by a thoughtless and dissipated life, wasted his small patrimony. This misfortune had contributed to tame his spirit, to open his eyes on the folly of his past conduct, and to direct him in the choice of more rational pursuits.

He was early distinguished by the favourable regards of a lady of great beauty and accomplishments. This blessing he did not prize as he ought. Though his devotion to Clara Lisle was fervent, he suffered the giddiness of youth, and the fascinations of pleasure, to draw him aside from the path of his true interest. Her regard for him made her overlook many of his foibles, and induced her to try various means to restore him to virtue and discretion. These efforts met with various success, till, at length, some flagrant and unexpected deviation, contrary to promises, and in defiance of her warnings, caused a breach between them that was irreparable.

The head of the nobler branch of Mr. Howard's family, was a cousin, a man of an excellent, though not of shining character. He had long been my friend's competitor for the favour of Miss Lisle. The lady's friends were his strenuous advocates, and used every expedient of argument

48

or authority, to subdue her prepossessions for another. None
of these had any influence, while my friend afforded her
any hopes of his reformation. His rashness and folly,
having, at length, extinguished these hopes, she complied,
after much reluctance and delay, with the wishes of
her family.

This event, communicated by the lady herself in a letter
to my friend, in which her motives were candidly stated,
and the most pathetic admonitions were employed to point
out the errors of his conduct, effected an immediate reformation. The blessing which he neglected or slighted, when
within his reach, now acquired inestimable value. His
regrets and remorses were very keen, and terminated in
a resolution to convert the wreck of his fortune into an
annuity, and retire for the rest of his life, to America. This
income, though small, was sufficient, economically
managed, to maintain him decently, at such a village
as Hatfield.

His residence here, at a distance from ancient companions, and from all the usual incitements to extravagance, completed, in a few years, a thorough change in
his character. He became, as I have formerly described him,
temperate, studious, gentle, and sedate. The irksomeness
of solitude, was somewhat relieved, by his acquaintance
with me, and by the efforts, which his growing kindness
for poor Ned, induced him to make for improving and
befriending the lad. These efforts, he imagined to be
crowned with remarkable success, and gradually concen-
tred all his social feelings in affection for me. He resolved
to be a father to me while living, and to leave his few
movables, all he had to leave, to me, at his death.

These prospects were somewhat disturbed, by
intelligence from home, that his cousin was dead.

Eighteen years absence from his native country, and from
Miss Lisle, had greatly strengthened his attachment to his
present abode, but had not effaced all the impressions of
his youth. The recollection of that lady's charms, her fidelity
to him in spite of the opposition of her family, and of his

own demerits, her generous efforts to extricate him from his difficulties, which even proceeded so far, as to pay, indirectly, and through the agency of others, a debt for which he had been arrested, always filled his heart with tenderness and veneration. These thoughts produced habitual seriousness, gratitude to this benefactor, an ardent zeal to fulfil her hopes by the dignity of his future deportment; but was not attended with any anger or regret at her compliance with the prudent wishes of her family, and her choice of one infinitely more worthy than himself. At this he sincerely rejoiced, and felt a pang, at the news of that interruption to her felicity, occasioned by her husband's death.

This event, however, came gradually to be viewed with somewhat different emotions. He began to reflect, that a tenderness so fervent as was once cherished for him, was not likely to be totally extinguished, by any thing but death. His cousin, though a man of worth, had been accepted from the impulse of generosity and pity, and not from that of love. She had been contented, and perhaps, happy in her union with him; but, if her first passion was extinct, he imagined there would be found no very great difficulty in reviving it. Both were still in the prime of life, being under thirty-eight years of age.

The correspondence, so long suspended, was now renewed between them; and Mr. Howard, with altered views, and renovated hopes, now embarked for that country which he had believed himself to have forever abjured. This new state of his affairs, by no means lessened his attachment to the fortunate youth, who had been, for eight years, the sole companion of his retirement. While his own destiny was unaccomplished, he thought it proper to forbear exciting any hopes in me. Should his darling purpose be defeated, he meant immediately to return. Should he meet with success, and his present views, as to the preference due to America, as a place of abode, continued, he meant to exert his influence with the elder and younger Clara, for his cousin had left behind him one child, a daughter, now in the bloom of youth, to induce them to emigrate. In every case, however, he was resolved that the farmer-boy should not be forgotten.

His projects were crowned, though not immediately, with all the success to be desired. The pair, whom so many years, and so wide an interval had severed, were now united, and the picture, which Mr. Howard drew, of the American climate and society, obtained his wife's consent to cross the ocean.

My dear Ned, said Mr. Howard to me, after relating these particulars, I have a pleasure in this meeting with you, that I cannot describe. You are the son, not of my instincts, but of my affections and my reason. Formerly I gave you my advice, my instructions, and company only, because I had nothing more to give. Now I am rich, and will take care that you shall never be again exposed to the chances of poverty. Though opulent, I do not mean to be idle. He that knows the true use of riches, never can be rich enough; but my occupation will leave me leisure enough for enjoyment; and you, who will share my labour, shall partake liberally of the profit. For this end, I mean to admit you as an inseparable member of my family, and to place you, in every respect, on the footing of my son.

My family consists of my wife and her daughter. The latter is now twenty-three, and you will be able to form a just conception of her person and mind when I tell you, that in both respects, she is exactly what her mother was at her age. There is one particular, indeed, in which the resemblance is most striking. She estimates the characters of others, not by the specious but delusive considerations of fortune or birth, but by the intrinsic qualities of heart and head. In her marriage choice, which yet remains to be made, she will forget ancestry and patrimony, and think only of the morals and understanding of the object. Hitherto, her affections have been wholly free, but . . . here Mr. Howard fixed his eyes with much intentness and significance, on my countenance . . . her parents will neither be grieved nor surprised, if, after a residence of

51

some time under the same roof with her *brother* Edward, she should no longer be able to boast of her freedom in that respect. If ever circumstances should arise to put my sincerity to the test, you shall never find me backward to convince you that I practise no equivocations and reserves, and prescribe no limitations or conditions, when I grant you the privilege of calling me father.

My stay with you at present must be short. I am now going, on business of importance, to Virginia. I shall call here on my return, which I expect will be soon, and take you with me to New-York, where I purpose to reside for some time. The interval may be useful to you, in settling and arranging your little matters, and equipping yourself for your journey.

Such, my friend, was the result of this meeting with Mr. Howard. Every thing connected with this event, was so abrupt and unexpected, that my mind was a scene of hurry and confusion, till his departure, next morning, left me at liberty to think on what had past. He left me with marks of the most tender affection, with particular advice in what manner to adjust my affairs, and with a promise of acquainting me by letter with all his motions.

I waited with some impatience for Mr. Howard's return. Many things had dropped from him, in our short interview, on which I had now leisure to reflect. His views, with regard to me, could not fail to delight my youthful fancy. I was dazzled and enchanted by the prospect which he set before me, of entering on a new and more dignified existence, of partaking the society of beings like Mrs. Howard and her daughter, and of aiding him in the promotion of great and useful purposes.

One intimation, however, had escaped him, which filled me with anxious meditations. The young Clara was the companion of his voyage hither. She had landed on this shore. To her presence and domestic intercourse, I was about to be introduced, and I was allowed to solicit her love. He was willing to bestow her upon me, and had, without doubt, gained the concurrence of her mother in this scheme. It was thus that he meant to insure the felicity, and establish the fortune, of his pupil.

There is somewhat in the advantages of birth and rank, in the habit of viewing objects through the medium of books, that gives a sacred obscurity, a mysterious elevation, to human beings. I had been familiar with the names of nobility and royalty, but the things themselves had ever been shrouded in an awe-creating darkness. Their distance had likewise produced an interval, which I imagined impossible for me to overpass. They were objects to be viewed, like the divinity, from afar. The only sentiments which they could excite, were reverence and wonder. That I should ever pass the mound which separated my residence, and my condition, from theirs, was utterly incredible.

The ideas annexed to the term *peasant,* are wholly inapplicable to the tillers of ground in America; but our notions are the offspring, more of the books we read, than of any other of our external circumstances. Our books are almost wholly the productions of Europe, and the prejudices which infect us, are derived chiefly from this source. These prejudices may be somewhat rectified by age, and by converse with the world, but they flourish in full vigour in youthful minds, reared in seclusion and privacy, and undisciplined by intercourse with various classes of mankind. In me, they possessed an unusual degree of strength. My words were selected and defined according to foreign usages, and my notions of dignity were modelled on a scale, which the *revolution* has completely taken away. I could never forget that my condition was that of a *peasant,* and in spite of reflection, I was the slave of those sentiments of self-contempt and humiliation, which pertain to that condition elsewhere, though chimerical and visionary on the western side of the Atlantic.

My ambition of dignity and fortune grew out of this supposed inferiority of rank. Experience had taught me, how slender are the genuine wants of an human being, and made me estimate, at their true value, the blessings of competence, and fixed property. Our fears are always proportioned to our hopes, and what is ardently desired, appears, when placed within our reach, to be an illusion designed to torment us. We are inclined to question the reality of that which our foresight had never suggested as near, though our wishes had perpetually hovered around it.

When the death of Wilmot put his sister in possession of a sum of money, which, when converted into land, would procure her and the man whom her affection had distinguished, a domain of four or five hundred fertile acres, my emotions I cannot describe. Many would be less affected in passing from a fisherman's hovel, to the throne of an opulent nation. It so much surpassed the ordinary bounds of my foresight, and even of my wishes, that, for a time, I was fain to think myself in one of my usual wakeful dreams. My doubts were dispelled only by the repetition of the same impressions, and by the lapse of time. I gradually became familiarized to the change, and by frequently revolving its benefits and consequences, raised the tenor of my ordinary sensations to the level, as it were, of my new condition.

From this unwonted height, Morton's reappearance had thrown us down to our original obscurity. But now my old preceptor had started up before me, and, like my good genius, had brought with him gifts immeasurable, and surpassing belief. They existed till now in another hemisphere; they occupied an elevation in the social scale, to which I could scarcely raise my eyes; yet they were now within a short journey of my dwelling. I was going to be ushered into their presence; but my privilege was not to be circumscribed by any sober limits. This heiress of opulence and splendour, this child of fortune, and appropriator of elegance and grace, and beauty, was proffered to me as a wife!

I reflected on the education which I had received from Mr. Howard; his affection for me, which had been unlimited; his relation to his wife's daughter, and the authority and respect, which that relation, as well as his personal

qualities, produced. I reflected on the futility of titular distinction; on the capriciousness of wealth, and its independ-
ance of all real merit, in the possessor, but still I could not
retain but for a moment, the confidence and self-respect
which flowed from these thoughts. I was still nothing more
than an obscure clown, whose life had been spent in the
barn-yard and corn-field, and to whose level, it was
impossible for a being qualified and educated like Clara,
ever to descend.

You must not imagine, however, that this descent was
desired by me. I was bound, by every tie of honour, though
not of affection, to Mary Wilmot. Incited by compassion
and by gratitude, I had plighted my vows to her, and had
formed no wish or expectation of revoking them. These
vows were to be completed, in a few months, by marriage;
but this event, by the unfortunate, though seasonable and
equitable claim of Morton, was placed at an uncertain distance. Marriage, while both of us were poor, would be an
act of the utmost indiscretion.

What, however, was taken away by Morton, might, I
fondly conceived, be restored to us by the generosity of Mr.
Howard. It was not, indeed, perfectly agreeable to the dictates of my pride, to receive fortune as the boon of any
one; but I had always been accustomed to regard Mr.
Howard more as my father than teacher, and it seemed
as if I had a natural right to every gift which was needful
to my happiness, and which was in his power to bestow.

Mary and her claims on me, were indeed, unknown to
my friend. He had no reason to be particularly interested
in her fate; and her claims interfered with those schemes
which he had apparently formed, with relation to Clara
and myself. How, I asked, might he regard her claims? In
what light would he consider that engagement of the
understanding, rather than of the heart, into which I had
entered? How far would he esteem it proper to adhere to
it; and what efforts might he make to dissolve it?

Various incidents had hindered me from thoroughly
explaining to him my situation, during his short stay at

Hatfield; but I resolved to seize the opportunity of our next meeting, and by a frank disclosure, to put an end to all my doubts. Meanwhile, I employed the interval of his absence, in giving an account of all these events to Mary, and impatiently waited the arrival of a letter. The period of my friend's absence was nearly expired, and the hourly expectation of his return prevented me from visiting Mary in person. Instead of his coming, however, I at length received a letter from him in these terms:

Richmond, Nov. 11.

I shall not call on you at Hatfield. I am weary of traversing hills and dales; and my detention in Virginia being longer than I expected, shall go on board a vessel in this port, bound for New-York. Contract, in my name, with your old friend, for the present accommodation of the girls, and repair to New-York as soon as possible. Search out No. ____, Broadway. If I am not there to embrace you, inquire for my wife or niece, and mention your name. Make haste; the women long to see a youth in whose education I had so large a share; and be sure, by your deportment, not to discredit your instructor, and belie my good report.

Howard.

Being, by this letter, relieved from the necessity of staying longer at Hatfield, I prepared to visit my friend at Abingdon. Some six or seven days had elapsed since my messenger had left with her my last letter, and I had not since heard from her. I had been enjoined to repair to New-York with expedition, but I could not omit the present occasion of an interview with Mary. Morton's claim would produce an essential change in her condition, and I was desirous of discussing with her the validity of this claim, and the consequences of admitting it.

I had not seen Morton since his first visit. I now, in my way to Abingdon, called at his father's house.

The old man appeared at the door. His son had visited and stayed with him a few days, but had afterwards returned to the city. He had gone thither to settle some affairs, and had promised to come back in a few weeks. He knew not in what affairs he was engaged; could not tell how far he had succeeded, or whereabout in the city he resided.

I proceeded to Abingdon, not without some expectation of Morton's having already accomplished his wishes, and persuaded my friend to refund the money; and yet, in a case of such importance, I could not easily believe that my concurrence, or at least, advice, would be dispensed with.

I went to her lodgings as soon as I arrived. I had procured her a pleasant abode, at the house of a lady who was nearly allied to my uncle, and where the benefits of decent and affectionate society could be enjoyed without leaving her apartments. Mrs. Bordley was apprized of the connection which subsisted between her inmate and me, and had contracted and expressed much affection for her guest. On inquiring for Miss Wilmot, of her hostess, she betrayed some surprise.

Mary Wilmot? she answered, that is a strange question from you: surely you know she is not here.

Not here? cryed I, somewhat startled; what has become of her?

You do not know then that she has left us for good and all?

No, indeed; not a syllable of any such design has reached me; but whither has she gone?

That is more than I can say. If you are uninformed on that head, it cannot be expected that I should be in the secret. I only know, that three days ago she told me of her intention to change her lodgings, and she did so accordingly, yesterday morning, at sun rise.

But what was her motive? What cause of dislike did she express to this house? I expected she would remain here, till she changed it for an house of her own.

Why indeed that may be actually the case now, for she went away with a very spruce young gentleman, in his chaise; but that cannot be. Poor creature! She was in no state for so joyous a thing as matrimony. She was very feeble; nay, she was quite ill: she had scarcely left her bed during five days before, and with difficulty got out of it, and dressed herself, when the chaise called for her. She would eat nothing, notwithstanding all my persuasion, and the pains I took to prepare some light nice thing, such as a weak stomach could bear. When she told me she meant to leave my house, I was as much surprised as you, and inquired what had offended or displeased her in my behaviour. She assured me that she had been entirely satisfied, and that her motives for leaving me had no connection with my deportment. There was a necessity for going, though she could not explain to me what it was. I ventured to ask where she designed to go, but she avoided answering me for some time; and when I repeated the question, she said, she could not describe her new lodgings. She knew not in what spot she was destined to take up her rest, and confessed, that there were the most cogent reasons for her silence on that head. I mentioned the coldness of the weather, and her own ill-health, but she answered, that no option had been left her, and that she must go, if it were even necessary to carry her from her bed to the carriage. All this, as you may well suppose, was strange, and I renewed my questions and intreaties, but she gave me no satisfaction, and persisted in her resolutions. Accordingly, on Thursday morning, a chaise stopped at the door, took her in, with a small trunk, and hastened away.

I was confounded and perplexed at this tale. No event was less expected than this. No intimation had even been dropped by Mary, that created the least suspicion of this design. She had left, as Mrs. Bordley proceeded to inform me, all her furniture, without direction to whom, or in what manner to dispose of it, and yet had said, that she never designed to return. The gentleman with whom she departed, was unknown to Mrs. Bordley, and had stopt so short a time as not to suffer her to obtain, by remarks or interrogatories, any gratification of her curiosity.

Having ineffectually put a score of questions to Mrs. Bordley, I entered the deserted apartments. The keys of closets and drawers no where appeared, though the furniture was arranged as usual. Inquiring of my companion for these, Ay, said she, I had almost forgotten. The last thing she said before the chair left the door, holding out a bunch of keys to me, was, Give these to . . . there her voice faultered, and I observed the tears flow. I received the keys, and though she went away without ending her sentence, I took for granted it was you she meant.

I eagerly seized the keys, and hoped, by their assistance, to find a clue to this labyrinth. I opened the closets and drawers and turned over their contents, but found no paper which would give me the intelligence I wanted. No script of any kind appeared; nothing but a few napkins and sheets, and the like cumbrous furniture. A writing-desk stood near the wall, but blank paper, wafers, and quills, were all that it contained. I desisted, at length, from my unprofitable labour, and once more renewed my inquiries of Mrs. Bordley.

She described the dress and form of the young man who attended the fugitive. I could not at first recognize in her description any one whom I knew. His appearance bespoke him to be a citizen, and he seemed to have arrived from the city, as well as to return thither. She dwelt with particular emphasis on the graces of the youth, and frequently insinuated that a new gallant had supplanted the old.

For some time, I was deaf to these surmises; but, at length, they insensibly revived in my fancy, and acquired strength. I began to account for appearances so as to justify my suspicion. She had not informed me of her motions; but that might arise from compunction and shame. There might even be something illicit in this new connection, to which necessity might have impelled her. The claims of Morton were made known to her by me, but possibly they had been previously imparted by himself. To shun that poverty to which this discovery would again reduce her, she listened to the offers of one, whose opulence was able to relieve her wants.

The notion that her conduct was culpable, vanished in a moment, and I abhorred myself for harbouring it. I remembered all the proofs of a pure and exalted mind, impatient of contempt and poverty, but shrinking with infinitely more reluctance from vice and turpitude, which she had given. I called to mind her treatment of a man, by name, Sedley, who had formerly solicited her love, and this remembrance gave birth to a new conjecture which subsequent reflection only tended to confirm.

Sedley had contracted a passion for Mary six or eight years ago. He was a man of excellent morals, and heir to a great fortune. He had patrimony in his own possession, and had much to hope for from his parents. These parents hated and reviled the object of their son's affections merely because she was poor, and their happiness seemed to depend on his renouncing her. To this he would never consent, and Mary might long ago have removed all the evils of her situation, had she been willing to accept Sedley's offers; but though she had the highest esteem for his virtues, and gratitude for his preference, her heart was another's. Besides, her notions of duty, were unusually scrupulous. Her poverty had only made her more watchful against any encroachments on her dignity, and she disdained to enter a family who thought themselves degraded by her alliance.

Sedley was a vehement spirit. Opposition whetted, rather than blunted his zeal; and Mary's conduct, while it heightened his admiration and respect, gave new edge to his desires. The youth whom she loved did not admit a mutual affection, and his poverty would have set marriage at an hopeless distance, even if it had been conceived. Sedley, therefore, believed himself the only one capable of truly promoting her happiness, and persisted in courting her favour longer and with more constancy that might have been expected from his ardent feelings and versatile age.

I need not repeat that Mary's affections were mine. To Sedley, therefore, I was the object of aversion and fear, and there never took place between us intercourse sufficient to subdue his prejudices. After her brother's death, marriage was resolved upon between us, and Sedley at length slackened the ardour of his pursuit. Still, however, he would not abjure her society.

Some secret revolution, perhaps, had been wrought in the mind of my friend. Her consent to marriage, had been extorted by me, for she was almost equally averse to marriage with one by whom she was not loved with that warmth which she thought her due, as with one who possessed every title to preference but her love. These scruples had been laid aside in consideration of the benefit which her brother's death, by giving her property, enabled her to confer upon me who was destitute. This benefit it was no longer in her power to confer. She would consider herself as severed from me forever, and in this state a renewal of Sedley's importunities, might subdue her reluctance. On comparing Mrs. Bordley's description of the voice, features, garb, and carriage of Mary's attendant, with those of Sedley, I fancied I discovered a strong resemblance between them. Some other coincidences, which came to light in the course of the day, made me certain as to the person of her companion. It was Sedley himself.

I was willing to gain all the knowledge of this affair which was within reach. Sedley's usual place of abode was his father's house in Virginia, but he chiefly passed his time in Philadelphia, where he resided with his sister, who was a lady of great merit, and left, by her husband's death, in opulent circumstances. This lady had made frequent overtures of friendship to Mary, but these had, for the most part, been declined. This reserve was not wholly free from pride. A mistaken sensibility made her shun those occasions for contempt or insult which might occur in her intercourse with the rich. The relation in which she stood to Sedley was another impediment. A just regard for his happiness compelled her to exclude herself as much as possible from his company. The kindness of Mrs. Valentine had not been diverted by these scruples and reserves, and some intercourse had taken place between them before Mary's retirement to Abingdon.

This change of views in my friend had given me much

disquiet, but some reflection convinced me that it was a cause of rejoicing rather than regret. Wedlock had been desired by me, more from zeal for the happiness of another, than for my own. I had lamented that destiny which made the affections of three persons merely the instruments of their misery, and had exerted my influence to give a new direction to my friend's passions. This undertaking was no less delicate than arduous, and no wonder, that in hands so unskilful as mine, the attempt should fail. I could not be much displeased that this end was effected, though I was somewhat mortified on finding that she did not deem me worthy of being apprized of her schemes. I reflected, however, that this information might only be delayed; and imagined a thousand plausible reasons which might induce her to postpone intelligence so unexpected, if not disagreeable to me.

Next morning I repaired to the city, and to Mrs. Valentine's house. I inquired of a female servant for Miss Wilmot, but was told that she had been there, a few hours, on the preceding Thursday, and had then gone, in company with her mistress and Mr. Sedley, to New-York. No time had been fixed for their return, but Mrs. Valentine had said that her absence might last for six or eight months. The steward, who might afford me more information, was out of town.

Thus my conjectures were confirmed; and having no reason for further delay, I immediately set out in the same road. My thoughts, disembarrassed from all engagements with Mary, persuaded of her union with Sedley, and convinced that this union would more promote her happiness than any other event, I returned without reluctance to Clara Howard. I was impatient to compare those vague and glittering conceptions which hovered in my fancy, with the truth; therefore adopted the swiftest conveyance, and arrived, in the evening of the same day, at Powle's Hook ferry.

My excursions had hitherto been short and rare, and the stage on which I was now entering, abounded with novelty and grandeur. The second city in our country was

62

familiar to my fancy by description, but my ideas were disjointed and crude, and my attention was busy in search-ing, in the objects which presented themselves, for simili-tudes which were seldom to be met with. A sort of tremulous, but pleasing astonishment, overwhelmed me, while I gazed through the twilight, on the river and the city on the further shore. My sensations of solemn and glowing expectation chiefly flowed from the foresight of the circumstances in which I was preparing to place myself.

Men exist more for the future than the present. Our being is never so intense and vivid, if I may so speak, as when we are on the eve of some anticipated revolution, momentous to our happiness. Our attention is attracted by every incident that brings us nearer to the change, and we are busy in marking the agreement between objects as they rise before us, and our previous imaginations. Thus it was with me. My palpitations increased as I drew near the house to which I had been directed, and I could scarcely govern my emotions sufficiently to inquire of the servant who appeared to my summons, for Mrs. Howard.

I was ushered into a lighted parlour, and presently a lady entered. She bore no marks of having passed the middle age, and her countenance exhibited the union of fortitude and sweetness. Her air was full of dignity and condescen-sion. Methought I wanted no other assurance but that which the sight of her conveyed, that this was the wife of my friend.

I was thrown, by her entrance, into some confusion, and was at a loss in what manner to announce myself. The moment she caught a distinct glance of my figure, her features expanded into a smile, and offering her hand, she exclaimed . . . Ahah! This, without doubt, is the young friend whom we have so anxiously looked for. Your name is Edward Hartley, and as such I welcome you, with the tenderness of a mother, to this home. Turning to a servant who followed her, she continued, call Clara hither. Tell her that a friend has arrived.

Before I had time to comment on this abrupt reception,

the door was again opened. A nymph, robed with the most graceful simplicity, entered, and advancing towards me, offered me her hand. . . . Here, said the elder lady, is the son and brother whom Mr. Howard promised to procure for us. Welcome him, my girl, as such.

Lifting her eyes from the floor, and casting on me bashful but affectionate looks, the young lady said, in an half-whisper, he is truly welcome . . . and again offered the hand which, confounded and embarrassed as I at first was, I had declined to accept. Now, however, I was less backward.

An unaffected and sprightly conversation followed, that tended to banish those timidities which were too apparent in my deportment. Mrs. Howard entered into a gay and almost humorous description of my person, such as she had received before my arrival, and remarked the differences between the picture and the original, intermingling questions, which, compelling me to open my lips in answer to them, helped me to get rid of my aukwardness. Presently supper was prepared, and dispatched with the utmost cheerfulness.

My astonishment and rapture were unspeakable. Such condescension and familiarity, surpassing all my fondest imaginations, from beings invested with such dazzling superiority, almost intoxicated my senses. My answers were disadvantageous to myself, for they were made in such a tumult and delirium of emotions, that they could not fail of being incoherent or silly.

Gradually these raptures subsided, and I acted and spoke with more sobriety and confidence. I had leisure also to survey the features of my friends. Seated at opposite sides of the table, with lights above and around us, every lineament and gesture were distinctly seen. It was difficult to say which person was the most lovely. The bloom and glossiness of youth had, indeed, disappeared in the elder, but the ruddy tints and the smoothness of health, joined to the most pathetic and intelligent expression, set the mother on a level, even in personal attractions, with the daughter. No music was ever more thrilling than the tones of Clara. They sunk, deeply, into my heart, while her eyes, casually turned on me, and beaming with complacency, contributed still more to enchant me.

In a few days, the effects of novelty gradually disappearing, I began to find myself at home. Mr. Howard's arrival, and the cordiality of his behaviour, contributed still more to place me at ease. Those employments he designed for me, now occurred. They generally engrossed the half of each day. They were light, dispatched without toil, or anxiety, and conduced, in innumerable ways, to my pleasure and improvement. They introduced me to men of different professions and characters, called forth my ingenuity and knowledge, and supplied powerful incitements to new studies and inquiries.

At noon, the day's business was usually dismissed, and the afternoon and evening were devoted to intellectual and social occupations. These were generally partaken by the ladies, and visits were received and paid so rarely, as to form no interruption to domestic pleasures. Collected round the fire, and busied in music or books, or discourse, the hours flew away with unheeded rapidity. The contrast which this scene bore to my past life, perpetually recurred to my reflections, and added new and inexpressible charms to that security and elegance by which I was at present surrounded.

Clara was the companion of my serious and my sportive hours. I found, in her character, simplicity and tenderness, united to powerful intellects. The name of children was often conferred upon us by my friend and his wife; all advances to familiarity and confidence between us were encouraged; our little plans of walking or studying together were sanctioned by smiles of approbation, and their happiness was evidently imperfect while ours was suspended or postponed.

In this intercourse, there was nothing to hinder the growth of that sentiment, which is so congenial with virtuous and youthful bosoms. My chief delight was in sharing the society and performing offices of kindness for Clara, and this delight the frankness of her nature readily shewed to be mutual. Love was not avowed or solicited, and did not frequently recur, in an undisguised shape, to my thoughts. My desires seemed to be limited to her presence, and to participating her occupations and amusements. Satisfied in like manner with this, no marks of impatience or anxiety were ever betrayed by her, but in my absence.

The fulness of content which I now experienced, did not totally exclude the remembrance of Mary. I had heard and seen nothing of Morton since my departure from Hatfield. The only way of accounting for this, was to suppose that Mary and he had met, and that the former, persuaded of the equity of his claim, had resigned to him the money which he had remitted to her brother.

The silence which she had observed, involved me in the deepest perplexity. I spared no pains to discover Mrs. Valentine's residence, but my pains were fruitless. My inquiries rendered it certain that, at least, no such person resided in New-York.

Thus occupied, the winter passed away. On a mild, but blustering evening in March, I happened to be walking, in company with Clara, on the battery. I chanced, after some time, to spy before me, coming in an opposite direction, the man whose fate had engaged so much of my attention. It was Morton himself. On seeing me, he betrayed much satisfaction, but no surprise. We greeted each other affectionately. Observing that he eyed my companion with particular earnestness, I introduced him to her.

This meeting was highly desirable, as I hoped to collect from it an explication of what had hitherto been a source of perplexity. I likewise marked a cheerfulnes in my friend's deportment, which shewed that some favourable change had taken place. He seemed no less anxious than I for a confidential interview; and an appointment of a meeting on the same evening was accordingly made.

Having conducted Clara home, I hastened to the place appointed. I was forthwith ushered into a parlour, where Morton was found in company with a lady of graceful and pensive mein, with a smiling babe in her arms, to whom he introduced me as to his wife. This incident confirmed my favourable prognostics, and I waited, with impatience, till the lady's departure removed all constraint from our conversation.

In a short time, she left us alone. I congratulate you, said I, on your reunion with your family, but cannot help expressing my surprise that you never favoured me with a second visit, or gave me any intelligence of your good fortune.

He apologized for his neglect, by saying, that the arrival of his wife and daughter, in New-York, obliged him, shortly after our interview, to hasten to this city, where succcessive engagements had detained him till now. He was, nevertheless, extremely desirous of a meeting, and intended, as soon as pleasant weather should return, to go to Hatfield, on purpose to see me. This meeting, however, had fortunately occurred to preclude the necessity of that journey. He then inquired into the health of Miss Wilmot, and her present situation. I was anxious to see her, he continued, on account of that affair, on which we conversed at our last meeting. As her brother's friend, I was, likewise, desirous of seeing her, and tendering her any service in my power, but when taking measures to bring about an interview, I received a letter from my wife, who, to my infinite surprise and satisfaction, had embarked for America, and arrived safely at New-York. My eagerness to see my family, made me postpone this interview for the present, and one engagement has since so rapidly succeeded another, that I have never been at leisure to execute this design.

What, said I, has no meeting taken place between Mary Wilmot and you? Has she not restored the money you claimed?

Surely, replied he, you cannot be ignorant that I have never received it. I doubted whether I ought to receive it, even if my title were good. It was chiefly to become acquainted with her, that I looked for her, and my good fortune has since enabled me to dispense with any thing else.

The property, left by her brother, may rightfully belong to her, notwithstanding present appearances. At any rate, her possession shall be unmolested by me.

He then proceeded to inform me, that his wife's parents being deceived by his long silence, and the intelligence of his shipwreck, into the opinion of his death, had relented, and settled an independent and liberal pension on their daughter, on condition of her chusing some abode at a distance from them. She proposed to retire, with her child, to some neat and rural abode in Cornwall, and was on the point of executing this design, when letters were received from her husband, at Algiers, which assured her of his safety, and requested her to embark for America, where it was his intention to meet her. She had instantly changed her plans, and selling her annuity on good terms, had transported herself and her property to New-York, where her husband being apprised of her arrival, hastened to join her.

Thus, continued Morton, you have, in my destiny, a striking instance of the folly of despair. My shipwreck, and my long absence, in circumstances which hindered all intercourse between me and my family, were the most propitious events that could have happened. Nothing but the belief of my death, and the consequent distresses of my wife, could have softened the animosity of her parents. Her disobedience, they thought, had been amply punished, and fate having taken from me, the power of receiving any advantage from their gift, they consented to make her future life secure, at least, from want.

It was also lucky, that their returning affection stopped just where it did. Their resentment was still so powerful as to make them refuse to see her, and to annex to their gift, the stern condition of residing at a distance from them. Hence she was enabled to embark for America, without detecting their mistake, as to my death. They carefully shut their ears against all intelligence of her condition, whether direct or indirect, and will probably pass their lives in ignorance of that, which, if known, would only revive their upbraidings and regrets.

I am not sorry for the hardships I have indured. They are not unpleasing to remembrance, and serve to brighten and endear the enjoyments of my present state, by contrast with former sufferings. I have enough for the kind of life which I prefer to all others, and have no desire to enlarge my stock. Meanwhile, I am anxious for the welfare of Miss Wilmot, and shall rejoice in having been, though undesignedly, the means of her prosperity.

I heard, in Philadelphia, that a marriage was on foot between her and you. I flattered myself, when I met you this evening, that your companion was she, and secretly congratulated you on the possession of so much gracefulness and beauty. In this, it seems, I was partly mistaken. This is a person very different from Mary Wilmot; but a friend, whom I met, shortly after parting from you, and to whom I described her, assured me that this was the object of your choice. Pray, what has become of Miss Wilmot?

I frankly confessed to him, my ignorance of her condition, and related what had formerly been the relation between her and me. I expressed my surprise at finding that she was still in possession of the money, after the representations I had made; and at the silence she had so long observed.

When I recollected in what manner, and in whose company, she had left Abingdon, I could not shut out some doubts, as to her integrity. She was, indeed, mistress of her own actions, and Sedley was not unworthy of her choice; but her neglect of my letter, and her keeping this money, were suspicious accompanyments. This belief was too painful, to attain my ready acquiescence, and I occasionally consoled myself, by imagining her conduct to proceed from some misapprehension, on the one or other part. Mrs. Valentine's reputation was unspotted, and under her guardianship, it was scarcely possible for any injury to approach my friend's person or morals.

My anxiety to discover the truth, was now increased. After being so long accustomed to partake her cares, and watch over her safety, I could not endure this profound ignorance. I was even uncertain, as to her existence. It was impossible, but that my friendship would be of some benefit. My sympathy could not fail to alleviate her sorrow, or enhance her prosperity.

But what means had I of removing this painful obscurity. I knew not which way to look for her. My discoveries must be wholly fortuitous.

Notwithstanding my own enjoyments, I allowed the image of Mary Wilmot to intrude into my thoughts too frequently. Some change in my temper was discerned by Clara, and she inquired into the cause. At first, I was deterred by indefinite scruples, from unfolding the cause, but some reflection shewed me that I was wrong, in so long concealing from her, a transaction of this moment. I, therefore, seized a favourable opportunity, and recounted all the incidents of my life, connected with this poor fugitive.

When I began, however, I was not aware of the embarrassment which I was preparing to suffer and inflict. We used to sit up much longer than our friends, and after they had retired to repose, taking their places on the sofa, allowed the embers to die gradually away, while we poured forth, unrestrained, the effusions of the moment. It was on one of these occasions that, after a short preface, I began my story. I detailed the origin of my intercourse with Miss Wilmot, the discovery of her passion for me, the contest between that passion and my indifference on one side, and the claims and solicitations of Sedley on the other. I was listened to with the deepest emotion. Curiosity enabled her to stifle it for some time; but when I came to the events of Wilmot's death, the discovery of his property, and the consequent agreement to marry, she was able to endure the recital no longer. She burst into tears, and articulated with difficulty: Enough, my friend, I know the rest. I know what you would say. Your melancholy is explained, and I see that my fate is fixed in eternal misery.

I was at once shocked, astonished, and delighted, by the discovery which was thus made, and made haste, by recounting subsequent transactions, to correct her error. She did not draw the same inferences from the flight and silence of the girl, or drew them with less confidence than I. She was not consoled by my avowals of passion for herself, and declared that she considered my previous contract as inviolable. Nothing could absolve me from it, but the absolute renunciation of Miss Wilmot herself.

I considered the disappearance and silence of Mary, as a sufficient renunciation of her claims, and once more dwelt upon the scruples and objections which she had formerly raised to our alliance; which had been, imperfectly, and for a time, removed by the death of her brother, and which, Morton's arrival, had restored to their original strength. Some regard, likewise, was due to my own felicity, and to that of one whose happiness deserved to be as zealously promoted as that of the fugitive. It was true, that I had tendered vows to Miss Wilmot, which my understanding, and not my heart; which gratitude, and not affection, had dictated. This tender, in the circumstances in which I was then placed, was necessary and proper; but these circumstances had now changed. My offer had been tacitly rejected. Not only my love, but my friendship, had been slighted and despised. My affections had never been devoted to another, and the sacrifice of inclination was limited to myself. This indifference, however, existed no more. It was supplanted by a genuine and ardent attachment for one in all respects more worthy. I was willing to hope that this attachment was mutual. Fortune and her parents, and her own heart, were all propitious to my love; and to stifle and thwart it for the sake of one, who had abjured my society and my friendship; who renounced my proffered hand, and cancelled all my promises; who had possibly made herself unworthy of my esteem, by the forfeiture of honour itself, or more probably had given up all her claims on my justice and compassion, by accepting another, would be, in the highest degree, absurd and unjustifiable.

These arguments wrought no effect upon Clara. It was her duty, she answered, to contend with selfish regards, and to judge of the feelings of others by her own. Whatever reluctance she might experience in resigning me to another, in whatever degree she might thwart the wishes and schemes of her parents, it was her duty to resign me, and she should derive more satisfaction from disinterested, than from selfish conduct. She would not attempt to disguise her feelings and wishes, and extenuate the sacrifice she was called on to make, but she had no doubt as to what was right, and her resolution to adhere to it would be immovable.

This resolution, and this inflexibility, were wholly unexpected. I was astonished and mortified, and having exhausted all my arguments in vain, gave way to some degree of acrimony and complaint, as if I were capriciously treated. At one time, I had thoughts of calling her parents to my aid, and explaining to them my situation with regard to Mary, and soliciting them to exert their authority in my behalf with Clara.

A deep and incurable sadness now appeared in my friend, and strong, though unostentatious proofs were daily afforded, that an exquisite sense of justice had dictated her deportment, and that she had laid upon herself a task to which her fortitude was scarcely equal. It appeared to me the highest cruelty to aggravate the difficulty of this task, by enlisting against her those whose authority she most revered, and whose happiness she was most desirous of promoting.

My eagerness to trace Miss Wilmot to her retreat, to find out her condition, and make her, if possible, my advocate with Clara, was increased by this unhappy resolution. I began to meditate anew upon the best means of effecting this. I blamed myself for having so long failed to employ all the means in my power, and resolved to begin my search without delay. Clara, whose conclusions respecting Miss Wilmot's motives were far more charitable than mine, was no less earnest in inciting me to this pursuit. She believed Miss Wilmot's conduct to have been consistent with integrity, that it flowed from a generous but erroneous self-denial, and that the re-establishment of intercouse between us, would terminate in the happiness of both.

The incidents formerly related, had made it certain that Miss Wilmot had flown away in company with Sedley. Sedley's patrimony and fixed abode were in Virginia. There, it was most probable, that he and the fugitive would be found. There, at least, should Sedley have abandoned his ancient residence, was it most likely that the means of tracing his footsteps, would be found. Mary, if not at present in his company, or in that of his sister, had not perhaps concealed her asylum from them, and might be discovered by their means. Fortunately, Mr. Howard had engagements at Richmond which would shortly require his own presence, or that of one in whom he could confide. He had mentioned this necessity in my presence in such a way as shewed that he would not be unwilling to transfer his business to me. Hitherto I had been unwilling to relinquish my present situation; but now I begged to be entrusted with his commission, as it agreed with my own projects.

In a few days I set out upon this journey. Passing, necessarily, at no great distance from Hatfield, I took that opportunity of visiting my uncle and sisters. You may imagine my surprise on finding, at my uncle's house, a letter for me, from Mary, which had arrived there just after my departure, in the preceding autumn, and had lain, during the whole winter, neglected and forgotten, in a drawer.

This letter was worthy of my friend's generous and indignant spirit, and fully accounted for her flight from Abingdon. She was determined to separate herself from me, to die in some obscure recess, whither I should never be able to trace her, and thus to remove every obstacle in the way of my pretentions to one, younger, lovelier and richer than herself. In this letter was enclosed an order for the money, which, as I had taught her too hastily to believe, belonged to another.

I believe you know that I am not a selfish or unfeeling wretch. What but the deepest regret, could I feel at the ignorance in which I had so long been kept of her destiny; what, but vehement impatience to discover the place of her retreat, and persuade her to accept my vows, or, at least, to take back the money to which Morton's title was not yet proved, which would save her at least from the horrors of that penury she was so little qualified to endure, and to which, for more than six inclement months, she had been, through unhappy misapprehension, subjected?

In this mood I hastened to this city, but my heroism quickly evaporated. I felt no abatement of my eagerness to benefit the unhappy fugitive, by finding her; counselling her; consoling her; repossessing her of the means of easy, if not of affluent subsistence; but more than this I felt myself incapable of offering. I knew full well, that, when acquainted with the whole truth, she never would accept me as hers; but I despaired of gaining any thing with respect to Clara, by that rejection. I despaired of ever lighting again on Miss Wilmot. Besides, my pride was piqued and wounded by resolutions that appeared to me absurd; to arise from prejudiced views and a narrow heart; from unreasonable regards bestowed upon one, of whose merits she had no direct knowledge, and blamable indifference to another whom she had abundant reason to love.

The letters that passed between us only tended to convince me that she was implacable, and I left the city for Virginia with a secret determination of never returning. I resolved to solicit Mr. Howard's permission to accompany some surveyors employed by him, who were to pass immediately into the western country. By this means, I hoped to shake off fetters that were now become badges of misery and ignominy.

The wisdom of man, when employed upon the future, is incessantly taught its own weakness. Had an angel whispered me, as I mounted the stage for Baltimore, that I should go no further on that journey than Schuylkill, and that, without any new argument or effort on my part, Clara would, of her own accord, call me back to her and to happiness, I should no doubt have discredited the intimation. Yet such was the event.

In order to rescue a drowning passenger I leaped into the river. The weather being bleak and unwholesome, I was seized, shortly after my coming out, with a fever, which reduced me, in a very few days, to the brink of the grave. Now was the solicitude of my Clara awakened. When in danger of losing me forever, she discovered the weakness of her scruples, and effectually recalled me to life, by entreating me to live for her sake.

I have not yet perfectly recovered my usual health. I am unfit for business or for travelling; and standing in need of some amusement which will relieve, without fatiguing my attention, I called to mind your claims on me, and determined to give you the account you desired.

When I received your letter, informing me of your design to meet me in New-York, I was utterly dispirited and miserable. My design of coming southward, I knew, would prevent an immediate meeting with you, and as I had then conceived the project of a journey to the western waters, I imagined that we should never have another meeting.

Now, my friend, my prospects are brighter, and I hope to greet you the moment of your arrival in New-York. I shall go thither as soon as I am able. I shall never repose till my happiness with Clara is put beyond the power of man to defeat.

But, alas! what has become of Mary Wilmot. Heaven grant that she be safe. While unacquainted with her destiny, my happiness will never be complete; day and night I torment myself with fruitless conjectures about her. Yet she went away with Sedley, a man of honour, and her lover, and with his sister, whose integrity cannot be questioned. With these she cannot be in danger, or in poverty. This reflection consoles me.

I long to see you, my friend. I hope to be of some service to you. You will see, by this long detail, that fortune has been kind to me. Indeed, when I take a view of the events of the last year, I cannot find language for my wonder. My blessings are so numerous and exorbitant, my merits so slender.

I wish thee patience to carry thee to the end of this long letter.

Adieu.
E. H.

LETTER XIV

TO E. HARTLEY
New-York, April 28.

WHY don't you come home, my love? Are you not quite well? Tell me when; the day, the hour, when I may expect you. I will put new elegance into my garb; new health into my cheeks; new light; new love; new joy into my eyes, against that happy hour.

Would to heaven I were with you. I represented to my father what an excellent nurse I should prove, but he would not suffer me to accompany him. I have a good mind to steal away to you, even now; but are you not already quite well? Yes, you are; or, very soon will be. Time and care are all that are required to make you so.

But, poor Mary. . . . Does not your heart, my Edward, bleed for poor Mary? Can I rob her of so precious a good; bereave her of the gem of which she has so long been in secure possession?

Can I riot in bliss, and deck myself in bridal ornaments, while she lives pining in dreary solitude, carrying to the grave an heart broken by the contumelies of the world; the horrors of indigence and neglect; and chiefly by the desertion of him on whom she doated? Do I not know what it is to love? Cannot I easily imagine what it is to bear about an unrequited passion? Have I not known, from infancy, the pleasures of affluence and homage? Cannot I conceive the mortifications to one thus bred up, of poverty and labour? Indeed, my friend, I conceive them so justly, that till Mary Wilmot is discovered, and is either been found happy, or been made happy, no selfish gratification, whatever, can insure my peace.

I should not thus be deeply interested for a mere stranger. I know your Mary. Your details, full of honesty and candour, have made me thoroughly acquainted with her. You have given me, in the picture of her life, the amplest picture of an human being that I ever was allowed to survey. Her virtue, my friend, has been tried. Not without foibles, she is, for which she was indebted to her education; but her signal excellence lies in having, in spite of a most pernicious education, so few faults.

My friend, you *must* find her. As you value my happiness, you *must*. Nay, as you value my love. If your zeal did not lead you to move heaven and earth in her cause, you would be, in my eyes, a wretch. Nay, if you did not. . . . But I am straying from the path. I must not think of her, lest my admiration and my pity for her get the better of my love for you.

Pray, make haste and be well, that you make as happy as she can be, your fond, your devoted

Clara.

LETTER XV

TO CLARA HOWARD
Philadelphia, April 30.

I WILL never yield to you, my friend, in zeal for one whom I reverence and love so much as Mary Wilmot. How I adore your generous, your noble spirit. While limited to the real good of that girl; while zealous to confer happiness on her, without an equivalent injury to others, I applaud, and will strive to emulate your generosity. . . .

An incident has just occurred, that seems to promise some intelligence concerning her. It has made me very uneasy. I am afraid she is not happy. I am afraid she is . . . is not happy; I mean, I fear she is . . . unhappy. But I know not what I would say. I am bewildered . . . by my terrors on her account. Let me tell you what I have heard. Judge for yourself. Unhappy the hour that I wrote the last letter from Hatfield. Yet, who could imagine that the intelligence contained in it would suggest so rash, so precipitate a flight!

This Sedley, whose fidelity, whose honour I have so often applauded, is, I am afraid, a miscreant; a villain. Mary . . . the very thought takes away my breath . . . is, I fear, a lost, undone creature. . . .

Yet how? Such a fall surely was impossible. Mary Wilmot, whose whole life has been exposed to my view; whom I have seen in the most unguarded moments; whose indifference to Sedley; whose unconquerable aversion to his most honourable and flattering offers, I have so often witnessed, could not forget herself; her dignity. I will not believe it.

But what am I saying? Let me recollect myself, and lay, distinctly, before you, the cause of my apprehensions.

This morning being disengaged, and the air mild, instead of going on with this letter, I stole abroad to enjoy the sweet breath of heaven. My feet carried me, unaware, to the door of the house in which I formerly passed a servitude of three years. My old master, Watkins, of time-measuring memory, has been some time dead. The widow turned her stock into revenue, and now lives at her ease. Though not eminently good, she is far from being a bad woman. She never behaved otherwise than kindly to "Neddy Sobersides," as she used to call me, and I feel somewhat like gratitude, which would not let me pass the door. So I called, to see the old dame.

I found her by a close-stove, in the parlour, knitting a blue stocking. . . . Lack a day, said she, why as I's a living soul, this is our Ned.

After the usual congratulations and inquiries were made, she proceeded: Why, what a fine story is this, Neddy, that we hear of you? Why, they say you've grown a rich man's son, and are going to be married to a fine rich, great lady, from some other country.

I avoided a direct answer. She continued: Ah! dear me, we all thought you were going to be married to poor Molly Wilmot, the mantua-maker. Nay, for the matter o' that, my poor dear man, I remember, said, as how, that if so be, we'd wait a year or so, we should see things turn up so, that you and her should be married already; at that time; and that, I remember, was just as your time was up. But Molly, (with a very significant air this was said) has carried her goods to a much worse market it seems.

Why, know you any thing of Miss Wilmot?

Why, I don't know but as I does. I doesn't know much to her advantage though, you may depend, Neddy.

I was startled. What do you know of her? Tell me, I beseech you, all you know.

Why, I don't know much, not I; but Peggy, my nurse,

said something or other about her, yesterday. She drank tea with me . . .

Pray, said I, impatiently, what said your nurse of Miss Wilmot?

Why, I don't know as I ought to tell . . . . But I will not tease you, Clara, as I was tired with the jargon of the old woman. I will give you the sum of her intelligence in my own words.

The nurse had lately been in the family of Mr. Kalm, of Germantown . . . between which and that of Mrs. Valentine, I have long known that much intimacy subsisted. Sedley, it seems, passed through this city about three weeks ago, and spent a day at Mr. Kalm's. At dinner, when the nurse was present, the conversation turned upon the marriage of Sedley, which, it seems, was just concerted with the daughter of a wealthy family in Virginia. The lady's name was mentioned, but the nurse forgot it.

Mrs. Kalm, who is noted for the freedom of her discourse, reminded Mr. Sedley of the mantua-maker who eloped with him from Abingdon last autumn, and jestingly inquired into her present condition. Sedley dealt in hints and innuendoes, which imported that he was on as good terms with Molly Wilmot as he desired to be; that all his wishes, with respect to her, were now accomplished; that she knew her own interest too well to allow any obstruction to his marriage to come from her; that she would speedily resume her customary station in society, as the *cause* of her present *disappearance* was likely to be soon removed.

I will not torment you or myself, by dwelling on further particulars. My informant was deplorably defective in the means of imparting any clear and consistent meaning. An hour was employed in recollecting facts and answering questions, all which, taken together, imported nothing less than that an improper connection had, for some months, subsisted between Sedley and my friend; a connection of such a nature as was consistent with his marriage with another.

Comfort me; counsel me, my angel. I gathered from the

beldame's tale, the probability at least, that Miss Wilmot was still in this city. Shall I seek her? shall I . . . Tell me, in short, what I must believe? what I shall do?

E.H.

.

LETTER XVI

TO E. HARTLEY
New-York, May 2.

AH! my friend! art thou so easily misled? Does
slander find in thee a dupe of her most silly and
extravagant contrivances? An old nurse's envious
and incoherent tale! At second hand, too! With all the
deductions and embellishments which must cleave to every
story, as it passes through the imagination of two gossips.

Art thou not ashamed of thyself, Edward? To impute
black pollution to the heart, whose fortitude, whose purity, so many years of trial have attested, on the authority
of a crazy beldame, repeating the malignant inferences,
and embellishing the stupid hints of an old nurse. Sedley
is a villain and a slanderer. Had *I* been present when he
thought proper to blast the fame of the innocent and absent, I should not have controuled my indignation. I should
have cast the furious *lie* in his teeth.

And is it possible, my friend, that on such evidence as
this, you build your belief that Mary has become an abandoned creature! I am ashamed of such credulity. She is in
the same city, you believe, yet sit idly in your chamber,
lamenting that depravity which exists only in your fancy,
and finding in such absurd and groundless suspicions, a
reason for withholding that property which, whether she
be vile as dirt, or bright as heaven, is equally her right.

Seek her out this moment. Never rest till you have found
her. Restore to her, her own property; tender her your
counsel; your aid. Mention me to her as one extremely
anxious to cultivate her good opinion, and enjoy her

friendship. Do this, Edward, instantly, I exhort, I intreat, I command you; and let me know the result.

C. H.

LETTER XVII

TO CLARA HOWARD
Philadelphia, May 4.

I HAVE just returned from Germantown, and find your letter on my table. Thank heaven, I have not merited all your rebukes. That anxiety to ascertain the truth, and that unwillingness to trust to such witnesses as gossips and nurses, which you think I ought to feel, I really have felt. My last was written in the first tumult of my thoughts. The moment I laid down the pen, and began more deliberately to reflect upon the subject, doubts and hopes thronged into my imagination. I resolved to bend every nerve to discover the retreat of Mary, and ascertain her true situation.

As Sedley was so well known to Mrs. Kalm, I resolved to visit that lady. I had no acquaintance with her, but I overlooked the impropriety of my application, and set out immediately to Germantown.

Being admitted to an apartment in which I found that lady alone, I introduced myself in some confused way, I scarcely know how, and inquired whether she knew the person whom Sedley was about to marry, and whether she could afford me any information of the place where Mary Wilmot was likely to be found.

She answered, with great civility, that Sedley's sister was her dear friend; that Mrs. Valentine resided, at this time, in New-England; that her brother, passing lately through this city, in order to join her, had spent part of a day with Mr. Kalm; that Sedley had given his friends leave to consider him as upon the eve of marriage, but had not thought proper to disclose to them the name and family of the lady; that they were totally in the dark on both these heads, but were inclined to believe that she was a woman of Boston; that as to Mary Wilmot, she knew nothing of her or her affairs.

Mrs. Kalm's curiosity was somewhat excited by the singularity of my introduction, and she soon became inquisitive in her turn. Encouraged by her frank and communicative humour, I ventured to explain, unreservedly, the motive of my inquiries. She smiled at the impression which the tale of the nurse and gossip had made on my fears.

Your uneasiness, said she, was without any foundation. Perhaps we might have jestingly talked of Miss Wilmot's elopement with Sedley, because his pretensions to that girl are pretty well known; but I am not now to be told that your friend was, on that journey, the companion, not of the brother, but the sister, and that Miss Wilmot's reputation and virtue, could not be safer under her own guardianship than under Mrs. Valentine's. Besides, there is not a man in the world, of stricter principles than Sedley. What you have heard, or something like it, might actually have passed at that dinner, but no one could have construed it in a way injurious to Sedley or your friend, but who was wholly unacquainted with the parties, or who was very hungry after slander.

Sedley certainly talked as if he knew more of Miss Wilmot than he just then thought fit to disclose. What he said was accompanied with nods and smiles of some significance; but I should just as readily have put an evil construction on his hints, had he been talking of his own sister. All the world knows that a woman of merit would be sure to receive from Sedley, exactly the treatment which an affectionate brother would be disposed to give.

As to Miss Wilmot's *disappearance,* I never knew, till now, there was any thing mysterious or suspicious in her conduct. It is true, she left her former residence, but, considering in whose company she left it, and the privacy and solitude in which she had previously lived, I was inclined to think she had risen into sight and notice, and instead of retiring from observation, had come forth more conspicuously than ever. This was necessarily the case, if she lived, or associated, as she probably did, with Mrs. Valentine.

When Sedley talked of the cause of her journey being removed, and her reassuming her station among us, I confess he was unintelligible to me. I knew of no cause for her journey, but her own pleasure, and perhaps, Mrs. Valentine's intreaties. The construction which a casual hearer seems to have put upon his words, was foolish and preposterous. Indeed, it is highly offensive to me, since it presupposed that I could patiently hear any one utter such insinuations at my table.

Mrs. Kalm seemed much hurt at the misapprehensions of the nurse, and was very earnest in vindicating Sedley's innocence. She bore testimony to the undeviating and exemplary propriety of Miss Wilmot's conduct, ever since it had been within the reach of her observation.

Thou wilt imagine, Clara, with what unspeakable delight I listened to her eulogy. I was astonished at my own folly, in drawing such extravagant conclusions. My own heart pleads guilty to thy charges of credulity and precipitation, but I hope I shall not be so grossly or so easily deceived a second time.

Mrs. Kalm could give me no account of the present situation of my friend, but she gave me Mrs. Valentine's address. From her, no doubt, I shall be able to obtain all the information I want. I was a stupid wretch, not sooner to inquire among that lady's numerous friends, where she was to be found. I will write to her immediately.

Congratulate me, my beloved, on this opening of brighter prospects for one who is equally and deservedly dear to both of us. Unless you make haste to write, I shall receive your congratulations in person, for I feel myself, already, well enough to travel, in your company, to the world's end. Adieu.

E. Hartley.

LETTER XVIII

TO CLARA HOWARD
Philadelphia, May 5.

THOUGH I am so soon to be with you, and have received no answer to my last, yet I cannot be alone in my chamber, and be within reach of pen and paper, without snatching them up and talking to my friend thus. This is a mode of conversing I would willingly exchange for the more lively and congenial intercourse of eyes and lips, but 'tis better than total silence.

What are you doing now? Busy, I suppose, in turning over the leaves of some book. Some painter of manners or of nature is before you. Some dramatist, or poet, or historian, furnishes you with occupation. The day, here, is celestially benign. Such, only, as our climate can know. It is not less splendid and serene with you. So, you have strolled into that field, which is not excelled, for the grandeur of its scenery, the balsamic and reviving virtue of its breezes, its commodiousness of situation, for the purpose of relieving those condemned to a city life, by any field on this globe. The battery . . . what a preposterous name! Yet not the only instance of a mound, serving at once the double purpose of pleasure and defence. Did you not say the *bulwarks* of Paris were pleasure-walks? You have been in Sicily and Provence. Did you ever meet with sun, sky, and water, more magnificent, and air more bland, than you are *now* contemplating and breathing? For methinks I see that lovely form gliding along the green, or fixed, in musing posture, at the rails, and listening to the ripling of the waters.

Perhaps, some duty keeps you at home. You expect a visitant; are seated at your toilet; adding all the inchantments of drapery; the brilliant hues and the flowing train of muslin, to a form whose excellence it is to be beautiful when unadorned, and yet to gain from every ornament, new beauty.

What a rare lot is yours, Clara! One of the most fortunate of women art thou. Wealth, affluence, is yours; but wealth is only the means of every kind of happiness; it is not happiness itself. But you have not only the tools, but the inclination and ability to use them. In no hands could riches be placed so as to produce more felicity to the possessor, and to those within reach of her munificence.

Which is the most unerring touchstone of merit, poverty or riches? Ingeniously to supply the place, or gracefully to endure the want of riches, is the privilege of great minds. To retain humility and probity, in spite of riches, and to effect the highest good of ourselves and others, by the use of them, is the privilege of minds still greater. The last privilege is Clara's. The first . . . vanity has sometimes said . . . no matter what. It was, indeed, vanity that said it. Vanity, that is now humbled into wisdom and self-distrust. So far from bearing poverty with dignity, I cannot justly call my former situation by that name, and was far from bearing even the moderate privations of that state with fortitude.

And are, indeed, these privations forever at an end? Is the harder test of wisdom, the true use of riches, now to be imposed upon me? It is. Clara Howard, and all that she inherits, will be mine. I ought to tremble for the consequences of exposure to such temptations. And, if I stood alone, I *should* tremble; but, in reality, whatever is your, or your father's gift, is not mine. Your power over it shall ever be unlimited and uncontrouled by me, and this, not more from the equity of your claim to the sole power, than from the absolute rectitude with which that power will be exercised by you. Had I millions of my own acquiring,

I should deem it no more than my duty to resign to you the employment of them.

Ah! my divine friend! I will be no more than your agent; your almoner; one whose aid may make charity less toilsome to you; may free the pleasures of beneficence from some of those pains by which they are usually attended. I will go before you, plucking up thorns, and removing asperities from the path that you chuse. All my recompense shall be the consciousness in whose service I labour, and whose pleasures I enhance.

They tell us that ambition is natural to man: that no possession is so pleasing as power and command. I do not find it so. I would fain be an universal benefactor. The power, that office or riches confers, is requisite to this end; but power in infirm hands, is productive only of mischief. I who know my own frailty, am therefore undesirous of power. So far from wishing to rule others, it is my glory and my boast to submit to one whom I deem unerring and divine. Clara's will is my law: her pleasure the science that I study; her smiles the reward that, next to an approving God, my soul prizes most dearly.

Indeed, my friend, before you honour me with your choice, you should contrive to exalt me or lower yourself. Some *parity* there ought to be between us. An angel in the heavens, like thee, is not a fit companion for a mere earthworm, like

Hartley.

LETTER XIX

TO E. HARTLEY
New-York, May 6.

AH hah! give them to me. Two letters at once. This is unexpected happiness. Charming papers! Lie *there* and still the little rebel, that will not allow me speech.

And thinkest thou my lips said this, as my father threw thy letters into my lap? No such thing. My heart was mutinous, 'tis true, but no one present . . . there were many present . . . was aware of its tumults, except, indeed, my mother. Her observant eye saw what was passing within. Or rather she guessed, from the superscription, what I felt, and therefore, considerately furnished me with an excuse for retiring.

Clara, my dear, I imagine your good woman has come. I think I saw her go down the steps. My friends will excuse you for a moment.

I hastily withdrew; and *then*, Edward, having gained the friendly covert of my chamber, I eagerly, rapturously, kissed and read thy letters.

I thought it would prove a mere slander; and yet I was uneasy. The mere possibility of its truth, shocked and distressed me, more than I can tell; but thy intelligence has not only removed the disquiet which thy foregoing letter had produced, but, in reality, has given me uncommon pleasure. I flatter myself that your letter to Mrs. Valentine will receive a speedy and satisfactory answer.

Human life, Edward, is a motley scene. Thou wilt not thank me for the novelty of that remark, but the truth of it

I think has received new illustration in the little incidents on which thy last letters have commented. Had not the old nurse's tale incited thee to inquiry, thou would'st not, at this moment, have been in the way to gain any knowledge of poor Mary. Had not thy sad prognostics filled me with melancholy, my mother's attention would not have been excited to the cause of my uneasiness.

I did not conceal from her the cause. I made her pretty well acquainted with the history of Mary. She was deeply interested in the story I told, and suggested many inquiries respecting her, which I had overlooked. She has made me extremely anxious as to some particulars, on which perhaps you can give me the desired information.

Pray tell me what you know of the history of her family before her father's leaving Europe. Where was he born? Where lived he? What profession did he follow? What know you of the history of Mary's mother?

Excuse me for confining myself, at present, to these inquiries. Tell me all you know on this subject, and I will then acquaint you with the motive of my inquisitiveness. I shall expect to hear from you, on Thursday morning.

Adieu. Be careful of thyself, if thou lovest thy

Clara.

LETTER XX

TO CLARA HOWARD
Philadelphia, May 8.

I AM at a loss, dear girl, to account for thy questions, but I will answer them to the utmost of my power. The same questions frequently occurred to me, in my intercourse with the Wilmots. It was natural, you know, to suppose that they had left relations in their native country, with whom it might be of some advantage to renew their intercourse.

Mary was ten years old, when her father took up his abode in Delaware, but he had been already five years in the country, so that, you will easily perceive, she was not likely to possess much personal knowledge of events previous to their voyage. Her mother's death happened just before their removal to Wilmington. It appears to have been the chief cause of that removal.

Your letter has put me on the task of recollection. I am sorry that I am able to collect and arrange very few circumstances, such as you demand. The Wilmots were either very imperfectly acquainted with the history of their parents, or were anxious to bury their history in oblivion. The first was probably the situation of the son, but I have often suspected, from the contradictions and evasions of which Mary was at different times guilty, when this subject was talked of between us, that the daughter pretended ignorance, for the sake of avoiding the mortification of telling the truth. When once urged pretty closely on this head, she, indeed, told me, the subject was a painful one to her; that she knew nothing of her European kindred which

93

would justify the searching them out; and that she would hold herself obliged to me, if I never recalled past events to her remembrance. After this injunction I was silent, but, in the course of numberless conversations, afterwards, hints were casually dropped, which afforded me, now and then, a glimpse into their family history.

When Mary spoke of her father, it was always with reverence for his talents, gratitude for his indulgence to her, and compassion for that frailty of character, which made him seek in dissipation, relief from sorrow on account of the death of a wife whom he adored; and a refuge, as she sometimes obscurely intimated, from some calamity or humiliation, which befel him in his native country.

My friend's heart always throbbed, and her eyes were filled with tears, whenever her mother was remembered. She took a mournful pleasure in describing her mother's person and manners, in which, she was prone to believe, all human excellence was comprized. Her own melancholy temper and gloomy destiny, she imagined to have descended to her by inheritance, and she once allowed me to collect from her discourse, that her mother had died the victim of some early and heavy disappointment.

We were once, the winter before last, conversing, by an evening fire, on that most captivating topic, ourselves. Having said something on my attachment to my country, and especially to the hill-side where I first drew breath, and inquired into her feelings in relation to the same objects,

Alas! said she, I should be puzzled to say to what country I belong. I am a German by my father; English by my mother. I was born at an hotel in Paris, I was nursed by a woman of Nice, where I passed my infancy; and my youth and womanhood, and probably my whole life, belong to America. Now, what is the country, Germany, England, France, Italy or America, which I have a right to call my own. The earliest object of my recollection is the face of my nurse, who accompanied us in all our wanderings, and who died just before my father, on Brandywine. The olives, the orange walks, and the sea-shore scenery of Savoy, are still fresh in my remembrance. Should I visit them again, no doubt my feelings would be strongly affected, but I never expect to visit them.

But your father's, your mother's natal spot, would have some charms, methinks, to one of your sensibility.

Some influence, no doubt, the contemplation would have, but no charms. Strange, if I should ever have an opportunity of trying their effect upon my feelings.

You are acquainted, then, with the birthplace of your father and mother.

Yes, I have heard them described so often, and with such minuteness, that I should recognize them, I think, at any distance of time. My father was born in the Grey-street, next to the chapel of St. Anne, at Altona. My mother and family have subsisted, from the days of William the Norman, at a spot, five miles from Taunton, in Devonshire.

I was in hopes that these particulars were preliminary to more interesting disclosures, but my friend now changed the subject of conversation, and would not be brought back to the point I wished.

Mr. Wilmot was a man of liberal education and cultivated taste. This appears from the representations of his daughter, and likewise from several books, which she preserved by connivance of his creditors, and which are enriched by many notes and memorandums in her father's hand-writing. These betoken an enlarged mind and extensive knowledge. She has, likewise, a sort of journal, kept by him when a mere youth, during two or three years residence in Bologne, in the character, as I suspect, of a commercial agent. This journal, which I have occasionally seen, affords many proofs of a sprightly and vigorous mind.

This, my friend, is the whole of my present recollections on this subject. I am anxious to know what has suggested your inquiry. Is your mother acquainted with any of the family in Europe? With the history of Wilmot before he came hither? Pray tell me all you know in your next.

Adieu.
E. H.

LETTER XXI

TO E. HARTLEY

New-York, May 10.

AS soon as I had read your letter, I hurried to my mother. All her conjectures are ascertained. A native of Holstein . . . . Family abode near Taunton . . . . Victim of some early distress. These circumstances place the truth beyond controversy. But I will tell you the story with somewhat more order.

I told you that my mother's curiosity was awakened by the effect of your gloomy prognostics. I told her every thing respecting Mary Wilmot, but her love for you.

Wilmot . . . Wilmot . . . said she. An English family . . . . Came over twenty-four years ago. I think I know something of them. Their story was a singular one; a disastrous one. I should like to know more of their history. I think it not improbable that these are the same Wilmots with those with whose history I am perfectly acquainted: Nay, more, who were no very distant relations of our own. Pray write to Ned, and get from him all he knows of their early adventures. Inquire if the father was from Holstein, and the mother fron Devonshire, and if Mary was born at Paris.

You see, my friend, your letter has satisfactorily confirmed these guesses; and now, will I relate to you, the early history of this family, in the words of my mother. Mary will be greatly astonished when she comes to find how much you know of her family . . . much more, 'tis probable, than she herself knows . . . and to discover that the nearest relation she has in the world is myself. Being alone with my

96

mother, on Thursday evening, she fulfilled the promise she had made, to tell me all she knew of the Wilmots, in these words:

Mary Anne was the only daughter of my father's only brother; consequently she was my cousin. She was nearly of my own age, and being the only child of a man, respectable for birth and property, and my near relation, and particularly of my own sex, we were intimately connected at an early age. She lost her mother in her infancy, and our family having several daughters, our house was thought more suited to her education than her father's. She lived with me and my sisters till she was eighteen years of age, receiving from us, our brothers, and our parents, exactly the same treatment which a real sister and daughter received.

There was no particular affection between Mary and myself. Our tempers did not chance to coincide. Her taste led her to one species of amusement, and mine to another. This difference stood in the way of that union of interests, which, however, took place between her and my elder sister. Still, there were few persons in the world for whom I had a more ardent esteem, or more tender affection, than for my cousin Mary Anne. She parted from us at the age of eighteen, in obedience to the summons of her father, who wished to place her at the head of his household. We lived in the north, and Mr. Lisle lived in Devonshire, so that we had little hope of any intercourse but by letter. This intercourse was very punctually maintained between her and my sister, and it was by means of this correspondence, that we obtained the knowledge of subsequent events.

On leaving our family, my cousin entered into a world of strangers; a sphere very incongenial with her temper and habits. So long a separation had deprived the parental character of all those claims to reverence and confidence, which are apt to arise when the lives of father and daughter are spent under the same roof. She saw in my uncle a man, who, in many essential particulars, both of speculation and of practice, was at variance with herself, and to whom nature had given prerogatives which her fearful temper foreboded would be oftener exerted to her injury than benefit. His inmates, his companions, his employments, his sports, were dissonant with all the feelings she was most accustomed to cherish. In short, her new situation was in the highest degree irksome.

She naturally looked abroad for that comfort which she could not find at home. She formed intimacies with several persons of her own sex, among others, with Miss Saunders, the daughter of a Bristol merchant, with whom she spent as much time as her father would allow her to spend. Her winter months were generally passed in the society of that young lady at Bristol; while her friend, in summer, was her guest in the country.

It was at the house of Mr. Saunders that she became acquainted with Veelmetz, or Wilmot, a young man of uncommon elegance and insinuation. He was a native of Germany, but had received his early education in England. He had, at this time, been for two or three years chief, or confidential clerk, in an English mercantile house, at Bologne, but made occasional excursions on behalf of his employer to the neighbouring countries. Some concerns detained him a few months at Bristol, and being on a familiar footing with the family of Saunders, he there became acquainted with my cousin.

On the first interview, my cousin was in love with the stranger. It is impossible to tell how far the laws of strict honour were observed by Wilmot in his behaviour to my cousin, either before or after the discovery of her attachment to him. Certain it is, that his heart was devoted to another at the period of his interview with Mary Anne; that she, at all times, earnestly acquitted him of any duplicity or treachery towards her, and ascribed the unfortunate cause of their mutual shame and embarrassment to some infatuation; in consequence of which a man, who concealed not his love and his engagement to another, and without the sanction or the promise of marriage, prevailed on her to forget her dignity and her duty.

Both parties deserved blame. Which deserved it most, and how far their guilt might be extenuated or atoned for by the circumstances attending it, it is impossible to tell. Mary Anne was a great, a mixed, and doubtless, a faulty character. The world, in general, was liberal of its eulogies on the probity, as well as on the graces and talents of Wilmot. His subsequent behaviour lay claim to some praise; but his fatal meeting with my cousin, proved that the virtue of both was capable of yielding, when the integrity of worse people would easily have stood firm.

About the same time, Wilmot returned to Bologne, and my cousin accompanied her father to Paris. The lady to whom the former was betrothed, was the daughter of the principal in that house, where Wilmot had long been a servant, and in which, in consequence of his merits, he was now shortly to become a son and partner. The nuptial day was fixed.

Before the arrival of that day, he wrote a letter to Mary Anne, acquainting her with his present situation, reminding her that he never practised any fraud or concealment in his intercourse with her; yet, nevertheless, offering to come, and either by an open application to her father, or by a clandestine marriage, prevent any evil that might threaten her safety or her reputation.

This letter placed my cousin in the most distressful dilemma that can be conceived. Her heart was still fondly devoted to him that made this offer. A fair fame was precious in her eyes. Her father's wrath was terrible. She knew that the accident, which Wilmot was willing to provide against, would soon and inevitably befal her. Yet, in her answer to his letter, the possibility of this accident was denied; her attachment was denied, and he was earnestly conjured to complete his own happiness and that of a worthier woman.

There were many generous pleas by which my cousin might have accounted for her conduct. She knew that the marriage he offered would never be crowned with her father's consent; that, on the contrary, his hatred and vengeance would pursue them forever. That Wilmot would thereby forfeit the honour already plighted to another; would inflict exquisite misery on that other and on himself, and would forever cut himself off from that road to fortune, which had now been opened to him.

She was candid enough to confess that these considerations, though powerful, did not singly dictate her conduct. Her heart was, in reality, full of grief. Despondency and horror took possession of her whole soul. She hoped to protract the discovery of her personal condition to a very late period, and then, when further concealment was hopeless, designed to put a violent end to life and all its cares.

Meanwhile, Wilmot's conscience being somewhat relieved by my cousin's answer, he gave himself up without restraint, to the pleasurable prospects before him. The day of happiness was near at hand. He had little leisure for any thing, but the offices of love and tenderness, and was engaged, on the evening of a fine day, to accompany his mistress, with a numerous party, on a rural excursion. The carriage, ready to receive them, was at the door, and he only waited, in a court before the house, till the lady had adjusted her dress for the occasion.

His mistress, Adela, having made the requisite adjustments, came out. She looked around for her lover in vain. Some accident, it was easily imagined, had called him for a few moments away. She collected patience to wait; but she waited and expected in vain. Night came, and one day succeeded another, but Wilmot did not appear. Inquiries were set on foot, and messengers were dispatched, but Wilmot had entirely vanished.

Some intelligence was, at last, gained of him. It appeared, that while walking to and fro in the court, two persons had come up to him, and after a short dialogue, had retired with him to an inn. There they had been closeted for a few minutes. After which they came forth, and mounting horses that stood at the gate, hastily left the city together.

The suspense and anxiety which this circumstance produced in the lady and her family, may be easily imagined.

Their conjectures wandered from one object to another, without obtaining satisfaction. They could gain from all their inquiries, no knowledge of the persons who had summoned the young man away. They inferred that the messengers were the bearers of no good tidings; since the attendants at the inn reported that Wilmot's countenance and motions betrayed the utmost consternation, on descending from the chamber where the conference was held.

Their suspense was at length terminated by the return of the fugitive himself. Wan, sorrowful, and drooping, an horseman languidly alighted, about ten days after Wilmot's disappearance, at the gate. It was Wilmot himself. The family flocked about, eager to express their joy, terror, and surprise. He received their greetings with affected cheerfulness, but presently requesting an interview with Adela, retired with her to her closet.

I suppose, my dear, you conjecture the true cause of all these appearances. My cousin's secret was betrayed, by an unfaithful confidant, to her father, whose rage, at the discovery, was without bounds. He rushed into his daughter's presence, in a transport of fury, and easily extorted from her the author of her disgrace. Without a moment's delay, he ordered horses, and in company with a friend, made all possible haste to Bologne. The daughter's uncertainty as to the cause and object of his journey, was ended by the return of Mr. Lisle, in company with Wilmot. The alternative offered to the youth, was to meet the father with pistols, or to repair his child's dishonour by marriage. Mr. Lisle's impetuosity overbore all my cousin's opposition, and Wilmot, the moment he discovered her true situation, was willing to repair the wrong to the utmost of his power.

The ceremony being performed, Mr. Lisle's pride was so far satisfied, but his rage demanded nothing less than eternal separation from his daughter. Wilmot was obliged to procure lodgings in a different quarter, and my poor cousin left her father's presence, for the last time, with his curses ringing in her ears.

The horror occasioned by these events, brought on a

101

premature labour, the fruit of which did not perish, as might have been expected, but has survived to this day, and is no other than your Mary Wilmot.

Poor Wilmot had an arduous office still to perform. These events, and his new condition, were to be disclosed to Adela. This it was easy to do by letter, but he rather chose to do full justice to his feelings in a formal interview. And this was the purpose for which he returned to Bologne.

It is not possible to imagine a more deplorable situation than that in which Wilmot was now placed. He was torn forever from the object of his dearest affections. At the moment when all obstacles were about to disappear, and a few days were to unite those hearts which had cherished a mutual passion from infancy, he was compelled to pay the forfeit of past transgressions, by binding himself to one who had his esteem, but not his love. Adela was the pride and delight of her family, and Wilmot had made himself scarcely a less fervent interest in their affections. That privilege he was now compelled to resign, and by the same act, to break the heart of the daughter, and excite unextinguishable animosity in the bosom of her friends. Every tie dear to the human heart, was now violently broken: every flattering scheme of honour and fortune, baffled and defeated. Nor had he the consolation to reflect, that by these sacrifices he had secured the happiness of, at least, one human being. My cousin was an involuntary actor in this scene. She had been overborne by her father's menaces, and even by the expostulations and entreaties of Wilmot himself. The irrevocable ceremony was hurried over without a moment's deliberation or delay, and before she had time to collect her thoughts and form her resolutions, to recover from the first confusions of surprise and affright, she found herself a wife and a mother.

It was, perhaps, merely the very conduct which my cousin's feelings taught her to pursue, that secured her ultimately some portion of happiness. All the fault of the first transgression she imputed to herself. Wilmot was the innocent and injured person: she only was the injurer and criminal. Those upbraidings which the anguish of his heart might have prompted him to use, were anticipated; dwelt upon and exaggerated; all the miseries of this alliance passed, in as vivid hues before her imagination, as before his. These images plunged her into the most profound and pitiable sorrow.

Wilmot's generosity would by no means admit, that her's only was the guilt. On the contrary, his candour, awakened by her example, was busy in aggravating his own crime. His heart was touched by the proofs of her extreme dejection; her disinterested regard. He reflected, that her portion of evil was at least equal to his own. Her sensibility to reputation, her sense of right, her dependance on her father for the means of subsistence, her attachment to her country and kindred, all contributed to heighten her peculiar calamity, since she believed her fame to be blasted forever; since her conscience reproached her with all the guilt of their intercourse; since her father had sworn never to treat her as his child; since she had lost, in her own opinion, the esteem of all her relations and friends, and solemnly vowed never to set foot in her native country.

Wilmot's efforts to console his wife, produced insensibly a salutary effect on his own feelings. Being obliged to search out topics of comfort for her use, they were equally conducive to his own, and a habit of regarding objects on their brightest side; of considering my cousin as merely a subject of tenderness and compassion, somewhat abated the edge of his own misfortunes.

My father took infinite, though unsolicited pains to reconcile the parent and child, but my uncle could not be prevailed on to do more than allow Wilmot a small annuity, with which he retired to the town of Nice, and by a recluse and frugal life, subsisted, if not with elegance, at least with comfort. Mary Anne was extremely backward to cultivate the society of her old friends. Their good offices she took pains to repel and elude, and her only source of consolation, with regard to them, appeared to be the hope that they had entirely forgotten her. We, her cousins,

103

were not, however, deterred by her repulses, but did every thing, in our power, to befriend her cause with her inexorable father, and to improve her domestic situation. We had the pleasure to find that Wilmot, though his vivacity, his ambitious and enterprizing spirit was flown, was an affectionate husband and provident father.

At my uncle's death we had hopes that Mary Anne's situation would be bettered. His will, however, bequeathed all his estate to his nephew, my elder brother, and the Wilmots were deprived even of that slender stipend which they had hitherto enjoyed. This injustice was, in some degree, repaired by my brother, who, as soon as the affairs of the deceased were arranged, sent a very large present to Wilmot. They did not make us acquainted with the motives of their new resolutions. We were merely informed, indirectly, that on the receipt of this sum, Wilmot repaired with his family to some port in France, and embarked for the colonies. Time insensibly wore away the memory of these transactions, and 'tis a long time since my sisters and I have been accustomed, in reviewing past events, to inquire "What has become of poor Mrs. Wilmot and her children?"

Such, Edward, was my mother's relation. Is it not an affecting one. And is, indeed, thy Mary the remnant of this family? They had several children, but most of them found an early grave in Europe, and the eldest, it seems, is the sole survivor. We must make haste, my friend, to raise her from obscurity and make her happy.

Is it not likely that Mary knows nothing of her mother's history? Being only ten years old at her death, the child would scarcely be made the confidant of such transactions. The father, it is likely, would be equally prone to silence, on such a topic.

Our fortune is strongly influenced by our ignorance. What can be more lonely and forlorn than the life thy poor friend has led. Yet had she returned to her mother's native country, and disclosed her relation to the present mistress of *Littlelisle,* she would have been instantly admitted to the house and bosom of a fond mother.

My uncle, to whom I told you the estate of Mary's grandfather was bequeathed, died unmarried and left this property to the sister, who was the intimate of Mary Anne, and who never lost the tenderest respect for her youthful friend. This happened some years after Wilmot's voyage to the colonies. My aunt being childless and a widow, was extremely solicitous to discover Mary Anne's retreat, and restore her, or her children to at least a part of that property, to the whole of which their title was, strictly speaking, better than her own. For this end, she made a great many inquiries in America, but none of them met with success.

I have written a long letter. Yet I could add much more, were I not afraid of losing this post. So let me hear thy comments on all these particulars, and tell me, especially, when I may certainly expect thy return. Adieu

Clara.

LETTER XXII

TO CLARA HOWARD
Philadelphia, May 11.

THANKS, a thousand thanks, my beloved friend, for thy story. It has absorbed and overwhelmed every other thought and feeling. Since I received it, I have done nothing but peruse and ponder on thy letter. It has opened cheerful prospects for my poor friend. Shall we not see her restored to her native country; to her original rank, and the affluence to which she is entitled by her birth, her education and her former sufferings? I trust, we shall.

'Tis impossible to guess how far she is acquainted with the history of her parents: but that and every other doubt will, I hope, speedily be put to flight.

I hope that this is the last letter I shall have occasion to write to you. The next time I shall address you, will be through no such wild and ambiguous medium.

May I find my Clara all gentleness; all condescension; all love. So, with all his heart, prays her

Edward.

LETTER XXIII

TO E. HARTLEY
New-York, May 11.

B Y the calm tenor of this letter you will hardly judge of the state of my mind before I sat down to write. To describe it would be doing wrong to myself and to you. I am not anxious to pass for better than I am; to hide my weakness, or to dwell upon my folly. In this letter to paint the struggles between reason and passion, would be making more arduous that task which I must assign to you.

I have formerly concealed these struggles. My motive was not shame. I aimed not to shun contempt, by concealing my defects; for, alas! the spirit with which I had to deal, modelled his opinions by a standard different from mine. That which was selfish and base in my eyes, was praiseworthy in his. I passed for obdurate and absurd, in proportion as I acted in a manner which appeared to me generous and just.

I concealed these struggles, because I hated to reflect upon my own faults; because they were past, and the better thoughts that succeeded were sources of complacency too precious to be lost, and attained and preserved with so much difficulty, that to review the conflicts which it cost me to gain them, would hazard their loss.

Thus it is, at present. I write to you, not to give utterance and new existence to anguish no longer felt. I write to you to tell my present views, and they cannot waver or change.

My friend, the bearer of this is your Mary. She is not happy. She is not another's. She is poor, but good, and no

107

doubt as much devoted to you as ever. Need I point out to you the road which you ought to take! Need I enforce, by arguments, that duty which compels you to consult her happiness, by every honest means?

Could I but inspire you, my friend, with the sentiments that now possess my heart: could I but make your convictions at once just and strong, and convert you into a cheerful performer of your duty, I should, indeed, be happy.

You will wonder by what means Mary has been made known to me. I will tell you. I went to pay a visit, long since due, to Mrs. Etheridge. It was but yesterday. After cursory discourse she mentioned that she expected in a few minutes to see a lady, who was going on the morrow to Philadelphia. I had written to you, and was not unwilling to make use of this opportunity. What, I asked, is her name? Her character? Her situation?

Mary Wilmot. She has just come from New-Haven, where she has passed the winter with a friend. She is amiable, but unfortunate.

You will imagine with what emotions I listened to these words. For some minutes I was too much surprised to think or to speak clearly. My companion noticed my emotion, but before she could inquire into the cause, a visitant was announced, and Miss Wilmot herself entered the room. Being introduced to each other, my name occasioned as much surprise and embarrassment as hers had given to me. The interview ended abruptly, but not till I had so far collected my thoughts, as to request her to be the bearer of a letter. She mentioned the place where it might be left and we parted.

I ought to have acted in a different manner. I ought to have asked her company home, have sought her confidence, have unbosomed myself to her, and removed every obstacle to her union with you, which might arise from an erring judgment or an unwise generosity.

But I was unfitted for this by the suddenness of our interview. I had not time to subdue those trembling and mixed feelings which the sight of her produced, before she withdrew, and I had not courage enough to visit her at her lodgings, and be the bearer of my own letter. So much the more arduous is the task which belongs to you. My deficiencies must be supplied by you. Act uprightly and ingenuously, my friend, I entreat you. Seek her presence, and shew her this and every other letter from me. Offer her, beseech her, compel her, to accept your vows.

Accuse me not of fickleness. Acquit me of mean and ungenerous behaviour. Dream not that reasoning or entreaty will effect any change in my present sentiments. I love you, Edward, as I ought to love you. I love your happiness; your virtue. I resign you to this good girl as to one who deserves you more than I; whose happiness is more dependent on the affections of another than mine is. What passion is now wanting in you time will shortly supply. In such a case, you must and will act and feel as you ought.

Let me not hear from you till you have seen her. I know whence will arise the failure of your efforts on such an interview. If she withstand your eloquence, it will be because you have betrayed your cause, or because she acts from a romantic and groundless generosity with regard to me. The last obstacle, it will be my province to remove. I will write to her, and convince her that by rejecting you on my account she does me injury and not benefit, and is an enemy to your happiness; for while Mary lives, and is not bound to another, I will never be to you any thing but

Your friend,
C. H.

LETTER XXIV

TO CLARA HOWARD
Philadelphia, May 13.

My Friend,

I DO not mean to reason with you. When I tell you that you are wrong, I am far from expecting your assent to my assertion. I say it not in a tone of bitterness or deprecation. I am calm, in this respect, as yourself. There is nothing to ruffle my calm. We fluctuate and are impatient, only when doubtful of the future. Our fate being sealed, and an end being put to suspense and to doubt, the passions are still. Sedateness and tranquillity at least are ours.

There is nothing, I repeat, to ruffle my calm. I am not angry with you, for I know the purity and rectitude of your motives. Your judgment only is misguided, but that is no source of impatience or repining to me. It is beyond my power, or that of time, to rectify your error.

I do not pity you. You aspire to true happiness, the gift of self-approbation and of virtuous forbearance. You have adopted the means necessary to this end, and the end is gained. Why then should I pity you? You would not derive more happiness from a different decision. Another would, indeed, be more happy, but you would, perhaps, be less. At any rate, your enjoyments would not be greater than they now are; for what gratification can be compared to that arising from the sense of doing as we ought?

I believe you in the wrong, and I tell you so. It is proper that the truth should be known. It is proper that my opinion, and the grounds of it should be known to you. Not

110

that after this disclosure, *you* will think or act differently. Of that I have not the least hope.

You are wrong, Clara. You study, it seems, the good of others. You desire the benefit of this girl; and since her happiness lies in being united to me, and in possessing my affections, you wish to unite us, and to transfer to her my love.

It cannot be done. Marry her I may, but I shall not love her. I cannot love her. This incapacity, you will think argues infirmity and vice in me, and lessens me in your esteem. It ought not to produce this effect. It is a proof of neither wickedness nor folly. I cannot love her, because my affections are already devoted to one more attractive and more excellent than she.

She has my reverence. If wedlock unites us, my fidelity will never be broken. I will watch over her safety with unfailing solicitude. She shall share every feeling and thought. The ties of the tenderest friendship shall be hers, but . . . nothing more.

You will say that more is due to her; that a just man will add to every office of a friend the sanction of ineffable passion. I will not discuss with you the propriety of loving *my wife,* when her moral and intellectual excellence is unquestionable, and when all her love is bestowed upon me. I will only repeat, that passion will never be felt.

What then will be the fruit of marriage? Nothing but woe to her whom you labour, by uniting us, to make happy. You rely, however, on the influence of time and intercourse to beget that passion which is now wanting. And think you that this girl will wed a man who loves her not?

She never will. Our union is impracticable, not from opposition or refusal on my side, but on hers. As to me, my concurrence shall be full, cheerful, zealous. Argument and importunity will not be wanting. If they fail, you will ascribe their failure to my coldness, ambiguity or artifice, or to mistaken generosity in her with regard to you. The last motive, after due representations, will not exist. The former cause may possess some influence, for I shall act with scrupulous sincerity. I shall counterfeit no passion and no warmth. The simple and unembellished truth shall be told to her, and this I know will be an insurmountable impediment.

But suppose, for a moment, this obstacle to disappear, and that Mary is happy as the wife of one who esteems her, indeed, but loves her not. Your end is accomplished. You proceed to reap the fruits of disinterested virtue, and contemplate the felicity which is your own work.

This girl is the only one of God's creatures worthy of benevolence. No other is entitled to the sacrifice of your inclination. None there are in whose happiness you find a recompence for evils and privations befalling yourself.

As to me, I am an inert and insensible atom, or I move in so remote a sphere that my pains or pleasures are independent of any will or exertion of yours. But no; that is a dignity of which I must not boast. I am so far sunk into depravity, that all my desires are the instigations of guilt, and all my pleasures those of iniquity. Duty tells you to withstand and to thwart, not to gratify my wishes.

I love you, and my happiness depends upon your favour. Without you, or with another, I can know no joy. But this, in your opinion, is folly and perverseness. To aspire to your favour, when it is beyond my reach, is criminal infatuation. Not to love her who loves me, and whose happiness depends upon my love, is, you think, cruel and unjust. Be it so. Great indeed, is my demerit. Worthless and depraved am I, but not single in iniquity and wretchedness; for the rule is fallacious that is not applicable to all others in the same circumstances. That conduct which in me is culpable, is no less culpable in others. Am I cruel and unjust, in refusing my love to one that claims it? So are you, whose refusal is no less obstinate as to me, as mine with respect to another; and who hearkens not to claims upon your sympathy, as reasonable as those of Mary on mine.

And how is it that Miss Wilmot's merits tower so far above mine? By placing her happiness in gaining affections which are obstinately withheld; by sacrificing the duty she owes herself, her fellow-creatures, and her God, to grief, because the capricious feelings of another have chosen a different object of devotion, does she afford no proof of infatuation and perverseness? Is she not at least sunk to a level with me?

But Mary Wilmot and I are not the only persons affected by your decision. There is another more entitled to the affections of this woman than I, because he loves her; because, in spite of coldness, poverty, and personal defects; in spite of repulse from her, the aversion of his family, and the inticements of those to whom his birth, fortune, and exterior accomplishments have made him desirable, continues to love her. With regard to this man is she not exactly in the same relation as I am to her? Is it not her duty to consult his happiness, and no longer to oppose his laudable and generous wishes? For him and for me, your benevolence sleeps. With regard to us you have neither consideration nor humanity. They are all absorbed in the cause of one, whose merits, whose claim to your sympathy and aid, if it be not less, is far from being greater than Sedley's or mine.

My path is, indeed, plain. I mean to visit Miss Wilmot; but before I see her, I shall transmit to her all the letters that have passed between you and me on this subject, and particularly a copy of *this*. She shall not be deceived. She shall judge with all the materials of a right judgment before her. I am prepared to devote myself to her will; to join my fate to hers to-morrow. I do not fear any lessening of my reverence for her virtues, of that tenderness which will be her due, and which it becomes him to feel in whose hands is deposited the weal or woe of a woman truly excellent. We have wherewith to secure the blessings of competence. With that we will seek the shores of the Ohio, and devote ourselves to rural affairs. You and yours I shall strive to forget. Justice to my wife and to myself, will require this at my hand. Adieu.

E. H.

LETTER XXV

TO MARY WILMOT
Philadelphia, May 14.

I AM impatient to see you, and assure myself from your own lips, of your welfare; but there is a necessity for postponing my visit till to-morrow evening. Then I will see you; meanwhile, read the inclosed papers. One is a narrative of occurrences since the date of my last letter to you from Hatfield. The rest are letters that have been written to Miss Howard, or received from her, down to the present hour. Read them, and reflect deeply and impartially on their contents. They require no preface or commentary. Make up your mind by evening, when I will attend you with an heart overflowing with the affection of a friend, and prepared to perform, with zeal and cheerfulness, whatever the cause of your felicity requires from

E. H.

LETTER XXVI

TO MISS HOWARD
Philadelphia, May 15.

I SIT down to relate what, perhaps, will afford you pain instead of pleasure. I know not whether I ought to give you pain, by this recital. Having no longer the power of living for my own happiness, I had wrought up my mind to the fervent wish of living for the sake of another. I found consolation in the thought of being useful to a human being.

Now my condition is forlorn and dreary. That sedate and mixed kind of happiness, on which I had set my wishes, is denied to me. My last hope, meagre and poor as it was, is extinguished forever. The fire that glowed in my bosom, languishes. I am like one let loose upon a perilous sea, without rudder or sail.

I have made preparation to leave this city to-morrow, by the dawn of day, on a journey from which I neither wish nor expect to return. I at this moment anticipate the dawn of comfort, from the scenes of the wilderness and of savage life. I begin to adopt, with seriousness, a plan which has often occurred to my juvenile reveries.

In my uncle's parlour there hangs a rude outline of the continent of North-America. Many an hour have I gazed upon it, and indulged that romantic love of enterprize, for which I have ever been distinguished. My eye used to leap from the shore of Ontario, to the obscure rivulets which form, by their conflux, the Allegheny. This have I pursued through all its windings, till its stream was lost in that of the Ohio. Along this river have I steered and paddled my canoe of bark, many hundreds of leagues, till the

Missisippi was attained. Down that mighty current I allowed myself to be passively borne, till the mouths of Missouri opened to my view. A more arduous task, and one hitherto unattempted, then remained for me. In the ardours of my fancy, all perils and hardships were despised, and I boldly adventured to struggle against the current of Missouri, to combat the dangers of an untried navigation, of hostile tribes, and unknown regions.

Having gained the remotest sources of the river, I proceeded to drag my barque over mountains and rocks, till I lighted upon the vallies and streams that tend to the north and west. On one of these I again embarked. The rivulets insensibly swelled into majestic streams. Lurking sands and overhanging cliffs gradually disappeared, and a river flowed beneath me, as spacious in its breadth and depth, and wandering through as many realms, as the Wolga or the Oronoco. After a tedious navigation of two thousand miles, I at last entered a bay of the ocean, and descried the shores of the great Pacific. This purpose being gained, I was little anxious to return, and allowed my fancy to range at will over the boundless field of contingencies, by some of which I might be transported across the ocean to China, or along the coast to the dominions of the Spaniards.

This scheme, suspended and forgotten for awhile, I have now resumed. To-morrow I go hence, in company with a person who holds an high rank in the Spanish districts westward of the Missisippi.

You will not receive this letter, or be apprised of my intentions, till after I am gone. I shall dispatch it at the moment of my leaving this city. I shall not write to Mr. Howard. I want not his aid or his counsel. I know that his views are very different from mine. I shall awaken opposition and remonstrance, which will answer no end but to give me torment and inquietude. To you I leave the task of informing him of my destiny, or allow him, if you please, to be wholly unacquainted with it. Either conduct is indifferent to me.

But there is one in whose welfare you condescend to take

some interest, and of whom I am able to communicate some tidings. Some commands which you laid upon me in relation to Mary have been fulfilled, and I shall now acquaint you with the result.

She sent me your letter not many hours after it was written, with a note, informing me of her place of abode, and requesting a meeting with me. A letter from you, by her hands, was a cause of sufficient wonder; but the contents of your letter were far more wonderful than the mode of its conveyance. The hand-writing assured me it was yours. The style and sentiments were alien to all that my fancy had connected with your name. With these tokens of profound indifference to my happiness, of ineffable contempt for my person and character, I compared the solicitude and tenderness which your preceding letter had breathed, and was utterly lost in horror and doubt. But this is not the strain in which I ought to write to you. Reason should set my happiness beyond the love or enmity of another not wiser or more discerning or benevolent than myself. If reason be inadequate to my deliverance, pride should hinder me from disclosing my humiliation; from confessing my voluntary servitude.

After my discomposure was somewhat abated, I proceeded to reflect on what was now to be done. Compliance with your dictates was obvious. Since I was no longer of importance to your happiness, it was time to remember what was due to that angelic sufferer.

I have already told you that I sent your letters, and promised to see her in the evening. I went at the appointed hour. I entered her apartment with a throbbing heart, for she is my friend. Near a year had passed since I had last seen her. This interval had been tormented with doubts of her safety, of her happiness, of her virtue, and even her existence. These doubts were removed, or about to be solved. My own eyes were to bear testimony to the truth of her existence.

I was admitted to her. I hastened to communicate my wishes. I enforced them by all the eloquence that I was master of, but my eloquence was powerless. She was too blind an admirer, and assiduous a follower of Clara Howard, to accept my proffers. I abruptly withdrew.

Heaven protect thee and her! I shall carry, I fear, the images of both of you along with me. Their company will not be friendly to courage or constancy. I shall shut them out as soon as I can.

E. H.

LETTER XXVII

TO MISS HOWARD
Philadelphia, May 13, Noon.

I FEEL some reluctance and embarrassment in addressing you in this manner, but am enabled, in some degree, to surmount them, by reflecting on the proofs which are now in my hands, of the interest which you take in my welfare, and of the inimitable generosity of your sentiments. I am likewise stimulated by the regard, which, in common with yourself, I feel for an excellent youth, to whose happiness this letter may essentially contribute.

I have seen you but for a moment. I was prepared to find in you all that could inspire veneration and love. That my prepossessions were fully verified, will, perhaps, redound little to the credit of my penetration or your beauty, since we seldom fail to discover in the features, tokens of all that we imagine to exist within.

I know you by more copious and satisfactory means; by several letters which Edward Hartley has put into my hands. By these it likewise appears, that you have some acquaintance with me, collected from the same source, and from the representations of my friend. The character and situation, the early history and unfortunate attachment of Mary, and that expedient which she adopted to free herself from useless importunities and repinings, are already known to you.

This makes it needless for me to mention many particulars of my early life; they authorise the present letter, and allow me, or, perhaps, to speak more truly, they enjoin me to confide in you a relation of some incidents that have lately occurred. Your sensibility would render them of some moment in your eyes, should they possess no relation but to a forlorn and unhappy girl; but their importance will be greater, inasmuch as they are connected with your own destiny, and with that of one, whom you justly hold dear. I shall claim your attention for as short a time as possible.

A letter, written last autumn, to Edward Hartley, informing him of the motives that induced me to withdraw from his society, has been shewn to you. It will, therefore, be needless to explain these motives anew. I console myself with believing, that they merited and obtained the approbation of so enlightened and delicate a judge as Clara Howard.

The place of my retreat was determined by the kind offers and solicitations of a lady, by name, Valentine. In other circumstances, similar solicitations from her had been refused, but now I was anxious to retire to a great and unknown distance from my usual home; to retire without delay, but my health was imperfect. I was a female without knowledge of the world, without the means of subsistence, and the season was cold and boisterous. Mrs. Valentine was opulent; her character entitled her to confidence and love; her engagements required her immediate departure; she would travel with all possible advantages; her new abode was at a great distance from my own; and she meant to continue absent during the ensuing year. There was but one consideration to make me hesitate.

Her brother had long offered me his affections. Mrs. Valentine had been his advocate, and endeavoured to win my favour, or at least, to facilitate his own exertions, by promoting our intercourse.

I had been hitherto unjust to the merits of this man. His constancy, his generosity, his gifts of person, understanding and fortune, might have won the heart of a woman less prepossessed in favour of another. My indifference, my aversion, were proportioned to that fervent love with which my heart was inspired by another. I thought it my duty to

120

avoid every means by which the impracticable wishes of
Sedley might be fostered. For this end, I had hitherto
declined most of those offers of friendship and intercourse
with which I had been honoured by his sister.

My unhappy situation had now reduced me to the
necessity of violating some of my maxims. I should never
have accompanied Mrs. Valentine, however, had I not been
previously assured that her brother designed to live at
a distance. It was impossible to object to his design of
accompanying us to the end of our journey.

That journey was accomplished. We arrived, at the eve
of winter, in the neighbourhood of Boston. The treatment
I received from my friend, was scrupulously delicate. She
acted with the frankness and affection of a sister; but I think
with shame, on that absurd pride which hindered me from
practising the same candour. I was born in an affluent
condition, but the misfortune of my parents, while they
trained me up in a thousand prejudices, left me, at the age
of eighteen, totally destitute of property or friends. There
was no human being on whom the customs of the world
would allow me to depend. My only relation was a younger
brother, who was still a boy, and who needed protection,
as much as myself. In this state, I had recourse for honest
bread, to my needle; but the bread thus procured was
mingled with many bitter tears. I conceived myself degraded by my labour; my penury was aggravated by
remembrance of my former enjoyments. I shrunk from the
salutation, or avoided the path, of my early companions.
I imagined that they would regard my fallen state with contempt, or with pity, no less hard to be endured than scorn.
I laboured sometimes by unjustifiable and disingenuous
artifices, to conceal my employments and my wants, and
masked my cares as well as I was able, under cheerful looks.

This spirit led me to conceal from Mrs. Valentine my
forlorn condition. I looked forward without hope, to the
hour when new labour would be requisite to procure for
me shelter and food. For these, I was at present indebted
to my friend; but I loved to regard myself merely as a

visitant, and anticipate the time when I should cease to lie under obligation. Meanwhile, there were many little and occasional sources of expense, to which my ill-supplied purse was unequal; while a thousand obstacles existed under this roof, to any profitable application of my time. Hence arose new cause of vexation, and new force to my melancholy.

All my stratagems could not conceal from my friend my poverty. For a time, she struggled to accommodate herself to my scruples, and to aid me, without seeming to know the extent of my necessities. These struggles were frustrated by my obstinate pride. I steadily refused either money or credit.

At length, she resolved to enter into full explanations with me, on this subject. She laid before me, with simplicity and candour, all her suspicions and surmises, and finally extorted from me a confession that I was not mistress of a single dollar in the world; that I had no kinsman to whom I could betake myself for the supply of my wants; no fund on which I was authorized to draw for a farthing.

This declaration was heard with the strongest emotion. She betrayed surprise and disappointment. After a pause, she expressed her astonishment at this news. She reminded me how little it agreed with past appearances. She had known me, during the latter part of my brother's life, and since. My brother's profession had apparently been useful to my subsistence, and since his death, though indeed the period had been short, I had lived in a neat seclusion, and at leisure.

These hints induced me to be more frank in my disclosures. I related what is already known to you, the fate of the money which I inherited from my brother, the doubtful circumstances that attended my brother's possession, and the irresistible claim of Morton.

Every word of my narrative added anew to my friend's surprise and disappointment. She continued for a long time silent, but much disquiet was betrayed by her looks. I mistook these for signs of disapprobation of my conduct,

122

and began to justify myself. Dear madam! Would you not, in my place, have acted in this manner?

Just so, Mary. Your conclusion was highly plausible.

I believe my conclusion, replied I, to be certain. I did not require any stronger proof of Morton's title.

And yet his claim was fallacious. This money was yours, and only yours.

This assertion was made with a confidence that convinced me of its truth, and caused my mind instantly to adopt a new method of accounting for the acquisition of this money. My eyes, fixed upon my companion, betrayed my suspicion that my benefactress was before me. Humiliation and gratitude were mingled in my heart. Tears gushed from my eyes, while I pressed her hand to my lips.

Ah! said I, if Morton were not the giver, who should know the defects of his title, but the real giver?

Your gratitude, Mary, is misplaced. You might easily imagine that my funds would never allow me to be liberal to that amount.

Is it not you? Whose then was the bounteous spirit? You are, at least, acquainted with the real benefactor.

I confess that I am, but may not be authorized to disclose the name.

I besought her to disclose her name.

The motive, said my friend, is obvious. It could only be the dread that, knowing your scrupulousness on this head, you would refuse the boon, and thus frustrate a purpose truly benevolent. This apprehension being removed, there can certainly be no reason for concealment. I am entirely of your opinion, that the author of every good deed should be known not only to the subject of the benefit, but to all mankind.

After much solicitation she, at length, confessed that this money was the gift of Mr. Sedley to my brother. She stated the motives of this uncommon liberality. Sedley had made his sister acquainted with his passion for me, and had engaged her counsel and aid. Her counsel had always been, to abandon a pursuit whose success was hopeless. . . .

123

Perceiving your reluctance, continued my friend, and finding it to arise from a passion for another, I earnestly
dissuaded him from persisting in claims which were hurtful to you without profiting himself. His passion sometimes
led him to accuse you of frowardness and obstinacy, and,
at those times, I had much ado to defend you, and to prove
your right to consult your own happiness.

But these moments, I must say in justice to my brother,
were few. I could generally reason him into better temper.
He could see, at least for a time, the propriety of ceasing
to vex you with entreaties and arguments, and was
generous enough to wish you happiness, even with another.
This spirit led him to inquire into the character and condition of your chosen friend. For this purpose he cultivated
the acquaintance of your brother, and discovered that the
only obstacle to your union with young Hartley, was your
mutual poverty. After many struggles, many fits of jealousy,
and anger, and melancholy, he determined to lay aside
every selfish wish, and to remove this obstacle to your happiness, by giving you possession of sufficient property.

This undertaking was in the highest degree arduous and
delicate. To make the offer directly to you, was chimerical.
No power on earth, he well knew, could persuade you to
receive a free gift in money from one whose pretensions
had been such as his. To bestow it upon Hartley, would
be exposing the success of his scheme to hazard. His scruples would be as likely to exclaim against such a gift, as
loudly as yours, especially when attended with those conditions which it would be necessary to prescribe. There was
likewise no certainty that his gift might not be diverted
by Hartley to other purposes than those which he sought.
Neither did he wish to ensure your marriage with another,
upon terms which should appear to lay you under obligations to that other. Besides, your union with Hartley, was,
in some degree, uncertain. A thousand untoward events
might occur to protract or prevent it, whereas your poverty was a present and constant evil.

After discussing a great number of expedients, he

adopted one, at length, which, perhaps, was as unskilful as any which he could have lighted on. By talking with your brother, he found him possessed of a quick, indignant, and lofty spirit; one that recoiled from pecuniary obligations; that placed a kind of glory in being poor, and in devoting his efforts to benevolent, rather than to lucrative purposes. He saw that direct offers of money, to any considerable amount, and accompanied with no conditions, or by conditions which respected his sister, would be disdainfully rejected. He determined, therefore, to leave him no option, and to put a certain sum in his possession without it being possible for him to discover the donor, or to refuse the gift. This sum was, therefore, sent to him, under cover of a short billet, without signature, and in a disguised hand.

This scheme was not disclosed to me till after it was executed. I did not approve it. I am no friend to indirect proceedings. I was aware of many accidents that might make this gift an hurtful one, or, at least, useless to the end Sedley proposed. Your brother's scruples, which hindered him from openly accepting it, were likely to prevent him from applying so large a sum to his own, or to your benefit. He would either let it lie idly in his coffers, under the belief that so ambiguous a transfer gave him no right to it, or he would, more probably, spend it on some charitable scheme. I was acquainted with his enthusiasm, in the cause of what he called the good of mankind, and that his notions of the goods and evils of life differed much from those of his sister.

This act, however, was not to be recalled, and it was useless to make my brother repent of his precipitation. I hoped that his intention would not be defeated, and watched the conduct of your brother very carefully, to discover the effect of his new acquisitions. The effect was such as I expected. Your brother's mode of life underwent no change; and the money, as there were easy means of discovering, lay in one of the banks, untouched.

My curiosity was awakened anew at your brother's death, and Sedley had the satisfaction of perceiving that your condition was visibly improved. You no longer hired out your labour. You lived in retirement, indeed, but with some degree of neatness; and your time was spent in improving and adorning your mind, and in those offices of kindness and charity, which, however arduous in themselves, are made light by the consciousness of dignity attending them.

I admire and love you, and that day which would make you my sister, I should count the happiest of my life. You have treated me with much distance and reserve, but I flattered myself that my overtures to intimacy, had been rejected not on my own account, but on that of my brother. Since you have been my companion, I have noticed the proofs of your poverty, with great uneasiness. I know, that your money, all but a few hundred dollars, still lies in one of the banks. Will you pardon me for having been attentive to your conduct? For my brother's sake, and for your own, I have watched all your movements, and could tell you the times and portions in which these hundreds have been drawn out; and have formed very plausible guesses as to the mode in which you have disposed of them.

How to reconcile your seeming poverty with the possession of some thousands, how to account for your acquiescence in my wishes to attend me hither, and for forbearing to use any more of this money for the supply of your own wants, has puzzled me a great deal. I perceive that you have dropped all intercourse with your former friend, and given up yourself a prey to melancholy. These things have excited, you will imagine, a great deal of reflection, but I have patiently waited till you yourself have thought proper to put aside the curtain that is drawn between us. This you have at length done, and I in my turn have disclosed what I am afraid my brother will never forgive me for doing.

I could not but be deeply affected by this representation. The generosity of Sedley and his sister, their perseverance in labouring for my good, when no personal advantage, not even the homage of a grateful spirit, could flow to themselves, made me feel the stings of somewhat like ingratitude. The merits and claims of Sedley came now to assume a new aspect. I had hitherto suffered different objects to engross my attention. I did not applaud or condemn myself for my conduct towards him, merely because I did not think of him. I was occupied by gloomy reveries, in which no images appeared but those of Hartley and my brother.

Now the subjects of my thoughts were changed. Time had insensibly, and, in some degree, worn out those deep traces, which I brought away with me from Abingdon. Pity and complacency, and reverence for Sedley; gratitude to his sister, from whom I had received so many favours, and who would deem herself amply repaid by my consent to make her brother happy, hourly gained ground in my heart.

These tendencies did not escape my friend, who endeavoured to strengthen and promote them. She insisted on the merits of her brother, arising from the integrity of his life, the elevation of his sentiments, and especially the constancy of his affection to me. She praised my self-denial with regard to Hartley, and hinted, that my duty to him was but half performed. It became me to shew that my happiness was consistent with self-denial. Marriage with Miss Howard will give him but little pleasure, she said, while he is a stranger to your fate, or while he knows that you are unhappy. For his sake, it becomes you, to shake off all useless repinings. To waste your days in this dejection, in longings after what is unattainable, and what you have voluntarily given up, is contemptible, and, indeed, criminal. You have profited but little by the lessons of that religion you profess, if you see not the impiety of despair, and the necessity of changing your conduct.

You have, indeed, fallen into a very gross error with regard to your friend. In some respects, you have treated him in an inhuman manner.

Good heaven, Mrs. Valentine, in what respect have I been inhuman?

Have you not detailed to me the contents of the letter which you left behind you at Abingdon? In that letter have

you not assured him that your heart was broken; that you
expected and wished for death . . . wishes that sprung from
the necessity there was of renouncing his love! Have you
not given him reason to suppose that you are enduring all
the evils of penury and neglect; that you are languishing
in some obscure corner, unknown, neglected, forgotten,
and despised by all mankind? Have you not done this?

Alas! it is too true.

Not to mention that this picture was by no means justified by the circumstances in which you left Abingdon, and
in which you could not but expect to pass the winter, amidst
all the comforts which my character, my station in society,
my friends, my fortune, and my friendship must bestow
. . . not to mention these things, which rendered your statement to him untrue, what must have been the influence
of this picture upon the feelings of that generous youth?
Can you not imagine his affliction?

O yes, indeed, I can. I was wrong: I now see my error.
I believed that I should not have survived to this hour. I
wanted to cut off every hope, every possibility of his union
with me.

And do you think that, by that letter, this end was
answered? Do not you perceive that Hartley's sympathy
for you must have been infinitely increased by that
distressful picture? that his resolution to find you out in
your retreat and compel you to be happy, would receive
tenfold energy? You imagine yourself to have resigned him
to Miss Howard, but your letter and your flight could only
bind him by stronger ties to yourself. Should this lady be
inclined to favour Hartley, of what materials must her heart
be composed, if she do not refuse, or at least, hesitate to
interfere with your claims? If she do not refuse, how must
her happiness be embittered by reflections on your forlorn
state? for no doubt the young man's sincerity will make
her mistress of your story.

Do not dwell upon this theme, said I. I am grieved for
my folly. I have been very wrong. Tell me rather, my

beloved monitor, what I ought to have done: what I may still do.

It would be useless to dwell on what is past, and cannot be undone. The future is fully in your power. Without doubt you ought to hasten to repair the errors you have committed.

By what means?

They are obvious. You must dismiss these useless, these pernicious regrets, which, in every view, religious or moral, are criminal. You must give admission to cheerful thoughts; fix your attention on the objects of useful knowledge; study the happiness of those around you; be affable and social, and entitle yourself to the friendship and respect of the many amiable persons who live near us. Above all, make haste to inform Hartley of your present condition; disclose to him your new prospects of being useful and happy; and teach him to be wise by your example.

But let your kindness be most shewn, where your power is greatest, and where you are most strongly bound by the ties of gratitude. Think of my brother, as he merits to be thought of. Hasten to reward him, for those years of anguish which your perverseness has given him, and which have consumed the best part of his life.

But how shall I gain an interview with Hartley? I know not where he is. You say that my draught has never been presented. It must be so; since the money is still there, in my own name. Some accident, perhaps, has befallen him. He may not be alive to receive the fruits of my repentance.

Set your heart at rest, replied my friend, with a significant smile; he is well.

Indeed? You speak as if you had the means of knowing. Surely, madam, you know nothing of him.

I know enough of him. He is now in New-York, in the same house with Miss Howard.

In the same house? And . . . perhaps . . . married?

Fie upon you, Mary. Is this the courage you have just avowed? To turn pale; to faulter, at the mere possibility of what you have so earnestly endeavoured to accomplish.

129

Forgive me. It was a momentary folly. He is then . . . *married.*

No. They live under the same roof; but it is nothing but a vague surmise that they will ever be married.

Dear lady! By what means . . .

Through my brother's letters; which, if you please to read them, will give you all the information that I possess. Why that sudden gravity? They will not taint your fingers, or blast your sight. They are worthy of my brother, and will depict, truly, that character which you could not fail to love, if you were but thoroughly acquainted with it.

This rebuke suppressed the objection which I was going to raise against perusing these letters. They were put into my hands. They contained no information respecting Hartley, but that he resided at New-York.

They contained chiefly, incidents and reflections relative to Sedley and to me. In this respect they were copious. I read them often, and found myself daily confirmed in the resolutions which I began to form. I need not dwell upon the struggles which I occasionally experienced, and those fits of profound melancholy into which I was still, sometimes, plunged. I shall only say, that listening only to the dictates of justice and gratitude, and to the pathetic remonstrances of my friend, I finally prevailed upon myself to consent to her brother's wishes.

I should have written to Hartley, informing him of my destiny, but I proposed to return to Philadelphia, with Mrs. Valentine, and hoped to meet him there, or at New-York.

I was not unaware of the effects of an interview with him. My soul was tremulous with doubt, and torn by conflicting emotions. I was ready, in dreary moments, to revoke my promise to Sedley, to trust once more to some kind chance that might make Hartley mine, or to consecrate my life to mournful recollections of my lost happiness. These were transient moments, and the bitter tears which attended them were soon dried up. I found complacency in the resolution to devote my life to Sedley's happiness, and to the society of his beloved sister.

130

Having arrived at New-York, I was told of Hartley's absence, and learned that he was then somewhere southward. I was informed by Mrs. Etheridge, with whom Sedley made me acquainted, of your general character. I wanted to see you; to know you; to repose my thoughts in your bosom; to be Hartley's advocate with you; but I could not procure sufficient courage to request an introduction to you. A thousand scruples deterred me. I thought, that to justify confidence and candour on such delicate topics, much time and many interviews would be necessary; but I could not remain in New-York beyond a day.

I went to Mrs. Etheridge strangely perplexed. Perhaps, I should have ventured to beseech that lady's company to your house; but the meeting that took place, on that occasion, confused me beyond the possibility of regaining composure. The superscription of your letter added to my surprise, and made me more willing to decline a meeting, since this letter would guide me to the very spot where Hartley was to be found.

I once more entered my native city. Sedley was prepared to meet and welcome me. He was apprised of my intention as to Hartley, and did not disapprove. He even wrote the billet by which I invited your friend to come to my lodgings.

My purpose was, to unfold the particulars contained in this letter to Hartley, and to introduce my two friends to each other. In answer to my billet, I received a voluminous pacquet, containing certain letters and narratives relative to him and to you.

How shall I describe my feelings on perusing them? They supply the place of a thousand conversations. They leave nothing to be said. They take away every remnant of hesitation. They inspire me with new virtue and new joy. I am not grieved that Hartley and his Clara are subjected to trials of their magnanimity, since I foresee the propitious issue of the trial. I am not grieved that the happiness of Mary has been an object of such value in your eyes, as to merit the sacrifice of your own. I exult that my feelings are akin

131

to yours, and that it is in my power to vie with you in generosity.

But Hartley's last letter gives me pain; the more, because, in the tenor of yours, which preceded it, there is an apparent harshness not, perhaps, to be mistaken by an unimpassioned reader, but liable to produce fallacious terrors in an heart deeply enamoured. I see the extent of this error in him, but am consoled by hoping that my reasoning, when we meet, or, at least, that time, will dispel this unfriendly cloud. I am impatient for his coming.

M. W.

LETTER XXVIII

TO MISS HOWARD
Philadelphia, May 13.

MY friend, we have met, but such a meeting! . . . The letters had told me of his sickness, but I expected not to behold a figure so wan, so feeble, so decayed. I expected much anxiety, much conflict in his features, between apprehension and hope; but not an aspect so wild, so rueful, so melancholy. His deportment and his words were equally adverse to my expectations.

After our first tears of congratulation were exhausted, he exclaimed in a tone of unusual vehemence:

Why, my friend, have you thus long abandoned me? You have been unjust to yourself and to me, and I know not how to pardon you, except on one condition.

What is that?

That we now meet to be united by the strongest ties, and never to part more. On that condition I forgive you.

I was prepared for this question; but the tones and looks with which it was accompanied, and especially its abruptness, disconcerted me. I was silent.

I came to this interview, resumed he, with one determination. I will not tremble, or repine, or upbraid, because my confidence in the success of my efforts, is perfect, and not to be shaken. I came to offer you the vows of an husband. They are now offered, and received. You have no power to decline them. Let me then salute you as . . . my wife.

133

I shrunk back, and spread out my hand to repulse him. I was still unable to speak.

I told you the purpose of my coming, said he, in a solemn tone. This purpose is the dearest to my heart. Of every other good I am bereaved, but to the attainment of this there can be no obstacle, but caprice, or inhumanity, or folly, such as I never can impute to you. If you love me, if you have regard to my welfare, if you wish me to love, grant me that good which is all that remains to endear existence. If you refuse this gift, I shall instantly vanish from society. I shall undertake a journey, in which my life will be exposed to numberless perils. If I pass them in safety, I shall be dead to all the offices and pleasures of civilized existence. I shall hasten to embrute all my faculties. I shall make myself akin to savages and tygers, and forget that I once was a man.

This is no incoherent intimation. It is the fixed purpose of my soul, to be changed only by your consenting to be mine. Ponder well on the consequences of a refusal. It decides my everlasting destiny.

Have you not read my letter? Have I not read yours and Clara's? How then can you expect my concurrence? Have you not anticipated my refusal?

I anticipated misery. Having found injustice and a callous heart in another, where I least expected to find them, I was prone, in the bitterness of disappointment, to ascribe them to every human creature; but that was rash and absurd. Mary cannot be unjust.

To whom do you impute an hard heart?

Not to you. You merit not the imputation. You will prove yourself compassionate and good. You will not scorn me; cast me off; drive me into hopeless exile, and inextricable perils. You are too good, and have been too long my friend; the partaker of my cares; the solace of my being; the rewarder of my tenderness. You will not reject me, banish me, kill me.

You know not what you say. Your thoughts are confused. You love and are beloved by another; by one who merits your eternal devotion and gratitude. They are due to her, and never will I rob her of them.

What mean you. Did not you say you had read the pacquets? and do not these inform you that I have no place in the affections of any human being but yourself? Convince me that I have, indeed, a place in yours; that I am not utterly deserted. Consent to be mine own, my beloved wife, and thus make me as happy as my fate will permit.

Alas, my friend! you are not in your right mind. Disappointment has injured your reason, or you could never solicit me thus; you could never charge Clara Howard with a hard heart.

Talk not of Clara Howard. Talk only of yourself and of me. Rid me of suspense and anxiety, by consenting to my wishes. Make me happy. Take away, at least, the largest portion of my misery, by your consent. Will you not be mine?

Never. Former objections time has rendered more strong; but your letters would have fixed my resolutions, had they wavered. These shew how far the happiness of Miss Howard and your own depend upon my perseverence; and persevere I must.

What mean you? Miss Howard's happiness, say you, depends upon your incompliance with her wishes? on your rejecting the prayers she has made, with the utmost degree of earnestness?

They are generous prayers, which suppose me weaker and more infatuated than I am. They are prayers which counteract their own purpose, since they exhibit an example of disinterestedness and self-oblivion, which I cannot fail to admire and to imitate. Our cases are, indeed, not parallel. Her love for you is answered and returned by equal love. To me your heart is indifferent, and I have resolved to conquer my perverse affections, or perish.

You have read her letters, her last letter, and yet you talk of her love! Once, I grant, it might have been, it was so, but that time of affability, of softness, of yielding, is gone. She is now rugged, austere, unfeeling. Her prepos-

135

terous abstractions and refinements have gained force through the coldness of her heart. There is no self-sacrifice, for she loves me not. There is no regard for my welfare or felicity, for she loves me not.

O, Edward! can you be so perverse; so unjust? You merit not the love of so pure a spirit. You merit not the happiness which such an one is qualified to give you. But your disappointment has disturbed your reason. I can pity and forgive you, and will intercede with her for your forgiveness. I see her merits and her superior claims too clearly, ever to consent to your separation.

You are discomposed, I continued. Surely you have been very sick. You seem to have just risen from the grave; you are so pale; so wan; so feeble. Your state of health has made you unfit to judge truly of the motives of your friend, and to adopt her magnanimity.

If you will have patience I can convince you that it is my duty to reject your offers, and that Clara Howard may still, if you please, be yours.

Then, replied he, you do reject them?

Do not look so wildly. I am sure, you are not well. You seem ready to sink upon the floor. You are cold, *very* cold. Let us defer this conversation a little while. I have much to say on the subject of my history, since we parted. That being known to you, you will see reason to judge differently of my motives in rejecting your offers. Instead of making that rejection more difficult by importunity and vehemence, you will see the justice of concurring with me, and of strengthening my resolution.

Impossible, said he, that any thing has happened to change my views. Are not your affections, merits, and integrity, the same as formerly? Answer me sincerely.

I will. I have no reason for concealment. Time has not lessened my merits, it is true, but . . .

That assurance is enough for me. I will eagerly listen to your story, but not until my fate is decided. Have pity on that sinking frame, and that wounded heart which you behold. There is but one cure, and that is deposited in your

136

hands. To every other my joy or sorrow; my life or death, is indifferent. Will you take me to your bosom; shall my image be fostered, and my soul find peace there; or shall I cast myself upon a sea of storms and perils, and vanish from this scene forever?

How you grieve me! I beseech you be not so impetuous. Listen to my story first, and then say in what manner I ought to act.

There is no room for delay. Say you will be mine, and then I shall enjoy repose. I shall be able to listen. Till then I am stretched upon the rack. Answer me; will you be mine?

O no! I replied; while I have an heart not wholly sordid and selfish, I cannot consent. My conscience will not let me.

Find consolation, he answered, in the approbations of that conscience, for a sentence that has ratified the doom of one who deserved differently from you. I perceive you are inflexible, and will therefore leave you.

But whither are you going? Will you not return to Clara?

To Clara! No. Far different is the path that I am to tread. I shall never see her more.

He now moved towards the door, as if going.

Edward! what can you mean? Stay. Do not go till you have heard me further. I entreat you, as you value my peace, and my life, hear me further.

Will you then consent? said he, returning with a more cheerful brow. How good you are! The same dear girl; the same angelic benignity as formerly. Confirm my happiness by new assurances. Confirm it by permitting this embrace.

I was compelled to avert my face; to repulse him from my arms. To what unlooked for trials have you subjected me! But I must not retract my resolutions. No, Edward, the bar between us is insuperable. I must never be yours.

Never! . . . never! . . . be mine! . . . Well, may the arms of a protecting Providence encircle thee! May some other rise to claim and possess thy love! May ye never, neither thou nor Clara, know remorse for your treatment to me! . . . Saying this, he snatched his hat from the table, and ran out of the house. I called, but he was gone beyond my hearing.

I was justly alarmed by this frantic demeanour. I knew not how to account for it, but by imagining that some remains of delirium still afflicted his understanding. I related this conversation to Sedley. I entreated him to pursue Edward to his lodgings, to prevail upon him to return hither, or to calm his mind, by relating what his abrupt departure had prevented me from saying.

Sedley cheerfully complied with my request, but Hartley was not to be found at his lodging. He waited his return till ten, eleven, and twelve o'clock, but in vain.

Meanwhile, I found some relief in imagining they had met; that Sedley's address and benevolence had succeeded in restoring our friend to better thoughts. My disappointment and alarm, at his return, on hearing that Hartley had not been met with, were inexpressible. That night passed away without repose. Early in the morning, I again entreated Sedley to go in search of the fugitive. He went, but presently returned to inform me that Hartley had set out, in the stage for Baltimore, at day-dawn.

I cannot comprehend his intimations of a journey to the wilderness; of embruting his faculties; of exposing his humanity, his life, to hazard. Could he have interpreted your letters into avowals of hatred or scorn, or even of indifference? One, indeed, who knew you less perfectly, might impute to you a rigour in judging; a sternness not suitable to the merits of this youth. Your letters are void of that extenuating spirit, that reluctance to inflict sufferings, which, perhaps, the wisest inflexibility will not be slow to feel, or unwilling to express . . . but Edward had sufficient knowledge to save him from a wrong construction.

Yet that, alas! is not true. He ought to have had that knowledge . . . but it was wanting.

Possibly he has not told you his designs. He cannot inform you of the truth with respect to me. My present situation should be known to you, to enable you to act with

138

propriety. I shall not prescribe to you. I am not mistress of your thoughts and motives. May heaven direct you right.

A friend will go to Baltimore on Tuesday, time enough for you to receive this, and to write to Hartley. If sent to me, I will intrust it to my friend. I have not time to add a word more.

Accept the reverence and love of

Mary.

LETTER XXIX

TO E. HARTLEY
New-York, May 15.

HARTLEY! how shall I address you? In terms of indignation or of kindness? Shall I entreat you to return, or exhort you to obey the wild dictates of your caprice? Shall I leave you to your froward destiny, and seek, in the prospect of a better world, a relief from the keen distress, the humiliating sorrows of this scene of weakness and error?

Shall I link my fate with one who is deaf to the most pathetic calls of his duty? Who forgets or spurns the most urgent obligations of gratitude? Whom the charms of nature, the attractions of science, the claims of helpless and fond sisters, who trust for shelter, for bread, for safety from contempt and servitude and vice, to his protection, his counsel, his presence, cannot detain from forests and wilds, where inevitable death awaits him?

Shall I bestow one drop of tender remembrance on him who upbraids and contemns me for sacrificing every selfish regard to his dignity; for stifling in my bosom, that ignoble passion, which makes us trample on the claims of others; which seeks its own gratification at the price of humanity and justice; which can smile in the midst of repinings and despair, of creatures no less worthy, no less susceptible of good?

You say that I love you not. Till this moment your assertion was untrue. My heart was not free, till *these* proofs of your infatuation and your folly were set before me. Till now, I was willing to account you not unworthy. I hoped

140

that time and my efforts, would reclaim you to some sense of equity and reason.

But now . . . must I then deem you utterly lost? Have you committed this last and irretrievable act? O no! it was surely but a momentary madness. The fit will be past before this letter reaches you. You will have opened your eyes to the cowardice, the ignominy, the guilt of this flight. You will hasten to close those wounds which have rent my heart. You will return to me with the speed of the wind, and make me, by the rectitude of your future conduct, forget that you have ever erred.

Has it come to this! now, that the impediment has vanished, that my feelings may be indulged at the cost of no one's peace; now that the duty which once so sternly forbad me to be yours, not only permits, but enjoins me to link together our fates; that the sweet voice of an approving conscience is ready to sanction and applaud every impulse of my heart, and make the offices of tenderness not only free from guilt, but coincident with every duty; that now . . .

Edward! let me hope that thou hast hesitated, doubted, lingered in thy fatal career. Let me foster this hope, that I may retain life. My fortitude, alas! is unequal to this test. No disaster should bereave me of serenity and courage; but to this, while I despise myself for yielding, I must yield. If this letter do not reach thee; if it fill not thy heart with remorse, thy eyes with tenderness; if it cure thee not of thy phrenzy, and bring thee not back . . .

It must . . . it will.

C. H.

LETTER XXX

TO E. HARTLEY
Philadelphia, May 15.

W HAT has become of that fortitude, my friend, which I was once accustomed to admire in you. You used to be circumspect, sedate, cautious; not precipitate in judging or resolving. What has become of all these virtues?

Why would you not give your poor friend a patient hearing? Why not hesitate a moment, before you plunged all whom you love into sorrow and distress? Was it impossible for six months of reflection to restore the strength of my mind, to introduce wiser resolutions and more cheerful thoughts, than those with which I parted from you?

I was then sick. My lonely situation, the racking fears your long silence had produced, a dreary and lowering sky, and the tidings your letter conveyed, of my return again to that indigence so much detested by my pride, were surely enough to sink me deeply in despondency; to make me, at the same time, desire and expect my death.

I saw the bright destiny that was reserved for you. My life, I thought, stood in the way of your felicity. I knew your impetuous generosity, your bewitching eloquence. I knew the frailty of my own heart. Hence my firm resolve to shun an interview with you, to see you no more, at least, till your destiny had been accomplished.

Happy was the hour in which I formed this resolution. By it I have not only secured that indirect happiness, arising from the contemplation of yours, but the ineffable bliss of requiting that love, of which my heart was so long insensible.

Yes, my friend, the place that you once possessed in my affections, is now occupied by another. By him, of whose claims I know you have always been the secret advocate; by that good, wise, and generous man, whom I always admitted to be second to yourself, but for whom my heart now acknowledges a preference.

Had you waited for an explanation of my sentiments, you would have saved me, your beloved Clara, yourself, and all your friends, the anxieties your present absence has produced. That rashness may excite remorse, but it cannot be recalled. Let it then be speedily forgotten, and let this letter put a stop to your flight.

Dear Edward! come back. All the addition of which my present happiness is capable, must come from you. The heart-felt approbation, the sweet ineffable complacensy with which my present feelings are attended, want nothing to merit the name of perfect happiness, but to be witnessed and applauded by you.

Your Clara, that noblest of women, joins me in recalling you, and is as eager to do justice to *your* passion, as *I* am to recompence the merits of Sedley. Therefore, my friend, if you value my happiness or Clara's, come back. Will you not obey the well known voice, calling you to virtue and felicity, of

Your sister
Mary.

LETTER XXXI

TO CLARA HOWARD
Wilmington, May 17.

I HAVE received and have read your letter. To say thus much is enough. From what a depth of humiliation and horror have I emerged! How quickly was I posting to my ignominy and my ruin! Your letter overtook me at this place, where a benignant fate decreed that I should be detained by sickness. Clara, thou hast judged truly. My eyes are open on my folly, and my infatuation. The mists that obscured my sight, are gone; I am once more a reasonable creature.

How shall I atone for my past misconduct, or compensate thee, my heavenly monitor, for the disquiet which thou hast endured for my sake? By hasting to thy feet, and pouring out before thee the tears of my repentance? Thy forgiveness is all that I dare claim. Thy tenderness I do not merit. Years of service and self-denial, are requisite to qualify me for receiving that best gift.

Your letter, with one from Mary, were left upon my pillow, by a traveller, passing through this town to Baltimore. I had swallowed laudanum, to secure me some sleep, on the night of my arrival hither. I was unable to proceed further, my mind and body being equally distempered. After a perturbed sleep, I awoke before the light, and lifting my head from the pillow, to acquaint myself with my situation, I perceived, by the light of a candle on the hearth, a pacquet lying beside me. I snatched it with eagerness, and found enclosed, thy letter, and one from Mary.

For a time, I imagined myself still dreaming. The contents of each letter so far surpassed and deceived every expectation, every wish, that I had formed; such pure and unmerited felicity was offered me, and by means so abrupt and inexplicable, that I might well hesitate to believe it real.

Next morning, on inquiry, I discovered that a midnight coach had arrived, in which a traveller, chancing to hear of my condition, and my name, entered my apartment while I slept, and left this pacquet, which, as I saw, was intended to have been conveyed to Baltimore.

My fever, though violent, proved to be merely an intermittent. By noon this day, though feeble and languid, I was freed from disease; I am also free from anxiety. The purest delight thrills in my bosom; mixed, now and then, and giving place to compunction for the folly of my late schemes. In truth, I have been sick. Since the perusal of thy letter by Mary, I have been half crazy, shivering and glowing by turns; bereft of appetite, and restless. Every object was tinged with melancholy hues.

But I shall not try to extenuate my fault. May thy smiles, my beloved Clara, and thy voice, musical and thrilling as it used to be, disperse every disquiet. No time shall be lost in returning to thee. My utmost haste will not enable me to offer thee, before Tuesday morning, the hand and heart of

E. H.

LETTER XXXII

TO E. HARTLEY
New-York, May 19.

YOU are coming, my friend. I shall chide you and thank you, in the same breath, for your haste. I hope you will incur no injury by a journey at night. Knowing that you mean not to lay by, I am unable to go to bed. The air was blustering in the evening, and now, at midnight, it blows a storm. It is not very cold, but an heavy rain is falling. I sit by my chamber-fire, occupied in little else than listening to it, and my heart droops, or gains courage, according to the pauses or increases of the wind and rain.

Would to Heaven thou hadst not this boisterous river to cross. It is said to be somewhat dangerous, in an high wind. This is a land of evils; the transitions of the seasons are so quick, and into such extremes. How different from the pictures which our fancy drew in our native land!

This wind and rain! How will you endure them in your crazy vehicle, thumping over rocks, and sinking into hollows? I wish you had not been in such haste. Twenty hours sooner or later, would be of no moment. And this river! . . . To cross it at any time, is full of danger; what must it be at night, and in a storm? Your adventurous spirit will never linger on the opposite shore till day dawns, and the wind has died away.

But well know I the dangers and toils of a midnight journey, in a stage-coach, in America. The roads are kneedeep in mire, winding through crags and pits, while the wheels groan and totter, and the curtains and roof admit the wet at a thousand seams.

It is *three,* and the day will soon come. How I long to see thee, my poor friend! Having once met, never, I promise thee, will we part more. This heart, with whose treasures thou art imperfectly acquainted, will pour all its sorrows and joys into thy honest bosom. My maturer age and more cautious judgment shall be counsellers and guides to thy inexperienced youth. While I love thee and cherish thee as a wife, I shall assume some of the prerogatives of an elder sister, and put my circumspection and forethought in the balance against they headlong confidence.

I revere thy genius and thy knowledge. With the improvements of time, very far wilt thou surpass the humble Clara; but in moral discernment, much art thou still deficient. Here I claim to be more than equal, but the difference shall not subsist long. Our modes of judging and our maxims, shall be the same; and this resemblance shall be purchased at the cost of all my patience, my skill and my love.

Alas! this rain is heavy! The gale whistles more loudly than ever. Would to heaven thou wast safely seated near me, at this quiet fire-side!——

LETTER XXXIII

TO MARY WILMOT
New-York, May 21.

REJOICE with me, my friend. Hartley is arrived, and has been little incommoded by his journey. He has brought with him your letter. Will you pardon me for omitting to answer it immediately, and as fully as it deserves? As soon as the tumults of my joy settles down into calm, unruffled felicity, I will comment upon every sentence. At present, I must devote myself to console this good lad for his sufferings, incurred, as he presumes to say, entirely on my account.

And so you have deferred the happiness of your Sedley for a whole month. I wonder he has any patience with you; but he that has endured, without much discontent, the delay of six or eight years (is it not so long?) ought to be ashamed of his impatience at a new delay of a few weeks.

Dear Mary, shall I tell you a secret? If you add one week of probation to the four already decreed, it is, by no means, impossible, that the same day may witness the happiness of both of us. May that day, whenever it shall come, prove the beginning of joy to Mary, and to her who, in every state, will be your affectionate

Clara.

THE END

JANE TALBOT,

A NOVEL

JANE TALBOT

LETTER I

TO HENRY COLDEN
Philadelphia, Monday evening, October 3.

I AM very far from being a wise girl. So conscience whispers me, and though vanity is eager to refute the charge, I must acknowledge that she is seldom successful. Conscience tells me it is folly, it is guilt to wrap up my existence in one frail mortal; to employ all my thoughts, to lavish all my affections upon one object; to doat upon a human being, who, as such, must be the heir of many frailties, and whom I know to be not without his faults; to enjoy no peace but in his presence, to be grateful for his permission to sacrifice fortune, ease, life itself for his sake.

From the humiliation produced by these charges, Vanity endeavours to relieve me by insinuating that all happiness springs from affection; that nature ordains no tie so strong as that between the sexes; that to love without bounds is to confer bliss not only on ourselves but on another; that conjugal affection is the genuine sphere not only of happiness but duty.

Besides, my heart will not be persuaded but that its fondness for you is nothing more than simple justice. Ought I not to love excellence, and does my poor imagination figure to itself any thing in human shape more excellent than thou?

But yet there are bounds beyond which passion cannot go without counteracting its own purposes. I am afraid

151

mine goes beyond those bounds. So far as it produces rapture, it deserves to be cherished, but when productive of impatience, repining, agony, on occasions too that are slight, trivial, or unavoidable, 'tis surely culpable.

Methinks, my friend, I would not have had thee for a witness of the bitterness, the tumult of my feelings, during this day; ever since you left me. You cannot conceive any thing more forlorn, more vacant, more anxious than this weak heart has been and still is. I was terrified at my own sensations, and, with my usual folly began to construe them into omens of evil; so inadequate, so disproportioned was my distress to the cause that produced it.

Ah! my friend! a weak — very weak creature is thy Jane. From excess of love arises that weakness: *that* must be its apology with thee, for, in thy mind, my fondness, I know, needs an apology.

Shall I scold you a little? I have held in the rein a long time, but my overflowing heart must have relief, and I shall find a sort of comfort in chiding you. Let me chide you then, for coldness, for insensibility — but no: I will not. Let me enjoy the rewards of self-denial and forbearance and seal up my accusing lips. Let me forget the coldness of your last salute, your ill-concealed effort to disengage yourself from my foolishly fond arms. You have got at your journey's end, I hope. Farewell.

J. Talbot.

LETTER II

TO HENRY COLDEN
Tuesday Morning, October 4.

I MUST write to you, you said, frequently, and copiously; you did not mean, I suppose that I should always be scribbling, but I cannot help it. I can do nothing but converse with you. When present, my prate is incessant; when absent, I can prate to you with as little intermission; for the pen, used as carelessly and thoughtlessly as I use it, does *but* prate.

Besides, I have not forgotten my promise. 'Tis true the story you wished me to give you, is more easily communicated by the pen, than by the lips. I admit your claim to be acquainted with all the incidents of my life, be they momentous or trivial. I have often told you that the retrospect is very mournful, but that ought not to prevent me from making it, when so useful a purpose as that of thoroughly disclosing to you the character of one, on whom your future happiness is to depend, will be effected by it. I am not surprized that calumny has been busy with my life, and am very little anxious to clear myself from unjust charges, except to such as you.

At this moment, I may add, my mood is not unfriendly to the undertaking. I can do nothing in your absence but write to you. To write what I have, ten thousand times, spoken, and which can be perfectly understood only when accompanied by looks and accents, seems absurd. Especially while there is a subject, on which my *tongue* can never expatiate, but on which it is necessary that you should know all that I can tell you.

153

The prospect of filling up this interval with the relation of the most affecting parts of my life, somewhat reconciled me to your necessary absence, yet I know my heart will droop: Even this preparation, to look back makes me shudder already. Some reluctance to recall tragical or humiliating scenes, and by thus recalling, to endure them, in some sense, a second time, I must expect to feel.

But let me lay down the pen for the present. Let me take my favourite and lonely path, and by a deliberate review of the past, refresh my memory and methodize my recollections. Adieu till I return.

J. T.

LETTER III

TO HENRY COLDEN
Tuesday Morning, 11 o'clock.

I AM glad I left not word how soon I meant to return,
for here has been, it seems, during my short absence,
a pair of gossips. They have just gone, lamenting the
disappointment, and leaving me a world of complimentary condolances.

I shall take care to prevent future interruption by shutting up the house and retiring to my chamber, where I am
resolved to remain till I have fully disburthened my heart.
Disburthen it, said I? I shall load it, I fear, with sadness,
but I will not regret an undertaking which my duty to you
makes indispensible.

One of the earliest incidents that I remember, is an expostulation with my father. I saw several strange people
enter the chamber where my mother was. Somewhat suggested to my childish fancy that these strangers meant to
take her away, and that I should never see her again. My
terror was violent, and I thought of nothing but seizing
her gown or hand, and holding her back from the rude
assailants. My father detained me in his arms, and endeavoured to soothe my fears, but I would not be appeased.
I struggled and shrieked, and, hearing some movements
in my mother's room, that seemed to betoken the violence
I so much dreaded, I leaped, with a sudden effort from
my father's arms, but fainted before I reached the door
of the room.

This may serve as a specimen of the impetuosity of my
temper. It was always fervent and unruly; unacquainted

155

with moderation in its attachments, violent in its indignation, and its enmity, but easily persuaded to pity and forgiveness.

When I recovered from my swoon, I ran to my mother's room, but she was gone. I rent the air with my cries, and shocked all about me with importunities to know whither they had carried her. They had carried her to the grave, and nothing would content me, but to visit the spot three or four times a day, and to sit in the room in which she died, in stupid and mopeful silence all night long.

At this time I was only five years old, an age at which, in general, a deceased parent is quickly forgotten; but, in my attachment to my mother, I shewed none of the volatility of childhood. While she lived, I was never at ease but when seated at her knee, or with my arms round her neck. When dead, I cherished her remembrance for years, and have paid, hundreds of times, the tribute of my tears at the foot of her grave.

My brother, who was three years older than myself, behaved in a very different manner. I used to think the difference between us was merely that of sex; that every boy was boisterous, ungrateful, imperious, and inhuman, as every girl was soft, pliant, affectionate. Time has cured me of that mistake, and as it has shewn me females, unfeeling and perverse, so it has introduced me to men full of gentleness and sensibility. My brother's subsequent conduct convinced me that he was at all times, selfish and irascible beyond most other men, and that his ingratitude and insolence to his mother were only congenial parts of the character he afterwards displayed at large.

My brother and I, passed our infancy in one unintermitted quarrel. We were never together, but he played some cruel and mischievous prank, which I never failed to resent to the utmost of my little power. I soon found that my tears only increased his exultation, and my complaints only grieved my mother. I, therefore, gave word for word and blow for blow, but being always worsted in such conflicts I shunned him whenever it was possible, and whatever his malice made me suffer, I endeavoured to conceal it from her.

My mother, on her death-bed, was anxious to see him, but he had strolled away after some boyish amusement, with companions as thoughtless as himself. The news of her death scarcely produced an hour's seriousness. He made my affliction a topic of sarcasm and contempt.

To soften my grief, my father consented to my living under the care of her whom I now call my mother. Mrs. Fielder was merely the intimate from childhood of my own mother, with whom, however, since her marriage, contracted against Mrs. Fielder's inclination and remonstrances, she had maintained but little intercourse. My mother's sudden death and my helpless age, awakened all her early tenderness, and induced her to offer an asylum to me. Having a considerable fortune and no family, her offer, notwithstanding ancient jealousies, was readily accepted by my father.

My new residence was, in many respects, the reverse of my former one. The treatment I received from my new parent, without erasing the memory of the old one, quickly excited emotions as filial and tender as I had ever experienced. Comfort and quiet, peace and harmony, obsequious and affectionate attendants and companions, I had never been accustomed to under the paternal roof.

From this period till I was nearly sixteen years of age, I merely paid occasional visits to my father. He loved me with as much warmth as his nature was capable of feeling, which I repaid him in gratitude and reverence. I never remitted my attention to his affairs, and studied his security and comfort as far as these were within my power.

My brother was not deficient in talents, but he wanted application. Very early he shewed strong propensities to active amusements and sensual pleasures. The school and college were little attended to, and the time that ought to have been appropriated to books and study, was wasted in frolics and carousals. As soon as he was able to manage a gun and a horse, they were procured, and these and the company to which they introduced him, afforded employment for all his attention and time.

My father had devoted his early years to the indefatigable pursuit of gain. He was frugal and abstemious, though not covetous, and amassed a large property. This property he intended to divide between his two children and to secure my portion to his nephew, whom his parents had left an orphan in his infancy, and whom my father had taken and treated as his own child by marrying him to me. This nephew passed his childhood among us. His temper being more generous than my brother's, and being taught mutually to regard each other as destined to a future union, our intercourse was cordial and affectionate.

We parted at an age at which nothing like passion could be felt. He went to Europe, in circumstances very favourable to his improvement, leaving behind him the expectation of his returning in a few years. Meanwhile, my father was anxious that we should regard each other, and maintain a correspondence as persons betrothed. In persons at our age, this scheme was chimerical. As soon as I acquired the power of reflection, I perceived the folly of such premature bonds, and though I did not openly oppose my father's wishes, held myself entirely free to obey any new impulse which circumstances might produce. My mother, so let me still call Mrs. Fielder, fully concurred in my views.

You are acquainted, my friend, with many events of my early life. Most of those not connected with my father and his nephew, I have often related. At present, therefore, I shall omit all collateral and contemporary incidents, and confine myself entirely to those connected with these two persons.

My father, on the death of his wife, retired from business, and took a house in an airy and secluded situation. His household consisted of an house keeper, and two or three servants, and apartments were always open for his son.

My brother's temper grew more unmanageable as he increased in years. My father's views with regard to him were such as parental foresight and discretion commonly dictate.

158

He wished him to acquire all possible advantages of education, and then to betake himself to some liberal profession, in which he might obtain honor as well as riches. This sober scheme by no means suited the restless temper of the youth. It was his maxim that all restraints were unworthy of a lad of spirit, and that it was far more wise to spend freely what his father had painfully acquired, than by the same plodding and toilsome arts, to add to the heap.

I scarcely know how to describe my feelings in relation to this young man. My affection for him was certainly without that tenderness which a good brother is sure to excite: I do not remember a single direct kindness that I ever received from him, but I remember innumerable ill offices and contempts. Still there was some inexplicable charm in the mere tie of kindred, which made me more deplore his errors, exult in his talents, rejoice in his success, and take a deeper interest in his concerns than in those of any other person.

As he advanced in age, I had new cause for my zeal in his behalf. My father's temper was easy and flexible: my brother was at once vehement and artful. Frank's arguments and upbraidings created in his father an unnatural awe, an apprehension and diffidence in thwarting his wishes and giving advice which usually distinguish the filial character. The youth perceived his advantages, and employed them in carrying every point on which his inclination was set.

For a long time this absurd indulgence was shewn in allowing his son to employ his time as he pleased: in refraining from all animadversions on his idleness and dissipation, and supplying him with a generous allowance of pocket money. This allowance required now and then to be increased. Every year and every month, by adding new sources of expense, added something to the stipend.

My father's revenue was adequate to a very splendid establishment, but he was accustomed to live frugally, and thought it wise to add his savings to the principal of his estate. These savings gradually grew less and less, till at length my brother's numerous excursions, a French girl whom he maintained in expensive lodgings, his horses, dogs, and *friends,* consumed the whole of it.

I never met my brother but by accident. These interviews were, for the most part, momentary, either in the street or at my father's house, but I was too much interested in all that befel him, not to make myself, by various means, thoroughly acquainted with his situation.

I had no power to remedy the evil, as my elder brother and as a man he thought himself entitled to govern and despise me. He always treated me as a frivolous girl, with whom it was waste of time to converse, and never spoke to me at all except to direct or admonish. Hence I could do nothing but regret his habits. Their consequences to himself it was beyond my power to prevent.

For a long time I was totally unaware of the tendencies of this mode of life. I did not suspect that my brother's passions would carry him beyond the bound of vulgar prudence, or induce him to encroach on those funds, from which his present enjoyments were derived. I knew him to be endowed with an acute understanding, and imagined that this would point out, with sufficient clearness, the wisdom of limiting his expences to his income.

In my daily conversations with my father, I never voluntarily introduced Frank as our topic, unless by the harmless and trite questions of ''when was he here?'' ''where has he gone?'' and the like. We met only by accident, at his lodgings: when I entered the room where he was, he never thought of bestowing more than a transient look on me, just to know who it was that approached. Circumstances, at length, however, occurred, which put an end to this state of neutrality.

I heard, twice or thrice a year, from my cousin Risberg. One day a letter arrived in which he obscurely intimated that the failure of remittances from my father, for more than half a year, had reduced him to great distress. My father had always taught him to regard himself as entitled to all the privileges of a son; had sent him to Europe, under

160

express conditions of supplying him with a reasonable stipend, till he should come of age, at which period it was concerted that Risberg should return and receive a portion with me, enabling him to enter advantageously on the profession of the law, to which he was now training. This stipend was far from being extravagant; or more than sufficient for the decent maintenance of a student at the temple, and Risberg's conduct had always been represented by those under whose eye he had been placed, as regular and exemplary.

This intimation surprised me a good deal. I could easily imagine the embarrassments to which a failure of this kind must subject a generous spirit, and thought it my duty to remove them as soon as possible. I supposed that some miscarriage or delay had happened to the money and that my father would instantly rectify any error or supply any deficiency. I hastened, therefore, to his house, with the opened letter. I found him alone and immediately shewed him that page of the letter which related to this affair. I anxiously watched his looks while he read it.

I observed marks of great surprise in his countenance, and as soon as he laid down the Letter I began to expatiate on the inconveniences which Risberg had suffered. He listened to me, in gloomy silence, and when I had done, made no answer but by a deep sigh and downcast look.

Pray, dear sir, continued I, what could have happened to the money which you sent. You had not heard, I suppose, of its miscarriage.

No, I had not heard of it before. I will look into it and see what can be done. Here further conversation was suspended by a visitant. I waited with impatience till the guest had retired, but he had scarcely left the room when my brother entered. I supposed my father would have immediately introduced this subject, and as my brother usually represented him in every affair of business, and could of course throw some light upon the present mystery, I saw no reason why I should be excluded from a conference in which I had some interest, and was, therefore, somewhat

surprised when my father told me he had no need of my
company for the rest of the day, and wished to be alone
with Francis. I rose, instantly to depart, but said, pray,
sir, tell my brother what has happened. Perhaps he can
explain the mystery.

What, cryed my Brother, with a laugh, has thy silly brain
ingendered a mystery which I am to solve? Thou mayest
save thyself the trouble of telling me, for, really, I have no
time to throw away on thee or thy mysteries.

There was always something in my brother's raillery
which my infirm soul could never support. I ought always
to have listened and replied without emotion, but a fluttering indignation usually deprived me of utterance. I found
my best expedient was flight, when I *could* fly, and silence
when obliged to remain; I therefore, made no answer to
this speech, but hastily withdrew.

Next morning earlier than usual, I went to my father.
He was thoughtful and melancholy. I introduced the subject that was nearest my heart, but he answered me reluctantly, and in general terms, that he had examined the
affair, and would take the necessary measures.

But dear sir, said I, how did it happen? How did the
money miscarry?

Never mind, said he, a little peevishly, we shall see things
put to rights, I tell you, and let that satisfy you.

I am glad of it. Poor fellow! Young, generous, disdain-
ing obligation, never knowing the want of money, how must
he have felt on being left quite destitute, penniless, running in arrear for absolute necessaries: in debt to a good
woman who lived by letting lodgings, and who dunned him
after so long a delay, in so indirect and delicate a manner —
What must he have suffered, accustomed to regard you as
a father, and knowing you had no personal calls for your
large revenue, and being so solemnly enjoined by you not
to stint himself in any rational pleasure, for you would be
always ready to exceed your stated remittances, when there
should be just occasion. Poor fellow! my heart bleeds for
him. But how long will it be before he hears from you? His

162

letter is dated seven weeks ago. It will be another six or eight weeks before he receives an answer, at least three months in all, and during all this time he will be without money. But perhaps he will receive it sooner.

My father frequently changed countenance, and shewed great solicitude. I did not wonder at this, as Risberg had always been loved as a son. A little consideration therefore ought to have shewed me the impropriety of thus descanting on an evil without remedy: yet I still persisted; at length, I asked to what causes I might ascribe his former disappointments, in the letter to Risberg, which I proposed writing immediately.

This question threw him into much confusion. At last he said, peevishly, I wish, Jane, you would leave these matters to me. I don't like your interference.

This rebuke astonished me. I had sufficient discernment to suspect something extraordinary, but was for a few minutes quite puzzled and confounded. He had generally treated me with tenderness and even deference, and I saw nothing peculiarly petulent or improper in what I had said.

Dear sir, forgive me, you know I write to my cousin, and as he stated his complaint to me, it will be natural to allude to them in my answer to his letter, but I will only tell him that all difficulties are removed, and refer him to your letter for further satisfaction; for you will no doubt write to him.

I wish you would drop the subject. If you write, you may tell him — but tell him what you please, or rather it would be best to say nothing on the subject — but drop the subject I beseech you.

Certainly, if the subject displeases you, I will drop it. — Here a pause of mutual embarrasment succeeded, which was, at length broken by my father.

I will speak to you to-morrow, Jane, on this subject. I grant your curiosity is natural, and will then gratify it. To-morrow, I may possibly explain why Risberg has not received what, I must own, he had a right to expect. We'll think no more of it at present, but play a game at *draughts*.

I was impatient, you may be sure, to have a second meeting. Next day my father's embarrassment and perplexity was very evident. It was plain that he had not forgot the promised explanation, but that something made it a very irksome task. I did not suffer matters to remain long in suspense, but asked him in direct terms what had caused the failure of which my cousin complained, and whether he was hereafter to receive the stipulated allowance?

He answered hesitatingly and with downcast eyes — why — he did not know. He was sorry. It had not been his fault. To say truth, Francis had received the usual sums to purchase the bills. Till yesterday, he imagined they had actually been purchased and sent. He always understood them to have been so from Francis. He had mentioned, after seeing Risberg's complaining letter, he had mentioned the affair to Francis. Francis had confessed that he had never sent the bills. His own necessities compelled him to apply the money given him for this purpose to his own use. To be sure, Risberg was his nephew; had always depended on him for his maintenance, but some how or another the wants of Francis had increased very much of late years, and swallowed up all that he could *rap* and *rend* without encroaching on his principal. Risberg was but his nephew, Frank was his own and only son. To be sure, he once thought that he had enough for his *three* children, but times, it seems, were altered. He did not spend on his own wants more than he used to do; but Frank's expenses were very great and swallowed up every thing. To be sure he pitied the young man, but he was enterprising and industrious, and could, no doubt, shift for himself; yet he would be quite willing to assist him, were it in his power, but really it was no longer in his power.

I was, for a time, at a loss for words to express my surprise and indignation at my brother's unfeeling selfishness. I could no longer maintain my usual silence on his conduct, but inveighed against it, as soon as I could find breath, with the utmost acrimony.

My father was embarrassed, confounded, grieved. He

sighed and even wept. — Francis, said he, at last, to be sure has not acted quite right. But what can be done? Is he not my child, and if he has faults, is he altogether without virtue? No, if he did not find a lenient and forgiving judge in me, his father, in whom could he look for one. Besides the thing is done, and therefore without remedy. This year's income is nearly exhausted, and I really fear before another quarter comes round, I shall want myself.

I again described in as strong and affecting terms as I could, Risberg's expectations and disappointment, and insinuated to him, that, in a case like this, there could be no impropriety in selling a few shares of his bank stock.

This hint was extremely displeasing, but I urged him so vehemently that he said, Francis will perhaps consent to it; I will try him this evening.

Alas! said I, my brother will never consent to such a measure. If he has found occasion for the money you had designed for my poor cousin, and of all your current income, his necessities will not fail to lay hold of this.

Very true, (glad, it seemed of an excuse for not thwarting his son's will,) Frank will never consent. So you see, it will be impossible to do any thing.

I was going to propose that he should execute this business without my brother's knowledge, but instantly perceived the impossibility of that. My father had for some years devolved on his son the management of all his affairs, and habit had made him no longer qualified to act for himself. Frank's opinion of what was proper to be done, was infallible, and absolute in all cases.

I returned home with a very sad heart. I was deeply afflicted with this new instance of my brother's selfishness and of my father's infatuation — poor Risberg! said I, what will become of thee. I love thee as my brother. I feel for thy distresses. Would to heaven I could remove them. And cannot I remove them? As to contending with my brother's haughtiness in thy favour, that is an hopeless task. As to my father, he will never submit to my guidance.

After much fruitless meditation, it occurred to me that

I might supply Risberg's wants from my own purse. My mother's indulgence to me was without bounds. She openly considered and represented me as the heiress of her fortunes, and confided fully in my discretion. The chief uses I had hitherto found for money were charitable ones. I was her almoner. To stand in the place of my father, with respect to Risberg, and supply his customary stipend from my own purse, was an adventurous undertaking for a young creature like me. It was impossible to do this, clandestinely; at least, without the knowledge and consent of Mrs. Fielder. I therefore resolved to declare what had happened, and request her counsel. An opportunity suitable to this did not immediately offer.

Next morning, as I was sitting alone in the parlour, at work, my brother came in. Never before had I received a visit from him. My surprise, therefore, was not small. I started up with the confusion of a stranger, and requested him, very formally, to be seated.

I instantly saw in his looks marks of displeasure, and though unconscious of meriting it, my trepidation increased. He took a seat without speaking, and after some pause addressed me thus.

So girl, I hear you have been meddling with things that do not concern you; sowing dissention between the old man and me; presuming to dictate to us how we are to manage our own property. He retailed to me, last night, a parcel of impertinence with which you had been teazing him, about this traveller Risberg, assuming, long before your time, the province of his care-taker. Why, do you think, continued he, contemptuously, he'll ever return to marry you? Take my word for't, he's no such fool. I *know* that he never will.

The infirmity of my temper, has been a subject of eternal regret to me; yet it never displayed itself with much force, except under the lash of my brother's sarcasms. My indignation on those occasions had a strange mixture of fear in it, and both together suffocated my speech. I made no answer to this boistrous arrogance.

But come, continued he, pray let us hear your very wise objections to a man's applying his own property to his own use. To rob himself, and spend the spoil upon another is thy sage maxim, it seems, for which, thou deservest to be dubbed a *she Solomon,* but let's see if thou art as cunning in defending as in coining maxims. Come, there is a chair; lay it on the floor, and suppose it a bar or rostrum, which thou wilt, and stand behind it, and plead the cause of foolish prodigality against common sense.

I endeavoured to muster up a little spirit, and replied, I could not plead before a more favourable judge. An appeal to my brother on behalf of foolish prodigality, could hardly fail of success. Poor common sense must look for justice at some other tribunal.

His eyes darted fire. Come, girl, none of your insolence. I did not come here to be insulted.

No, you rather came to commit than receive an insult.

Paltry distinguisher! to jest with you, and not chide you for your folly, is to insult you, is it? Leave off romance, and stick to common sense, and you will never receive any thing but kindness from me. But come, if I must humour you, let me hear how you have found yourself out to be wiser than your father and brother.

I do not imagine, brother, any good will result from our discussing this subject. Education, or sex, if you please, has made a difference in our judgments, which argument will never reconcile.

With all my heart. A truce everlasting let there be, but in truth, I merely came to caution you against intermeddling in *my* affairs, to tell you to beware of sowing jealousy and ill will between the *old man* and me. Prate away on other subjects as much as you please, but on this affair of Risberg's, hold your tongue for the future.

I thank you for your brotherly advice, but I am afraid I never shall bring myself to part with the liberty of *prating* on every subject that pleases me: at least, my forbearance will flow from my own discretion, and not from the imperious prohibition of another.

167

He laughed. Well said, oddity. I am not displeased to see you act with some spirit: but I repeat my charge: *be quiet*. Your interference will do no good.

Indeed, I firmly believe that it will not; and *that* will be a motive for my silence, that shall always have its due weight within me. Risberg, I see, must look elsewhere for a father and a brother.

Poor thing! do; put its finger in its eye and weep. Ha! ha! ha! poor Risberg! how would he laugh to see these compassionate tears. It seems he has written in a very doleful strain to thee: talked very pathetically about his debts, to his laundress and his landlady. I have a good mind to leave thee in this amiable ignorance, but I'll prove for once a kind brother, by telling you that Risberg is a profligate and prodigal; that he neglects every study, but that of dice: that this is the true reason why I have stood in the way of the old man's bounty to him. I have unquestionable proofs of his worthlessness, and see no reason to throw away money upon London prostitutes and gamblers. I never mentioned this to the old man, because I would not needlessly distress him, for I know he loves Jack at least as well as his own children. I tell it you to justify my conduct, and hope that I may for once trust to your good sense not to disclose it to your father.

My heart could not restrain its indignation at these words.

'Tis false, I exclaimed, 'tis an horrid calumny against one who cannot defend himself; I will never believe the depravity of my absent brother, till I have as good proof of it, as my present brother has given me of his.

Bravo! my girl, who could have thought you could give the lie with such a grace? why don't you spit in the face of the vile calumniator? — But I am not angry with you, Jane: I only pity you: yet I'll not leave you before I tell you my mind. I have no doubt Risberg means to return. He knows on what footing you are with Mrs. Fielder, and will take care to return; but, mind me, Jane, you shall never throw yourself and your fortune away upon Risberg, while I have a voice or an arm to prevent it; and now — good bye to you.

So ended this conversation. He left me in an hurry and confusion of spirits not to be described. For a time I felt nothing but indignation and abhorrence for what, I thought, a wicked and cruel calumny, but in proportion as I regained my tranquillity, my reflections changed. Did not my brother speak truth? Was there not something in his manner very different from those of an impostor? How unmoved was he by the doubts which I ventured to insinuate of his truth! Alas! I fear 'tis too true.

I told you before that we parted at an age when love could not be supposed to exist between us. If I know myself, I felt no more for him than for a mere brother; but then I felt all the solicitude and tenderness of a sister. I knew scarcely how to act in my present situation; but at length determined to disclose the whole affair to my mother. With her approbation I enclosed an order on a London merchant in a letter to this effect:

"I read your letter, my friend, with the sentiments of one who is anxious for your happiness. The difficulties you describe, will, I am afraid, be hereafter prevented only by your own industry. My father's and brother's expenses consume the whole of that income in which you have hitherto had a share, and I am obliged to apprize you that the usual remittances will no longer be made. You are now advancing to manhood, and, I hope will soon be able to subsist upon the fruits of your own learning and industry.

"I have something more to say to you, which I scarcely know how to communicate. Somebody here has loaded your character with very heavy imputations. You are said to be addicted to gaming, sensuality and the lowest vices. How much grief this intelligence has given to all who love you, you will easily imagine. To find you innocent of these charges would free my heart from the keenest solicitude it has hitherto felt. I leave to you the proper means of doing this, if you can do it, without violation of truth.

169

"I am very imperfectly acquainted with your present views. You orginally designed, after having compleated your academical and legal education, to return to America. If this should still be your intention, the enclosed will obviate some of your pecuniary embarrassments, and my mother enjoins me to tell you that, as you may need a few months longer to make the necessary preparations for returning, you may draw on her for an additional sum of five hundred dollars. Adieu."

My relation to Risberg was peculiarly delicate. His more lively imagination had deceived him already into belief that he was in love. At least, in all his letters, he seemed fond of recognizing that engagement which my father had established between us, and exaggerated the importance to his happiness of my regard. Experience had already taught me to set their just value on such professions. I knew that men are sanguine and confident, and that the imaginary gracefulness of passion naturally prompts them to make their words outstrip their feelings. Though eager in their present course, it is easy to divert them from it, and most men of an ardent temper can be dying of love for half a dozen different women in the course of a year.

Women feel deeply, but boast not. The supposed indecency of forwardness makes their words generally fall short of their sentiments, and passion, when once thoroughly imbibed, is as hard to be escaped from, as it was difficultly acquired. I felt no passion, and endeavoured not to feel any for Risberg, till circumstances should make it proper and discreet. My attachment was to his interest, his happiness, and not to his person, and to convince him of this, was extremely difficult. To persuade him that his freedom was absolute and entire: that no tie of honour or compassion bound him to me, but that on the contrary, to dispose of his affections elsewhere, would probably be most conducive to the interest of both.

These cautious proceedings were extremely unpleasing to my Cousin, who pretended to be deeply mortified at any thing betokening indifference and terribly alarmed at the

170

possibility of losing me. On the whole, I confess to you that I thought my Cousin and I were destined for each other, and felt myself, if I may so speak, not in love with him, but prepared, at the bidding of discretion, to love him.

My brother's report therefore greatly distressed me. Should my Cousin prove a reprobate, no power on earth should compel me to be his. If his character should prove blameless, and my heart raise no obstacles, at a proper time, I should act with absolute independence of my brother's inclinations. The menace, that while he had voice or arm he would hinder my choice of Risberg, made the less impression as it related to an event, necessarily distant and which probably might never happen.

The next letter from Risberg put an end to all further intercrouse between us. It informed us of his being on the eve of marriage into an opulent family. It expressed much indignation at the calumny which had prevailed with my father to withdraw his protection: declared that he deemed himself by no means equitably or respectfully treated by him: Expressed gratitude to my mother for the supply she had remitted, which had arrived very seasonably and prevented him from stooping to humiliations which might have injured his present happy prospects; and promised to repay the sum as soon as possible. This promise was punctually performed, and Risberg assured me that he was as happy as a lovely and rich wife could make him.

I was satisfied with this result, and bestowed no further thought on that subject. From morn to midnight have I written, and have got but little way in my story. Adieu.

171

LETTER IV

TO HENRY COLDEN
Wednesday Morning, October 5.

I CONTINUED my visits to my father as usual. Affairs proceeded nearly in their old channel. Frank and I never met but by accident, and our interviews began and ended merely with a good morrow. I never mentioned Risberg's name to my father, and observed that he as studiously avoided lighting on the same topic.

One day a friend chanced to mention the greatness of my fortune, and congratulated me on my title to two such large patrimonies as those of Mrs. Fielder and my father. I was far from viewing my condition in the same light with my friend. My mother's fortune, was indeed large and permanent, but my claim to it was merely through her voluntary favour, of which a thousand accidents might bereave me. As to my father's property, Frank had taken care very early to suggest to him that I was amply provided for in Mrs. Fielder's good graces, and that it was equitable to bequeath the whole inheritance to him. This disposition indeed was not made without my knowledge; but tho' I was sensible that I held of my maternal friend by a very precarious tenure; that my character and education were likely to secure a much wiser and more useful application of money than my brother's habits, it was impossible for me openly to object to this arrangement; so that as things stood, tho' the world, in estimating my merits, never forgot that my father was rich, and that Frank and I were his only children, I had in reality no prospect of inheriting a farthing from him.

Indeed, I always entertained a presentiment that I should one day be poor, and have to rely for subsistence on my own labour. With this persuasion, I frequently busied my thoughts in imagining the most lucrative and decent means of employing my ingenuity, and directed my enquiries to many things of little or no use, but on the irksome supposition that I should one day live by my own labour. But this is a digression.

In answer to my friend's remarks, I observed that my father's property was much less considerable than some people imagined, that time made no accession to it, and that my brother's well known habits, were likely to reduce it much below its present standard, long before it would come to a division.

There, Jane, you are mistaken, said my friend, or rather you are willing to mislead me; for you must know that tho' your father appears to be idle, yet your brother is speculating with his money at an enormous rate.

And pray, said I, for I did not wish to betray all the surprise that this intelligence gave me, in what speculations is he engaged?

How should I tell you, who scarcely know the meaning of the word. I only heard my father say that young Talbot, though seemingly swallowed up in pleasure, knew how to turn a penny as well as another, and was employing his father's wealth in *speculation*; That, I remember, was his word, but I never, for my part, took the trouble to enquire what *speculation* meant. I know only that it is some hazardous or complicated way of getting money.

These hints, tho' the conversation passed immediately to other subjects, made a deep impression on my mind. My brother's character, I knew to be incompatible with any sort of industry, and had various reasons for believing my father's property to be locked up in bank stock. If my friend's story were true, there was a new instance of the influence which Frank had acquired over his father. I had very indistinct ideas of speculation, but was used to regard it as something very hazardous, and almost criminal.

I told my mother all my uneasiness. She thought it worth while to take some means of getting at the truth, in conversation with my father. Agreeably to her advice, on my next visit, I opened the subject, by repeating exactly what I heard. I concluded by asking if it were true.

Why yes, said he, it is partly true, I must confess. Some time ago Frank laid his projects before me, and they appeared so promising and certain of success, that I ventured to give him possession of a large sum.

And what scheme, sir, was it, if I may venture to ask.

Why child, these are subjects so much out of thy way, that thou wouldst hardly comprehend any explanation that I could give.

Perhaps so: but what success, dear sir, have you met with?

Why I can't but say, that affairs have not been quite as expeditious in their progress as I had reason, at first, to expect. Unlooked for delays and impediments will occur in the prosecution of the best schemes, and these, I must own, have been well enough accounted for.

But, dear sir, the scheme I doubt not was very beneficial that induced you to hazard your whole fortune. I thought you had absolutely withdrawn yourself from all the hazards and solicitudes of business.

Why indeed, I had so, and should never have engaged again in them, of my own accord. Indeed, I trouble not myself with any details at present. I am just as much at my ease as I used to be. I leave every thing to Frank.

But sir, the hazard; the uncertainty of all projects. Would you expose yourself at this time of life, to the possibility of being reduced to distress. And had you not enough already?

Why what you say, Jane, is very true; these things did occur to me, and they strongly disinclined me, at first, from your brother's proposals; but, I don't know how it was, he made out the thing to be so very advantageous; the success of it so infallible; and his own wants were so numerous that my whole income was insufficient to supply them: the

174

Lord knows how it has happened. In my time, I could live upon a little. Even with a wife and family; my needs did not require a fourth of the sum that Frank, without wife or child, contrives to spend, yet I can't object neither. He makes it out that he spends no more than his rank in life, as he calls it, indispensibly requires. Rather than encroach upon my funds, and the prospects of success being so very flattering, and Frank so very urgent and so very sanguine, whose own interest it is to be sure of his footing, I even, at last, consented.

But I hope, dear sir, your prudence provided in some degree against the possibility of failure. No doubt, you reserved something which might serve as a stay to your old age in case this hopeful project miscarried. Absolutely to hazard *all* on the faith of any project whatever, was unworthy of one of your experience and discretion.

My father, Henry, was a good man. Humane, affectionate, kind, and of strict integrity, but I scarcely need to add, after what I have already related, that his understanding was far from being vigorous, or his temper firm. His foibles, indeed, acquired strength as he advanced in years, while his kindness and benevolence remained undiminished.

His acquiescence in my brother's schemes can hardly be ranked with follies; you, who know what scheme it was, who know the intoxicating influence of a specious project, and especially, the wonderful address and plausibility of Catling, the adventurer, who was my brother's prime minister and chief agent in that ruinous transaction, will not consider their adopting the phantom as any proof of the folly of either father or son. But let me return. To my compliment to his experience and discretion, my father replied — why, truly, I hardly know how it may turn out in the long run. At first indeed, I only consented to come down with a few thousands, the total loss of which would not break my heart; but this, it seems, though it was all they at first demanded, did not prove quite sufficient. Some debts they were obliged to contract, to no great amount, indeed, and these must be paid or the scheme relinquished.

175

Having gone so far into the scheme it was absurd to let a trifle stop me. I must own, had I foreseen all the demands that have been made, from time to time, I should never have engaged in it, but I have been led on from one step to another, till I fear, it would avail me nothing to hesitate or hold back: and Frank's representations are so very plausible!

Does your whole subsistence then, my dear sir, depend on the success of this scheme? Suppose it should utterly fail, what will be the consequences to yourself.

Fail! That is impossible. It cannot fail, but through want of money, and I am solemnly assured that no more will be necessary.

But how often, Sir, has this assurance been given? No doubt with as much solemnity the first time as the last.

My father began to grow impatient — It is useless, Jane, to start difficulties and objections now. It is too late to go back, even if I were disinclined to go forward, and I have no doubt of ultimate success. Be a good girl, and you shall come in for a share of the profit. Mrs. Fielder and I, between us, will make you the richest heiress in America. Let that consideration reconcile you to the scheme.

I could not but smile at this argument. I well knew that my brother's rapacity was not to be satisfied with millions. To sit down and say, "I have enough" was utterly incompatible with his character. I dropped the conversation for the present.

My thoughts were full of uneasiness. The mere sound of the word "project" alarmed me. I had little desire of knowing the exact nature of the scheme, being no wise qualified to judge of its practicability; but a scheme in which my brother was the agent, in which my father's whole property was hazarded, and which appeared, from the account I had just heard, at least, not to have fulfilled the first expectations, could not be regarded with tranquillity.

I took occasion to renew the subject with my father, some time after this. I could only deal in general observations on the imprudence of putting independence and subsistence

176

to hazard; though the past was not to be recalled, yet the future was his own, and it would not be unworthy of him to act with caution. I was obliged to mingle this advice with much foreign matter, and convey it in the most indirect and gentle terms. His pride was easily offended at being thought to want the council of a girl.

He replied to my remarks with confidence, that no farther demand would be made upon him. The last sum was given with extreme reluctance, and nothing but the positive assurance that it would absolutely be the last, had prevailed with him.

Suppose, sir, said I, what you have already given should prove insufficient. Suppose some new demand should be made upon you.

I cannot suppose that, after so many solemn and positive assurances.

But were not assurances as positive and solemn on every former occasion as the last.

Why yes, I must own they were, but new circumstances arose that could not be foreseen.

And, dear sir, may not new circumstances arise hereafter that could not be foreseen.

Nay, nay (with some impatience) I tell you there cannot be any.

I said no more on this subject at this time, but my father, notwithstanding the confidence he expressed, was far from being at ease.

One day I found him in great perturbation. I met my brother, who was going out as I entered, and suspected the cause of his disquiet. He spoke less than usual, and sighed deeply. I endeavoured, by various means, to prevail on him to communicate his thoughts, and, at last succeeded. My brother, it seems had made a new demand upon his purse, and he had been brought reluctantly, to consent to raise the necessary sum by a Mortgage on his house, the only real property he possessed. My brother had gone to procure a lender and prepare the deeds.

I was less surprised at this intelligence than grieved. I

thought I saw my father's ruin was inevitable, and knew not how to prevent or procrastinate it. After a long pause, I ventured to insinuate that, as the thing was yet to be done, as there was still time for deliberation —

No, no, interrupted he, I must go on. It is too late to repent. Unless new funds are supplied, all that we have hitherto done will go for nothing, and Frank assures me that one more sacrifice, and all will be well.

Alas! sir, are you still deceived by that language. Can you still listen to assurances, which experience has so often shewn to be falacious. I know nothing of this fine project, but I can see, too clearly, that unless you hold your hand you will be undone. Would to heaven you would hesitate a moment — I said a great deal more to the same purpose, and was at length interrupted by a message from my brother, who desired to see me a few minutes in the parlour below. Tho' at a loss as to what could occasion such an unusual summons, I hastened down.

I found my brother with a strange mixture of pride, perplexity and solicitude in his looks. His "how d'ye" was delivered in a graver tone than common, and he betrayed a disposition to conciliate my good will, far beyond what I had ever witnessed before. I waited with impatience to hear what he had to communicate.

At last, with many pauses and much hesitation he said; — Jane, I suppose your legacy is untouched. Was it two or three thousand Mrs. Mathews put you down for in her will?

The sum was three thousand dollars. You know that, though it was left entirely at my own disposal, yet the bequest was accompanied with advice to keep it unimpaired till I should want it for my own proper subsistence. On that condition I received, and on that condition shall keep it.

I am glad of it with all my heart, replied he, with affected vivacity. I was afraid you had spent it by this time on dolls, trinkets, and baby-things. The sum is entire you say? In your drawer? I am surprised you could resist the temptation to spend it. I wonder nobody thought of robbing you.

You cannot suppose brother, I would keep that sum in my possession. You know it was in Bank at my Aunt's death, and there it has remained.

At what bank pr'ythee?

I told him.

Well, I am extremely glad thou hadst wit enough to keep it snug, for now the time has come to put it to some use. My father and I have a scheme on foot by which we shall realize immense profit. The more engines we set to work, the greater and more speedy will be the ultimate advantage. It occurred to me that you had some money, and that, unless it were better employed, it would be but justice to allow you to throw it into stock. If therefore, you are willing, it shall be done. What say you Jane?

This proposal was totally unexpected. I harboured not a moment's doubt as to the conduct it became me to pursue, but how to declare my resolutions, or state my reasons for declining his offer, I knew not.

At last, I stammered out, that, my Aunt had bequeathed me this money, with views as to the future disposition of it, from which I did not think myself at liberty to swerve.

And pray, said he, with some heat, what were these profound views?

They were simple and obvious views. She knew my sex and education laid me under peculiar difficulties as to subsistence. As affairs then stood, there was little danger of my ever being reduced to want or dependance, but still there was a possibility of this. To ensure me against this possible evil she left me this sum, to be used only for subsistence, and when I should be deprived of all other means.

Go on, said my brother. Repeat the clause in which she forbids you, if at any time the opportunity should be offered of doubling or trebling your money, and thereby effectually securing that independence which she wished to bequeath to you, to profit by the offer. Pray, repeat that clause.

Indeed, said I, innocently, there is no such clause.

I am glad to hear it. I was afraid that she was silly enough to insert some such prohibition. On the contrary, the

179

scheme I propose to you, will merely execute your Aunt's great purpose. Instead of forbidding, she would have earnestly exhorted you, had she been a prophetess, as well as a saint, to close with such an offer as I now make you, in which, I can assure you, I have your own good as well as my own in view.

Observing my silent and perplexed air — Why Jane, said he, surely you cannot hesitate. What is your objection? Perhaps you are one of those provident animals who look before they leap, and having gained a monopoly of wisdom, will take no scheme upon trust. You must examine with your own eyes. I will explain the affair to you if you chuse, and convince you beyond controversy that your money may be trebled in a twelvemonth.

You know brother, I can be no judge of any scheme that is at all intricate.

There is no intricacy here. All is perfectly simple and obvious. I can make the case as plain to you, in three minutes, as that you have two thumbs. In the English Cottons, in the first place, there is —

Nay, Brother, it is entirely unnecessary to explain the scheme. My determinations will not be influenced by a statement which no mortal eloquence will make intelligible to me.

Well then, you consent to my proposal?

I would rather you would look elsewhere for a partner in your undertaking.

The girl's a fool — Why? what do you fear? suspect? You surely cannot doubt my being faithful to your interest. You will not insult me so much as to suppose that I would defraud you of your money. If you do, for, I know, I do not stand very high in your opinion, if you doubt my honesty, I will give you the common proofs of having received your money. Nay, so certain am I of success, that I will give you my note; bond; what you please; for thrice the amount, payable in one year.

My brother's bond will be of no use to me; I shall never go to law with my brother.

Well then, what will satisfy you?

I am easily satisfied, Brother. I am contented with things just as they are. The sum, indeed, is a trifle, but it will answer all my humble purposes.

Then you will, replied he, struggling with his rage, you will not agree?

My silence was an unequivocal answer.

You turn out to be what I always thought you, a little, perverse, stupid, obstinate — but take time (softening his tone, a little,) take time to consider of it.

Some unaccountable oddity, some freak must have taken hold of you, just now, and turned your wits out of door. 'Tis impossible you should deliberately reject such an offer. Why, girl, three thousand dollars has a great sound, perhaps, to your ears, but you'll find it a most wretched pittance, if you should ever be obliged to live upon it. The interest would hardly buy you garters and topknots. You live, at this moment, at the rate of six times the sum. You are now a wretched and precarious dependant on Mrs. Fielder, her marriage, (a very likely thing for one of her habits, fortune and age,) will set you afloat in the world, and then where will be your port. Your legacy, in any way you can employ it, will not find you bread. Three times the sum might answer, perhaps, and that, if you will fall on my advice, you may now attain in a single twelvemonth. Consider these things, and I will call on you in the evening for your final answer.

He was going, but I mustered resolution enough to call him back. Brother one word. All deliberation in this case is superfluous. You may think my decision against so plausible a scheme, perverse and absurd, but, in this instance, I am fully sensible that I have a right to do as I please, and shall exert that right whatever censure I may incur.

So, then, you are determined not to part with your paltry legacy?

I am determined not to part with it.

His eyes sparkled with rage, and stamping on the floor, he exclaimed — Why then let me tell you, Miss, you are

181

a damned idiot. I knew you were a fool, but could not believe that your folly would ever carry you to these lengths — much more in this style did poor Frank utter on this occasion. I listened trembling, confounded, vexed; and as soon as I could recover presence of mind, hastened out of his presence.

This dialogue occupied all my thoughts during that day and the following. I was sitting, next evening, at twilight pensively, in my own apartment, when, to my infinite surprise, my brother was announced. At parting with him the day before, he swore, vehemently, that he would never see my face again if he could help it. I suppose this resolution had given way to his anxiety to gain my concurrence with his schemes, and would fain have shunned a second interview. This however was impossible. I therefore composed my tremours as well as I was able, and directed him to be admitted. The angry emotions of yesterday had disappeared from his countenance, and he addressed me, with his customary carelessness. After a few trifling preliminaries, he asked me, if I had considered the subject of our yesterday's conversation. I answered that I had supposed that subject to have been dismissed forever. It was not possible for time or argument to bring us to the same way of thinking on it. I hoped therefore that he would not compel me to discuss it a second time.

Instead of flying into rage, as I expected, he fixed his eyes thoughtfully on the floor, and after a melancholy pause, said — I expected to find you invincible on that head. To say truth, I came not to discuss that subject with you anew. I came merely to ask a trifling favour — Here he stopt. He was evidently at a loss how to proceed. His features became more grave, and he actually sighed.

My heart, I believe, thou knowest, Harry, is the sport, the mere plaything of gratitude and pity. Kindness will melt my firmest resolutions in a moment. Intreaty will lead me to the world's end. Gentle accents, mournful looks in my brother, was a claim altogether irresistible. The mildness,

the condescension which I now witnessed, thrilled to
my heart. A grateful tear rushed to my eye, and I almost
articulated, dear, dear brother, be always thus kind and
thus good, and I will lay down my life for you.

It was well for us both that my brother had too much
pride or too little cunning to profit by the peculiarities of
my temper. Had he put a brotherly arm around me, and
said, in an affectionate tone, dear sister, oblige me, I am
afraid I should have instantly complied with the most indiscreet and extravagant of his requests.

Far otherwise, however, was his deportment. This condescension was momentary. The words had scarcely
escaped him before he seemed to recollect them as having
been unworthy of his dignity. He reassumed his arrogant
and careless air, half whistled "Ca ira" and glanced at the
garden, with a tall poplar, that. How old?

Not very old, for *I* planted it.

Very likely. Just such another giddy head and slender
body as the planter's. — But now I think of it, Jane, since
your money is idle, suppose you lend me five hundred
dollars of it till to-morrow. Upon my honor, I'll repay it
then. My calls just now are particularly urgent. See here,
I have brought a *check* ready filled. It only wants your
signature.

I felt instant and invincible repugnance to this request.
I had so long regarded my brother as void of all discretion, and as habitually misapplying money to vicious purposes, that I deemed it a crime of no inconsiderable degree,
to supply the means of his prodigality. Occasions were daily
occurring in which much good was effected by a few dollars,
as well as much evil produced by the want of them. My
imagination pondered on the evils of poverty much oftener
than perhaps was useful, and had thence contracted a terror of it not easily controuled. My legacy I had always
regarded as a sacred deposit; an asylum in distress which
nothing but the most egregious folly would rob or dissipate.
Yet now I was called upon to transfer, by one stroke of

the pen, to one who appeared to me to be engaged in ruinous vices or chimerical projects, so large a portion as five hundred dollars.

I was no niggardly hoarder of the allowance made me by my mother, but so diffident was I of my own discernment, that I never laid out twenty dollars without her knowledge and concurrence. Could I then give away *five hundred* of this sacred treasure, bestowed on me for very different purposes, without her knowledge? It was useless to acquaint her with my brother's request, and solicit her permission. She would never grant it.

My brother, observing me hesitate, said — Come, Jane; make haste. Surely this is no such mighty favour that you should stand a moment. 'Twill be all the same to you, since I return it to-morrow. May I perish, if I don't.

I still declined the offered pen — For what purpose, brother, surely I may ask? so large a sum.

He laughed; a mere trifle, girl. 'Tis a bare nothing; but much or little, you shall have it again, I tell you, to-morrow. Come; time flies. Take the pen, I say, and make no more words about the matter.

Impossible! till I know the purpose. Do not urge me to a wrong thing.

His face reddened with indignation. A wrong thing! you are fool enough to tire the patience of a saint. What do I ask, but the loan of a few dollars, for a single day? Money that is absolutely idle; for which you have no use. You know that my father's property is mine; that my possessions are twenty times greater than your own: yet you refuse to lend this paltry sum for one day. Come, Jane, sister; you have carried your infatuation far enough. Where a raw girl should gain all these scruples and punctilios I can't imagine. Pray, what is your objection?

In these contests with my brother, I was never mistress of my thoughts. His boisterous, negligent, contemptuous manners, awed, irritated, embarrassed me. To say any thing which implied censure of his morals or his prudence, would be only raising a storm which my womanish spirit could not withstand. In answer to his expostulations, I only repeated — impossible! I cannot.

Finding me inflexible, he once more gave way to indignation — What a damn'd oaf! to be thus creeping and cringing to an idiot; a child; an ape. Nothing but necessity, cruel necessity would have put me on this task. Then turning to me, he said in a tone half supplicating; half threatening; let me ask you once more; will you sign this check? Do not answer hastily: for much, very much depends on it. By all that is sacred I will return it to you to-morrow. Do it, and save me and your father from infamy; from ruin; from a prison; from death. He may have cowardice enough to live and endure his infamy, but I have spirit enough to die and escape it.

This was uttered with an impetuosity that startled me. The words ruin, prison, death, rung in my ears, and almost out of breath, I exclaimed — what do you mean? my father go to prison? my father ruined? what do you mean?

I mean what I say. Your signing this check may save me from irretrievable ruin. This trifling supply, which I can no where else procure, if it comes to night, may place us out of danger. If delayed till to-morrow morning, there will be no remedy. I shall receive an adequate sum to-morrow afternoon, and with that I will replace this.

My father ruined! In danger of a goal! Good Heaven! Let me fly to him. Let me know from himself the full extent of the evil — I left my seat with this purpose, but he stopped me. Are you mad, girl? He does not know the full extent of the evil. Indeed the evil will be perfectly removed by this trifling loan. He need not know it.

Ah! my poor father, said I, I see thy ruin, indeed. Too fatally secure hast thou been; too doating in thy confidence in others. These words half articulated, did not escape my brother. He was, at once, astonished and enraged by them, and even in these circumstances could not suppress his resentment.

He had, however, conjured up a spirit in me which made me deaf to his invective. I made towards the door.

185

Where are you going? You shall not leave the room till you have signed this paper.

Nothing but force shall keep me from my father. I will know his true situation, this instant from his own lips. Let me go. I *will* go.

I attempted to rush by him, but he shut the door and swore I should not leave the room till I had complied with his request.

Perceiving me thoroughly in earnest, and indignant in my turn at his treatment, he attempted to soothe me, by saying, that I had misunderstood him in relation to my father; that he had uttered words at random; that he was really out of cash at this moment: I should inexpressibly oblige him by lending him this trifling sum till to-morrow evening.

Brother, I will deal candidly with you. You think me childish, ignorant and giddy. Perhaps, I am so, but I have sense enough to resolve, and firmness enough to adhere to my resolution, never to give money without thoroughly knowing and fully approving of the purposes to which it is to be applied. You tell me, you are in extreme want of an immediate supply. Of what nature is your necessity? What has occasioned your necessity? I will not withhold, what will really do you good; what I am thoroughly convinced will do you good, but I must first be convinced.

What, would you have more than my word? I tell you it will save your — I tell you it will serve me essentially. It is surely, needless to enter into long and intricate details, which, ten to one, you will not understand.

As you please, said I. I have told you that I will not act in the dark.

Well then, I will explain my situation to you as clearly as possible.

He then proceeded to state transactions of which I understood nothing. All was specious and plausible, but I easily perceived the advantages under which he spoke, and the gross folly of suffering my conduct to be influenced by representations, of whose integrity I had no means of judging.

I will not detain you longer by this conversation. Suffice it to say, that I positively refused to comply with his wishes. The altercation that ensued was fortunately interrupted by the entrance of two or three visitants, and after lingering a few minutes, he left the house gloomy and dissatisfied.

I have gone into these incidents with a minuteness that I fear has tired you; but I will be more concise for the future. These incidents are chiefly introductory to others of a more affecting nature, and to those I must now hasten. Meanwhile I will give some little respite to my fingers.

LETTER V

TO HENRY COLDEN
Thursday Morning, October 6.

AS soon as my visitants had gone, I hastened to my father's. I immediately introduced the subject of which my heart was full. I related the particulars of my late interview with my brother; intreated him with the utmost earnestness to make the proper enquiries into the state of my brother's affairs, with whose fate it was too plain, that his own was inextricably involved.

He was seized with extreme solicitude on hearing my intelligence. He could not keep his chair one moment at a time, but walked about the floor trembling. He called his servant, and directed him in a faultering voice to go to my brother's house and request him to come immediately.

I was sensible that what I had done was violently adverse to my brother's wishes. Nevertheless, I urged my father to an immediate explanation, and determined to be present at the conference.

The messenger returned. My brother was not at home. We waited a little while, and then dispatched the messenger again, with directions to wait till his return. We waited, in vain, till nine; ten; eleven o'clock. The messenger then came back, informing us that Frank was still abroad. I was obliged to dismiss the hope of a conference this night, and returned in an anxious and melancholy mood to Mrs. Fielder's.

On my way, while ruminating on these events, I began to fear that I had exerted an unjustifiable degree of caution: I knew that those who embark in pecuniary schemes are often reduced to temporary streights and difficulties: that ruin and prosperity frequently hang on the decision of the moment: that a gap may be filled up by a small effort seasonably made, which if neglected, rapidly widens and irrevocably swallows up the ill-fated adventurer.

It was possible that all my brother had said was literally true; that he merited my confidence in this instance, and that the supply he demanded would save both him and my father from the ruin that impended over them. The more I pondered on the subject, the more dissatisfied I became with my own scruples. In this state of mind I reached home. The servant, while opening the door, expressed her surprise at my staying out so late, telling me, that my brother had been waiting my return for several hours, with marks of the utmost impatience. I shuddered at this intelligence, though just before I had almost formed the resolution of going to his house and offering him the money he wanted.

I found him, in my apartment. — Good God! cried he, where have you been till this time of night?

I told him frankly where I had been, and what had detained me. He was thunderstruck. Instead of that storm of rage and invective which I expected, he grew pale with consternation: and said in a faint voice:

Jane you have ruined me beyond redemption. Fatal, fatal rashness. It was enough to have refused me a loan which tho' useless to you, is as indispensible to my existence as my heart's blood. Had you quietly lent me the trifling pittance I asked, all might yet have been well; my father's peace have been saved and my own affairs been compleatly re-established.

All arrogance and indignation were now laid aside. His tone and looks betokened the deepest distress. All the firmness, reluctance and wariness of my temper vanished in a moment. My heart was seized with an agony of compunction. I came close to him and taking his hand involuntarily said — Dear brother! Forgive me.

Strange what influence calamity possesses in softening the character. He made no answer, but putting his arms

189

around me, pressed me to his breast while tears stole down his cheek.

Now was I thoroughly subdued. I am quite an April girl, thou knowest, Harry, and the most opposite emotions fill, with equal certainty my eyes. I could scarcely articulate — O! my dear brother, forgive me. Take what you ask. If it can be of any service to you, take all I have.

But how shall I see my father. Infinite pains have I taken to conceal from him a storm which I thought could be easily averted; which his knowledge of it would only render more difficult to resist, but my cursed folly, by saying more than I intended to you, has blasted my designs.

I again expressed my regret for the rashness of my conduct, and intreated him to think better of my father, than to imagine him invincible to argument. I promised to go to him in the morning, and counteract, as much as I could, the effects of my evening conversation. At length he departed, with somewhat renovated spirits, and left me to muse upon the strange events of this day.

I could not free myself from the secret apprehension of having done mischief rather than good, by my compliance. I had acted without consulting my mother, in a case where my youth and inexperience stood in the utmost need of advice. On the most trivial occasions I had hitherto held it a sacred duty, to make her the arbitress and judge of my whole conduct, and now shame for my own precipitance and regard for my brother's feelings seemed to join in forbidding me to disclose what had passed. A most restless and unquiet night did I pass.

Next morning was I to go to my father, to repair as much as possible the breach I had thoughtlessly made in his happiness. I knew not what means to employ for this purpose. What could I say? I was far from being satisfied, myself, with my brother's representations. I hoped, but had very little confidence that any thing in my power to do, would be of permanent advantage.

These doubts did not make me defer my visit. I was greatly surprised to find my father as cheerful and serene as usual, which he quickly accounted for, by telling me that

he had just had a long conversation with Frank, who had
convinced him that there was no ground for the terrors I
had inspired him with the night before. He could not
forbear a little acrimony on the impropriety of my interference, and I tacitly acquiesced in the censure. I found
that he knew nothing of the sum I had lent, and I thought
not proper to mention it.

That day, notwithstanding his promises of payment,
passed away without hearing from my brother. I had never
laid any stress upon the promise, but drew a bad omen
from this failure.

A few days elapsed without any material incident. The
next occasion on which my brother was introduced into
conversation with Mrs. Fielder, took place one evening after
my friend had returned from spending the day abroad.
After a pause in which there was more significance than
usual — pray have you seen Frank lately?

I made some vague answer.

He has been talked about this afternoon very little, as
usual, to his advantage.

I trembled from head to foot.

I fear continued she, he is going to ruin, and will drag
your father down the same precipice.

Dearest madam! what new circumstance. —

Nothing very new. It seems Mr. Frazer — his wife told
the story — sold him, a twelve month ago, a curricle and
pair of horses. Part of the money after some delay, was paid.
The rest was dunned for unavailingly a long time. At
length, Curricle and horses scoured the roads under the
management of Monsr. Petitgrave, brother to Frank's
housekeeper, the handsome mustee. This gave Frazer
uneasiness and some importunity extorted from Frank a
note, which being due *last Tuesday* was at Frank's importunity, withdrawn from bank to prevent protest. Next day
however it was paid.

I ventured to ask if Mrs. Frazer had mentioned any
sum.

Yes: a round sum: *five hundred dollars.*

Fortunately, the dark prevented my mother from perceiving my confusion. It was Tuesday Evening on which I had lent the money to Frank. He had given me reason to believe that his embarrassments arose from his cotton-weaving scheme, and that the sum demanded from me was to pay the wages of craving but worthy labourers.

While in the first tumult of these reflections, some one brought a letter. It was from my brother; this was the tenour —

"I fear, Jane, I have gained but little credit with you for punctuality. I ought to have fulfilled my promise, you will say. I will not excuse my breach of it, by saying, (though I might say so, perhaps, with truth,) that you have no use for the money: that I have pressing use for it, and that a small delay, without being of any importance to you, will be particularly convenient to me: no. The true and all sufficient reason why I did not return the money, was — because I had it not. To convince you that I am really in need, I enclose you a check for another five hundred, which you'll much oblige me by signing. I can repay you both sums together by Saturday — if you needs must have it so soon. The bearer waits."

In any state of my thoughts, there was little likelihood of my complying with a request made in these terms. With my present feelings, it was difficult to forbear returning an angry and reproachful answer. I sent him back these lines.

"I am thoroughly convinced that it is not in my power to afford you any effectual aid in your present difficulties. It will be very easy to injure myself. The request you make can have no other tendency. I must therefore decline complying."

The facility with which I had yielded up my first resolutions, probably encouraged him to this second application, and I formed very solemn resolutions not to be seduced a second time.

In a few minutes after dispatching my answer, he appeared. I need not repeat our conversation. He extorted from me without much difficulty, what I had heard thro' my mother, and methinks, I am ashamed to confess it — by exchanging his boisterous airs for pathetic ones — by appealing to my sisterly affection, and calling me his angel and Saviour; and especially by solemnly affirming that Frazer's story was a calumny, I, at length, did as he would have me: yet only for *three* hundred; I would not go beyond that sum.

The moment he left me, I perceived the weakness and folly of my conduct in the strongest light. I renewed all my prudent determinations: yet strange to tell, within less than a week, the same scene of earnest importunity on his side, and of foolish flexibility on mine was re-acted.

With every new instance of folly, my shame and self condemnation increased, and the more difficult I found it to disclose the truth to my mother.

In the course of a very few days, one half of my little property, was gone. A sum sufficient, according to my system of economy, to give me decent independence of the world for, at least, three years, had been dissipated by the prodigality of a profligate woman. At the time, indeed, I was ignorant of this. It was impossible not to pay some regard to the plausible statements and vehement asseverations of my brother, and to suffer them to weigh something against charges which might possibly be untrue. As soon as accident had put me in full possession of the truth on this head, I was no longer thus foolishly obsequious.

The next morning after our last interview I set out, as usual, to bid good morrow to my father. My uneasy thoughts led me unaware to extend my walk, till I reached the door of a watch-maker with whom my servant had some time before, left a watch to be repaired. It occurred to me that since I was now on the spot, I might as well stop and make some enquiry about it. On entering the shop I almost repented of my purpose, as two persons were within the bar, if I may call it so, seated in a lounging posture, by a small stove, smoking segars and gazing at me with an air of indolent impertinence. I determined to make my stay as short as possible, and hurried over a few questions to the artist, who knew me only as the owner of the watch. My attention was quickly roused by one of the loungers, who, having satisfied his curiosity, by gazing at me, turned to the other and said; well; you have hardly been to Frank's this morning, I suppose.

Indeed, but I have; was the reply.

Why, damn it, you pinch too hard. Well, and what success.

Why, what do you think?

Another *put-off,* another *call-again,* to be sure.

I would not go till he downed with the stuff.

No! (with a broad stare) it an't possible.

Seeing is believing I hope — producing a piece of paper.

Why so it is. A check — but — what's that name? — let's see, stooping to examine the signature — *"Jane Talbot"* who the Devil is she?

Don't you know her? She's his sister. A devilish rich girl.

But how? does *she* lend him money?

Yes, to be sure. She's his sister you know.

But how does she get money? Is she a widow?

No, She is a girl, I've heard, not eighteen. 'Tis not my look out how she gets money, so as her check's good, and that I'll fix as soon as the door's open.

Why damn it, if I dont think it a forgery. How should such a girl as that get so much money.

Can't conceive. Coax or rob her aunt of it, I suppose. If she's such another as Frank, she is able to outwit the devil. I hope it may be good. If it isn't, he shan't be his own man one day longer.

But how did you succeed so well.

He asked me yesterday, to call once more. So I called, you see, by times, and finding that he had a check for a little more than my debt I teazed him out of it, promising to give him the balance. I pity the fellow from my soul. It was all for trinkets and furniture bought by that prodigal jade, Mademoiselle Couteau. She would ruin a prince if she had him as much at her command as she has Frank. Little does the sister know for what purpose she gives

194

her money; however, that, as I said before, be her look out.

During this dialogue my eye was fixed upon the artist, who with the watch open in one hand, and a piece of wire in the other, was describing, with great formality, the exact nature of the defect, and the whole process of the cure; but though I looked stedfastly at him, I heard not a syllable of his dissertation. I broke away when his first pause allowed me.

The strongest emotion in my heart was resentment. That my name should be prostituted by the foul mouths of such wretches, and my money be squandered for the gratification of a meritricious vagabond, were indignities not to be endured. I was carried involuntarily towards my brother's house. I had lost all that awe in his presence, and trepidation at his scorn which had formerly been so troublesome. His sarcasms or revilings had become indifferent to me, as every day's experience had of late convinced me that, in no valuable attribute was he, any wise, superior to his sister. The consciousness of having been deceived and wronged by him, set me above both his anger and his flattery. I was hastening to his house to give vent to my feelings, when a little consideration turned my steps another way. I recollected that I should probably meet his companion, and that was an encounter which I had hitherto carefully avoided — I went according to my first design, to my father's — I was in hopes of meeting Frank there, some time in the day, or of being visited by him at Mrs. Fielder's.

My soul was in a tumult that unfitted me for conversation. I felt hourly increasing remorse at having concealed my proceedings from my mother. I imagined that had I treated her from the first, with the confidence due to her, I should have avoided all my present difficulties. Now the obstacles to confidence appeared insurmountable, and my only consolation was, that by inflexible resolution, I might shun any new cause for humiliation and regret.

I had purposed to spend the greater part of the day at my father's, chiefly in the hope of a meeting with my brother, but, after dinner, my mother sent for me home. Something methought very extraordinary, must have happened, as my mother was well; as, according to the messenger's account, she had just parted with a gentleman who seemed to have visited her on private business, my heart misgave me.

As soon as I got home, my mother took me into her chamber, and told me, after an affecting preface, that a gentleman in office at —— Bank, had called on her and informed her that checks of my signing to a very large amount had lately been offered, and that the last made its appearance to day and was presented by a man with whom it was highly disreputable for one in my condition to be thought to have any sort of intercourse.

You may suppose that after this introduction, I made haste to explain every particular. My mother was surprised and grieved. She rebuked me, with some asperity, for my reserves. Had I acquainted her with my brother's demands, she could have apprised me of all that I had since discovered. My brother, she asserted was involved beyond any one's power to extricate him, and his temper, his credulity were such, that he was forever doomed to poverty.

I had scarcely parted with my mother, on this occasion, to whom I had promised to refer every future application, when my brother made his appearance. I was prepared to overwhelm him with upbraidings for his past conduct, but I found my tongue tied in his presence. I could not bear to inflict so much shame and mortification, and besides, the past being irrevocable, it would only aggravate the disappointment which I was determined every future application should meet with. After some vague apology for nonpayment, he applied for a new loan. He had borrowed he said, of a deserving man, a small sum, which he was now unable to repay. The poor fellow was in narrow circumstances: was saddled with a numerous family: had been prevailed upon to lend, after extreme urgency on my brother's part; was now driven to the utmost need and by a prompt repayment would probably be saved from ruin. A

196

minute and plausible account of the way in which the debt originated, and his inability to repay it shewn to have proceeded from no fault of his.

I repeatedly endeavoured to break off the conversation, by abruptly leaving the room, but he detained me by importunity; by holding my hand; by standing against the door.

How irresistible is supplication! The glossings and plausibilities of eloquence are inexhaustible. I found my courage wavering. After a few ineffectual struggles, I ceased to contend. He saw that little remained to compleat his conquest, and to effect that little, by convincing me that his tale was true, he stepped out a moment, to bring in his creditor, whose anxiety had caused him to accompany Frank to the door.

This momentary respite gave me time to reflect. I ran thro' the door now no longer guarded; up stairs I flew into my mother's chamber, and told her from what kind of persecution I had escaped.

While I was speaking, some one knocked at the door. It was a servant, dispatched by my brother to summon me back. My mother went in my stead. I was left, for some minutes, alone.

So persuasive had been my brother's Rhetorick, that I began to regret my flight.

I felt something like compunction at having deprived him of an oppertunity to prove his assertions. Every gentle look and insinuating accent reappeared to my memory, and I more than half repented my inflexibility.

While buried in these thoughts, my mother returned. She told me that my brother was gone, after repeatedly requesting an interview with me, and refusing to explain his business to any other person.

Was there any body with him, madam?

Yes. One Clarges: a Jeweller. An ill looking suspicious person.

Do you know any thing of this Clarges?

Nothing, but what I am sorry to know. He is a dissolute fellow, who has broken the hearts of two wives, and thrown his children for maintenance on their maternal relations. 'Tis the same who carried your last check to the Bank.

I, just then, faintly recollected the name of Clarges, as having occurred in the conversation at the Watchmaker's, and as being the name of him who had produced the paper. This, then, was the person who was to have been introduced to me as the friend in need, the meritorious father of a numerous family, whom the payment of a just debt was to relieve from imminent ruin! How loathsome; how detestible; how insecure, are fraud and treachery. Had he been confronted with me, no doubt he would have recognized the person whom he stared at, at the watchmaker's.

Next morning I received a note, dated on the preceding evening. These were the terms of it.

"I am sorry to say, Jane, that the ruin of a father and brother may justly be laid at your door. Not to save them, when the means were in your power, and when entreated to use the means, makes you the author of their ruin. The crisis has come. Had you shewn a little mercy, the crisis might have terminated favourably. As it is, we are undone. You do not deserve to know the place of my retreat. Your unsisterly heart will prompt you to intercept, rather than to aid or connive at my flight. Fly, I must, whither, it is pretty certain, will never come to your knowledge. Farewell."

My brother's disappearance, the immediate ruin of my father, whose whole fortune was absorbed by debts contracted in his name, and for the most part without his knowledge, the sudden affluence of the adventurer who had suggested his projects to my brother, were the immediate consequences of this event. To a man of my father's habits and views, no calamity can be conceived greater than this. Never did I witness a more sincere grief; a more thorough dispair. Every thing he once possessed, was taken away from him and sold. My mother however, prevented all the most opprobrious effects of poverty, and all in my power to alleviate his solitude, and console him in his distress, was done.

Would you have thought, after this simple relation, that there was any room for malice and detraction to build up their inventions?

My brother was enraged that I refused to comply with any of his demands; not grateful for the instances in which I did comply. Clarges resented the disappointment of his scheme as much as if honour and integrity had given him a title to success.

How many times has the story been told, and with what variety of exaggeration, that the sister refused to lend her brother money, when she had plenty at command, and when a seasonable loan would have prevented the ruin of her family, while, at the same time, she had such an appetite for toys and baubles, that ere yet she was eighteen years old, she ran in debt to Clarges the Jeweller, for upwards of five hundred dollars worth.

You are the only person to whom I have thought myself bound to tell the whole truth. I do not think my reluctance to draw the follies of my brother from oblivion, a culpable one. I am willing to rely, for my justification from malicious charges, on the general tenour of my actions, and am scarcely averse to buy my brother's reputation at the cost of my own. The censure of the undistinguishing, and undistinguished multitude, gives me little uneasiness. Indeed the disapprobation of those who have no particular connection with us, is a very faint, dubious, and momentary feeling. We are thought of, now and then, by chance, and immediately forgotten. Their happiness is unaffected by the sentence casually pronounced on us, and we suffer nothing since it scarcely reaches our ears, and the interval between the judge and the culprit, hinders it from having any influence on their actions. Not so, when the censure reaches those who love us. The charge engrosses their attention, influences their happiness, and regulates their deportment towards us. My self-regard, and my regard for you, equally leads me to vindicate myself to you, from any charge, however chimerical or obsolete it may be.

My brother went to France. He seemed disposed to

forget that he ever had kindred or country: never informed us of his situation and views. All our tidings of him came to us indirectly. In this way we heard that he procured a commission in the republican troops, had made some fortunate campaigns, and had enriched himself by lucky speculations in the forfeited estates.

My mother was informed, by some one lately returned from Paris, that Frank had attained possession of the whole property of an emigrant Compte de Puysegur, who was far from being the poorest of the ancient nobles: that he lived, with princely luxury in the Count's hotel; that he had married, according to the new mode, the Compte's sister, and was, probably, for the remainder of his life, a Frenchman. He is attentive to his countrymen, and this reporter partook of several entertainments at his house.

Methinks the memory of past incidents must sometimes intrude upon his thoughts. Can he have utterly forgotten the father whom he reduced to indigence; whom he sent to a premature grave? Amidst his present oppulence one would think it would occur to him to enquire into the effects of his misconduct, not only to his own family but on others.

What a strange diversity there is among human characters. Frank is, I question not, gay, volatile, impetuous as ever. The jovial carousal and the sound sleep are never molested, I dare say, by the remembrance of the incidents I have related to you.

Methinks had I the same heavy charges to make against my conscience, I should find no refuge but death, from the goadings of remorse. To have abandoned a father to the goal or the hospital, or to the charity of strangers; a father too who had yielded him an affection and a trust without limits; to have wronged a sister out of the little property on which she relied for support, to her unprotected youth or helpless age: A sister who was virtually an orphan; who had no natural claim upon her present patroness, but might be dismissed pennyless from the house that sheltered her, without exposing the self-constituted mother to any reproach.

And has not this event taken place already? What can I expect but that, at *least,* it will take place as soon as she hears of my resolution with regard to thee? She ought to know it immediately. I myself ought to tell it, and this was one of the tasks which I designed to perform in your absence; yet, alas! know not how to set about it.

My fingers are for once thoroughly weary. I must lay down the pen — But first — why don't I hear from you? Every day since Sunday, when you left me, have I dispatched an enormous pacquet; and have not received a sentence in answer. 'Tis not well done, my friend, to forget and neglect me thus. You gave me some reason, indeed, to expect no very sudden tidings from you, but there is inexpiable treason in the silence of four long days. If you do not offer substantial excuses for this delay, woe be to thee.

Take this letter, and expect not another syllable from my pen till I hear from you.

LETTER VI

TO HENRY COLDEN
Thursday Night.

WHAT a little thing subverts my peace; dissipates my resolutions: — am I not an honest foolish creature, Hal? I uncover this wayward heart to thy view as promptly as if the disclosure had no tendency to impair thy esteem, and forfeit thy love: that is, to devote me to death; to ruin me beyond redemption.

And yet, if the unveiling of my follies should have this effect, I think I should despise thee for stupidity, and hate thee for ingratitude; for whence proceed my irresolution, my vicissitudes of purpose, but from my love, and, that man's heart must be made of strange stuff that can abhor or contemn a woman for loving him too much. Of such stuff the heart of my friend, thank heaven, is *not* made. Though I love him far — *far* too much, he will not trample on, or scoff at me.

But how my pen rambles. — No wonder! for my intellects are in a strange confusion. There is an acute pain just here. Give me your hand and let me put it on the very spot. Alas! there is no dear hand within my reach. I remember feeling just such a pain but once before: then you chanced to be seated by my side. I put your hand to the spot, and, strange to tell, a moment after I looked for the pain and 'twas gone — utterly vanished! Cannot I imagine so strongly as to experience that relief which your hand pressed to my forehead would give? Let me lay down the pen and try. —

Ah! my friend! when present, thou'rt an excellent

physician, but as thy presence is my cure, so thy absence is my only, my fatal malady.

My desk is, of late, always open: my paper spread: my pen moist. I must talk to you, tho' you give me no answer, though I have nothing but gloomy forebodings to communicate, or mournful images to call up. I must talk to you, even when you cannot hear; when invisible; when distant many a mile. It is some relief even to corporeal agonies. Even the pain, which I just now complained of, is lessened since I took up the pen — O! Hal! Hal! If you ever prove ungrateful or a traitor to me, and there be a state retributive hereafter, terrible will be thy punishment.

But why do I talk to thee thus wildly? why deal I in such rueful prognostics? I want to tell you why, for I have a reason for my present alarms: They all spring from one source — my doubts of thy fidelity. Yes, Henry, since your arrival at Wilmington, you have been a frequent visitant of Miss Secker, and have kept a profound silence towards me.

Nothing can be weaker and more silly than these disquiets. Cannot my friend visit a deserving woman a few times, but my terrors must impertinently intrude — Cannot he forget the pen, and fail to write to me, for half a week together, but my rash resentments must conjure up the phantoms of ingratitude and perfidy.

Pity the weakness of a fond heart, Henry, and let me hear from you, and be your precious and long withheld letter my relief from every disquiet. I believe, and do *not* believe what I have heard, and what I have heard teems with a thousand mischiefs, or is fair and innocent according to my reigning temper. — Adieu; but let me hear from you immediately.

LETTER VII

TO JANE TALBOT
Wilmington, Saturday, October 8.

I THOUGHT I had convinced my friend, that a letter from me ought not to be expected earlier than Monday. I left her to gratify no fickle humour, or because my chief pleasure lay any where but in her company. She knew of my design to make some stay at this place, and that the business that occasioned my stay, would leave me no leisure to write.

Is it possible that my visits to Miss Secker have given you any concern? why must the source of your anxiety be always so mortifying and opprobrious to me? that the absence of a few days and the company of another woman, should be thought to change my sentiments, and make me secretly recant those vows which I offered to you, is an imputation on my common sense which — I suppose I deserve. You judge of me from what you know of me. How can you do otherwise? If my past conduct naturally creates such suspicions, whom am I to blame but myself? reformation should precede respect, and how should I gain confidence in my integrity, but as the fruit of perseverance in well doing.

Alas! how much has he lost who has forfeited his own esteem!

As to Miss Secker, your ignorance of her, and I may add, of yourself, has given her the preference. You think her your superior, no doubt, in every estimable and attractive quality, and therefore suspect her influence on a being so sensual and volatile as poor Hal. Were she really more lovely, the faithless and giddy wretch might possibly forget you, but Miss Secker is a woman whose mind and person are not only inferior to yours, but wholly unfitted to inspire love. If it were possible to smile in my present mood, I think I should indulge *one smile* at the thought of falling in love with a woman who has scarcely had education enough to enable her to write her name; who has been confined to her bed about eighteen months, by a rheumatism contracted by too assiduous application to the wash-tub, and who often boasts, that she was born not above forty-five years ago, in an upper story of the mansion at Mount Vernon.

You do not tell me who it was that betrayed me to you. I suspect however it was Miss Jessup. She was passing through this town in her uncle's carriage on Wednesday, on her way home. Seeing me come out of the poor woman's lodgings, she stopped the coach, prated for five minutes, and left me with ironical menaces of telling you of my frequent visits to a single lady, of whom it appeared that she had some knowledge. Thus you see that your disquiets have had no foundation but in the sportive malice of your talkative neighbour.

Hannah Secker chanced to be talked of at Mr. Henshaw's as a poor creature, who was sick and destitute, and lay, almost deserted, in a neighbouring hovel. She existed on charity, which was the more scanty and reluctant, as she bore but an indifferent character either for honesty or gratitude.

The name, when first mentioned, struck my ear as something that had once been familiar, and, in my solitary evening walk, I stopped at her cottage. The sight of her, though withered by age and disease, called her fully to mind. Three years ago she lived in the city, and had been very serviceable to me in the way of her calling. I had dismissed her, however, after receiving several proofs that a pair of silk stockings and a muslin cravat offered too mighty a temptation for her virtue. You know I have but little money to spare from my own necessities, and all the service I could render her was to be her petitioner and advocate with some opulent families in this place — but enough, and too much of Hannah Secker.

Need I say that I have read your narrative, and that I fully acquit you of the guilt laid to your charge. That was done, indeed, before I heard your defence, and I was anxious to hear your story, merely because all that relates to you is, in the highest degree, interesting to me.

This letter, notwithstanding my engagements, should be longer, if I were not in danger, by writing on, of losing the post. So, dearest love, farewell, and tell me in your next, which I shall expect on Tuesday, that every pain has vanished from your head and from your heart. You may as well delay writing to your mother till I return. I hope it will be permitted me to do so very shortly. Again, my only friend, farewell.

Henry Colden.

LETTER VIII

TO HENRY COLDEN
Philadelphia, Monday October 10.

I AM ashamed of myself, Henry. What an inconsistent creature am I! I have just placed this dear letter of your's next to my heart. The sensation it affords, at this moment, is delicious: almost as much so as I once experienced from a certain somebody's hand, placed on the same spot. But that somebody's hand was never (if I recollect aright) so highly honoured as this paper. Have I not told you that your letter is deposited *next* my heart?

And with all these proofs of the pleasure your letter affords me, could you guess at the cause of those tears which even now, have not ceased flowing? Your letter has so little tenderness — is so *very* cold — but let me not be ungrateful for the preference you grant me, merely because it is not so enthusiastic and unlimited as my own.

I suppose, if I had not extorted from you some account of this poor woman, I should never have heard a syllable of your meeting with her. It is surely possible for people to be their own calumniators, to place their own actions in the worst light; to exaggerate their faults and conceal their virtues. If the fictions and artifices of vanity be detestible, the concealment of our good actions is surely not without guilt. The conviction of our guilt is painful to those that love us; wantonly and needlessly to give this pain is very perverse and unjustifiable. If a contrary deportment argue vanity, self detraction seems to be the offspring of pride.

Thou art the strangest of men, Henry. Thy whole

207

conduct, with regard to me has been a tissue of self-upbraidings. You have disclosed not only a thousand misdeeds (as you have thought them) which could not possibly have come to my knowledge by any other means, but have laboured to ascribe even your commendable actions to evil or ambiguous motives. Motives are impenetrable, and a thousand cases have occurred in which every rational observer would have supposed you to be influenced by the best motives, but where if credit be due to your own representations, your motives were far from being laudable.

Why is my esteem rather heightened than depressed by this deportment. In truth, there is no crime which remorse will not expiate, and no more shining virtue in the whole catalogue than sincerity. Besides, your own account of yourself, with all the exaggerations of humility, proved you, on the whole, and with the allowances necessarily made by every candid person, to be a very excellent man.

Your deportment to me ought chiefly to govern my opinion of you, and have you not been uniformly generous, sincere and upright? not quite passionate enough, perhaps; no blind and precipitate enthusiast; Love has not banished discretion, or blindfolded your sagacity, and as I should forgive a thousand errors on the score of love, I cannot fervently applaud that wisdom which tramples upon love. Thou hast a thousand excellent qualities, Henry, that is certain, yet a little more impetuosity and fervour in thy tenderness would compensate for the want of the whole thousand. *There* is a frank confession for thee! I am confounded at my own temerity in making it. Will it not injure me, in thy esteem, and of all evils which it is possible for me to suffer, the loss of *that* esteem, would soonest drive me to desperation.

The world has been liberal of its censure, but surely a thorough knowledge of my conduct could not condemn me. When my father and mother united their entreaties to those of Talbot, my heart had never known a preference. The man of their choice was perfectly indifferent to me, but every individual of his sex was regarded with no less indifference. I did not conceal from him the state of my feelings, but was always perfectly ingenuous and explicit. Talbot acted like every man in love. He was eager to secure me on these terms, and fondly trusted to his tenderness and perseverance, to gain those affections, which I truly acknowledged to be free. He would not leave me for his European voyage till he had extorted a solemn promise.

During his absence, I met you. The nature of those throbs, which a glance of your very shadow was sure to produce, even previous to the exchange of a single word between us, was entirely unknown to me. I had no experience to guide me. The effects of that intercourse which I took such pains to procure, could not be foreseen. My heart was too pure to admit even such a guest as apprehension, and the only information I possessed respecting you, impressed me with the notion that your heart already belonged to another.

I sought nothing but your society and your esteem. If the fetters of my promise to Talbot, became irksome after my knowledge of you, I was unconscious of the true cause. This promise never for a moment lost its obligation with me. I deemed myself as much the wife of Talbot, as if I had stood with him at the altar.

At the prospect of his return, my melancholy was excruciating, but the cause was unknown to me. I had nothing to wish, with regard to you, but to see you occasionally; to hear your voice, and to be told that you were happy. It never occurred to me that Talbot's return would occasion any difference in this respect. Conscious of nothing but rectitude in my regard for you; always frank and ingenuous in disclosing my feelings, I imagined that Talbot would adopt you as warmly for his friend as I had done.

I must grant that I erred in this particular, but my error sprung from ignorance unavoidable. I judged of others by my own heart and very sillily imagined that Talbot would continue to be satisfied with that cold and friendly regard for which only my vows made me answerable — Yet my husband's jealousies and discontents were not unreason-

able. He loved me with passion, and if that sentiment can
endure to be unrequited, it will never tolerate the preference
of another, even if that preference be less than love.

In compliance with my husband's wishes — Ah! my
friend! why cannot I say that I *did* comply with them; what
a fatal act is that of plighting hands, when the heart is
estranged. Never, never let the placable and compassionate
spirit, be seduced into an union, to which the affections
are averse. Let it not confide in the after birth of love. Such
an union is the direst cruelty even to the object who is
intended to be benefited.

I have not yet thoroughly forgiven you for deserting me.
My heart swells with anguish at the thought of your setting
more lightly by my resentment than by that of another;
of your willingness to purchase any one's happiness at the
cost of mine. You are too wise; too dispassionate by far.
Don't dispise me for this accusation, Henry. You know my
unbiassed judgment has always been with you. Repeated
proofs have convinced me that my dignity and happiness
are safer in your keeping than in my own.

You guess right my friend. Miss Jessup told me of your
visits to this poor sick woman. There is something
mysterious in the character of this Polly Jessup. She is particularly solicitous about every thing which relates to you.
It has occurred to me, since reading your letter, that she
is not entirely without design in her prattle. Something
more, methinks, more than the mere tatling, gossipping,
inquisitive propensity, in the way in which she introduces
you into conversation.

She had not alighted ten minutes before she ran into my
apartment, with a face full of intelligence. The truth respecting the wash-woman was very artfully disguised, and
yet so managed as to allow her to elude the imputation of
direct falsehood. She will, no doubt, in this, as in former
cases cover up all under the appearance of a good natured
jest; yet, if she be in jest, there is more of malice, I suspect,
than of good nature in her merriment.

Make haste back, my dear Hal. I cannot bear to keep

my mother in ignorance of our resolutions, and I am utterly at a loss in what manner to communicate them, so as to awaken the least reluctance. O! what would be wanting to my felicity if my mother could be won over to my side. And is so inestimable a good utterly hopeless. Come, my friend, and dictate such a letter as may subdue those prejudices, which, while they continue to exist, will permit me to chuse only among deplorable evils.

Jane Talbot.

LETTER IX

TO JANE TALBOT

New-York, October 13.

I HAVE just heard something which has made me very uneasy. I am afraid of seeming to you impertinent. You have declared your resolution to persist in conduct which my judgment disapproved. I have argued with you and admonished you, hitherto, in vain, and you have (tacitly indeed) rejected my interference: yet I cannot forbear offering you my counsel once more.

To say truth, it is not so much with a view to change your resolution, that I now write, as to be informed what your resolution is. I have heard what I cannot believe, yet, considering your former conduct, I have misgivings that I cannot subdue. Strangely as you have acted of late I am willing to think you incapable of what is laid to your charge. In few words, Jane, they tell me that you mean to be actually married to Colden.

You know what I think of that young man. You know my objections to the conduct you thought proper to pursue in relation to Colden, in your husband's life time. You will judge then with what emotions such intelligence was received.

Indiscreet as you have been, there are I hope, bounds which your education will not permit you to pass. Some regard, I hope, you will have for your own reputation. If your conscience object not to this proceeding, the dread of infamy, at least, will check your career.

You may think that I speak harshly, and that I ought to wait, at least, till I knew your resolution, before I spoke of it in such terms; but if this report be groundless, my censures cannot affect you. If it be true, they may serve, I hope, to deter you from persisting in your scheme.

What more can I say? You are my nearest relation; not my daughter, it is true, but, since I have not any other kindred, you are more than a daughter to me. That love which a numerous family or kindred would divide among themselves, is all collected and centered in you. The ties between us have long ceased to be artificial ones, and I feel, in all respects, as if you actually owed your being to me.

You have hitherto consulted my pleasure but little. I have all the rights, in regard to you, of a mother, but these have been hitherto despised or unacknowledged. I once regarded you as the natural successor to my property, and tho' your conduct has forfeited these claims, I now tell you, and you know that my word is sacred, that all I have shall be yours, on condition that Colden is dismissed.

More than this I will do. Every assurance possible I will give, that all shall be your's at my death, and all I have, I will share with you, *equally,* while I live. Only give me your word that, *as soon* as the transfer is made, Colden shall be thought of and conversed with, either personally or by letter, no more. I want only your promise; on that I will absolutely rely.

Mere lucre ought not perhaps, to influence you, in such a case, and if you comply, through regard to my peace, or your own reputation, I shall certainly esteem you more highly than if you are determined by the present offer, yet, such is my aversion to this alliance, that the hour in which I hear of your consent to the conditions which I now propose to you, will be esteemed one of the happiest of my life.

Think of it, my dear Jane, my friend, my child, think of it. Take time to reflect, and let me have a deliberate answer, such as will remove the fears that at present afflict, beyond my power of expression, your

H. Fielder.

213

LETTER X

TO MRS. FIELDER
Philadelphia, October 15.

I HAVE several times taken up the pen, but my distress has compelled me to lay it down again. Heaven is my witness that the happiness of my revered mamma is dearer to me than my own; no struggle was ever greater between my duty to you and the claims of another.

Will you not permit me to explain my conduct? will you not acquaint me with the reasons of your aversion to my friend? — let me call him by that name. Such indeed, has he been to me: the friend of my understanding and my virtue. My soul's friend; since, to suffer, without guilt, in this world, entitles us to peace in another, and since to him I owe that I have not been a guilty, as well as an unfortunate creature.

Whatever conduct I pursue with regard to him, I must always consider him in this light: at least, till your proofs against him are heard. Let me hear them I beseech you. Have compassion on the anguish of your poor girl, and reconcile, if possible, *my* duty to *your* inclination, by stating what you know to his disadvantage. You must have causes for your enmity, which you hide from me. Indeed, you tell me that you have: you say that if I knew them they would determine me. Let then every motive be set aside through regard to my happiness, and disclose to me this secret.

While I am ignorant of these charges; while all that I know of Colden tends to endear his happiness to me, and while his happiness depends upon my acceptance of his vows, *can* I, *ought* I, to reject him?

Place yourself in my situation. You once loved and was once beloved. I am, indeed, your child. I glory in the name which you have had the goodness to bestow upon me. Think and feel for your child, in her present unhappy circumstances; in which she does not balance between happiness and misery; that alternative, alas! is not permitted; but is anxious to discover which path has fewest thorns, and in which her duty will allow her to walk.

How greatly do you humble me! and how strongly evince your aversion to Colden, by offering, as the price of his rejection, half your property. How low am I fallen in your esteem, since you think it possible for such a bribe to prevail, and what calamities must this alliance seem to threaten, since the base selfishness of accepting this offer, is better in your eyes, than my marriage!

Sure I never was unhappy till now. Pity me, my mother. Condescend to write to me again, and by disclosing all your objections to Colden, reconcile, I earnestly intreat you, *my* duty to your inclination.

Jane Talbot.

LETTER XI

TO MRS. FIELDER
Philadelphia, October 17.

YOU will not write to me. Your messenger assures me that you have cast me from your thoughts forever, you will speak to me and see me no more. That must not be. I am preparing, inclement as the season is, to pay you a visit. Unless you shut your door against me I *will* see you. You will not turn me out of doors, I hope.

I will see you and compel you to answer me, to tell me why you will not admit my friend to your good opinion.

J. Talbot.

LETTER XII

TO JANE TALBOT
New York, October 19.

YOU need not come to see me, Jane. I will not see you. Lay me not under the cruel necessity of shutting my door against you, for *that* must be the consequence of your attempt.

After reading your letter, and seeing full proof of your infatuation, I resolved to throw away my care no longer upon you. To think no more of you. To act just as if you never had existence. Whenever it was possible, to shun you. When I met you, by chance or perforce, to treat you merely as a stranger. I write this letter to acquaint you with my resolution. Your future letters cannot change it, for they shall all be returned to you unopened.

I know you better than to trust to the appearance of half yielding reluctance which your letter contains. Thus it has always been, and as often as this dutious strain flattered me with hopes of winning you to reason, have I been deceived and disappointed.

I trust to your discernment: your seeming humility no longer. No child are you of mine. You have, henceforth, no part in my blood, and may I very soon forget that so lost and betrayed a wretch ever belonged to it.

I charge you, write not to me again.

H. F.

LETTER XIII

TO MRS. FIELDER

Philadelphia, October 24.

IMPOSSIBLE! Are you not my mother? more to me
than any mother. Did I not receive your protection and
instruction in my infancy and my childhood? When
left an orphan by my own mother, your bosom was open
to receive me. *There* was the helpless babe cherished, and
there was it taught all that virtue, which it has since endeavoured to preserve unimpaired in every trial.

You must not cast me off. You must not hate me. You
must not call me ungrateful and a wretch. Not to have merited these names is all that enables me to endure your displeasure. As long as that belief consoles me, my heart will
not break.

Yet that, even that, will not much avail me. The distress
that I now feel, that I have felt ever since the receipt of
your letter cannot be increased.

You forbid me to write to you, but I cannot forbear as
long as there is hope of extorting from you the cause of
your aversion to my friend. I solicit not this disclosure with
a view or even in the hope of repelling your objections.
I want, I had almost said, I *want* to share your antipathies.
I want only to be justified in obeying you. When known,
they will, perhaps, be found sufficient. I conjure you, once
more, tell me your objections to this marriage.

As well as I can, I have examined myself. Passion may
influence me, but I am unconscious of its influence. I think
I act with no exclusive regard to my own pleasure, but as
it flows from and is dependant on the happiness of others.

If I am mistaken in my notions of duty, God forbid that I should shut my ears against good counsel. Instead of loathing or shunning it, I am anxious to hear it. I know my own shortsighted folly: my slight experience. I know how apt I am to go astray. How often my own heart deceives me, and hence I always am in search of better knowledge: hence I listen to admonition, not only with docility but gratitude. My inclination ought perhaps to be absolutely neuter, but if I know myself, it is with reluctance that I withhold my assent from the expostulator. I am delighted to receive conviction from the arguments of those that love me.

In this case, I am prepared to hear and weigh, and be convinced by any thing you think proper to urge.

I ask not pardon for my faults, nor compassion on my frailty. That I love Colden I will not deny, but I love his worth; his merits real or imaginary enrapture my soul. Ideal his virtues may be, but to me they are real, and the moment they cease to be so, that the illusion disappears, I cease to love him, or, at least, I will do all in my power to do. I will forbear all intercourse or correspondence with him — for his, as well as my own sake.

Tell me then, my mother, what you know of him. What heinous offence has he committed, that makes him unworthy of my regard.

You have raised, without knowing it, perhaps, or designing to effect it in this way, a bar to this detested alliance. While you declare, that Colden has been guilty of base actions, it is impossible to grant him my esteem as fully as an husband should claim. Till I know what the actions are which you impute to him, I never will bind myself to him by indissoluble bands.

I have told him this and he joins with me to intreat you to communicate your charges to me. He believes that you are misled by some misapprehension; some slander. He is conscious that many of his actions have been, in some respects, ambiguous, capable of being mistaken by careless or distant or prejudiced observers. He believes that you have been betrayed into some fatal error in relation to *one* action of his life.

If this be so, he wishes only to be told his fault, and will spare no time and no pains to remove your mistake, if you should appear to be mistaken.

How easily, my good mamma, may the most discerning and impartial be misled! The ignorant and envious have no choice between truth and error. Their tales must want something to compleat it, or must possess more than the truth demands. Something you have heard of my friend injurious to his good name, and you condemn him unheard.

Yet this displeases me not. I am not anxious for his justification, but only to know so much as will authorize me to conform to your wishes.

You warn me against this marriage for my own sake. You think it will be disastrous to me. — The reasons of this apprehension would, you think, appear just in my eyes should they be disclosed, yet you will not disclose them. Without disclosure I cannot, — as a rational creature, I *cannot* change my resolution. If then I marry and the evil come that is threatened, whom have I to blame? at whose door must my misfortunes be laid if not at her's, who had it in her power to prevent the evil and would not?

Your treatment of me can proceed only from your love, and yet all the fruits of the direst enmity may grow out of it. By untimely concealments may my peace be forfeited forever. Judge then between your obligations to me, and those of secrecy into which you seem to have entered with another.

My happiness, my future conduct are in your hand. Mould them; govern them as you think proper. I have pointed out the means, and once more conjure you, by the love which you once bore; which you still bear to me, to use them.

Jane Talbot.

LETTER XIV

TO JANE TALBOT
New-York, October 27.

INSOLENT creature that thou art, Jane, and cunning as insolent! To elude my just determination by such an artifice! To counterfeit a strange hand, in the direction of thy letter, that I might thereby be induced to open it.

Thou wilt not rest, I see, till thou hast torn from my heart every root; every fibre of my once cherished tenderness: Till thou hast laid my head low in the grave. To number the tears and the pangs which thy depravity has already cost me — but thy last act is destined to surpass all former ones.

Thy perseverance in wickedness, thy inflexible imposture amazes me beyond all utterance. Thy effrontery in boasting of thy innocence; in calling this wretch thy *friend*, thy *soul's* friend, the means of securing the favour of a pure and all-seeing judge, exceeds all that I supposed possible to human nature. And that thou, Jane, the darling of my heart, and the object of all my care and my pride, should be this profligate, this obdurate creature!

When very young you were ill of a fever. The physician gave up, for some hours, all hope of your life. I shall never forget the grief which his gloomy silence gave me. All that I held dear in the world, I then thought, I would cheerfully surrender to save your life.

Poor short-sighted wretch that I was. That event, which, had it then happened, would, perhaps have bereaved me of reason, would have saved me from a portion far more bitter. I should have never lived to witness the depravity of one, whom my whole life had been employed in training to virtue.

Having opened your letter, and somewhat debated with myself, I consented to read. I will do more than read: I will answer it minutely. I will unfold that secret, by which, you truly think, my aversion to your present scheme has been chiefly caused.

I have hitherto been silent thro' compassion to you; through the hope that all might yet be well; that you might be influenced by my persuasions to forbear an action, that will insure forever your ruin. I now perceive the folly of this compassion and these hopes. I need not be assiduous to spare you the shame and mortification of hearing the truth. Shame is as much a stranger to your heart as remorse. Say what I will; disclose what I will, your conduct will be just the same. A show of much reluctance and humility will, no doubt, be made, and the tongue will be busy in imploring favour which the heart disdains.

In the foresight of this, I was going to forbid your writing, but you care not for my forbidding. As long as you think it possible to reconcile me to your views, and make me a partaker in your infamy, you will harrass me with importunity; with feigned penitence and preposterous arguments — But one thing at least is in my power. I can shun you, and I can throw your unopened letters into the fire, and that, believe me, Jane, I shall do.

But I am wasting time. My indignation carries me away from my purpose. Let me return to it, and having told you all my mind, let me dismiss the hateful subject forever.

I knew the motives that induced you to marry Lewis Talbot. They were good ones. Your compliance with mine and your father's wishes in that respect, shewed that force of understanding which I always ascribed to you. Your previous reluctance: your scruples, were indeed unworthy of you, but you conquered them and that was better; perhaps, it evinced more magnanimity than never to have had them.

You were happy, I long thought, in your union with a man of probity and good sense. You may be sure, I thought of you often, but only with pleasure. Certain indications, I early saw in you of a sensibility that required strict government: an inattention to any thing but feeling: a proneness to romantic friendship and a pining after good not consistent with our nature. I imagined that I had kept at a distance all such books and companions as tend to produce this phantastic character, and whence you imbibed this perverse spirit, at so early an age, is, to me, inconceivable. It cost me many a gloomy foreboding.

My disquiets increased as you grew up, and that age arrived when the heart comes to be entangled with what is called love. I was anxious to find for you a man of merit, to whose keeping your happiness might safely be entrusted. Talbot was such an one, but thy wayward heart refused to love him. He was not all your fancy had conceived of excellent and lovely. He was a mere man, with the taste and habits suitable and common to his education and age. He was addicted to industry, was regular and frugal in his manners and economy. He had nothing of that specious and glossy texture which captivates inexperience and youth, and serves as a substitute for every other virtue. While others talked about their duty he was contented with performing it, and he was satisfied with ignorance of theories as long as his practice was faultless.

He was just such an one as I wished for the darling of my heart, but you thought not so. You did not object to his age, though almost double your own: to his person or aspect, tho' they were by no means worthy of his mind: to his profession or condition; but your heart sighed after one who could divide with you your sympathies. Who saw every thing just as you saw it. Who could emulate your enthusiasm, and echo back every exclamation which chance should dictate to you.

You even pleaded religion as one of your objections. Talbot, it seems, had nothing that deserved to be called religion. He had never reasoned on the subject. He had read no books and had never looked into his bible since he was fifteen years old. He seldom went to Church, but because it was the fashion, and when there, seldom spared a thought from his own temporal concerns, to a future state and a governing deity. All those expansions of soul, produced by meditation on the power and goodness of our maker, and those raptures that flow from accommodating all our actions to his will, and from consciousness of his approbation and presence, you discovered to be strangers to his breast, and, therefore, you scrupled to unite your fate with his.

It was not enough that this man has never been seduced into disbelief. That his faith was steadfast and rational, without producing those fervours and reveries and rhapsodies, which unfit us for the mixed scenes of human life, and breed in us absurd and phantastic notions of our duty or our happiness: that his religion had produced all its practical effects, in honest, regular, sober and consistent conduct.

You wanted a zealot; a sectary: one that should enter into all the trifling distinctions and minute subtilties that make one christian the mortal foe of another, while, in their social conduct, there is no difference to be found between them.

I do not repeat these things to upbraid you for what you then were, but merely to remind you of the inconsistency of these notions with your subsequent conduct. You then, at the instance of your father and at my instance gave them up, and that compliance, supposing your scruples to have been undissembled, made you a still greater interest in our affections.

You never gave me reason to suppose that you repented of this compliance. I never saw you after your engagement, but you wore a cheerful countenance; at least, till your unfortunate connection with Colden. To that connection must be traced every misfortune and depravity that has attended you since.

When I heard from Patty Sinclair, of his frequent visits to you during your retirement at Burlington, I thought of it but little. He was, indeed, a new acquaintance. You were unacquainted with his character and history, except so far

224

as you could collect them from his conversation, and no confidence could of course, be placed in that. It was therefore, perhaps, somewhat indiscreet, to permit such *very* frequent visits; such *very* long walks. To neglect the friends whom you lived with, for the sake of exclusive conversations and lonely rambles, noon and night, with a mere stranger. One, not regularly introduced to you. Whose name you were obliged to enquire of himself. You too, already a betrothed woman: your lover absent: yourself from home, and merely on terms of hospitality! all this did not look well.

But the mischief, it was evident, was to be known by the event. Colden might have probity and circumspection. He might prove an agreeable friend to your future husband and a useful companion to yourself. Kept within due limits, your complacency for this stranger; your attachment to his company, might occasion no inconvenience: How little did I then suspect to what extremes you were capable of going, and even then had actually gone!

The subject was of sufficient importance to induce me to write to you. Your answer was not quite satisfactory; yet on the whole, laid my apprehensions at rest. I was deceived by the confidence you expressed in your own caution, and the seeming readiness there was to be governed by my advice.

Afterwards, I heard, through various channels, without any efforts on my part, intelligence of Colden. At first I was not much alarmed. Colden, it is true, was not a faultless or steadfast character. No gross or enormous vices were ascribed to him. His habits, as far as appearances enabled one to judge, were temperate and chaste. He was contemplative and bookish and was vaguely described as being somewhat visionary and romantic.

In all this there was nothing formidable. Such a man might surely be an harmless companion. Those with whom he was said to associate most intimately were highly estimable. Their esteem was a test of merit, not to be disposed of or hastily rejected.

Things, however, quickly took a new face. I was informed that after your return to the city, Colden continued to be a very constant visitant. Your husband's voyage left you soon after at liberty, and your intercourse with this person, only became more intimate and confidential.

Reflecting closely on this circumstance, I began to suspect some danger lurking in your path. I now remembered that impetuosity of feeling which distinguished your early age: those notions of kindred among souls: of friendship and harmony of feelings which, in your juvenile age, you loved to indulge.

I reflected that the victory over these chimeras, which you gained by marriage with Talbot, might be merely temporary: and that in order to call these dormant feelings into action, it was only requisite to meet with one, contemplative, bookish and romantic as yourself.

Such a one, it was greatly to be feared, you had now found in this young man; just such qualities he was reported to possess, as would render him dangerous to you, and you dangerous to him. A poet, not in theory only, but in practise: accustomed to intoxicate the women with melodious flattery; fond of being *intimate;* avowedly devoted to the sex: eloquent in his encomiums upon female charms; and affecting to select his *friends* only from that sex.

What effect might such a character have upon your peace, even without imputing any ill attention to him? both of you might work your own ruin, while you designed nothing but good, and even supposing that your intercourse should be harmless, or even beneficial with respect to yourselves, what was to be feared for Talbot? An intimacy of this kind could hardly escape his observation on his return. It would be criminal, indeed, to conceal it from him.

These apprehensions were raised to the highest pitch by more accurate information of Colden's character which I afterwards received. I found, on enquiring of those who had the best means of knowing, that Colden had imbibed that pernicious philosophy which is now so much in vogue. One who knew him perfectly; who had long been in habits

226

of the closest intimacy with him, who was still a familiar correspondent of his, gave me this account.

I met this friend of Colden's, Thomson his name is, of whom I suppose you have heard something, in this city. His being mentioned as the intimate companion of Colden, made me wish to see him, and fortunately I prevailed upon him to be very communicative.

Thomson is an excellent young man: he loves Colden much, and describes the progress of his friend's opinions with every mark of regret. He even showed me letters that had passed between them, and in which every horrid and immoral tenet was defended by one and denied by the other. These letters showed Colden as the advocate of suicide; a scoffer at promises; the despiser of revelation, of providence and a future state; an opponent of marriage, and as one who denied (shocking!) that any thing but mere habit and positive law, stood in the way of marriage; nay, of intercourse without marriage, between brother and sister, parent and child!

You may readily believe that I did not credit such things on slight evidence. I did not rely on Thomson's mere words, solemn and unaffected as these were; nothing but Colden's hand-writing could in such a case, be credited.

To say truth, I should not be much surprised had I heard of Colden, as of a youth whose notions, on moral and religious topics, were, in some degree, unsettled: that in the fervour and giddiness incident to his age, he had not tamed his mind to investigation: had not subdued his heart to regular and devout thoughts: that his passions or his indolence had made the truths of religion somewhat obscure, and shut them out, not properly from his conviction but only from his attention.

I expected to find, united with this vague and dubious state of mind, tokens of the influence of a pious education: a reverence, at least, for those sacred precepts on which the happiness of men rests, and at least, a practical observance of that which, if not fully admitted by his understanding, was yet very far from having been rejected by it.

227

But widely and deplorably different was Colden's case. A most fascinating book* fell at length into his hands, which changed, in a moment, the whole course of his ideas. What he had before regarded with reluctance and terror, this book taught him to admire and love. The writer has the art of the grand deceiver; the fatal art of carrying the worst poison under the name and appearance of wholesome food; of disguising all that is impious or blasphemous or licentious under the guise and sanctions of virtue.

Colden had lived before this without examination or enquiry. His heart, his inclination was, perhaps, on the side of religion and true virtue, but this book carried all his inclination, his zeal and his enthusiasm, over to the adversary, and so strangely had he been perverted, that he held himself bound, he conceived it to be his duty, to vindicate, in private and public, to preach, with vehemence, his new faith. The rage for making converts seized him, and that Thomson was not won over to the same cause, proceeded from no want of industry in Colden.

Such was the man whom you had admitted to your confidence; whom you had adopted for your bosom friend. I knew your pretensions to religion, the stress which you laid upon piety as the basis of morals. I remembered your objections to Talbot on this score, not only as a husband, but as a friend. I could, therefore, only suppose that Colden had joined dissimulation to his other errors, and had gained and kept your good opinion by avowing sentiments which his heart secretly abhored.

I cannot describe to you, Jane, my alarms upon this discovery. That your cook had intended to poison you, the next meat which you should eat in your own house, would have alarmed me I assure you, much less. The preservation of your virtue was unspeakably of more importance in my eyes than of your life.

I wrote to you, and what was your reply? I could scarcely

*Godwin's Political Justice

believe my senses. Every horrid foreboding realized! already such an adept in this accursed sophistry! the very cant of that detestible sect adopted!

I had plumed myself upon your ignorance. He had taken advantage of that, I supposed, and had won your esteem by counterfeiting a moral and pious strain. To make you put him forever at a distance, it was needed only to tear off his mask. This was done, but, alas, too late for your safety. The poison was already swallowed.

I had no patience with you, to listen to your trifling and insidious distinctions; such as, though you could audaciously urge them to me, possessed no weight; *could* possess no weight in your understanding. What was it to me whether he was ruffian or madman; whether in destroying you, he meant to destroy or to save? Is it proper to expose your breast to a sword, because the wretch that wields it, supposes madly that it is a straw, which he holds in his hand?

But I will not renew the subject. The same motives that induced me to attempt to reason with you then, no longer exists. The anguish, the astonishment which your letters, as they gradually unfolded your character, produced in me, I endeavoured to show you at the time. Now I pass them over to come to a more important circumstance.

Yet how shall I tell it thee, Jane. I am afraid to entrust it to paper. Thy fame is still dear to me. I would not be the means of irretrievably blasting thy fame. Yet what may come of relating some incidents on paper?

Faint is my hope, but I am not without some hope, that thou canst yet be saved: be snatched from perdition. Thy life I value not in comparison with something higher. And if, through an erring sensibility, the sacrifice of Colden cost thee thy life, I shall yet rejoice. As the wife of Colden, thou wilt be worse than dead to me.

What has come to me, I wonder? I began this letter with a firm and as I thought inflexible soul. Despair had made me serene, yet now thy image rises before me, with all those bewitching graces which adorned thee when thou wast innocent and a child. All the mother seizes my heart and my tears suffocate me.

Shall I shock, shall I wound thee, my child, by lifting the veil from thy mis-conduct, behind which thou thinkest thou art screened from every human eye? How little dost thou imagine that I know *so much*!

Now will thy expostulations and reasonings have an end. Surely they *will* have an end. Shame at last; Shame at last will overwhelm thee and make thee dumb.

Yet my heart sorely misgives me. I shudder at the extremes to which thy accursed seducer may have urged thee. What thou hast failed in concealing, thou mayest be so obdurately wicked as to attempt to justify.

Was it not the unavoidable result of confiding in a man avowedly irreligious and immoral: Of exposing thy understanding and thy heart to such stratagems as his philosophy made laudable and necessary? But I know not what I would say. I must lay down the pen, till I can reason myself into some composure. I will write again to-morrow.

H. Fielder.

LETTER XV

TO THE SAME

O MY lost child! In thy humiliations at this moment I can sympathize. The shame that must follow the detection of it is more within my thoughts at present, than the negligence or infatuation that occasioned thy faults.

I know all. Thy intended husband knew it all. It was from him that the horrible tidings of thy unfaithfulness to marriage vows first came.

He visited this city on purpose to obtain an interview with me. He entered my apartment with every mark of distress. He knew well the effect of such tidings on my heart. Most eagerly would I have laid down my life to preserve thy purity spotless.

He demeaned himself as one who loved thee, with a rational affection, and who, however deeply he deplored the loss of thy love, accounted thy defection from virtue of infinitely greater moment.

I was willing to discredit even his assertion. Far better it was that the husband should prove the defamer of his wife, than that my darling child should prove a profligate! but he left me no room to doubt by shewing me a letter.

He shewed it me on condition of my being everlastingly silent to you in regard to its contents. He yielded to a jealousy which would not be conquered, and had gotten this letter by surreptitious means. He was ashamed of an action which his judgment condemned as ignoble and deceitful.

Far more wise and considerate was this excellent and injured man than I. He was afraid, by disclosing to you the knowledge he had thus gained, of rendering you desperate and hardened. As long as reputation was not gone, he thought your errors were retrievable. He distrusted the success of his own efforts, and besought me to be your guardian: As to himself he resigned the hope of even gaining your love, and entreated me to exert myself for dissolving your connection with Colden, merely for your own sake.

To show me the necessity of my exertions he had communicated this letter, believing that my maternal interest in your happiness, would prevent me from making any but a salutary use of it. Yet he had not put your safety into my hands, without a surety. He was so fully persuaded of the ill consequences of your knowing how much was known, that he had given me the proofs of your guilt, only on my solemn promise to conceal them from you.

I saw the generosity and force of his representations, and while I endeavoured by the most earnest remonstrances, to break your union with Colden, I suffered no particle of the truth to escape me. But you were hard as a rock. You would not forbid his visits, nor reject his letters.

I need not repeat to you what followed; by what means I endeavoured to effect that end, which your obstinate folly refused.

When I gave this promise to Talbot, I foresaw not his speedy death and the consequences to Colden and yourself. I have been affrighted at the rumour of your marriage, and to justify the conduct I mean to pursue, I have revealed to you, what I promised to conceal, merely because I foresaw not the present state of your affairs.

You will not be surprised that on your marriage with this man, I should withdraw from you what you now hold from my bounty. No faultiness in you shall induce me to leave you without the means of decent subsistence, but I owe no benevolence to Colden. My duty will not permit me to give any thing to your paramour. When you change your name you must change your habitation and leave behind you whatever you found.

Think not, Jane, that I cease to love thee. I am not so inhuman as to refuse my forgiveness to a penitent; yet I ask not thy penitence to insure thee my affection. I have told thee my conditions and adhere to them still.

To preclude all bickerings and cavils, I enclose the letter which attests your fall.

H. Fielder.

LETTER XVI

(Enclosed letter)

TO HENRY COLDEN
Tuesday Morning.

Y OU went away this morning before I was awake, I think you might have staid to breakfast, yet on second thoughts, your early departure was best. *Perhaps,* it was so.

You have made me very thoughtful, to day. What passed last night has left my mind at no liberty to read and to scribble as I used to do. How your omens made me shudder!

I want to see you. Can't you come again this evening? but no, you must not. I must not be an encroacher. I must judge of others, and of their claims upon your company, by myself and my own claims. Yet I should be glad to see that creature who would dare to enter into competition with *me.*

But I may as well hold my peace. My rights will not be admitted by others. Indeed no soul but yourself can know them in all their extent, and, what is all I care for, *you* are far from being strictly just to me.

Don't be angry, Hal. Skip the last couple of sentences, or think of them as not mine. I disown them, to-morrow, at six, the fire shall be stirred, the candles lighted, and the sofa placed in order due. I shall be at home to *nobody; mind that.*

I am loath to mention one thing, however, but I must. Though nothing be due to the absent man, somewhat is due to myself. I have been excessively uneasy the whole day. I am terrified at certain consequences. What may not happen if, No; the last night's scene must not be repeated; at least, for a month to come. The sweet oblivion of

234

the future and past lasted only for the night. Now I have liesure to look forward, and am resolved (dont laugh at my resolves; I am quite in earnest. —) to keep thee at a distance for at least a fortnight to come. It shall be a whole month, if thou dost not submit with a good grace.

Jane Talbot.

LETTER XVII

TO MR. HENRY COLDEN

New York, October 22.

Sir.

I ADDRESS myself to you as the mother of an unhappy girl, who has put herself into your power. But I write not to upbraid you or indulge my own indignation, but merely to beseech your compassion for her whom you profess to love.

I cannot apologize for the manner in which I have acted in regard to your connection with Jane Talbot. In that respect, I must take to myself all the blame you may chuse to impute to me.

I call not into question the disinterestedness of your intentions in proposing marriage to this woman, nor, if the information which I am going to give you, should possess any influence, shall I ascribe that influence to any thing but a commendable attention to your true interest and a generous regard to the welfare of my daughter.

Be it known to you, then, sir, that Mrs. Talbot possesses no fortune in her own right. Her present dwelling, and her chief means of subsistence, are derived from me; she holds them at my option, and they will be instantly and entirely withdrawn, on her marriage with you.

You cannot be unacquainted with the habits and views in which my daughter has been educated. Her life has passed at ease and in luxury and you cannot but perceive the effect of any material change in her way of life.

It would be a wretched artifice to pretend any particular esteem for you, or to attempt to persuade you that any part of this letter is dictated by any regard to your interest, except as that is subservient to the interest of one, whom I can never cease to love.

Yet I ardently hope that this circumstance may not hinder you from accepting bills upon London to the amount of three hundred pounds sterling. They shall be put into your hands the moment I am properly assured that you have engaged your passage to Europe, and are determined to be nothing more than a distant well-wisher to my daughter.

I am anxious that you should draw from the terms of this offer, proof of that confidence in your word, which you might not perhaps have expected from my conduct towards you in other respects. Indeed, my conscience acquits me of any design to injure you. On the contrary, it would give me sincere pleasure to hear of your success in every laudable pursuit.

I know your talents and the direction which they have hitherto received. I know that London is a theatre best adapted to the lucrative display of these talents, and that the sum I offer you will be an ample fund, till your own exertions may be turned to account.

If this offer be accepted, I shall not only hold myself everlastingly obliged to you, but I shall grant you an higher place in my esteem. Yet, through deference to scruples, which you may possibly possess, I most cheerfully plight to you my honor, that this transaction shall be concealed from Mrs. Talbot, and from all the world.

Though property is necessary to our happiness, and my daughter's habits render the continuance of former indulgences, necessary to her content, I will not be so unjust to her, as to imagine that this is *all* which she regards. Respect from the world and the attachment of her ancient friends are, also, of some value in her eyes. Reflect, sir, I beseech you, whether you are qualified to compensate her for the loss of property; of good name — my own justification, in case she marries you, will require me to be nothing more than *just* to her — and of *all* her ancient friends, who will abhor in her, the faithless wife and the ungrateful child. I need not inform *you* that *your* family will never receive into their bosom one whom her own kindred have rejected. *I am, &c.*

H. Fielder.

LETTER XVIII

TO MRS. FIELDER
Philadelphia, October 28.

I NEED not hesitate a moment to answer this letter. I will be all that my revered mamma, wishes me to be. I have vowed an eternal separation from Colden, and to enable me to keep this vow, I entreat you to permit me to come to you.

I will leave this house in any body's care you direct. My Molly and the boy Tom I shall find it no easy task to part with, but, I will, nevertheless, send the former to her mother, who is thrifty and well to live. I beg you to permit me to bring the boy with me. I wait your answer.

Jane Talbot.

LETTER XIX

TO HENRY COLDEN
Philadelphia, October 28.

O MY friend! where are you at this trying moment?
why did you desert me? now, if ever, does my feeble
heart stand in need of your counsel and courage.
Did I ever lean these throbbing brows against your arm,
and pour my tears into your bosom, that I was not com-
forted. Never did that adored voice fail to whisper sweet
peace to my soul. In every storm, thy calmer and more
strenuous spirit, has provided me the means of safety. —
But now I look around for my stay, my monitor; my
encourager, in vain.

You will make haste to dispatch the business that detains
you. You will return, and fly, on the wings of love, to thy
Jane. Alas! she will not be found. She will have fled far
away, and in her stead will she leave this sullen messenger
to tell thee that thy Jane has parted from thee forever!

Do not upbraid me, Hal. Do not call me ungrateful or
rash. Indeed, I shall not be able to bear thy reproaches.
I know they will kill me quite.

And don't expostulate with me. Confirm me rather in
my new resolution. Even if you think it cruel or absurd,
aver that it is just. Persuade me that I have done my duty
to my mother, and assure me of your cheerful acquiescence.

Too late is it now, even if I would, to recall my promise.

I have promised to part with you. In the first tumult of
my soul, on receiving the inclosed letters, I wrote an answer,
assuring Mrs. Fielder of my absolute concurrence with
her will.

240

Already does my heart, calling up thy beloved image; reflecting on the immense debt which I owe to your generosity; on the disappointment which the tidings of my journey will give you; already do I repent of my precipitation.

I have sought repose but I find it not. My pillow is moist with the bitterest tears that I ever shed. To give vent to my swelling heart, I write to you, but I must now stop. All my former self is coming back upon me, and while I think of you as of my true and only friend, I shall be unable to persist. I will not part with thee my friend. I cannot do it. Has not my life been solemnly devoted to compensate thee for thy unmerited love? For the crosses and vexations thou hast endured for my sake?

Why shall I forsake thee? To gratify a wayward and groundless prejudice? To purchase the shortlived and dubious affection of one who loves me in proportion as I am blind to thy merit; as I forget thy benefits: as I countenance the envy and slander that pursue thee?

Yet what shall I bring to thy arms: A blasted reputation, poverty: contempt. The indignation of mine and of *thy* friends. For thou art poor and so am I. Thy kindred have antipathies for me as strong as those that are fostered against thyself ——

Jane Talbot.

LETTER XX

TO HENRY COLDEN
October 28, Evening.

I WILL struggle for sufficient composure to finish this letter. I have spent the day in reflection, and am now, I hope, calm enough to review this most horrid and inexplicable charge.

Look, my friend at the letter she has sent me. It is my hand writing. The very same which I have so often mentioned to you as having been, after so unaccountable a manner, mislaid.

I wrote some part of it, alone, in my own parlour. You recollect the time. The day after that night which an heavy storm of rain, and my fatal importunity prevailed on you to spend under this roof.

Mark the deplorable consequences of an act, which the coldest charity would not have declined. On such a night I would have opened my doors to my worst enemy. Yet because I turned not forth my best friend, on such a night, see to what a foul accusation I have exposed myself.

I had not finished, but it came into my mind that something in that which I had a little before received from you, might be seasonably noticed, before I shut up my billet. So I left my paper on the table open, while I ran up stairs to get your letter which I had left in a drawer in my chamber.

While turning over cloaths and papers I heard the street door open, and some one enter. This did not hinder me from continuing my search. I thought it was my gossipping neighbour, Miss Jessup, and had some hopes that,

242

finding no one in the parlour, she would withdraw, with as little ceremony as she entered.

My search was longer than I expected, but finding it at last, down I went, fully expecting to find a visitant, not having heard any steps returning to the door.

But no visitant was there, and the paper was gone! I was surprised, and a little alarmed. You know my childish apprehensions of robbers.

I called up Molly who was singing at her work in the kitchen. She had heard the street door opened and shut, and footsteps over head, but she imagined them to be mine. A little heavier too, she recollected them to be, than mine. She likewise heard a sound as if the door had been opened and shut softly. It thus appeared that my unknown visitant had hastily and secretly withdrawn and my paper had disappeared.

I was confounded at this incident. Who it was that could thus purloin an unfinished letter and retire in order to conceal the theft, I could not imagine. Nothing else had been displaced. It was no ordinary thief; no sordid villain.

For a time, I thought perhaps, it might be some facetious body, who expected to find amusement in puzzling or alarming me. Yet I was not alarmed; for what had I to fear or to conceal? the contents were perfectly harmless, and being fully satisfied with the purity of my own thoughts, I never dreamed of any construction being put on them, injurious to me.

I soon ceased to think of this occurrence. I had no cause as I then thought, to be anxious about consequences. The place of the lost letter was easily supplied by my loquacious pen, and I came, at last, to conjecture that I had carelessly whisked it into the fire, and that the visitant had been induced to withdraw, by finding the apartment empty. Yet I never discovered any one who had come in and gone out in this manner. Miss Jessup, whom I questioned afterwards, had spent that day elsewhere. And now, when the letter and its contents were almost forgotten, does it appear before me, and is offered in proof of this dreadful charge.

After reading my mother's letter, I opened with trembling hand that which was inclosed. I instantly recognized the long lost billet. All of it appeared, on the first perusal, to be mine. Even the last mysterious paragraph was acknowledged by my senses. In the first confusion of my mind, I knew not what to believe or reject, my thoughts were wandering, and my repeated efforts had no influence in restoring them to order.

Methinks, I then felt as I should have felt if the charge had been true. I shuddered as if to look back would only furnish me with proofs of a guilt of which I had not hitherto been conscious: proofs that had merely escaped remembrance, or had failed to produce their due effect, from some infatuation of mind.

When the first horror and amazement were passed, and I took up the letter and pondered on it once more, I caught a glimpse suddenly: suspicion darted all at once into my mind: I strove to recollect the circumstances attending the writing of this billet.

Yes: it was clear. As distinctly as if it were the work of yesterday, did I now remember, that I stopped at the words *nobody; mind that.* The following sentences are strange to me. The character is similar to what precedes, but the words were never penned by me.

And could Talbot — Yet what end? a fraud so — Ah! let me not suspect my *husband* of *such* a fraud. Let me not have reason to abhor his memory.

I fondly imagined that with his life, my causes of disquiet were at an end, yet now are my eyes open to an endless series of calamities and humiliations which his decease has made sure.

I cannot escape from them. There is no help for me. I cannot disprove. What testimony can I bring to establish my innocence: to prove that another hand has added these detestable confessions?

True it is you passed that night under my roof. Where was my caution? you, Henry, knew mankind better than

244

I: why did you not repel my importunities, and leave me in spite of my urgencies for your stay?

Poor thoughtless wretch that I was, not to be aware of the indecorum of allowing one of your sex, not allied to me by kindred — I, too, alone, without any companion but a servant, to pass the night in the same habitation.

What is genuine of this note, acknowledges your having lodged here. Thus much I cannot, and need not deny; yet how shall I make those distinctions visible to Mrs. Fielder; how shall I point out that spot in my billet, where the forgery begins? and at whose expense must I vindicate myself? Better incur the last degree of infamy myself, since it will not be deserved, than to load him that is gone with reproach. Talbot sleeps, I hope, in peace, and let me not, for any selfish or transitory good, molest his ashes. Shall I not be contented with the approbation of a pure and all-seeing judge?

But if I *would* vindicate myself, I have not the power: I have forfeited my credit with my mother. With her my word will be of no weight: surely it ought to weigh nothing. Against evidence of this kind, communicated by an husband, shall the wild and improbable assertion of the criminal be suffered to prevail? I have only my assertion to offer.

Yet, my good God! in what a maze hast thou permitted my unhappy feet to be entangled! With intentions void of blame, have I been pursued by all the consequences of the most atrocious guilt.

In an evil hour, Henry, was it that I saw thee first. What endless perplexities have beset me since that disasterous moment. I cannot pray for their termination, for prayer implies hope.

For thy sake, God is my witness, more than for my own, have I determined to be no longer thine. I hereby solemnly absolve you from all engagements to me. I command you, I beseech you, not to cast away a thought on the ill-fated Jane. Seek a more worthy companion, and be happy.

Perhaps you will feel, not pity, but displeasure, in recieving this letter. You will not deign to answer me, perhaps,

245

or will answer me with sharp rebuke. I have only lived to trouble your peace, and have no claim to your forbearance: yet, methinks, I would be spared the misery of hearing your reproaches, re-echoed as they will be by my own conscience. I fear they will but the more unfit me for the part that I wish henceforth to act.

I would carry, if possible, to Mrs. Fielder's presence a cheerful aspect. I would be to her that companion which I was in my brighter days. To study her happiness shall be henceforth my only office, but this, unless I can conceal from her an aching heart, I shall be unable to do. Let me not carry with me the insupportable weight of your reproaches.

Jane Talbot.

LETTER XXI

TO JANE TALBOT
Baltimore, October 31.

Y OU had reason to fear my reproaches, yet you have strangely erred in imagining the cause for which I should blame you. You are never tired, my good friend, of humbling me by injurious suppositions.

I do, indeed, reproach you for conduct that is rash; unjust; hurtful to yourself; to your mother; to me; to the memory of him who, whatever were his faults, has done nothing to forfeit your reverence.

You are charged with the blackest guilt that can be imputed to woman. To know you guilty produces more anguish in the mind of your accuser, than any other evil could produce, and to be convinced of your innocence, would be to remove the chief cause of her sorrow, yet you are contented to admit the charge: to countenance her error by your silence. By stating the simple truth, circumstantially and fully; by adding earnest and pathetic assurances of your innocence; by shewing all the letters that have passed between us, the contents of which will shew that such guilt was impossible; by making your girl bear witness to the precaution you used on that night, to preclude misconstructions, surely you may hope to disarm her suspicions.

But this proceeding has not occurred to you. You have mistrusted the power of truth, and even are willing to perpetuate the error. And why? because you will not blast the memory of the dead. The loss of your own reputation: the misery of your mother, whom your imaginary guilt

makes miserable, are of less moment in your eyes than —
what? let not he, my girl, who knows thee best, have most
reason to blush for thee.

Talbot, you imagine, forged this calumny. It was a wrong
thing and much unhappiness has flowed from it. This calumny, you have it, at length, in your power to refute. Its
past effects cannot be recalled, but here the evil may end,
the mistake may be cleared up, and be hindered from
destroying the future peace of your mother.

Yet you forbear from tenderness to *his* memory, who,
if you are consistent with yourself, you must believe to look
back on that transaction with remorse, to lament every evil
which it has hitherto occasioned, and to rejoice in the means
of stopping the disastrous series.

My happiness is just of as little value. Your mother's
wishes, though allowed to be irrational and groundless, are
to be gratified by the disappointment of mine, which appear to be just and reasonable, and since one must be
sacrificed, that affection with which you have inspired me;
and those benefits you confess to owe to me; those sufferings believed by you to have been incurred by me for your
sake, do not, it seems, entitle me to preference.

On this score, however, my good girl, set your heart at
ease. I never assumed the merits you attributed to me. I
never urged the claims you were once so eager to admit.
I desire not the preference. If, by abjuring me, your happiness could be secured; if it were possible for you to be
that cheerful companion of your mother, which you seem
so greatly to wish: if, in her society, you could stifle every
regret, and prevent your tranquillity from being invaded
by self-reproach, most gladly would I persuade you to go
to her, and dismiss me from your thoughts forever.

But I know, Jane, that this cannot be. You never will
enjoy peace under your mother's roof. The sighing heart
and the saddened features, will forever upbraid her, and
bickering and repining will mar every domestic scene. Your
mother's aversion to me is far from irreconcileable, but that
which will hasten reconcilement will be *marriage*. You cannot

forfeit her love as long as you preserve your integrity, and those scruples which no argument will dissipate, will yield to reflection on an evil (as she will regard it) that cannot be remedied.

Admitting me, in this respect, to be mistaken, your mother's resentment will ever give you disquiet. True, but will your union with me, console you nothing? in pressing the hoped-for fruit of that union to your breast; in that tenderness which you will hourly receive from me, will there be nothing to compensate you for sorrows in which there is no remorse, and which, indeed, will owe their poignancy to the generosity of your spirit?

You cannot unite yourself to me, but with some view to my happiness. Will your contributing to that happiness be nothing?

Yet I cannot seperate my felicity from your's. I can enjoy nothing at the cost of your peace. In whatever way you decide, may the fruit be content.

I ask you not for proofs of love; for the sacrifice of others to me. My happiness demands it not. It only requires you to seek your own good. Nothing but ceaseless repinings can follow your compliance with your mother's wishes; but there is something in your power to do. You can hide these repinings from her, by living at a distance from her. She may know you only through the medium of your letters, and these may exhibit the brightest side of things. She wants nothing but your divorce from me, and that may take place without living under her roof.

You need not stay here. The world is wide and she will eagerly consent to the breaking of your shackles by change of residence. Much and the best part of your country you have never seen. Variety of objects will amuse you, and new faces and new minds eraze the deep impressions of the past. Colden and his merits may sink into forgetfulness, or be thought of with no other emotion than regret that a being so worthless was ever beloved — But I wander from the true point. I meant not to introduce myself into this letter — Self! That vile debaser whom I detest as my worst enemy, and who assumes a thousand shapes and practises a thousand wiles to entice me from the right path.

Ah! Jane. Could thy sagacity discover no other cause of thy mother's error than Talbot's fraud? Could thy heart so readily impute to him so black a treachery? Such a prompt and undoubting conclusion, it grieves me to find thee capable of.

How much more likely that Talbot was himself deceived. For it was not by him that thy unfinished letter was purloined. At that moment he was probably some thousands of miles distant. It was five weeks before his return from his Hamburg voyage, when that mysterious incident happened.

Be of good cheer, my sweet girl. I doubt not all will be well. We shall find the means of detecting and defeating this conspiracy, and of re-establishing thee in thy mother's good opinion. At present, I own, I do not see the means; but to say truth, my mind is clouded by anxieties; enfeebled by watching and fatigue.

You know why I came hither. I found my friend in a very bad way, and have no hope but that his pangs, which must end within a few days, may, for his sake, terminate very soon. He will not part with me, and I have seldom left his chamber since I came.

Your letter has disturbed me much, and I seize this interval when the sick man has gained a respite from his pain to tell you my thoughts upon it. I fear I have not reasoned very clearly. Some peevishness, I doubt, has crept into my style. I rely upon your wonted goodness to excuse it.

I have much to say upon this affecting subject, but must take a future opportunity.

I also have received a letter from Mrs. Fielder, of which I will say no more, since I send you enclosed *that,* and my answer. I wish it had come at a time when my mind was more at ease, as an immediate reply seemed to be necessary. Adieu.

Henry Colden.

LETTER XXII

TO MRS. FIELDER

Baltimore, November 2.

Madam.

I T would indeed be needless to apologize for your behaviour to me. I not only acquit you of any enmity to me, but beg leave to return you my warmest thanks for the generous offers which you make me in this letter.

I should be grosly wanting in that love for Mrs. Talbot which you believe me to possess, if I did not partake in that gratitude and reverence which she feels for one, who has performed for her every parental duty. The esteem of the good is only of less value in my eyes than the approbation of my own conscience. There is no price which I would not pay for your good opinion, consistent with a just regard to that of others and to my own.

I cannot be pleased with the information which you give me. For the sake of my friend, I am grieved that you are determined to make her marriage with me, the forfeiture of that provision which your bounty has hitherto supplied her.

Forgive me if I say that in exacting this forfeiture you will not be consistent with yourself. On her marriage with me, she will stand in much more need of your bounty than at present, and her merits, however slender you may deem them, will then be, at least, *not less* than they now are.

If there were any methods by which I might be prevented from sharing in gifts bestowed upon my wife, I would eagerly concur in them.

I fully believe that your motive in giving me this timely warning was a generous one. Yet, in justice to myself and your daughter, I must observe that the warning was superfluous, since Jane never concealed from me the true state of her affairs, and since I never imagined you would honour with your gifts a marriage contracted against your will.

Well do I know the influence of early indulgences. Your daughter is a strong example of that influence, nor will her union with me, if, by that union she forfeit your favour, be any thing more than a choice among evils, all of which are heavy.

My own education and experience sufficiently testify the importance of riches, and I should be the last to despise or depreciate their value. Still, much as habit has endeared to me the goods of fortune, I am far from setting them above all other goods.

You offer me, Madam, a large alms. Valuable to me as that sum is, and eagerly as I would accept it in any other circumstances, yet, at present, I must, however reluctantly, decline it. A voyage to Europe and such a sum, if your daughter's happiness were not in question, would be the utmost bound of my wishes.

"Shall I be able to compensate her —" you ask.

No, indeed, Madam, I am far from deeming myself qualified to compensate her for the loss of property, reputation and friends. I aspire to nothing but to console her under that loss, and to husband as frugally as I can, those few meagre remnants of happiness which shall be left to us.

I have seen your late letter to her. I should be less than man if I were not greatly grieved at the contents; yet, Madam, I am not cast down below the hope of convincing you that the charge made against your daughter is false. You could not do otherwise than believe it. It is for us to show you by what means, you, and, probably, Talbot himself, have been deceived.

To suffer your charge to pass, for a moment, uncontradicted, would be unjust, not more to ourselves than to you. The mere denial will not, and ought not to change your opinion. It may even tend to raise higher the acrimony

252

of your aversion to me. It must ever be irksome to a generous spirit to deny, without the power of disproving, but a tacit admission of the charge would be unworthy of those who know themselves innocent.

Beseeching your favourable thoughts, and grateful for the good which, but for the interference of higher duties, your heart would prompt you to give, and mine would not scruple to accept, I am &c.

Henry Colden.

LETTER XXIII

TO HENRY COLDEN
Philadelphia, November 2.

AH! My friend! how mortifying are those proofs of thy excellence. How deep is that debasement into which I am sunk, when I compare myself with thee. It cannot be the want of love that makes thee so easily give me up. My feeble and jealous heart is ever prone to suspect; yet I ought at length to be above these ungenerous surmises.

My own demerits; my fickleness: my precipitation are so great, and so unlike thy inflexible spirit, that I am ever ready to impute to thee that contempt for me, which I know I so richly deserve. I am astonished that so poor a thing as I am, thus continually betraying her weakness, should retain thy affection; yet at any proof of coldness or indifference in thee, do I grow impatient; melancholy: a strange mixture of upbraiding for myself, and resentment for thee, occupies my feelings.

I have read thy letter. I shuddered when I painted to myself thy unhappiness on receiving tidings of my resolution to join my mother. I felt that thy reluctance to part with me, would form the strongest obstacle to going, and yet, being convinced that I must go, I wanted thee to counterfeit indifference, to feign compliance.

And such a wayward heart is mine that now these assurances of thy compliance have come to hand, I am not satisfied. The poor contriver wished to find in thee an affectation of indifference. Her humanity would be satisfied with that appearance, but her pride demanded that it should

254

be no more than a veil, behind which the inconsolable, the bleeding heart should be distinctly seen.

You are too much in earnest in your equanimity. You study my exclusive happiness with too unimpassioned a soul. You are pleased when I am pleased; but not, it seems, the more so from any relation which my pleasure bears to you: no matter what it is that pleases me: so I am but pleased, you are content.

I don't like this oblivion of self. I want to be essential to your happiness. I want to act with a view to your interests and wishes; these wishes requiring my love and my company for your own sake.

But I have got into a maze again. Puzzling myself with intricate distinctions. I can't be satisfied with telling you that I am not well, but I must be inspecting with these careful eyes into causes, and labouring to tell you of what nature my malady is.

It has always been so. I have always found an unaccountable pleasure in dissecting, as it were, my heart; uncovering, one by one, its many folds, and laying it before you, as a country is shewn in a map. This voluble tongue, and this prompt pen! what volumes have I talked to you on that bewitching theme myself!

And yet, loquacious as I am, I never interrupted you when you were talking. It was always such a favour when these rigid fibres of yours relaxed: and yet I praise myself for more forbearance than belongs to me. The little impertinent has often stopped your mouth; at times too when your talk charmed her most; but then it was not with words.

But have I not said this a score of times before? and why do I indulge this prate now?

To say truth, I am perplexed and unhappy. Your letter has made me so. My heart flutters too much to allow me to attend to the subject of your letter. I follow this rambling leader merely to escape from more arduous paths, and I send you this scribble because I must write to you. Adieu.

Jane Talbot.

LETTER XXIV

TO THE SAME

Nov. 3.

WHAT is it, my friend, that makes thy influence over me so absolute? No resolution of mine can stand against your remonstrances. A single word, a look, approving or condemning, transforms me into a new creature. The dread of having offended you, gives me the most pungent distress. Your "Well done" lifts me above all reproach. It is only when you are distant, when your verdict is uncertain, that I shrink from contumely, that the scorn of the world, though unmerited, is a load too heavy for my strength.

Methinks I should be a strange creature, if left to myself. A very different creature, doubtless, I should have been, if placed under any other guidance. So easily swayed am I by one that is the lord of my affections. No will, no reason have I of my own.

Such sudden and total transitions! in solitude I ruminate and form my schemes. They seem to me unalterable, yet a word from you scatters all my laboured edifices, and I look back upon my former state of mind, as on something that passed when I was a lunatic or dreaming.

It is but a day since I determined to part with you; since a thousand tormenting images engrossed my imagination; yet now am I quite changed: I am bound to you by links stronger than ever. No, I will not part with you.

Yet how shall I excuse my non-compliance to my mother? I have told her that I would come to her, that I waited only for her directions as to the disposal of her property. What

256

will be her disappointment when I tell her that I will not come: when she finds me, in spite of her remonstrances, still faithful to my engagements to thee.

Is there no method of removing this aversion? of outrooting this deadly prejudice? And must I, in giving myself to thee, forfeit her affection.

And now this dreadful charge! no wonder that her affectionate heart was sorely wounded by such seeming proofs of my wickedness.

I thought at first — shame upon my inconsistent character! my incurable blindness! I should never have doubted the truth of my first thoughts, if you had not helped me to a more candid conjecture. I was unjust enough to load *him* with the guilt of this plot against me, and imagined there was duty in forbearing to detect it.

Now, by thy means, do I judge otherwise. Yet how my friend shall I unravel this mystery? my heart is truly sad. How easily is my woman's courage lowered, and how prone am I to despond.

Lend me thy aid, thy helping hand, my beloved. Decide and act for me, and be my weakness fortified; my hope restored by thee. Let me lose all separate feelings, all separate existence, and let me know no principle of action, but the decision of your judgement; no motive or desire but to please; to gratify you.

Our marriage, you say, will facilitate reconcilement with my mother. Do you think so? then let it take place, my dear Hal. Heaven permit that marriage may tend to reconcile; but let it reconcile or not, if the wish be your's, it shall occupy the chief place in my heart. The time, the manner, be it your's to prescribe. My happiness, on that event will surely want but little to compleat it, and if you bid me not despair of my mother's acquiescence, I *will* not despair.

I am to send your letter, after reading, to my mother, I suppose. I have read it, Hal, more than once. And for my sake thou declinest her offers. When you thus refuse no sacrifice on my account, shall I hesitate, when it becomes my turn? shall I ever want gratitude, thinkest thou? shall

257

I ever imagine that I have done enough to evince my gratitude?

But how do I forget thy present situation. Thy dying friend has scarcely occurred to me. Thy afflictions, thy fatigues, are absorbed in my own selfish cares.

I am very often on the brink of hating myself. So much thoughtlessness of others; such callousness to sorrows not my own: my hard heart has often reproached thee for sparing a sigh or a wish from me: that every gloom has not been dispelled by my presence, was treason, forsooth, against my majesty, and the murmurs that delighted love should breathe, to welcome thy return, was changed into half vindictive reluctance; not quite a frown, and upbraidings in which tenderness was almost turned out of door by anger.

In the present case, for instance, I have scarcely thought of thy dying friend once. How much thy disquiets would be augmented by the letters which I sent thee never entered my thoughts. To hide our sorrows from those who love us, seems to be no more than generous. Yet I never hid any thing from thee. All was uttered that was felt. I considered not attending circumstances. The bird, as soon as it was scared, flew into the bosom that was nearest, and merely occupied with dangers of its own, was satisfied to find a refuge there.

And yet, — See now, Vanity, the cunning advocate, entering with his — *And yet.* Would I listen to him, what a world of palliations and apologies would he furnish. How would he remind me of cases in which my sympathy was always awakened with attention. How often — But I will not listen to the flatterer.

And now I think of it, Hal, you differ from me very much in that respect. Every mournful secret must be wrung from you. You hoard up all your evil thoughts, and brood over them alone. Nothing but earnest importunity ever got from you any of your griefs.

Now this is cruel to yourself and unjust to me. It is denying my claim to confidence. It is holding back from me a part of yourself. It is setting light by my sympathy.

And yet — the prater Vanity once more, you see — but I will let him speak out this time. Here his apology is your's, and myself am only flattered indirectly.

And yet when I have extorted from you any secret sorrow, you have afterwards acknowledged that the disclosure was of use. That my sympathising love was grateful to you, and my counsel of some value: that you drew from my conduct on those occasions new proofs of my strength of mind, and of my right, a right which my affection for you gave me, to share with you all your thoughts.

Yet on the next occasion that offers, you are sure to relapse into your habitual taciturnity, and my labours to subdue it, are again to be repeated. I have sometimes been tempted to retaliate and convince you, by the effects of my concealments upon you, of the error of your own scheme.

But I never could persist, in silence, for five minutes together. Shut up as the temple of my heart is, to the rest of mankind, all its doors fly open of their own accord, when you approach.

Now am I got into my usual strain: in which I could persevere forever. No wonder it charms me so much, since, while thus pursuing it, I lose all my cares in a sweet oblivion, but I must stop, at last, and recall my thoughts to a less welcome subject.

Painful as it is, I must write to my mother. I will do it now, and send you my letter. I will endeavour, hereafter, to keep alive, a salutary distrust of myself, and do nothing without your approbation and direction. Such submission becomes thy

Jane.

LETTER XXV

TO MRS. FIELDER
Philadelphia, November 4.

I TREMBLE thus to approach my honoured mother, once more, since I cannot bring into her presence the heart that she wishes to find. Instead of acknowledgment of faults, and penitence suitable to their heinous nature, I must bring with me a bosom free from self-reproach, and a confidence which innocence only can give, that I shall be sometime able to disprove the charge brought against me.

Ah my mother! could such guilt as this ever stain a heart, fashioned by your tenderest care! did it never occur to you that possibly some mistake might have misled the witness against me!

The letter which you sent me is partly mine. All that is honest and laudable is mine, but that which confesses dishonour has been added by another hand. By whom my hand writing was counterfeited, and for what end, I know not. I cannot name any one, who deserves to be suspected.

I might proceed to explain the circumstances attending the writing and the loss of this letter so fatal to me: but I forbear to attempt to justify myself by means which I know before hand, will effect nothing; unless it be to aggravate, in your eyes, my imaginary guilt.

If it were possible for you to suspend your judgment: if the most open and earnest and positive averments of my innocence could induce you, not to reverse, but merely to postpone your sentence, you would afford me unspeakable happiness.

You tell me, that the loss of your present bounty will be the consequence of my marriage. My claims on you are long ago at an end. Indeed, I never had any claims. Your treatment of me has flowed from your unconstrained benevolence. For what you have given: for the tenderness which you continually bestowed on me, you have received only disappointment and affliction.

For all your favours, I seem to you ungrateful: yet long after that conduct was known, which, to you, proves my unworthiness, your protection has continued, and you are so good as to assure me that it shall not be withdrawn as long as I have no protector but you.

Dear as my education has made the indulgences of competence to me, I hope, I shall relinquish them without a sigh. Had you done nothing more than screen my infancy and youth from hardship and poverty, than supplied the mere needs of nature, my debt to you could never be paid.

But how much more than this have you done for me? you have given me, by your instructions and example, an understanding and an heart. You have taught me to value a fair fame beyond every thing but the peace of virtue; you have made me capable of a generous affection for a benefactor equal to yourself; capable of acting so as, at once, to *deserve,* and to *lose* your esteem: and enabled me to relinquish cheerfully those comforts and luxuries which cannot be retained but at the price of my integrity.

I look forward to poverty without dismay. Perhaps I make light of its evils, because I have never tried them. I am indeed a weak and undiscerning creature. Yet nothing but experience will correct my error, if it be an error.

So sanguine am I, that I even cherish the belief that the privation of much of that ease which I have hitherto enjoyed, will strengthen my mind, and somewhat qualify me for enduring those evils which I cannot expect always to escape.

You know, my mother, that the loss of my present provision, will not leave me destitute. If it did, I know your generosity too well, to imagine that you would withdraw from me all the means of support.

Indeed my own fund, slender as it is, in comparison with what your bounty supplies me, is adequate to all my personal wants; I am sure it would prove so on the trial. So that I part with your gifts with less reluctance, though with no diminution of my gratitude.

If I could bring to you, my faith unbroken, and were allowed to present to you my friend, I would instantly fly to your presence: but, that is a felicity too great for my hope. The alternative, however painful, must be adopted by

Your ever grateful

Jane.

LETTER XXVI

TO MRS. TALBOT
Baltimore, November 5.

I HIGHLY approve of your letter. It far exceeded the expectations I had formed of you. You are, indeed, a surprising creature.

One cannot fail to be astonished at the differences of human characters; at the opposite principles by which the judgments of men are influenced.

Experience, however, is the antidote of wonder. There was a time when I should have reflected on the sentiments of your mother, with a firm belief that no human being could be practically influenced by them.

She offers, and surely with sincerity, to divide her large property with you: to give away half her estate during her own life, and while, indeed, she is yet in her prime; and to whom give it? to one who has no natural relation to her: who is merely an adopted child: who has acted for several years, in direct repugnance to her will: in a manner she regards as not only indiscreet, but flagrantly criminal. Whom one guilty act has (so it must appear to your mamma) involved her in a continued series of falsehoods and frauds.

She offers this immense gift to you, on no condition but a mere verbal promise to break off intercourse with the man you love, and with whom you have been actually criminal.

She seems not aware how easily promises are made that are not designed to be performed: how absurd it would be to rely upon your integrity in this respect, when you have shewn yourself (so, it must appear to her) grossly defective in others of infinitely greater moment. How easily might a heart like yours be persuaded to recall its promises; or violate this condition, as soon as the performance of her contract has made you independent of her and of the world.

You promise; — it is done in half a dozen syllables — that you will see the hated Colden no more. All that you promise, you intend. To-morrow she enriches you with half her fortune. Next day, the seducer comes, and may surely expect to prevail on you to forget this promise, since he has conquered your firmness in a case of unspeakably greater importance.

This offer of hers surely indicates, not only love for you, but reverence for your good faith inconsistent with the horrid imputation she has urged against you.

As to me, what a portrait does her letter exhibit. And yet this scoffer at the obligation of a promise, is offered four or five thousand dollars on condition that he plights his word to embark for England, and to give up all his hopes of you.

Villain as he is; a villain not by habit or by passion, but by *principle;* a cool blooded systematic villain; yet she will give him affluence and the means of depraving thousands, by his example and his rhetoric, on condition that he refuses to marry the woman whom he has made an adulteress. Who has imbibed, from the contagion of his discourse, all the practical and speculative turpitude which he has to impart.

This conduct might be considered only as proving her aversion to me. So strong is it, as to impel her to indiscreet and self-destructive expedients: and so I should likewise reason if these very expedients did not argue a confidence in my integrity somewhat inconsistent with the censure passed on my morals.

After all, is there not reason to question the sincerity of her hatred? Is not thy mother a dissembler, Jane? does she really credit the charge she makes against thee? does she really suppose me that insane philosopher which her letter describes?

Yet this is only leaping from a ditch into a quicksand.

It is quite as hard to account for her dissimulation, as for her sincerity. Why should she pretend to suspect *you* of so black a deed, or me of such abominable tenets?

And yet, an observer might say, it is one thing to promse and another to perform in her case as well as in ours. She tells us what she *will do,* provided we enter into such engagements, but, if we should embrace her offers, is it certain that she would not hesitate, repent, and retract.

Passion may dictate large and vehement offers upon paper, which deliberating prudence would never allow to be literally adhered to.

Besides, may not these magnificent proposals be dictated by a knowledge of our characters, which assured her that they would never be accepted. But, with this belief, why should the offers be made?

The answer is easy. These offers, by the kindness and respect for us which they manifest, engage our esteem and gratitude, and by their magnitude, shew how deeply she abhors this connection, and hence dispose us to do that, for pity's sake, which mere lucre would never recommend.

And here is a string of guesses to amuse thee Jane. Their truth or falsehood is of little moment to us, since these offers ought not to influence our conduct.

One thing is sure; that is, thy mother's aversion to me. And yet I ought not to blame her. That I am an Atheist in morals, the Seducer of her daughter, she fully believes, and these are surely sufficient objections to me. Would she be a discerning friend; or virtuous mother if she did not with this belief remonstrate against your alliance with one so wicked.

The fault lies not with her. With whom then does it lie? Or, what only is important, where is the remedy? Expostulation and remonstrance will avail nothing. I cannot be an hypocrite, I cannot dissemble that I have *once* been criminal; and that I am, at present, conscious of a thousand weaknesses and self distrusts. There is but one meagre and equivocal merit that belongs to me. I stick to the truth: Yet this is a virtue of late growth. It has not yet acquired firmness to resist the undermining waves of habit, or to be motionless amidst the hurricane of passions.

You offer me yourself. I love you. Shall I not then accept your offer? Shall my high conception of your merits, and my extreme contempt and distrust of myself, hinder me from receiving so precious a boon? Shall I not make happy by being happy? Since you value me so much beyond my merits: since my faults though fully disclosed to you, do not abate your esteem, do not change your views in my favour, shall I withhold my hand?

I am not obdurate. I am not ungrateful. With you I never was an hypocrite. With the rest of the world I have ceased to be so. If I look forward without confidence, I look back with humiliation and remorse. I have always wished to be good, but till I knew you, I despaired of ever being so, and even now my hopes are perpetually drooping.

I sometimes question, especially since your actual condition is known, whether I should accept your offered hand: But mistake me not, my beloved creature. My distrust does not arise from any doubts of my own constancy. That I shall grow indifferent or forgetful or ungrateful to you, can never be.

All my doubts are connected with you. Can I compensate you for those losses which will follow your marriage. The loss of your mother's affection; the exchange of all that splendour and abundance you have hitherto enjoyed for obscurity and indigence.

You say I *can*. The image of myself in my own mind is a sorry compound of hateful or despicable qualities. I am even out of humour with my person, my face. So absurd am I in my estimates of merit, that my homely features and my scanty form, had their part in restraining me from aspiring to one supreme in loveliness, and in causing the surprise that followed the discovery of your passion.

In your eyes, however, this mind and this person are venerable and attractive. My affection, my company, are chief goods with you. The possession of all other goods cannot save you from misery, if this be wanting. The loss of of all others will not bereave you of happiness if this be possessed.

Fain would I believe you. You decide but reasonably. Fortune's goods ought not to be so highly prized, as the reason of many prizes them, and as my habits, in spite of reason's dissent, and remonstrances compel me to prize them. They contribute less to your happiness, and that industry and frugality which supplies their place, you look upon without disgust; with even some degree of satisfaction.

Not so I; I cannot labour for bread; I cannot work to live. In that respect I have no parallel. The world does not contain my likeness. My very nature unfits me for any profitable business. My dependence must ever be on others or on fortune.

As to the influence of some stronger motive to industry than has yet occurred: I am without hope. There can be no stronger ones to a generous mind, than have long been urgent with me: being proof against these, none will ever conquer my reluctance.

I am not indolent, but my activity is vague; profitless; capricious. No lucrative or noble purpose impels me. I aim at nothing but selfish gratification. I have no relish, indeed, for sensual indulgences. It is the intellectual taste that calls for such banquets as imagination and science can furnish; but though less sordid than the epicure, the voluptuary, or the sportsman, the principle that governs them and me, is the same: equally limited to self; equally void of any basis in morals or religion.

Should you give yourself to me, and rely upon my *labour* for shelter and food, deplorable and compleat would be your disappointment. I know myself too well to trust myself with such an office. My love for you would not strengthen my heart or my hands. No; it would only sink me, with more speed, into despair. Quickly, and by some fatal deed, should I abandon you, my children, and the world.

Possibly, I err. Possibly I underrate my strength of mind and the influence of habit, which makes easy to us every path; but I will not trust to the *possible*.

Hence it is that, if by marriage you should become wholly dependant on me, it could never take place. Some freak of fortune may indeed place me above want, but my own efforts never will. Indeed, in this forbearance; in this self-denial, there is no merit. While admitted to the privileges of a betrothed man; your company, your confidence, every warrantable proof of love mine; I may surely dispense with the privileges of wedlock. Secretly repine I might: occasionally I might murmur. But my days would glide along, with fewer obstacles, at least, than if I were that infirm and disconsolate wretch — *your husband.*

But this unhappy alternative is not ours. Thou hast something which thy mother cannot take away: sufficient for thy maintenance: thy frugal support. Meaner, and more limited indeed than thy present and former affluence: such as I, of my own motion, would never reduce thee to: such as I can object to only on thy own account.

How has the night run away! my friend's sister arrived here yesterday. They joined in beseeching me to go to a separate chamber and strive for some refreshment. I have slept a couple of hours, and that has sufficed. My mind, on waking, was thronged with so many images, connected with my Jane, that I started up, at last, and betook myself to the pen.

Yet how versatile and fleeting is thought! In this long letter I have not put down one thing that I intended. I meant not to repeat what has been so often said before, and especially I meant not to revolve, if I could help it, any gloomy ideas.

Thy letters gave me exquisite pleasure. They displayed all thy charming self to my view. I pressed every precious line to my lips with nearly as much rapture as I would have done the pratler herself, had she been talking to me all this tenderness instead of writing it.

I took up the pen that I might tell thee my thanks, yet rambled almost instantly into mournful repetitions. I have half a mind to burn the scribble, but I cannot write more just now, and this will show you, at least, that I am not unmindful of you. Adieu.

Colden.

LETTER XXVII

TO MRS. TALBOT
Baltimore, November 6.

LET me see! this is the beginning of November. Yes; it was just a twelve-month ago, that I was sitting at this silent hour, at a country fire just like this. My elbow, then as now, was leaning on a table, supplied with books and writing tools.

What shall I do, thought I, then, to pass away the time till ten. Can't think of going to bed till that hour, and if I sit here, idly basking in the beams of this cheerful blaze, I shall fall into a listless, uneasy doze, that without refreshing me, as sleep would do, will unfit me for sleep.

Shall I read? nothing here that is new. Enough that is of value, if I could but make myself inquisitive; treasures which, in a curious mood, I would eagerly rifle, but now the tedious page only adds new weight to my eye-lids.

Shall I write? what? to whom? there are Sam and Tom, and brother Dick, and sister Sue — they all have epistolary claims upon me still unsatisfied. Twenty letters that I ought to answer. Come, let me briskly set about the task —

Not now: some other time. To-morrow. What can I write about? havn't two ideas that hang together intelligibly. 'Twill be common-place trite stuff. Besides, writing always plants a thorn in my breast.

Let me try my hand at a reverie: a meditation — on that hearth-brush. Hair — what sort of hair? of a hog — and the wooden handle — of poplar or cedar or white oak. At one time a troop of swine munching mast in a grove of oaks, transformed by those magicians, carpenters and butchers, into hearth-brushes. A whimsical metamorphosis upon my faith.

Pish! what stupid musing! I see I must betake myself to bed at last, and throw away upon oblivion one more hour than is common.

So it once was, but how is it now? no wavering and deliberating what I shall do to — lash the drowsy moments into speed. In my haste to set the table and its gear in order for scribble, I overturn the inkhorn, spill the ink and stain the floor.

The damage is easily repaired, and I sit down, with unspeakable alacrity, to a business that tires my muscles, sets a *gnawer* at work upon my lungs, fatigues my brain and leaves me listless and spiritless.

How you have made yourself so absolute a mistress of the goose-quill, I can't imagine; how you can maintain the writing posture, and pursue the writing movement for ten hours together, without benumbed brain, or aching fingers, is beyond my comprehension.

But you see what zeal will do for me. It has enabled me to keep drowsiness, fatigue and languor at bay, during a long night. Converse with thee, heavenly maid, is an antidote even to sleep, the most general and inveterate of all maladies.

By and bye, I shall have as voluble a pen as thy own. And yet to *that,* my crazy constitution says — nay. 'Twill never be to me other than an irksome, ache-producing implement. It need give pleasure to others, not a little, to compensate for the pain it gives myself.

But this, thou'lt say, is beside the purpose. It is, and I will lay aside the quill a moment to consider. I left off my last letter, with a head full of affecting images, which I have waited impatiently for the present opportunity of putting upon paper. Adieu then, for a moment, says thy

Colden.

LETTER XXVIII

TO THE SAME
10 o'Clock at Night.

NOW let us take a view of what is to come. Too often I endeavour to escape from fore sight when it presents to me nothing but evils, but now I must, for thy sake, be less a coward.

In six weeks Jane becomes mine. Till then, thy mother will not cast thee out of her protection, and will she *then?* will she not allow of thy continuance in thy present dwelling? and though so much displeased as to refuse thee her countenance and correspondence, will she, *indeed,* turn thee out of doors? She threatens it, we see, but, I suspect, it will never be more than a threat, employed, perhaps, only to intimidate and deter; not designed to be enforced; or, if made in earnest, yet, when the irrevocable deed is done, will she not hesitate to inflict the penalty? Will not her ancient affection; thy humility, thy sorrow, thy merits — such as, in spite of this instance of contumacy, she cannot deny thee — will not these effectually plead for thee?

More than ever will she see that thou needest her bounty: and since she cannot recall what is past, will she not relent and be willing to lessen the irremediable evil all she can.

There is one difficulty that I know not how to surmount. Giving to the wife will be only giving to the husband. Shall one whom she so much abhors, be luxuriously supplied from her bounty?

The wedded pair must live together, she will think: and shall this hated encroacher find refuge from beggary and vileness under *her* roof? be lodged and banqueted at *her* expense? *that,* her indignant heart will never suffer.

Would to Heaven she would think of me with less abhorrence. I wish for treatment conformable to her assumed relation to thee, for all our sakes. As to me, I have no pride; no punctilio, that will stand in the way of reconciliation. At least there is no deliberate and stedfast sentiment of that kind. When I reason the matter with myself, I perceive a sort of claim to arise from my poverty and relation to thee, on the one hand, and, on the other, from thy merit, thy affinity to her, and her capacity to benefit.

Yet I will never supplicate — not meanly supplicate for an alms. I will not live, nor must thou, when thou art mine, in *her* house. Whatever she will give thee, money, or furniture, or clothes, receive it promptly, and with gratitude: but let thy home be thy own. For lodging and food, be thou the payer.

And where shall *be* thy home? You love the comforts, the ease, the independence of an household. Your own pittance will not suffice for this. All these you must relinquish for my sake. You must go into a family of strangers. You must hire a chamber, and a plate of such food as is going — You must learn to bear the humours, and accommodate yourself to the habits of your inmates.

Some frugal family and humble dwelling must content thee. A low roof, a narrow chamber and an obscure avenue, the reverse of all the specious, glossy and abundant that surround thee now, will be thy portion: all that thou must look for as *my* wife. And how will this do, Jane? Is not the price too great?

And my company will not solace thee under these inconveniences. I must not live with thee; only an occasional visitor; one among an half dozen at a common fire: With witnesses of all we say. Thy pittance will do no more than support thyself. *I* must house myself and feed elsewhere. *Where,* I know not. *That* will depend upon the species of employment I shall be obliged to pursue for my subsistence. Scanty and irksome it will be, at best.

Once a day, I may see thee. Most of my evenings may possibly be devoted to thy company. A Soul harassed by unwelcome toil, eyes dim with straining at tiresome or painful objects, shall I bring to thee. If, now and then, we are alone, how can I contribute to thy entertainment. The day's task will furnish me with nothing new. Instead of alleviating by my cheerful talk, thy vexations and discomforts, I shall demand consolation from thee.

And yet imperious necessity may bereave us even of that joy. I may be obliged to encounter the perils of the seas once more. Three-fourths of the year, the ocean may divide us, thou in solitude, the while, pondering on the dangers to which I may be exposed, and I, a prey to discontent, and tempted in some evil hour, to forget thee, myself and the world.

How my heart sinks at this prospect! Does not thine Jane? Dost thou not fear to take such a wretched chance with me? I that know myself; my own imbecility; I ought surely to rescue thee from such a fate, by giving thee up.

I can write no more, just now. I wonder how I fell into this doleful strain. It was silly in me to indulge it. These images are not my customary inmates. Yet now that they occur to me, they seem but rational and just. I want, methinks, to know how they appear to thee. Adieu.

Henry Colden.

LETTER XXIX

TO THE SAME

Wilmington, November 7.

I HAVE purposely avoided dwelling on the incidents that are passing here. They engross my thoughts at all times, but those devoted to the pen, and to write to thee is one expedient for loosening their hold.

An expedient not always successful. My mind wanders in spite of me, from my own concerns and from thine, to the sick bed of my friend. A reverie, painful and confused, invades me, now and then: my pen stops, and I am obliged to exert myself anew to shake off the spell.

Till now, I knew not how much I loved this young man. Strange beings we are! separated as we have been, for many a-year; estranged as much by difference of sentiments as local distance, his image visiting my memory not once a month, and then a transitory, momentary visit: had he died a year ago, and I not known it, the stream of my thoughts would not have been ruffled by a single impediment. Yet now that I stand over him, and witness his decay ——

Many affecting conversations we have had. I cannot repeat them now. After he is gone, I will put them all upon paper and muse upon them often.

His closing hour is serene. His piety now stands him in some stead. In calling me hither, he tells me that he designed, not his own gratification, but my good. He wished to urge upon me the truths of religion, at a time when his own conduct might visibly attest their value. By their influence in making that gloomy path which leads to the grave, joyous and lightsome; he wishes me to judge of their excellence.

275

His pains are incessant and sharp. He can seldom articulate without an effort that increases his pangs: yet he talks
much: in cogent terms, and with accurate conceptions;
and in all he says, evinces a pathetic earnestness for
my conviction.

I listen to him with an heart as unbiassed as I can prevail
on it to be: as free, I mean, from its customary bias; for
I strive to call up feelings and ideas similar to his. I know
how pure to him would be the satisfaction of leaving the
world, with the belief of a thorough change in me.

I argue not with him. I say nothing but to persuade him
that I am far from being that contumacious enemy to his
faith, which he is prone to imagine me to be.

Thy mother's letter has called up more vividly than usual,
our ancient correspondence, and the effects of that
disclosure. Yet I have not mentioned the subject to him.
I never mentioned it. I could not trust myself to mention
it. There was no need. The letters were written by me. I
did not charge him to secrecy, and if I had, he would not
have been bound to compliance. It was his duty to make
that use of them which tended to prevent mischief; which
appeared, to him, to have that tendency; and this he has
done. His design, I have no doubt, was benevolent and just.

He saw not all the consequences that have followed, 'tis
true; but that ignorance would justify him, even if these
consequences were unpleasing to him; but they would not
have displeased, had they been foreseen. They would
only have made his efforts more vigorous; his disclosures
more explicit.

His conduct, indeed, on that occasion, as far as we know
it, seems irregular and injudicious. To lay before a stranger
private letters from his friend, in which opinions were
avowed and defended, that he knew would render the writer
detestable to her that read.

He imagined himself justified in imputing to me
atrocious and infamous errors. He was grieved for my
debasement, and endeavoured, by his utmost zeal and eloquence, to rectify these errors. This was generous and just;

276

but needed he to proclaim these errors, and blazon this infamy?

Yet ought I to wish to pass upon the world for other than I am? can I value that respect which is founded in ignorance? can I be satisfied with caresses from those, who, if they knew me fully, would execrate and avoid me?

For past faults and rectified errors, are not remorse and amendment adequate atonements? If any one despise me for what I *was,* let me not shrink from the penalty. Let me not find pleasure in the praise of those whose approbation is founded in ignorance of what I *am.* It is unjust to demand, it is sordid to retain praise that is not merited, either by our present conduct or our past. Why have I declined such praise? Because I value it not.

Thus have I endeavoured to think in relation to Thomson. My endeavour has succeeded. My heart entirely acquits him. It even applauds him for his noble sincerity.

Yet I could never write to him, or talk to him on this subject. My tongue; my pen will be sure to faulter. I know that he will boldly justify his conduct, and I feel that he ought to justify, yet the attempt to justify would awaken — indignation, selfishness. In spite of the suggestions of my better reason, I know we should quarrel.

We should not quarrel *now,* if the topic were mentioned. Of indignation against him, even for a real fault: much less for an imaginary one, I am, at this time, not capable; but it would be useless to mention it. There is nothing to explain; no misapprehensions to remove; no doubts to clear up. All that he did, I, in the same case, ought to have done.

But I told you, I wished not to fill my letters with the melancholy scene before me. This is a respite, a solace to me; and thus, and in reading thy letters, I employ all my spare moments.

Write to me, my love. Daily, hourly, and cheerfully, if possible. Borrow not; be not thy letters tinged with the melancholy hue of this.

Write speedily and much, if thou lovest thy

Colden.

LETTER XXX

TO HENRY COLDEN
Philadelphia, Nov. 9.

WHAT do you mean, Hal, by such a strain as this? I wanted no additional causes of disquiet. Yet you tell me to write cheerfully; I would have written cheerfully, if these letters, so full of dark forebodings, and rueful prognostics, had not come to damp my spirits.

And is the destiny that awaits us so very mournful? Is thy wife necessarily to lose so many comforts, and incur so many mortifications? are my funds so small, that they will not secure to me the privilege of a separate apartment, in which I may pass my time with whom, and in what manner I please?

Must I huddle with a dozen squalling children and their notably noisy, or sluttishly indolent dam, round a dirty hearth, and meagre winter's fire? must sooty rafters, a sorry truckle bed, and a mud incumbered alley be my nuptial lot.

Out upon thee, thou egregious painter! Well for thee thou art not within my arm's length. I should certainly bestow upon thee a hearty — *kiss* or two. — My blundering pen! I recall the word. I meant *cuff;* but my saucy pen, pretending to know more of my mind than I did myself, turned (as its mistress, mayhap, would have done, hadst thou been near me, *indeed*) her *cuff* into a *kiss.*

What possessed thee, my beloved, to predict so ruefully. A very good beginning too! more vivacity than common! But I hardly had time to greet the sunny radiance — 'tis a long time since my cell was gilded by so sweet a beam:

278

— when a *black usurping mist* stole it away, and all was dreary as it was wont to be.

Perhaps thy being in a house of mourning may account for it. Fitful and versatile, I know thee to be. Changeable with scene and circumstance. Thy views are just what any eloquent companion pleases to make them. She, thou lovest, is thy deity; her lips thy oracle. And hence my cheerful omens of the future: the confidence I have in the wholesome efficacy of my government. I that have the *will* to make thee happy, have the power too. I know I have: and hence my promptitude to give away all for thy sake: to give myself a *wife's* title to thy company: a conjugal share in thy concerns: and claim to reign over thee.

Make haste and atone, by the future brightness of thy epistolary emanations, for the pitchy cloud that overspreads these sick man's dreams.

How must thou have rummaged the cupboard of thy fancy for musty scraps and flinty crusts to feed thy spleen withall: inattentive to the dainties which a blue-eyed Hebe had culled in the garden of Hope, and had poured from out her basket into thy ungrateful lap.

While thou wast mumbling these refractory and unsavoury bits, I was banqueting on the rosy and delicious products of that Eden, which love, when not scared away by evil omens, is always sure (the poet says) to *plant* around us. I have tasted nectarines of her raising, and I find her, let me tell thee, an admirable *Horticulturist.*

Thou art so far off, there is no sending thee a basket full, or I would do it. They would wilt and wither ere they reached thee; the atmosphere thou breathest would strike a deadly worm into their hearts before thou couldst get them to thy lips.

But to drop the basket and the bough, and take up a plain meaning — I will tell thee how I was employed when thy letter came: but first I must go back a little.

In the autumn of *ninety seven* and when death had spent his shafts in my own family, I went to see how a family fared, the father and husband of which kept a shop in Front street, where every thing a lady wanted was sold, and where I had always been served with great dispatch and affability.

Being one day (I am going to tell you how our acquaintance began) — Being one day detained in the shop by a shower, I was requested to walk into the parlour. I chatted ten minutes with the good woman of the house, and found in her so much gentleness and good sense, that, afterwards, my shopping visits were always, in part, social ones. My business being finished at the compter, I usually went back, and found, on every interview, new cause for esteeming the family. The treatment I met with was always cordial and frank, and though our meetings were thus merely casual, we seemed, in a short time, to have grown into a perfect knowledge of each other.

This was in the summer you left us, and the malady breaking out a few months after, and all *shopping* being at an end, and alarm and grief taking early possession of my heart, I thought but seldom of the Hennings. A few weeks after death had bereaved me of my friend, I called these and others, whose welfare was dear to me, to my remembrance; and determined to pay them a visit and discover how it fared with them. I hoped they had left the city, yet Mrs. Henning had told me that her husband, who was a devout man, held it criminal to fly on such occasions, and that she, having passed safely through the pestilence of former years, had no apprehensions from staying.

Their house was inhabited, but I found the good woman in great affliction. Her husband had lately died after a tedious illness, and her distress was augmented by the solitude in which the flight of all her neighbours and acquaintances had left her. A friendly visit could at no time have been so acceptable to her, and my sympathy was not more needed to console her, than my council to assist her in the new state of her affairs.

Laying aside ceremony, I enquired freely into her condition, and offered her my poor services. She made me fully acquainted with her circumstances, and I was highly pleased at finding them so good. Her husband had always been industrious and thrifty, and his death left her enough to support her and her Sally in the way they wished.

Enquiring into their views and wishes, I found them limited to the privacy of a small but neat house, in some cleanly and retired corner of the city. Their stock in trade, I advised them to convert into money, and placing it in some public fund, live upon its produce. Mrs. Henning knew nothing of the world. Though an excellent manager within doors, any thing that might be called business was strange and arduous to her, and without my direct assistance she could do nothing.

Happily, at this time, just such a cheap and humble, but neat, new and airy dwelling as my friend required, belonging to Mrs. Fielder, was vacant. You know the house. 'Tis that where the Frenchman Catineau lived. Is it not a charming abode? at a distance from noise, with a green field opposite, and a garden behind; of two stories; a couple of good rooms on each floor; with unspoilt water, and a kitchen, below the ground, indeed, but light, wholesome and warm.

Most fortunately too that incorrigible creole had deserted it. He was scared away by the fever, and no other had put in a claim. I made haste to write to my mother, who, though angry at me on my own account, could not reject my application in favour of my good widow.

I even prevailed on her to set the rent forty dollars lower than she might have gotten from another, and to give a lease of it at that rate for five years. You can't imagine my satisfaction in compleating this affair, and in seeing my good woman quietly settled in her new abode, with her daughter Sally, and her servant *Alice,* who had come with her from Europe, and had lived with her the dear Lord knows how long.

Mrs. Henning is no common woman, I assure you. Her temper is the sweetest in the world. Not cultivated or enlightened is her understanding, but naturally correct. Her life has always been spent under her own roof; and never saw I a scene of more quiet and order than her little homestead exhibits. Though humbly born, and perhaps, meanly brought up, her parlour and chamber add to the purest cleanliness, somewhat that approaches to elegance.

The mistress and the maid are nearly of the same age, and though equally innocent and good humoured, the former has more sedateness and reserve than the latter. She is devout in her way, which is methodism, and acquires from this source nothing but new motives to charity to her neighbours, and thankfulness to God.

Much; indeed, all these comforts she ascribes to me: Yet her gratitude is not loquacious. It shews itself less in words than in the pleasure she manifests on my visits; the confidence with which she treats me; laying before me all her plans and arrangements, and intreating my advice in every thing. Yet she has brought with her, from her native country, notions of her inferiority to the better born and better educated, but too soothing to my pride. Hence she is always diffident, and never makes advances to intimacy but when expressly invited and encouraged.

It was a good while before all her new arrangements were compleated. When they were, I told her, I would spend the day with her, for which she was extremely grateful. She sent me word, as soon as she was ready to receive me, and I went.

Artless and unceremonious was the good woman in the midst of all her anxiety to please. Affectionate, yet discreet in her behaviour to her Sally and her Alice, and of me as tenderly observant as possible.

She shewed me all her rooms from cellar to garret, and every thing I saw delighted me. Two neat beds in the front room above, belong to her and Sally. The back room is decked in a more fanciful and costly manner.

Why this, my good friend, said I, on entering it, is quite superb. Here is carpet and coverlet and curtains that might satisfy a prince; You are quite prodigal; and for whose accommodation is all this?

O! any lady that will favour me with a visit. It is a spare room, and the only one I have, and I thought I would launch out a little for once. One wishes to set the best they have before a guest, though indeed, I dont expect many to visit me, but it is some comfort to think one has it in one's power to lodge a friend, when it happens so, in a manner that may not discredit one's intentions. I have no relations in this country, and the only friend I have in the world, besides God, is you, Madam. But still, it may sometimes happen you know that one may have occasion to entertain somebody. God be thanked I have enough, and what little I have to spare, I have no right to hoard up.

But might you not accomodate a good quiet kind of body in this room, at so much a-year or week?

Why, Ma'am, if you think that's best; but I thought one might indulge one's self in living one's own way. I have never been used to strangers, and always have had a small family. It would be a very new thing to me, to have an inmate. I am afraid I should not please such a one. And then, Ma'am, if this room's occupied, I have no decent place to put any accidental person in. It would go hard with me to be obliged to turn a good body away, that might be here on a visit, and might be caught by a rain or a snow storm.

Very true. I did not think of that; and yet it seems a pity that so good a room should be unemployed: perhaps for a year together.

So it does, Ma'am, and I cant but say, if a proper person should offer, who wanted to be snug and quiet, I should have no great objection. One that could put up with our humble ways, and be satisfied with what I could do to make them comfortable. I think I should like such a one well enough.

One, said I, who would accept such accommodation as a favour. A single person for example. A woman: A young woman. A stranger in the country, and friendless like yourself.

O! very true, Madam, said the good woman, with sparkling benignity, I should have no objection in the world to such a one. I should like it of all things. And I should not mind to be hard with such a one. I should not stickle about terms. Pray, Ma'am, do you know any such. If you do, and will advise me to take her, I would be very glad to do it.

Now, Hal, what thinkest thou? cannot I light on such a young, single, slenderly provided woman as this. One whose heart pants for just such a snug retreat, as Mrs. Henning's roof would afford her.

This little chamber, set out with perfect neatness; looking out on a very pretty piece of verdure and a cleanly court yard; with such a good couple to provide for her; with her privacy unapproachable but at her own pleasure; Her quiet undisturbed by a prater, a scolder, a bustler, or a whiner. No dirty children to offend the eye or squalling ones to wound the ear. With admitted claims to the gratitude, confidence and affection of her hostess; might not these suffice to make a lowly, unambitious maiden happy?

One who, like Mrs. Henning, had only *one* friend upon earth. Whom her former associates refused to commune with or look upon. Whose loneliness was uncheered, except by her own thoughts, and by her books. Perhaps now and then at times when oceans did not sever her from him, by that one earthly friend.

Might she not afford him as many hours of her society as his engagements would allow him to claim. Might she not, as an extraordinary favour, admit him to partake with her the comforts of her own little fire, if winter it be; or, in summertime, to join her at her chamber window, and pass away the starlight hour in the unwitnessed community of fond hearts?

Suppose, to obviate unwelcome surmises and too scrupulous objections, the girl makes herself a wife, but because their poverty will not enable them to live together, the girl merely admits the chosen youth on the footing of a visitor.

Suppose her hours are not embittered by the feelings of dependance. She pays an ample compensation for her entertainment, and by her occasional company, her superior strength of mind and knowledge of the world's ways, she materially contributes to the happiness and safety of her hostess.

Suppose, having only one visitor, and he sometimes wanting in zeal and punctuality, much of her time is spent alone. Happily she is exempt from the humiliating necessity of working to live; and is not obliged to demand a share of the earnings of her husband. Her task, therefore, will be to find amusement. Can she want the means, think'st thou?

The sweet quiet of her chamber; the wholesome airs from abroad; or the cheerful blaze of her hearth, will invite her to mental exercise. Perhaps, she has a taste for books, and besides that pure delight which knowledge on its own account affords her, it possesses tenfold attractions in her eyes, by its tendency to heighten the esteem of him whom she lives to please.

Perhaps, rich as she is in books, she is an economist of pleasure, and tares herself away from them, to enjoy the vernal breezes, or the landscape of Autumn in a twilight ramble. Here she communes with bounteous nature, or lifts her soul in devotion to her God, to whose benignity she resigns herself as she used to do to the fond arms of that parent she has lost.

If these do not suffice to fill up her time, she may chance to reflect on the many ways in which she may be useful to herself. She may find delight in supplying her own wants; by maintaining cleanliness and order all about her; by making up her own dresses, especially as she disdains to be out done in taste and expertness at the needle by any female in the land.

By limiting in this way, and in every other, which her judgment may recommend, her own expenses, she will be able to contribute somewhat to relieve the toils of her beloved. The pleasure will be hers of reflecting, not only that her love adds nothing to his fatigues and cares; not only that her tender solicitudes and seasonable counsel, cherish his hopes and strengthen his courage, but that the employment of her hands makes his own seperate subsistence an easier task. To work for herself will be no trivial gratification to her honest pride, but to work for her beloved, will, indeed, be a cause of exultation.

Twenty things she may do for him which others must be paid for doing, not in caresses, but in money; and this service, though not small, is not perhaps the greatest she is able to perform. She is active and intelligent, perhaps, and may even aspire to the profits of some trade. What is it that makes one calling more lucrative than another? Not superior strength of shoulders or sleight of hand; not the greater quantity of brute matter that is reduced into form or set into motion. No. The difference lies in the mental powers of the artist, and the direction accidentally given to these powers.

What should hinder a girl like this from growing rich by her diligence and ingenuity. She has, perhaps, acquired many arts with no view but her own amusement. Not a little did her mother pay to those who taught her to draw and to sing. May she not levy the same tribute upon others that were levied on her, and make a business of her sports.

There is, indeed, a calling that may divert her from the thoughts of mere lucre. She may talk and sing for another and dedicate her best hours to a tutelage, for which there is a more precious requital than money can give.

Do'st not see her, Hal. I do — as well as this gushing sensibility will let me — rocking in her arms and half stifling with her kisses or delighting with her lullaby, a precious little creature —

Why my friend, do I hesitate? do I not write for thy eye, and thine only? and what is there but pure and sacred in the anticipated transports of a mother.

The conscious heart might stifle its throbs in thy presence, but why not indulge them in thy absence, and tell thee its inmost breathings, not without a shame-confessing glow, yet not without drops of the truest delight that were ever shed.

Why, how now, Jane? whence all this interest in the scene

286

thou pourtrayest? One would fancy that this happy out-cast, this self dependant wife was no other than *thyself*!

A shrewd conjecture truly. I suppose, Hal, thou wilt be fond enough to guess so too. By what penalty shall I deter thee from so rash a thing? yet thou art not here — I say it to my sorrow — to suffer the penalty which I might chuse to inflict.

I will not say what it is, lest the *fear* of it should keep thee away.

And now that I have finished the history of Mrs. Henning and her boarder, I will bid thee — good night.

Good —— good night, my love.

Jane Talbot.

LETTER XXXI

TO HENRY COLDEN
Philadelphia, Nov. 11.

HOW shall I tell you the strange — *strange* incident! every fibre of my frame still trembles. I have endeavoured, during the last hour, to gain tranquillity enough for writing, but without success: yet I can forbear no longer; I must begin.

I had just closed my last to you, when somebody knocked. I heard footsteps below, as the girl ushered in the visitant, which were not quite unknown to me. The girl came up. — A gentleman is waiting.

A gentleman! thought I. An odd hour this — it was past ten — for any man but one to visit *me*. His business must be very urgent. So, indeed, he told the girl, it was, for she knew me averse to company at any time, and I had withdrawn to my chamber for the night; but he would not be eluded. He must see me, he said, this night.

A tall and noble figure, in a foreign uniform, arose from the sofa at my entrance. The half extinct lamp on the mantle, could not conceal from me — *my brother!*

My surprise almost overpowered me. I should have sunk upon the floor, had he not stepped to me, and sustained me in his arms.

I see you are surprised, Jane, said he, in a tone not without affection in it. You did not expect, I suppose, ever to see me again. It was a mere chance brought me to America. I shall stay here a moment and then hie me back again. I could not pass through the city without an "How d'ye" to the little girl for whom I have still some regard.

The violence of my emotions found relief in a flood of tears. He was not unmoved, but embracing me with tenderness, he seated me by him on the sofa.

When I had leisure to survey his features, I found that time had rather improved his looks. They were less austere; less contemptuous than they used to be; perhaps, indeed, it was only a momentary remission of his customary feelings.

To my rapid and half coherent questions, he replied: — I landed — you need not know where. My commission requires secrecy, and you know I have personal reasons for wishing to pass thro' this city without notice. My business did not bring me further southward than New-London; but I heard your mother resided in New-York, and could not leave the country without seeing you. I called on her yesterday, but she looked so grave and talked so obscurely about you, that I could not do less than come hither. She told me you were here. How have been affairs since I left you?

I answered this question vaguely.

Pray, with much earnestness, are you married yet?

The confusion with which I returned an answer to this, did not escape him.

I asked Mrs. Fielder the same question, and she talked as if it were a doubtful point. She could not tell, she said, with a rueful physiognomy. Very probably it might be so — I could not bring her to be more explicit. As I proposed to see you, she said, you were the fittest person to explain your own situation. This made me the more anxious to see you. Pray, Jane, how do matters stand between you and Mrs. Fielder? are you not on as good terms as formerly?

I answered, that some difference had unhappily occurred between us, that I loved and revered her as much as ever, and hoped that we should soon be mother and daughter again.

But the cause — the cause, Jane. Is a lover the bone of contention between you? that's the rock on which family harmony is sure to be wrecked. But tell me, what have you quarrelled about?

How could I explain on such a subject, thus abruptly introduced, to *him?* I told him it was equally painful and useless to dwell on my contentions with my mother, or on my own affairs. Rather let me hear, said I, how it fares with you; what fortunes you have met with in this long absence.

Pretty well; pretty well. Many a jade's trick did fortune play me before I left this spot, but, ever since, it has been all smooth and bright with me — But this marriage — Art thou a wife or not? I heard I think some talk about a Talbot. What's become of him? they said you were engaged to him.

It is long since the common destiny has ended all Talbot's engagements.

Dead, is he? well; a new aspirer, I suppose, has succeeded, and he is the bone of contention. Who's he?

I could not bear that a subject of such deep concern to me, should be discussed thus lightly, and, therefore, begged him to change the subject.

Change the subject? with all my heart, if we can find any more important; but that's impossible. So, we must ev'n stick to this; a little longer. Come, what's his parentage; fortune; age; character; profession; 'Tis not likely I shall find fault where Mrs. Fielder does. Young men and old women seldom hit upon the same choice in an husband, and, for my part, I am easily pleased.

This is a subject, brother, on which it is impossible that we should think alike; nor is it necessary. Let us then talk of something in which we have a common concern: something that has a claim to interest you.

What subject, girl, can have a stronger claim on my attention than the marriage of my sister — I am not so giddy and unprincipled as to be unconcerned on that head. So make no more ado, but tell your *brother* candidly what are your prospects?

After some hesitation — My real brother; one who had the tenderness becoming that relation, would certainly deserve my confidence. But —

But what? come, never mince the matter. I have scarcely

290

been half a brother hitherto I grant you. More of an enemy, perhaps, than friend, but no reason why I should continue hostile or indifferent. So tell me who the lad is and what are his pretensions?

I endeavoured to draw him off to some other subject, but he would not be diverted from this. By dint of interrogatories he, at last, extorted from me a few hints respecting you. Finding that you were without fortune or profession, and that my regard for you had forfeited all favour with my mother: the enquiry was obvious, How we meant to live? It was impossible to answer this question in any manner satisfactory to him. He has no notion of existence unconnected with luxury and splendor.

Have you made any acquisitions, continued he, since I saw you? has any good old aunt left you another legacy? — this was said with the utmost vivacity and self-possession. A strange being is my brother. Could he have forgotten by whom I was robbed of my former legacy?

Come, come, I know thou art a romantic being. One accustomed to *feed on thoughts* instead of pudding. Contentment and a cottage are roast beef and a palace to thee; but, take my word for it, this inamorato of thine will need a more substantial diet. By marrying him you will only saddle him with misery. So drop all thoughts of so silly a scheme; write him a "good bye;" make up your little matters, and come along with me. I will take you to my country; introduce you to a new world; and bring to your feet hundreds of generous souls, the least of whom is richer, wiser, handsomer than this tame-spirited droning animal — what's his name? but no matter. I suppose I know nothing of him.

I was rash enough to tell him your name and abode, but I treated his proposal as a jest. I quickly found that he was serious. He soon became extremely urgent. Recounted the advantages of his condition; the charming qualities of his wife; the security and splendor of his new rank. He endeavoured to seduce my vanity by the prospect of the conquests I should make in that army of colonels, philosophers, and commissioners, that formed the circle of his friends — any man but a brother, said he, must own that you are a charming creature. So you need only come and see, in order to conquer.

His importunities increased as my reluctance became more evident. Thoughtless as I supposed him to be, he said, the wish to find me out, carry me to France, and put me in fortune's way, was no inconsiderable inducement with him to accept the commission which brought him to America. He insinuated that brothership and eldership gave him something like a title to paternal authority, and insisted on obedience.

The contest became painful. Impatience and reproach on his side awakened the like sentiments in me, and it cost me many efforts to restrain my feelings. Alternately he commanded and persuaded: was willing to be governed by my mother's advice; would carry me forthwith to New-York: would lay before her his proposal; and be governed by her decision. The public vessel that brought him lay at Newport waiting his return. Every possible accommodation and convenience was possessed by the ship. It was nothing but a sailing palace, in which the other passengers were merely his guests selected by himself.

I was a fool for refusing his offer. A simpleton. The child of caprice, whom no time could render steadfast except in folly: into whom no counsel or example could instil an atom of common sense. He supposed *my man* was equally obstinate and stupid, but he would soon see of what stuff *he* was made. He would hurry to Baltimore, and take the boy to task for his presumption and insolence in aspiring to Jane Talbot without her brother's consent.

He snatched up his hat, but this intimation alarmed me. Pray, stay one moment, brother. Be more considerate. What right can you possibly have to interfere with Mr. Colden's concerns. Talk to me, as much and in what style you please, but I beseech you insult not a man who never offended you.

Perceiving my uneasiness on this head, he took advantage of it to renew his solicitations for my company to France. Swore solemnly that no man should have his sister without his consent, and that he would force the boy to give me up.

This distressing altercation ended by his going away, declaring, in spite of my entreaties, that he would see you, and teach your insolence a lesson not easily forgotten.

To sleep after this interview was impossible. I could hardly still my throbbing heart sufficiently to move the pen. You cannot hear from me in time to avoid this madman, or to fortify yourself against an interview. I cannot confute the false or cunning glosses he may make upon my conduct. He may represent me to you as willing to accompany him; as detained only by my obligation to you from which it is in your power to absolve me.

Till I hear from you I shall have no peace. Would to heaven there was some speedier conveyance.

Jane Talbot.

LETTER XXXII

TO JANE TALBOT

Baltimore, Nov. 14.

LET me overlook your last letter* for the present, while I mention to you a most unexpected and surprising circumstance. It has just happened. I have parted with my visitant but this moment.

I had strolled to the bank of the river, and was leaning idly on a branch of an appletree that hung pretty low, when I noticed some one coming hastily towards me: there was something striking and noble in the air and figure of the man.

When he came up, he stopped. I was surprised to find myself the object of which he was in search. I found afterwards that he had enquired for me at my lodgings, and had been directed to look for me in this path. A distinct view of his features saved him the trouble of telling me that he was your brother. However, that was information that he thought proper immediately to communicate. He was your brother, he said: I was Colden: I had pretensions to you, which your brother was entitled to know, to discuss, and to pronounce upon. Such, in about as many words, was his introduction to me, and he waited for my answer with much impatience.

I was greatly confused by these sudden and unceremonious intimations; at last I told him that all that he had said respecting my connection with his sister, was true. It

*Letter XXX.

294

was a fact that all the world was welcome to know. Of course I had no objection to her brother's knowing it.

But what were my claims; what my merits; my profession; my fortune! On all these heads a brother would naturally require to be thoroughly informed.

As to my character, sir, you will hardly expect any satisfactory information from *my* own mouth. However, it may save you the trouble of applying to others, when I tell you, that my character has as many slurs and blots in it as any you ever met with. A more versatile, inconsistent, prejudiced and faulty person than myself, I do not believe the earth to contain. Profession, I have none, and am not acquiring any, nor expect ever to acquire. Of fortune I am wholly destitute; not a farthing have I, either in possession or reversion.

Then pray, sir, on what are built your pretensions to my sister?

Really, sir, they are built on *nothing*. I am, in every respect, immeasurably her inferior. I possess not a single merit that entitles me to grace from her.

I have surely not been misinformed. She tacitly admitted that she was engaged to be your wife.

'Tis very true. She is so.

But what, then, is the basis of this engagement.

Mutual affection, I believe, is the only basis. Nobody who knows Jane Talbot will need to ask why she is beloved? Why she requites that passion in the present case is a question which she only can answer.

Her passion, sir, (contemptuously) is the freak of a child; of folly and caprice. By your own confession you are beggarly and worthless, and therefore it becomes you to relinquish your claim.

I have no claim to relinquish. I have urged no claims. On the contrary, I have fully disclosed to her every folly and vice that cleaves to my character.

You know, sir, what I mean.

I am afraid not perfectly. If you mean that I should

profess myself unworthy of your sister's favour, 'tis done. It has been done an hundred times.

My meaning, sir, is simply this: that you, from this moment, give up every expectation of being the husband of Mrs. Talbot. That you return to her every letter, and paper that has passed between you; that you drop all intercourse and correspondence.

I was obliged to stifle a laugh which this whimsical proposal excited. I continued, through this whole dialogue, to regard my companion with a stedfast, and cheerful gravity.

These are injunctions, said I, that will hardly meet with compliance, unless, indeed, they were imposed by the lady herself. I shall always have a supreme regard for her happiness, and whatever path she points out to me, I will walk in it.

But *this* is the path in which her true interest requires you to walk.

I have not yet discovered that to be *her* opinion: the moment I do, I will walk in it accordingly.

No matter what *her* opinion is. She is froward and obstinate. It is *my* opinion that her true happiness requires all connection between you to cease from this moment.

After all, sir, though, where judgments differ, one only can be right, yet each person must be permitted to follow his own. You would hardly, I imagine, allow your sister to prescribe to you in your marriage choice, and I fear she will lay claim to the same independence for herself. If you can convert her to your way of thinking, it is well. I solemnly engage to do whatever she directs.

This is insolence. You trifle with me. You pretend to misconstrue my meaning.

When you charge me with insolence, I think you afford pretty strong proof that you mistake *my* meaning. I have not the least intention to offend you.

Let me be explicit with you. Do you instantly and absolutely resign all pretensions to my sister?

I will endeavour to be explicit in my turn. Your sister,

notwithstanding my defects and disadvantages, offers me her love: vows to be mine. I accept her love; She is mine: nor need we to discuss the matter any further.

This, however, by no means put an end to altercation. I told him I was willing to hear all that he had to say upon the subject. If truth were on his side, it was possible he might reason me into a concurrence with him. In compliance with this concession, he dwelt on the benefits which his sister would receive from accompanying him to France, and the mutual sorrow, debasement and perplexity likely to flow from an union between us, unsanctioned by the approbation of our common friends.

The purpose of all this is to prove, said I, that affluence and dignity without me, will be more conducive to your sister's happiness, than obscurity and indigence *with* me.

It was.

Happiness is mere matter of opinion; Perhaps Jane thinks already as you do.

He allowed that he had talked with you ineffectually on that subject.

I think myself bound to believe her in a case where she is the proper judge, and shall eagerly consent to make her happy in her own way. *That,* sir, is my decision.

I will not repeat the rest of our conversation. Your letters have given me some knowledge of your brother, and I endeavoured by the mildness, sedateness and firmness of my carriage to elude those extremes to which his domineering passions were likely to carry him. I carefully avoided every thing that tended in the least to exasperate. He was prone enough to rage, but I quietly submitted to all that he could *say.* I was sincerely rejoiced when the conference came to an end.

Whence came your brother thus abruptly? Have you seen him? Yet he told me that you had. Alas! what must you have suffered from his impetuosity.

I look with impatience for your next letter, in which you will tell what has happened.

LETTER XXXIII

TO HENRY COLDEN
Philadelphia, November 17.

I HAVE just sent you a letter, but my restless spirit can find no relief but in writing.

I torment myself without end in imagining what took place at your meeting with my brother. I rely upon your equanimity, yet to what an insupportable test will my brother's passions subject you. In how many ways have I been the cause of pain and humiliation to you! Heaven, I hope, will sometime grant me the power to compensate you for all that I have culpably, or innocently made you suffer. —

What's this? A letter from my brother! The superscription is his

* * *

Let me hasten, my friend, to give you a copy of this strange epistle. It has neither date nor signature.

"I have talked with the man whom you have chosen to play the fool with. I find him worthy of his mistress: a tame, coward-hearted, infatuated blockhead.

It was silly to imagine that any arguments would have weight with you or with him. I have got my journey for my pains. Fain would I have believed that you were worthy of a different situation, but I dismiss that belief, and shall henceforth leave you to pursue your own dirty road, without interruption.

Had you opened your eyes to your true interest, I think I could have made something of you. My wealth and my influence should not have been spared, in placing you in a station worthy of my sister. Every one however, must take his own way — though it lead him into a slough or a ditch.

I intended to have virtually divided my fortune with you: to have raised you to princely grandeur; but no: you are enamoured of the dirt, and may cling to it as closely as you please.

It is but justice, however, to pay what I owe you. I remember I borrowed several sums of you: the whole amounted to fifteen hundred dollars. *There* they are, and much good may they do you. That sum and the remnant which I left you may perhaps set the good man up in a village shop: may purchase an assortment of tapes, porringers and twelve-to-the-pound candles. The gleanings of the year may find you in skimmed milk and hasty pudding three times a day, and you may enjoy between whiles the delectable amusements of mending your husband's stockings at one time, and serving a neighbour with a pennyworth of snuff at another.

Fare thee well, Jane. Farewell forever: for it must be a stronger inducement that can possibly happen, that shall ever bring me back to this land. I would see you ere I go, but we shall only scold: So, once more, farewell, simpleton.''

What think you of this letter? The inclosed bills were most unexpected and acceptable presents. I am now twice as rich as I was. This visit of my brother I was disposed to regret, but on the whole I ought, I think, to regard it with satisfaction. By thus completely repairing the breach made in my little patrimony, it has placed me in as good a situation as I ever hoped to enjoy; Besides, it has removed from my brother's character some of the stains which used to discolour it. Ought I not to believe him sincere in his wishes to do me service. We cannot agree exactly in our notion of duty or happiness, but that difference takes not away from him the merit of a generous intention. He would have done me good in his way.

Methinks, I am sorry he has gone. I would fain have parted with him as a sister ought. A few tears and a few blessings were not unworthy such an occasion. Most fervently should I have poured my blessings upon him. I wish he had indulged me with another visit; Especially as we were to part, it seems, forever. One more visit and a kind embrace from my only brother would have been kept in melancholy, sweet remembrance.

Perhaps we shall meet again. Perhaps, some day, thou and I shall go to France. We will visit him together, and witness, with our own eyes, his good fortune. Time may make him gentle; kind; considerate; brotherly. Time has effected greater wonders than that; for I will always maintain that my brother has a noble nature: stifled and obscured it may be, but not extinguished.

LETTER XXXIV

TO HENRY COLDEN
Philadelphia, Nov. 18.

HOW little is the equanimity or patience that nature has allotted me? thy entrance now would find me quite peevish. Yet I do not fear thy entrance. Always anxious as I am to be amiable in your eyes, I am at no pains to conceal from you that impatience which now vexes my soul, because it is your absence that occasions it.

I sat alone on the sofa below, for a whole hour. Not once was the bell rung — not once did my fluttering heart answer to footsteps in the passage. I had no need to start up at the opening of the parlour door, and to greet, as distinctly as the joyous tumult of my bosom would suffer me, the much loved, long expected visitant.

Yet deceived, by my fond heart, into momentary forgetfulness of the interval of an hundred miles that lies between us, more than once cast I a glance behind me, and started, as if the hoped for peal had actually been rung.

Tired, at length, of my solitude, where I had enjoyed your company so often, I covered up the coals, and withdrew to my chamber. And here, said I, tho' I cannot talk to him, yet I can write.

But first, I read over again this cruel letter of my mother. I weighed all the contents, and especially those heavy charges against you.

How does it fall out that the same object is viewed by two observers with such opposite sensations. That what one hates, the other should doat upon? two of the same sex: one cherished from infancy; reared; modelled; taught to

301

think; feel, and even to speak, by the other: acting till now, and even now, acting, in all respects, but one, in inviolable harmony; that two such should jar and thwart each other, in a point, too, in respect to which, the whole tendency and scope of the daughter's education was to produce a fellow feeling with the mother. How hard to be accounted for! how deeply to be rued!

I sometimes catch myself trembling with solicitude lest I should have erred. Am I not betrayed by passion? can I claim the respect due to that discernment which I once boasted?

I cannot blame my mother. She acts and determines, as I sometimes believe, without the benefits of my knowledge. Did she know as much as I know, surely she would think as I do.

In general, this conclusion seems to be just; but there are moments when doubts insinuate themselves. I cannot help remembering the time when I reasoned like my mother: when the belief of a christian seemed essential to every human excellence. All qualities, without that belief, were not to be despised as useless, but to be abhorred as pernicious. There would be no virtue, no merit, divorced from religion. In proportion to the speciousness of his qualities was he to be dreaded. The fruit, whatever form it should assume, was nothing within but bane, and was to be detested and shunned in proportion as the form was fair and its promises delicious.

I seldom trusted myself to enquire how it was my duty to act towards one whom I loved, but who was destitute of this grace, for of such moment was the question to me, that I imagined the decision would necessarily precede all others. I could not love, till I had investigated this point, and no force could oblige me to hold communion with a soul, whom this defect despoiled of all beauty and devoted to perdition.

But what now is the change that time and passion have wrought. I have found a man without religion. What I supposed impossible, has happened. I love the man. I cannot give him up. The mist that is before my eyes, does not change what was once vice into virtue. I do not cease to regard unbelief as the blackest stain; as the most deplorable calamity that can befall a human creature, but still I *love* the man, and that fills me with unconquerable zeal to rescue him from this calamity.

But my mother interferes. She reminds me of the horror which I once entertained for men of your tenets. She enjoins me to hate you, or to abhor myself for loving one worthy of nothing but hatred.

I cannot do either. My heart is still yours, and it is a voluntary captive. I would not free it from its thraldom, if I could. Neither do I think its captivity dishonors it. Time, therefore, has wrought some change. I can now discover some merit: something to revere and to love, even in a man without religion. I find my whole soul penetrated with zeal for his welfare. There is no scheme which I muse upon with half the constancy or pleasure, as that of curing his errors, and I am confident of curing them.

Ah Jane! says my mother; rash and presumptuous girl! What a signal punishment hangs over thee. Thou wilt trust thyself within the toils of the grand deceiver. Thou wilt enter the list with his subtleties. Vain and arrogant, thou fearest not thy own weakness. Thou wilt stake thy eternal lot upon thy triumph in argument against one, who, in spite of all his candour and humility, has his pride and his passions engaged on the side of his opinions.

Subtle wretch! does she exclaim, accomplished villain! How nicely does he select: how adroitly manage his tools! He will oppose, only to yield more gracefully. He will argue only that the rash simpleton may the more congratulate herself upon her seeming victory! How easy is the verbal assent! the equivocating accent! The hesitating air! These he will assume whenever it is convenient to lull your fears and gratify your vanity, and nothing but the uniformity of his conduct, his continuance in the same ignominious and criminal path, will open your eyes, and shew you that only grace from above can reach his obdurate heart, or dart a ray into his benighted faculties.

Will you be surprised that I shudder when my mother urges me in this strain, with her customary energy. Always wont to be obsequious to the very turn of her eye, and to make her will, not only the regulator of my actions, but the criterion of my understanding; it is impossible not to hesitate; to review all that has passed between us, and re-consider anew the motives that have made me act as I have acted.

Yet the review always confirms me in my first opinion. You err, but are not obstinate in error. If your opinions be adverse to religion, your affections are not wholly estranged from it. Your understanding dissents, but your heart is not yet persuaded to refuse. You have powers, irresistable in whatever direction they are bent: capable of giving the highest degree of misery or happiness to yourself and to others. At present they are mis-directed or inactive. They are either pernicious or useless.

How can I, who have had ample opportunities of knowing you, stand by with indifference while such is your state? I love you, it is true. All your felicity and all your woe become mine. I have a selfish interest in your welfare. I cannot bear the thought of passing through *this* world, or of entering any future world, without you. My heart has tried in vain to create a separate interest: to draw consolation from a different source. Hence indifference to your welfare is impossible. But would not indifference, even if no extraordinary tie subsisted between us, be criminal? What becomes of our obligation to do good to others, if we do not exert ourselves, when all the means are in our power, to confer the most valuable of all benefits: to remove the greatest of all ills?

Of what stuff must that heart be made which can behold, unmoved, genius and worth, destitue of the joys and energies of religion; wandering in a maze of passions and doubts; devoured by phantastic repinings and vague regrets: Drearily conscious of wanting a foundation whereon to repose; a guide in whom to trust. What heart can gaze at such a spectacle without unspeakable compassion.

Not to have our pity and our zeal awakened, seems to me to argue the utmost depravity of heart. No stronger proof can be given that we ourselves are destitute of true religion. The faith or the practice must be totally wanting. We may talk devoutly; we may hie, in due season, to the house of prayer; while there, we may put on solemn visages and mutter holy names. We may abstain from profane amusements, or unauthorised words; we may shun, as infectious, the company of unbelievers. We may study homilies and creeds; but all this, without *rational* activity for others good, is not religion. I see, in all this, nothing that I am accustomed to call by that name.

I see nothing but a narrow selfishness: sentiments of fear degrading to the Deity: a bigotry that contracts the view; that freezes the heart; that shuts up the avenues to benevolent and generous feeling. This buckram stiffness does not suit me. Out upon such monastic parade. I will have none of it.

But then, it seems, there is danger to ourselves from such attempts. In trying to save another from drowning, may we not sometimes be drawn in ourselves? Are we not taught to deprecate, not only evil, but temptation to evil?

What madness to trust our convictions, in a point of such immense importance, to the contest of argument with one of superior subtlety and knowledge. Is there not presumption in such a trust?

Excellent advice is this to the mass of women: to those to whom habit or childish fear or parental authority has given their faith: who never doubted or enquired or reasoned for themselves. How easily is such a fabric to be overturned. It can only stand by being never blown upon. The least breath disperses it in air; The first tide washes it away.

Now, I entertain no reverence for such a bubble. In some sense, the religion of the timorous and uninquisitive, is true. In another sense it is false. Considering the proofs on which it reposes, it is false, since it merely originates in deference to the opinions of others, wrought into belief by means of habit. It is on a level, as to the proof which supports it, with the wildest dreams of savage superstition, or the fumes of a dervise's fanaticism.

As to me, I was once just such a pretty fool in this respect, as the rest of my sex. I was easily taught to regard religion not only as the safe-guard of every virtue, but even as the test of a good understanding. The name of *infidel* was never mentioned but with abhorrence or contempt. None but a profligate, a sensualist, a ruffian, could disbelieve. Unbelief was a mere suggestion of the grand deceiver, to palliate or reconcile us to the unlimited indulgence of our appetites, and the breach of every moral duty. Hence it was never stedfast or sincere. An adverse fortune or a death-bed, usually put an end to the illusion.

Thus I grew up, never beset by any doubts; never venturing on enquiry. My knowledge of you, put an end to this state of superstitious ignorance. In you I found, not one that disbelieved, but one that doubted. In all your demeanor there was simplicity and frankness. You concealed not your sentiments; you obtruded them not upon my hearing. When called upon to state the history of your opinions, it was candidly detailed; with no view of gaining my concurrence, but merely to gratify my curiosity.

From my remonstrances you never averted your ear. Every proof of an unprejudiced attention, and even of a bias favorable to my opinions, was manifest. Your own experience had half converted you already. Your good sense was for a time the sport of a specious theory. You became the ardent and bold champion of what you deemed truth. But a closer and longer view insensibly detected flaws and discords where all had formerly been glossy smoothness and ravishing harmony. Diffidence and caution, worthy of your youth and inexperience, had resumed their place; and those errors, of which your own experience of their consequences had furnished the antidote, which your own reflections had

306

partly divested of illusion, had only been propitious to your advancement in true wisdom.

What had I to fear from such an adversary? What might I not hope from perseverance? What expect but new clearness to my own convictions; new and more accurate views of my powers and habits?

In order to benefit you, I was obliged to scrutinize the foundation of my own principles. I found nothing but a void. I was astonished and alarmed; and instantly set myself to the business of enquiry. How could I hope to work on your convictions without a suitable foundation for my own?

And see now my friend the blindness of our judgements. I who am imagined to incur such formidable perils from intercourse with you, am, in truth, indebted to you alone for all my piety: all of it that is permanent and rational. Without those apprehensions which your example inspired, without that zeal for your conversion which my attachment to you has produced, what would now have been my claims to religious knowledge?

Had I never extorted from you your doubts, and the occasion of these doubts; had I never known the most powerful objections to religion from your lips, I should have been no less ignorant of the topics and arguments favourable to it.

And I think I may venture to ascribe to myself no less a progress in candour than in knowledge. My belief is stronger than it ever was, but, I no longer hold in scorn or abhorrence those who differ from me. I perceive the speciousness of those fallacies by which they are deluded. I find it possible for men to disbelieve and yet retain their claims to our reverence, our affection, and especially our good offices.

Those whom I once thought were only to be hated and shunned, I now find worthy of compassionate efforts for their good. Those whom I once imagined sunk beneath the reach of all succour, and to merit scarcely the tribute of a sigh for their lost estate, now appear to be easily raised to tranquillity and virtue, and to have irresistable claims to our help.

In no respect has your company made me a worse, in every respect it has made me a better woman. Not only my piety has become more rational and fervent, but a new spring has been imparted to my languishing curiosity. To find a soul, to whom my improvement will give delight; eager to direct and assist my enquiries; delicately liberal no less of censure when merited, than of praise where praise is due; entering, almost without the help of language from me, into my inmost thoughts: assisting me, if I may so speak, to comprehend myself; and raising to a stedfast and bright flame, the spark that my wayward fancy, left to itself, would have instantaneously emitted and lost —

But why do I again attempt this impossible theme. While reflecting on my debt to thee, my heart becomes too big for its mansion. My hand faulters, and the characters it traces, run into an illegible scrawl.

My tongue only is fitted for such an office; and Heaven grant that you may speedily return to me, and put an end to a solitude which every hour makes more irksome. Adieu.

LETTER XXXV

TO MRS. TALBOT
Baltimore, November 20.

HOW truly did my Angel say, that she whom I love is my deity, and her lips my oracle and that to her pertains not only the will to make me happy, by giving me stedfastness and virtue, but the power also!

I have read your letter oftener than a dozen times already, and at every reading my heart burns more and more. That weight of humiliation and despondency, which without your arm to sustain me, would assuredly sink me to the grave, becomes light as a feather, and while I crush your testimonies of love in my hand, I seem to have hold of a stay of which no storm can bereave me.

One of my faults, thou sayest, is a propensity to reason. Not satisfied with looking at that side of the post that chances to be near me, I move round and round it, and pause and scrutinize till those whose ill fate it is to wait upon my motions, are out of patience with me.

Every one has ways of his own. A transient glance at the post, satisfies the mob of passengers. 'Tis my choice to stand awhile and gaze.

The only post indeed, which I closely examine is myself, because my station is most convenient for inspecting *that*. Yet though I have a fuller view of myself than any other can have of me, my imperfect *sight*, that is, my erring judgement, is continually blundering.

If all my knowledge relate to my own character, and that knowledge is egregiously defective, how profound must be my ignorance of others, and especially of her, whom I presume to call mine?

No paradox ever puzzled me so much as your conduct. On my first interview with you I loved you, yet what kind of passion was that, which knew only your features and the sound of your voice. Every successive interview has produced, not only something new or unexpected, but something in seeming contradiction to my previous knowledge.

She will act, said I, in such and such circumstances, as those of her delicate and indulgent education must always act. That wit, that eloquence, that knowledge, must only make her despise such a witless, unendowed, unaccomplished, wavering and feeble a wretch as I am.

To be called your friend: to be your occasional companion; to be a tolerated visitor was more than I expected. When I found all this anxiously sought and eagerly accepted I was lost in astonishment. At times, may I venture to confess, that your regard for me, brought your judgment into question! It failed to inspire me with more respect, for myself, and not to look at me with my own eyes degraded you in my opinion.

How have you laboured to bestow on me that inestimable gift Self confidence! And some success has attended your efforts. My deliverance from my chains is less desperate than once it was. I may judge of the future, perhaps, by the past. Since I have already made such progress in exchanging distant veneration for familiar tenderness, and in persuading myself that he must possess some merit whom a soul like thine idolises, I may venture to anticipate the time when all my humiliation may vanish, and I shall come to be thought worthy of thy love, not only by thee, but by myself.

What a picture is this thou drawest! Yet such is my weakness, Jane, that I must shudder at the prospect. To tear thee from thy present dwelling and its comforts; to make thee a tenant of thy good widow, and a seamstress for me!

Yet what (thou sayest,) is a fine house, and a train of

310

servants, music and pictures? What silly prejudice to con-
nect dignity and happiness with high ceilings and damask
canopies, and golden superfluity.

Yet so silly am I, when reason deserts the helm, and habit
assumes it. The change thou hast painted, deceives me for
a moment, or rather is rightly judged of, while I look at
nothing but thy colouring, but when I withdraw my eye
from that, and the scene rises before me in the hues it is
accustomed to derive from my own fancy, my soul droops,
and I pray heaven to avert such a destiny.

I tell thee all my follies, Jane. Art thou not my sweet
physician, and how canst thou cure the malady, when thou
knowest not all its symptoms?

I love to regard myself in this light. As one owing his
virtue, his existence, his happiness his every thing to thee,
and as proposing no end to himself, but thy happiness in
turn: but the discharge of an endless debt of gratitude.

On my account, Jane, I cannot bear you should lose any
thing. It must not be. Yet what remedy? How is thy
mother's aversion to be subdued — how can she be made
to reason on my actions as you reason? yet not so, neither.
None but she that loves me, can make such constructions
and allowances as you do.

Why may she not be induced to give up the hope of dis-
uniting us, and while she hates me, continue her affection
for thee. Why rob thee of those bounties hitherto dispensed
to thee, merely because *I* must share in them. My partaking with thee contributes indispensibly to thy happiness.
Not for my own sake, then, but merely for thine, ought
competence to be secured to thee.

But is there no method of excluding me from all
participation. She may withhold from me all power of a
landlord, but she cannot prevent me from subsisting on
thy bounty.

Yet why does she now allow you to possess what you do?
can she imagine that my happiness is not as dear to you
now, as it will be in consequence of any change? If I share

nothing with you now, it is not from any want of benevolent importunity in you.

There is a strange inconsistency and contradiction in thy mother's conduct.

But something may surely be done to lighten her antipathies. I may surely confute a false charge. I may convince her of my innocence in one respect.

Yet see my friend the evils of which one error is the parent. My conduct towards the poor Jessy appears to your mother a more enormous wickedness than this imputed injustice to Talbot. The frantic indiscretion of my correspondence with Thomson, has ruined me, for he that will commit the greater crime, will not be thought to scruple the less.

And then there is such an irresistible crowd of evidence in favor of the accusation! when I first read Mrs. Fielder's letter the consciousness of my innocence gave me courage, but the longer I reflect upon the subject, the more deeply I despond. My own errors will always be powerful pleaders against me at the bar of this austere judge.

Would to heaven I had not yielded to your urgency. The indecorum of compliance stared me in the face at the time. Too easily I yielded to the inchantments of those eyes, and the pleadings of that melting voice.

The charms of your conversation: the midnight hour whose security was heightened by the storm that raged without: so perfectly screened from every interruption: and the subject we had been talking on so affecting and attractive to me, and so far from being exhausted; And you so pathetically earnest in intreaty, so absolutely forbidding my departure.

And was I such a shortsighted fool as not to insist on your retiring at the usual hour! The only thing that could make the expedient suggested by me effectual, was that. Your Molly lying with you, could avail you nothing, unless you actually passed the night in your chamber.

As it was, no contrivance could be more unfortunate, since it merely enabled her the more distinctly to remark the hour when you came up. Was it *three* or *four* when you left the parlour?

The unbosoming of souls which that night witnessed, so sweetly as it dwelt upon my memory, I now regard with horror, since it has involved you in such evil.

But the letter — that was a most disastrous accident. I have read very frequently this fatal billet. Who is it that could imitate your hand so exactly? The same fashion in the letters, the same colour in the ink, the same style, and the sentiments expressed, so fully and accurately coalescing with the preceding and genuine passages — no wonder that your mother, being so well acquainted with your pen, should have no doubt as to your guilt, after such testimony.

There must be a perpetrator of this iniquity. Talbot it could not be; for where lay the letter in the interval between its disappearance and his return; and what motive could influence him to commit or to countenance such a forgery?

Without doubt there was some deceiver. — Some one stole the letter, and by his hand was this vile conclusion added, and by him was it communicated to Talbot. But hast thou such an enemy in the world? Whom have you offended, capable of harbouring such deadly vengeance?

Pray my friend, fit down to the recollection of your past life, and enquire who it was that possessed your husband's confidence; who were his intimate companions, endeavor to discover; tell me the names and characters of all those who were accustomed to visit your house, either on your account or his. Strange if among all these, there is no foundation for some conjecture, however shadowy.

Thomson is no better, yet grows worse hardly perceptibly. Adieu.

Henry Colden.

LETTER XXXVI

TO HENRY COLDEN
Philadelphia, Nov. 23.

YOU impose on me a painful task. Persuaded that reflection was useless, I have endeavored to forget this fatal letter and all its consequences. I see you will not allow me to forget it; but I must own it is weakness to endeavor to shun the scrutiny.

Some one, my friend, must be in fault; and what fault can be more atrocious than this. To defraud, by forgery, your neighbour of a few dollars, is a crime which nothing but a public and ignominious death will expiate: Yet how trivial is that offence, compared with a fraud like this, which robs an helpless woman of her reputation; introduces mortal enmity between her and those whose affection is necessary to render life tolerable.

Whenever I think of this charge, an exquisite pain seizes my heart. There must be the blackest perfidy somewhere. I cannot bear to think that any human creature is capable of such a deed. A deed which the purest malice must have dictated, since there is none surely in the world, whom I have ever intentionally injured.

I cannot deal in conjectures. The subject, I find, by my feelings since I began this letter, is too agonizing — too bewildering. It carries back my thoughts to a time of misery, to which distance, instead of smoothing it into apathy, only adds a new sting.

A spotless reputation was once dear to me, but have I now torn the passion from my heart. I am weary of pursuing a phantom. No one has pursued it with more eagerness

314

and perseverance than I; and what has been the fruit of my labor but reiterated mortification and disappointment?

An upright demeanor, a self-acquitting conscience, are not sufficient for our safety. Calumny and misapprehension have no bounds to their rage and their activity.

How little did my thoughtless heart imagine the horrid images which beset the minds of my mother and my husband. Happy ignorance! Would to Heaven it had continued! Since knowledge puts it not in my power to remove the error, it ought to be avoided as the greatest evil.

While I know my own motives, and am convinced of their purity, let me hold in contempt the opinions of the world respecting me. They can never have a basis in truth. Be they favorable or otherwise, they cannot fail to be built on imperfect knowledge. The praise of others is therefore as little to be sought or prized as their censure to be dreaded or shunned.

Heaven knows how much I value the favor and affection of my mother, but dear as it is, I must give it up. How can I retain it? I cannot confute the charge. I must not acknowledge a guilt that does not belong to me. Added, therefore, to her belief of my guilt, must be the persuasion of my being an hardened and obdurate criminal.

What will she think of my two last letters? The former tacitly confessing my unworthiness, and promising compliance with all her wishes: the next asserting my innocence, and refusing her generous offers. My first, she will probably ascribe to an honorable compunction, left to operate without your controul. In the second she will trace your influence. Left to myself, she will imagine me capable of acting as she wishes; but, guided by you, she will lose all hopes of me, and resign me to my fate.

Indeed I have given up my mother. There is no other alternative but that of giving up you; and in this case I can hesitate, indeed, but I cannot decide against you.

I am placed in a very painful situation. I feel as if every hour spent under this roof was an encroachment on another's rights. My mother's bounty is not withheld, merely because my rebellion against her will is not completed; but I that feel no doubt, and whom mere consideration of her pleasure, important as it is, will never make swerve from my purpose; ought I to enjoy goods to which I have forfeited all title? Ought I to wait for an express command to be gone from her doors? Ought I to lay her under the necessity of declaring her will?

Yet if I change my lodgings immediately, without waiting her directions, will she not regard my conduct as contemptuous? Shall I not then be a rebel indeed; one that scorns her favor, and is eager to get rid of all my obligations?

How painful is such a situation: yet there is no escaping from it that I can see. I must, per force, remain as I am. But perhaps her next letter will throw some light upon my destiny. I suppose my positive assertions will shew her that a change of purpose cannot be hoped for from me.

The bell rings. Perhaps it is the post-man, and the intelligence I wish for has arrived — Adieu.

J. Talbot.

LETTER XXXVII

TO THE SAME

November 26.

WHAT shall I say to thee, my friend. How shall I communicate a resolution fatal, as thy tenderness will deem it, to thy peace; yet a resolution suggested by an heart which has, at length, permitted all selfish regards to be swallowed up by a disinterested consideration of thy good.

Why did you conceal from me your father's treatment of you, and the consequences which your fidelity to me has incurred from his rage? I will never be the cause of plunging you into poverty so hopeless. Did you think I would; and could you imagine it possible to conceal from me forever his aversion to me.

How much misery would your forbearance have laid up in store for my future life. When fate had put it out of my power to absolve you from his curses, some accident would have made me acquainted with the full extent of the sufferings and contumelies with which, for my sake, he had loaded you.

But, thanks to Heaven, I am apprized in time of the truth. Instead of the bearer of a letter from my mother, whose signal at the door put an end to my last letter, it was my mother herself.

Dear and welcome as those features and that voice once were, now would I rather have encountered the eyes of a basalisk and the notes of the ill-boding raven.

She hastened with all this expedition to thank me; to urge me to execute; to assist me in performing the promises of

317

my first letter. The second, in which these promises were recalled, never reached her hand. She left New-York, as it now appeared, before its arrival. The interval had been spent on the road, where she had been detained by untoward and dangerous accidents.

Think, my friend, of the embarrassments attending this unlooked for and inauspicious meeting. Joy at my supposed compliance with her wishes, wishes that imaged to themselves my happiness, and only mine, enabled her to support the hardships of this journey. Fatigue and exposure, likely to be fatal to one of so delicate, so infirm a constitution, so lately and imperfectly recovered from a dangerous malady, could not deter her.

Fondly, rapturously did she fold to her bosom, the long lost and late recovered child. Tears of joy she shed over me, and thanked me for the tranquil and serene close which my return to virtue, as she called my acquiescence, had secured to her life. That life would at all events be short, but my compliances, if they could not much protract it, would at least render its approaching end peaceful.

All attempts to reason with my mother were fruitless. She fell into alarming agonies when she discovered the full import of that coldness and dejection which my demeanor betrayed. Fatigued and indisposed as she was, she made preparation to depart: she refused to pass one night under the same roof; her *own* roof; and determined to be gone, on her return home, the very next morning.

Will not your heart comprehend the greatness of this trial, and pity and excuse a momentary wavering; a yielding irresolution? Yet it was but momentary. An hour's solitude and deep reflection fortified my heart against the grief and supplication even of my mother.

Next day she was more calm. She condescended to reason, to expostulate. She carefully shunned the mention of atrocious charges. She dwelt only on the proofs which your past life and your own confessions had afforded of unsteady courage and unwarrantable principles; your treatment of the Woodbury girl; your correspondence with

318

Thomson; your ignoble sloth; your dependance upon others; your helplessness.

From these accusations, I defended you in silence. My heart was your secret advocate. I did not verbally repell any of these charges. That of inglorious dependance for subsistence upon others, I admitted; but I could not forbear urging that this dependance was on a father. A father who was rich; who had no other child than yourself; whose own treatment of you, had planted and reared in you this indisposition to labor; to whose property, your title, ultimately, could not be denied.

And has he then, she exclaimed, deceived you in that particular? Has he concealed from you his father's resolutions? That his engagement with you, has already drawn down his father's anger, and even his curses. On his persisting to maintain an inviolable faith to you, he was ignominiously banished from his father's roof. All kindred and succour were disclaimed, and on you depends the continuance of that decree, and whether that protection and subsistence which he has hitherto enjoyed, and of which his character stands in so much need, shall be lost to him forever.

You did not tell me *this*, my friend. In claiming your love, far was I from imagining that I tore you from your father's house, and plunged you into that indigence which your character and education so totally unfit you for sustaining or escaping from.

My mother removed all doubt which could not but attend such unwelcome tidings, by shewing me her own letter to your father, and his answer to it.

Well do I recollect your behaviour on the evening when my mother's letter was received by your father. At that time, your deep dejection was inexplicable. And did you not — my heart bleeds to think how much my love has cost you — Did you not talk of a fall on the ice when I pointed to a bruize on your forehead. That bruize, and every token of dismay, your endeavors at eluding or diverting my attention from your sorrow and solemnity, are now explained.

Good Heaven! And was I indeed the cause of that violence, that contumely; the rage, and even curses of a father? And why concealed you these maledictions and this violence from me? Was it not because you well knew that I would never consent to subject you to such a penalty?

Hasten then, I beseech you, to your father; lay this letter before him; let it inform him of my solemn and irrevocable resolution to sever myself from you forever.

But this I will, myself, do. I will acquaint him with my resignation to *his* will and that of my mother, and beseech him to restore you to his favor.

Farewell, my friend. By that name, at least, I may continue to call you. Yet no. I must never see you nor hear from you again; unless it be in answer to this letter.

Let your pity stifle the emotions of indignation or grief, and return me such an answer as may tend to reconcile me to the vow, which, whether difficult or easy, must not be broken.

J. T.

LETTER XXXVIII

TO HENRY COLDEN, SENIOR

November 26.

Sir,

I WAS not informed till to-day, of the correspondence that has passed between you and my mother, nor of your aversion to the alliance which was designed to take place between your son and me.

It is my duty to inform you that, in my opinion, your approbation was absolutely necessary to such an union; and consequently, since your concurrence is withheld, it will never take place. Every tie or engagement between us, is, from this moment dissolved, and all intercourse, by letter or otherwise will here end.

Your son, in opposing your wishes, imagined himself consulting my happiness. In that he was mistaken; and I have now removed his error, by acquainting him with my present determination.

I am deeply grieved that his attachment to me has forfeited your favor. I hope that there is no other obstacle to reconcilement, and that the termination of all intercourse between us may remove that obstacle.

Jane Talbot.

I join my daughter in assuring you that the alliance for which a mutual aversion was entertained, cannot take place; and that all her engagements with your son are dissolved. I join her likewise in entreating you to forget his disobedience, and restore him to your protection and favor.

M. Fielder.

LETTER XXXIX

TO MRS. TALBOT

November 28.

I T BECOMES me to submit without a murmur to a resolution dictated by a disinterested regard to my happiness.

That you may find in that persuasion; in your mother's tenderness and gratitude; in the affluence and honor, which this determination has secured to you; abundant consolation for every evil that may befall yourself or pursue me, are my only wishes.

Far was I from designing to conceal from you entirely my father's aversion to our views. I frequently apprised you of the inferences to be naturally drawn from his known character, but I trusted to his generosity, to the steadiness of my own deportment — to your own merits, when he should become personally acquainted with you: to his good sense, when reflecting on an evil in his power to lessen, though not wholly to remove — for a change in his opinions; or, at least, in his conduct.

There was sufficient resemblance in the characters of both our parents to make me rely on the influence of time and reflection in our favour. Your mother could not cease to love you. I could not by any accident be wholly bereaved of my father's affection. No conduct of theirs had robbed them of my esteem. Why then did I persist in thwarting their wishes? why encourage you in your opposition? because I imagined that, in thwarting their present views, which were founded in error, I consulted their lasting happiness, and made myself a title to their future gratitude, by challenging their present rebukes.

I told you not of my father's passionate violences, disgraceful to himself and productive of unspeakable anguish to me. Why should I revive the scene? why be the historian of my father's dishonor? why needlessly add to my own and to your affliction?

My concealments arose not from the fear that the disclosure would estrange you from me. I supposed you willing to grant me the same independence of a parent's controul which you claimed for yourself. I saw no difference between forbearing to consult a parent in a case where we know that his answer will condemn us, and slighting his express forbidding.

I say thus much to account for, and, if possible, excuse that concealment with which you reproach me. Tender and reluctant, indeed, are these reproaches, but as I deem it a sacred duty to reveal to you the utmost of my follies, what but injustice to you would be the tacit admission of injurious but groundless charges.

My actual faults are of too deep a dye to allow me to sport with your good opinion, or permit me to be worse thought of by you than I deserve.

You exhort me to seek reconcilement, with my father. What mean you? I have not been the injurer. Not an angry word, accusing look or vengeful thought has come from me. I have exercised the privilege of a rational and moral being. I have loved, not according to another's estimate of merit, but my own. Of what then am I to repent? where lies my transgression? if his treatment of me be occasioned by antipathy for you, must I adopt his antipathy, and thus creep again into favour? Impossible! if it arise from my refusing to give up an alliance which his heart abhors, your letter to him, which you tell me you mean to write, and which will inform him that every view of that kind is at an end, will remove the evil.

Fear not for me, my friend. Whatever be my lot, be

assured that I never can taste pure misery while the thought
abides with me that you are not unhappy.

And what now remains but to leave with you the blessing
of a grateful and devoted heart, and to submit, with what
humility I can, to the destiny which you have prescribed.

I should not deserve your love, if I did not now relinquish it with an anguish next to despair: neither should
I have merit in my own eyes, if I did not end this letter
with acquitting you, the author of my loss, of all shadow
of blame. Farewell —— *forever.*

H. Colden.

LETTER XL

TO JAMES MONTFORD
November 28.

I TOLD you of your brother Stephen's talk with me about accompanying him on his Northwest voyage. I mentioned to you what were my objections to the scheme. It was a desperate adventure: a sort of forlorn hope: to be pursued in case my wishes in relation to Jane should be crossed. I had not then any, or much apprehension of change in her resolutions. So many proofs of a fervent and invincible attachment to me had she lately given, that I could not imagine any motive strong enough to change her purpose. Yet now, my friend, have I arranged matters with your brother, and expect to bid an everlasting farewell to my native shore some day within the ensuing fortnight.

I call it an everlasting farewell, for I have, at present, neither expectation nor desire of returning. A three years wandering among boistrous seas, and through various climates, added to that inward care, that spiritless dejected heart which I shall ever bear about me, would surely never let me return, even if I had the wish; but I have not the wish. If I live at all, it must be in a scene far different and distant from that in which I have been hitherto reluctantly detained.

And why have I embraced this scheme? There can be but one cause.

Having just returned from following Thomson's remains to the grave, I received a letter from Jane. Her mother had just arrived. She came, it seems, in consequence of her

daughter's apparent compliance with her wishes. The letter, retracting my friend's precipitate promise, had miscarried or had lingered by the way. What I little suspected,
my father had acquainted Mrs. Fielder with his conduct
towards me, and this, together with her mother's importunities, had prevailed on Jane once more to renounce me.

There never occurred an event in my life which did not,
some way, bear testimony to the usefulness and value of
sincerity. Had I fully disclosed all that passed between my
father and me, should I not easily have diverted Jane from
these extremities. Alone; at a distance from me; and with
her mother's eloquence at hand, to confirm every wayward
sentiment, and fortify her in every hostile resolution, she
is easily driven into paths, and perhaps kept steadily in
them, from which proper explanations and pathetic
arguments, had they been early and seasonably employed
by me, would have led her easily away.

I begin to think it is vain to strive against maternal influence. What but momentary victory can I hope to attain?
What but poverty, dependance, ignominy, will she share
with me? And if her strenuous spirit set nought by these,
and I know she is capable of rising above them, how will
she support her mother's indignation and grief.

I have now, indeed, no hope of even momentary victory.
There are but two persons in the world who command her
affections. Either when present, (the other absent or silent)
has absolute dominion over her. Her mother no doubt is
apprized of this, and has now pursued the only effectual
method of securing submission.

I have already written an answer; I hope such an one
as, when the present tumults of passion have subsided,
when the eye sedately scrutinizes, and the heart beats in
an even tenour, may be read without shame or remorse.

I shall also write to her mother. In doing this, I must
keep down the swelling bitterness. It may occupy my solitude, torment my feelings, but why should it infect my pen?

I have sometimes given myself credit for impartiality in
judging of others. Indeed I am inclined to think myself no

blind or perverse judge even of my own actions. Hence indeed, the greater part of my unhappiness. If my conduct had always conformed, instead of being adverse, to my principles, I should have moved on tranquilly and self satisfied, at least, but, in truth, the being that goes by my name was never more thoroughly contemned by another than by myself — but this is falling into the old strain; irksome, tiresome and useless to you as to me. Yet I cannot write just now in any other: therefore I will stop.

Adieu, my friend. There will be time enough to hear from you ere my departure. Let me hear then from you.

LETTER XLI

TO HENRY COLDEN

Philadelphia, Dec. 3.

Sir,

MY Daughter informs me that the letter she has just dispatched to you, contains her resolution of never seeing you more. I likewise discover that she has requested, and expects a reply from you, in which, she doubts not, you will confirm her resolution.

You, no doubt, regard me as your worst enemy. No request from me can hope to be complied with, yet I cannot forbear suggesting the propriety of your refraining from making any answer to my daughter's letter.

In my treatment of you I shall not pretend any direct concern for your happiness. I am governed, whether erroneously or not, merely by views to the true interest of Mrs. Talbot, which in my opinion, forbids her to unite herself to you. But if that union be calculated to bereave her of happiness, it cannot certainly be conducive to yours. If you consider the matter rightly, therefore, instead of accounting me an enemy, you will rank me among your benefactors.

You have shewn yourself, in some instances, not destitute of generosity. It is but justice to acknowledge that your late letter to me avows sentiments such as I by no means expected, and makes me disposed to trust your candour to acquit my intention at least of some of the consequences of your father's resentment.

I was far from designing to subject you to violence or ignominy, and meant nothing by my application to him but your genuine and lasting happiness.

I dare not hope that it will ever be in my power to appease that resentment which you feel for me. I cannot expect that you are so far raised above the rest of men, that any action will be recommended to you by its tendency to oblige me: Yet I cannot conceal from you that your reconcilement with your father will give me peculiar satisfaction.

I ventured on a former occasion to make you an offer, on condition of your going to Europe, which I now beg leave to repeat. By accepting the inclosed bill, and embarking for a foreign land without any further intercourse, personally or by letter, with my daughter, and after reconciliation with your father, you will confer a very great favour on one, who, notwithstanding appearances, has acted in a manner that becomes

Your true friend,
M. Fielder.

LETTER XLII

TO MRS. FIELDER

Baltimore, Dec. 5.

Madam,

I PRETEND not to be raised above any of the infirmities of human nature, but am too sensible of the errors of my past conduct, and the defects which will ever cleave to my character, to be either surprised or indignant at the disapprobation of a virtuous mind. So far from harbouring resentment against you, it is with reluctance I decline the acceptance of your bill. I cannot consider it in any other light than as an alms which my situation is far from making necessary, and by receiving which I should defraud those whose poverty may plead a superior title.

I hasten to give you pleasure by informing you of my intention to leave America immediately. My destiny is far from being certain, but, at present, I both desire and expect never to revisit my native land.

I design not to solicit another interview with Mrs. Talbot. You dissuade me from making any reply to her letter, from the fear, no doubt, that my influence will be exerted to change her resolution. Dismiss, I entreat you, madam, every apprehension of that kind. Your daughter has deliberately made her election. If no advantage be taken of her tenderness and pity, she will be happy in her new scheme. Shall I, who pretend to love her, subject her to new trials and mortifications? Am I able to reward her, by my affection, for the loss of every other comfort. What can I say in favour of my own attachment to her, which may not be urged in favour of her attachment to her mother. The happiness of one or other must be sacrificed, and shall I

not rather offer, than demand the sacrifice? and how poor
and selfish should I be if I did not strive to lessen the difficulties of her choice, and persuade her that in gratifying
her mother, she inflicts no lasting misery on me?

I regard in its true light, what you say with respect to
reconcilement with my father, and am always ready to comply with your wishes in the only way that a conviction of
my own rectitude will permit. I have patiently endured
revilings and blows, but I shall not needlessly expose myself
to new insults. Though willing to accept apology and grant
an oblivion of the past, I will never avow a penitence which
I do not feel, or confess that I deserved the treatment
I received.

Truly can I affirm that your daughter's happiness is of
all earthly things most dear to me. I fervently thank Heaven
that I leave her exempt from all the hardships of poverty,
and in the bosom of one who will guard her safety with
a zeal equal to my own. All that I fear is, that your efforts
to console her will fail. I know the heart, which, if you
thought me worthy of the honour, I should account it my
supreme felicity to call mine. Let it be a precious deposit
in your hands.

And now, Madam, permit me to conclude with a solemn
blessing on your head, and on her's, and with an eternal
farewell to you both.

H. Colden.

LETTER XLIII

TO JAMES MONTFORD
Philadelphia, Dec. 7.

I HOPE you will approve of my design to accompany
Stephen. The influence of variety and novelty will no
doubt be useful. Why should I allow my present feelings, which assure me that I have lost what is indispensible,
not only to my peace, but my life, to supplant the invariable
lesson of experience, which teaches that time and absence
will dull the edge of every calamity? And have I not found
myself peculiarly susceptible of this healing influence?

Time and change of scene will, no doubt, relieve me,
but, in the mean time, I have not a name for that wretchedness into which I am sunk. The light of day, the company of mankind is, at this moment, insupportable. Of all
places in the world, *this* is the most hateful to my soul. I
should not have entered the city, I should not abide in it
a moment, were it not for a thought that occurred just
before I left Baltimore.

You know the mysterious and inexplicable calumny
which has heightened Mrs. Fielder's antipathy against me.
Of late, I have been continually ruminating on it, and
especially since Mrs. Talbot's last letter. Methinks it is
impossible for me to leave the country till I have cleared
her character of this horrid aspersion. Can there be any
harmony between mother and child; must not suspicion
and mistrust perpetually rankle in their bosoms, while this
imposture is believed?

Yet how to detect the fraud — Some clue must be discer-
nible; perseverance must light on it, at last. The agent in

332

this sordid iniquity must be human: must be influenced by the ordinary motives: must be capable of remorse or of error; must have moments of repentance or of negligence.

My mind was particularly full of this subject in a midnight ramble which I took just before I left Baltimore. Something, I know not what, recalled to mind a conversation which I had with the poor washwoman at Wilmington. Miss Jessup, whom you well know by my report, passed through Wilmington just as I left the sick woman's house, and stopped a moment just to give me an "How'de'ye" and to drop some railleries, founded on my visits to Miss Secker, a single and solitary lady. On reaching Philadelphia she amused herself with perplexing Jane, by jesting exaggerations on the same subject, in a way that seemed to argue somewhat of malignity; yet I thought nothing of it at the time.

On my next visit to the sick woman, it occurred to me, for want of other topics of conversation, to introduce Miss Jessup. Did she know any thing, I asked, of that lady.

O Yes, was the answer. A great deal. She lived a long time in the family. She remembered her well, and was a sufferer by many of her freaks.

It is always disagreeable to me to listen to the slanderous prate of servants: I am careful, whenever it intrudes itself, to discourage and rebuke it; but just at this time I felt some resentment against this lady, and hardly supposed it possible for any slanderer to exaggerate her contemptible qualities. I suffered her therefore to run on in a tedious and minute detail of the capricious, peevish and captious deportment of Miss Jessup.

After the rhetoric of half an hour, all was wound up, in a kind of satyrical apology, with — No wonder, for the girl was over head and ears in love, and her man would have nothing to say to her. An hundred times has she begged and prayed him to be kind, but he slighted all her advances, and always after they had been shut up together, she wreaked her disappointment and ill humour upon us.

Pray, said I, who was this ungrateful person?

His name was Talbot. Miss Jessup would not give him up, but teazed him with letters and prayers till the man at last, got married, ten to one for no other reason than to get rid of her.

This intelligence was new. Much as I had heard of Miss Jessup, a story like this had never reached my ears. I quickly ascertained that the Talbot spoken of was the late husband of my friend.

Some incident interrupted the conversation here. The image of Miss Jessup was displaced to give room to more important reveries, and I thought no more of her till this night's ramble. I now likewise recollected that the only person suspected of having entered the apartment where lay Mrs. Talbot's unfinished letter, was no other than Miss Jessup herself, who was always gadding at unseasonable hours. How was this suspicion removed? By Miss Jessup herself, who, on being charged with the theft, asserted that she was elsewhere engaged at the time.

It was, indeed, exceedingly improbable that Miss Jessup had any agency in this affair. A volatile, giddy, thoughtless character, who betrayed her purposes on all occasions, from a natural incapacity to keep a secret; and yet had not this person succeeded in keeping her attachment to Mr. Talbot from the knowledge, and even the suspicion of his wife? Their intercourse had been very frequent since her marriage, and all her sentiments appeared to be expressed with a rash and fearless confidence. Yet, if Hannah Secker's story deserved credit, she had exerted a wonderful degree of circumspection, and had placed on her lips a guard that had never once slept.

I determined to stop at Wilmington next day, on my journey to you, and glean what further information Hannah could give. I ran to her lodgings as soon as I alighted at the inn.

I enquired how long and in what years she lived with Miss Jessup; what reason she had for suspecting her mistress of an attachment to Talbot; what proofs Talbot gave of aversion to her wishes.

On each of these heads, her story was tediously minute and circumstantial. She lived with Miss Jessup and her mother, before Talbot's marriage with my friend; after the marriage, and during his absence on the voyage which occasioned his death.

The proofs of Miss Jessup's passion were continually occurring in her own family, where she suffered the ill humor, occasioned by her disappointment, to display itself without controul. Hannah's curiosity was not chastised by much reflection, and some things were overheard which verified the old maxim, that "Walls have ears." In short, it appears that this poor lady doated on Talbot; that she reversed the usual methods of proceeding and submitted to his mercy; that she met with nothing but scorn and neglect; that even after his marriage with Jane, she sought his society, pestered him with invitations and letters, and directed her walks in such a way as to make their meeting in the street occur as if by accident.

While Talbot was absent she visited his wife very frequently, but the subjects of their conversation and the degree of intimacy between the two ladies were better known to me than to Hannah.

You may think it strange that my friend never suspected or discovered the state of Miss Jessup's feelings. But, in truth, Jane is the least suspicious or inquisitive of mortals. Her neighbour was regarded with no particular affection: her conversation is usually a vein of impertinence or levity; her visits were always unsought and eluded as often as decorum would permit; her talk was seldom listened to, and she and all belonging to her were dismissed from recollection as soon as politeness gave leave. Miss Jessup's deficiencies in personal and mental graces and Talbot's undisguised contempt for her, precluded every sentiment like jealousy.

Jane's life, since the commencement of her acquaintance with Miss Jessup, was lonely and secluded. Her friends were not of her neighbour's cast, and these tattlers who knew any thing of Miss Jessup's follies were quite unknown to her. No wonder, then, that the troublesome impertinence of this poor woman had never betrayed her to so inattentive an observer as Jane.

After many vague and fruitless inquiries, I asked Hannah if Miss Jessup was much addicted to the pen.

Very much. Was always scribbling. Was never by herself three minutes but the pen was taken up: would write on any pieces of paper that offered: was frequently rebuked by her mother for wasting so much time in this way: the cause of a great many quarrels between them: the old lady spent the whole day knitting: supplied herself in this way, with all the stockings she herself used; knit nothing but worsted, which she wore all the year round: all the surplus beyond what she needed for her own use, she sold at a good price to a Market street shopkeeper: Hannah used to be charged with the commission: always executed it grumblingly: the old lady had stipulated with a Mr. H —— to take at a certain price, all she made: Hannah was dispatched with the stockings, but was charged to go beforehand to twenty other dealers, and try to get more. Used to go directly to Mr. H ——, and call on her friends by the way, persuading the old lady that her detention was occasioned by the number and perseverance of her applications to the dealers in hose: till, at last, she fell under suspicion; was once followed by the old lady, detected in her fraud, and dismissed from the house with ignominy. The quondam mistress endeavoured to injure Hannah's character by reporting that her agent had actually got a higher price for the stockings than she thought proper to account for to her employer; had gained, by this artifice, not less than three farthings a pair, on twenty-three pairs: all a base lie as ever was told —

You say that Miss Jessup was a great scribbler. Did she write well: fast: neatly?

They say she did: very well. For her part, she could not write; and was therefore no judge, but Tom, the waiter and

336

coachman, was very fond of reading and writing, and used to say that Miss Hetty would make a good clerk. Tom used to carry all her messages and letters; Was a cunning and insinuating fellow; cajoled his mistress by flatteries and assiduities: got many a smile: many a bounty and gratuity, for which the fellow only laughed at her behind her back.

What has become of this Tom?

He lives with her still, and was in as high favour as ever. Tom had paid her a visit, the day before, being in attendance on his mistress on her late journey. From him, she supposed that Miss Hetty had gained intelligence of Hannah's situation, and of her being succoured, in her distress, by me.

Tom, you say, was her letter carrier. Did you ever hear from him with whom she corresponded? did she ever write to Talbot?

O yes. Just before Talbot's marriage, she often wrote to him. Tom used to talk very freely in the kitchen about his mistress' attachment, and always told us, what reception he met with. Mr. Talbot seldom condescended to write any answer.

I suppose, Hannah, I need hardly ask whether you have any specimen of Miss Jessup's writing in your possession?

This question considerably disconcerted the poor woman. She did not answer me till I had repeated the question.

Why — yes — she had — something — she believed.

I presume it is nothing improper to be disclosed: if so, I should be glad to have a sight of it.

She hesitated: was very much perplexed. Denied and confessed alternately that she possessed some of Miss Jessup's writing; at length began to weep very bitterly.

After some solicitation on my part, to be explicit, she consented to disclose what she acknowledged to be a great fault. The substance of her story was this:

Miss Jessup, on a certain occasion, locked herself up for several hours in her chamber. At length she came out, and went to the street door, apparently with an intention of going abroad. Just then an heavy rain began to fall. This incident produced a great deal of impatience, and after waiting some time, in hopes of the shower's ceasing, and frequently looking at her watch, she called for an umbrella. Unhappily, as poor Hannah afterwards thought, no umbrella could be found. Her own had been lent to a friend the preceding evening, and the mother would have held herself most culpably extravagant to uncase hers, without a most palpable necessity. Miss Hetty was preparing to go out unsheltered, when the officious Tom interfered, and asked her if *he* could do what she wanted. At first, she refused his offer, but the mother's importunities to stay at home becoming more clamorous, she consented to commission Tom to drop a letter at the post office. This he was to do with the utmost dispatch, and promised that not a moment should be lost. He received the letter, but instead of running off with it immediately, he slipped into the kitchen, just to arm himself against the storm by an hearty draught of strong beer.

While quaffing his nectar, and chattering with his usual gaiety, Hannah, who had long owed a grudge both to mistress and man, was tempted to convey the letter from Tom's pocket, where it was but half deposited, into her own. Her only motive was to vex and disappoint those whose chief pleasure it had always been to vex and disappoint her. The tankard being hastily emptied, he hastened away to the post office. When he arrived there, he felt for the letter. It was gone: dropped, as he supposed, in the street. In great confusion he returned, examining very carefully the gutters and porches, by the way. He entered the kitchen in great perplexity, and enquired of Hannah, if a letter had not fallen from his pocket before he went out.

Hannah, according to her own statements, was incapable of inveterate malice. She was preparing to rid Tom of his uneasiness, when he was summoned to the presence of his lady. He thought proper to extricate himself from all difficulties by boldly affirming that the letter had been left according to direction, and he afterwards endeavoured to

338

persuade Hannah that it had been found in the bottom of his pocket.

Every day increased the difficulty of disclosing the truth. Tom and Miss Jessup, talked no more on the subject, and time, and new provocations from her mistress, confirmed Hannah in her resolution of retaining the paper.

She could not read, and was afraid of trusting any body else with the contents of this epistle. Several times she was about to burn it, but forbore from the persuasion that a day might arrive when the possession would be of some importance to her. It had laid, till almost forgotten, in the bottom of her crazy chest.

I rebuked her with great severity, for her conduct, and insisted on her making all the atonement in her power, by delivering up the letter to the writer. I consented to take charge of it for that purpose.

You will judge of my surprise, when I received a letter, with the seal unbroken, directed to Mrs. Fielder of New-York. Jane and I had often been astonished at the minute intelligence which her mother received of our proceedings: at the dexterity this secret informant had displayed in mis-representing and falsely construing our actions. The in-former was anonymous, and one of the letters had been extorted from her mother by Jane's urgent solicitations. This I had frequently perused and the penmanship was still familiar to my recollection. It bore a striking resemblance to the superscription of this letter, and was equally remote from Miss Jessup's ordinary hand writing. Was it rash to infer from these circumstances that the secret enemy, whose malice had been so active and successful, was at length discovered?

What was I to do? Should I present myself before Miss Jessup with this letter in my hand, and lay before her my suspicions, or should I carry it to Mrs. Fielder, to whom it was directed? My curiosity was defeated by the careful manner in which it was folded, and this was not a case in which I deemed myself authorized to break a seal.

After much reflection, I determined to call upon Miss

Jessup. I meant not to restore her the letter, unless the course our conversation should take, made it proper. I have already been at her house. She was not at home. I am to call again at eight o'clock in the evening.

In my way thither I passed Mrs. Talbot's house. There were scarcely any tokens of its being inhabited. No doubt, the mother and child, have returned together to New-York. On approaching the house, my heart, too heavy before, became a burthen almost insupportable. I hastened my pace, and averted my eyes.

I am now shut up in my chamber at an Inn. I feel as if in a wilderness of savages, where all my safety consisted in solitude. I was glad not to meet with an human being whom I knew.

What shall I say to Miss Jessup when I see her. I know not. I have reason to believe her the author of many slanders, but look for no relief from the mischiefs they have occasioned, in accusing or upbraiding the slanderer. She has likewise disclosed many instances of guilty conduct, which I supposed impossible to be discovered. I never concealed them from Mrs. Talbot, to whom a thorough knowledge of my character was indispensible; but I was unwilling to make any other my confessor. In this, I cannot suppose her motives to have been very benevolent, but, since she adhered to the truth, it is not for me to arraign her motives.

May I not suspect that she had some hand in the forgery lately come to light. A mind like hers, must hate a successful rival. To persuade Talbot of his wife's perfidy, was at least to dissolve his alliance with another; and since she took so much pains to gain his favor, even after his marriage, is it not allowable to question the delicacy and punctiliousness, at least, of her virtue?

Mrs. Fielder's aversion to me, is chiefly founded on a knowledge of my past errors. She thinks them too flagrant to be atoned for, and too inveterate to be cured. I can never hope to subdue perfectly that aversion, and though Jane can never be happy without me, *I,* alone, cannot make her

happy. On my own account, therefore, it is of little moment
what she believes. But her own happiness is deeply
concerned in clearing her daughter's character of this
blackest of all stains.

Here is some one coming up the stairs, towards my apartment. Surely it cannot be to me that this visit is intended —

* * *

Good Heaven! What shall I do?

It was Molly that has just left me.

My heart sunk at her appearance. I had made up my
mind to separate my evil destiny from that of Jane; and
could only portend new trials and difficulties from the appearance of one whom I supposed her messenger.

The poor girl, as soon as she saw me, began to sob bitterly, and could only exclaim — O, sir! O, Mr. Colden.

This behaviour was enough to terrify me. I trembled in
every joint while I faultered out — I hope your mistress is well.

After many efforts, I prevailed in gaining a distinct
account of my friend's situation. This good girl, by the sympathy she always expressed in her mistress's fortunes; by
her silent assiduities and constant proofs of discretion and
affection, had gained Mrs. Talbot's confidence; yet no farther than to indulge her feelings with less restraint in
Molly's presence than in that of any other person.

I learned that the night after Mrs. Fielder's arrival, was
spent by my friend in sighs and restlessness. Molly lay in
the same chamber, and her affectionate heart was as much
a stranger to repose as that of her mistress. She frequently
endeavored to comfort Mrs. Talbot, but in vain.

Next day she did not rise as early as usual. Her mother
came to her bed-side, and enquired affectionately after her
health. The visit was received with smiling and affectionate
complacency. Her indisposition was disguised, and she
studied to persuade Mrs. Fielder that she enjoyed her usual
tranquillity. She rose, and attempted to eat, but quickly desisted, and after a little while retired and locked herself up
in her chamber. Even Molly was not allowed to follow her.

341

In this way, that and the ensuing day past. She wore an air of constrained cheerfulness in her mother's presence; affected interest in common topics; and retired at every convenient interval to her chamber, where she wept incessantly.

Mrs. Fielder's eye was watchful and anxious. She addressed Mrs. Talbot in a tender and maternal accent; seemed solicitous to divert her attention by anecdotes of New-York friends; and carefully eluded every subject likely to recall images which were already too intimately present. The daughter seemed grateful for these solicitudes, and appeared to fight with her feelings the more resolutely because they gave pain to her mother.

All this was I compelled to hear from the communicative Molly.

My heart bled at this recital. Too well did I predict what effect her compliance would have on her peace.

I asked if Jane had not received a letter from me.

Yes — Two letters had come to the door at once, this morning; one for Mrs. Fielder and the other for her daughter. Jane expected its arrival, and shewed the utmost impatience when the hour approached. She walked about her chamber, listened, with a start, to every sound; continually glanced from her window at the passengers.

She did not conceal from Molly the object of her solicitude. The good girl endeavored to sooth her, but she checked her with vehemence. Talk not to me, Molly. On this hour depends my happiness — my life. The sacrifice my mother asks, is too much or too little. In bereaving me of my love she must be content to take my existence also. They never shall be separated.

The weeping girl timorously suggested that she had already given me up.

True, Molly, in a rash moment, I told him that we meet no more: but two days of misery has convinced me that it cannot be. His answer will decide my fate as to this world. If he accept my dismissal, I am thenceforth undone. I will

342

die. Blessing my mother, and wishing her a less stubborn child, *I will die.*

These last words were uttered with an air the most desperate, and an emphasis the most solemn. They chilled me to the heart, and I was unable longer to keep my seat. Molly, unbidden, went on.

Your letter at last came. I ran down to receive it. Mrs. Fielder was at the street door before me, but she suffered me to carry my mistress' letter to her. Poor lady! She met me at the stair-head, snatched the paper eagerly, but trembled so she could not open it. At last she threw herself on the bed, and ordered me to read it to her. I did so. At every sentence she poured forth fresh tears, and exclaimed, wringing her hands — O! what — what an heart have I madly cast away.

The girl told me much more, which I am unable to repeat. Her visit was self-prompted. She had caught a glympse of me as I passed the door, and without mentioning her purpose to her mistress, set out as soon as it was dusk.

Cannot you do something, Mr. Colden, for my mistress? continued the girl. She will surely die if she has not her own way; and to judge from your appearance, it is as great a cross to you as to her.

Heaven knows, that, with me, it is nothing but the choice of dreadful evils. Jane is the mistress of her own destiny. It is not I that have renounced her, but she that has banished me. She has only to recall the sentence, which she confesses to have been hastily and thoughtlessly pronounced — and no power on earth shall sever me from her side.

Molly asked my permission to inform her mistress of my being in the city, and conjured me not to leave it, during the next day, at least. I readily consented, and requested her to bring me word in the morning in what state things were.

She offered to conduct me to her then. It was easy to effect an interview without Mrs. Fielder's knowledge: but I was sick of all clandestine proceedings, and had promised Mrs. Fielder not to seek another meeting with her daughter. I was likewise anxious to visit Miss Jessup, and ascertain what was to be done by means of the letter in my pocket.

Can I, my friend, can I, without unappeasable remorse, pursue this scheme of a distant voyage. Suppose some fatal dispair should seize my friend. Suppose — it is impossible. I will not stir till she has had time to deliberate; till resignation to her mother's will, shall prove a task that is practicable.

Should I not be the most flagrant of villains if I deserted one that loved me. My own happiness is not a question. I cannot be a selfish being and a true lover. Happiness, without her, is indeed a chimerical thought, but my exile would be far from miserable, while assured of her tranquillity, and possession would confer no peace, if her whom I possessed, were not happier than a different destiny would make her.

Why have all these thoughts been suspended for the last two days. I had wrought myself up to a firm persuasion that marriage was the only remedy for all evils: that our efforts to regain the favor of her mother would be most likely to succeed, when that which she endeavored to prevent, was irretrievable. Yet that persuasion was dissipated by her last letter. *That* convinced me that her lot would only be made miserable by being united to mine. Yet now — is it not evident that our fates must be inseperable?

What a phantastic impediment is this aversion of her mother! And yet, can I safely and deliberately call it phantastic? Let me sever myself *from* myself, and judge impartially. Be my heart called upon to urge its claims to such affluence, such love, such treasures of personal and mental excellence as Jane has to bestow, would it not be dumb. It is not so absurd as to plead its devotion to her, as an atonement for every past guilt, and as affording security for future uprightness.

On my own merit I am, and ever have been mute. I have plead with Mrs. Fielder not for myself but for Jane. It is her happiness that forms the object of my supreme regard. I am eager to become hers, because *her,* not because *my* happiness, though my happiness certainly *does,* demand it.

I am then resolved. Jane's decision shall be deliberate. I will not biass her by prayers or blandishments. Her resolution shall spring from her own judgment, and shall absolutely govern me. I will rivet myself to her side, or vanish forever according to her pleasure.

I wish I had written a few words to her by Molly, assuring her of my devotion to her will: And yet, stands she in need of any new assurances. She has banished me. I am preparing to fly. She recalls me, and it is impossible to depart.

I must go to Miss Jessup's. I will take up the pen ('tis my sole amusement —) when I return —

* * *

I went to Miss Jessup's; her still sealed letter in my pocket: my mind confused: perplexed: sorrowful: wholly undetermined as to the manner of addressing her, or the use to be made of this important paper. I designedly prolonged my walk in hopes of forming some distinct conception of the purpose for which I was going, but only found myself each moment, sinking into new perplexities. Once I had taken the resolution of opening her letter and turned my steps towards the fields, that I might examine it at leisure, but there was something disgraceful in the violation of a seal, which scared me away from this scheme.

At length, reproaching myself for this indecision and leaving my conduct to be determined by circumstances I went directly to her house.

Miss Jessup was unwell; was unfit to see company: desired me to send up my name. I did not mention my name to the servant but replied I had urgent business, which a few minutes conversation would dispatch. I was admitted.

I found the lady, in a careless garb, reclining on a sofa, wan, pale and of a sickly aspect. On recognising me, she assumed a languidly smiling air, and received me with much civility. I took my seat near her. She began the talk.

345

I am very unwell; Got a terrible cold, coming from Dover: been laid up ever since; a teazing cough; no appetite: and worse spirits than I ever suffered: Glad you've come to relieve my solitude: not a single soul to see me; Mrs. Talbot never favours a body with a visit. Pray how's the dear girl? Hear her mother's come; heard, it seems, of your intimacy with Miss Secker: Determined to revenge your treason to her goddess! vows she shall, henceforth, have no more to say to you.

While waiting for admission, I formed hastily the resolution in what manner to conduct this interview. My deportment was so solemn, that the chatterer glancing at my face in the course of her introductory harangue, felt herself suddenly chilled and restrained.

Why what now? Colden. You are mighty grave methinks. Do you repent already of your new attachment. Has the atmosphere of Philadelphia, reinstated Jane in all her original rights?

Proceed, madam. When you are tired of raillery, I shall beg your attention to a subject in which your honour is deeply concerned: to a subject which allows not of a jest.

Nay, said she, in some little trepidation, if you have any thing to communicate, I am already prepared to receive it.

Indeed Miss Jessup, I *have* something to communicate. A man of more refinement and address than I can pretend to, would make this communication in a more circuitous and artful manner; and a man, less deeply interested in the establishment of truth, would act with more caution and forbearance. I have no excuse to plead: no forgiveness to ask, for what I am now going to disclose. I demand nothing from you, but your patient attention, while I lay before you the motives of my present visit.

You are no stranger to my attachment to Mrs. Talbot. That my passion is requited is likewise known to you. That her mother objects to her union with me, and raises her objections on certain improprieties in my character and conduct, I suppose, has already come to your knowledge.

You may naturally suppose that I am desirous of gaining

her favour, but it is not by the practice of fraud and iniquity, and therefore I have not begun with denying or concealing my faults. Very faulty: very criminal have I been: to deny that would be adding to the number of my transgressions, but I assure you, Miss Jessup, there have been limits to my follies: there is a boundary beyond which I have never gone. Mrs. Fielder imagines me much more criminal that I really am, and her opinion of me, which if limited, in the strictest manner by my merits, would amply justify her aversion to my marriage with her daughter, is, however, carried further than justice allows.

Mrs. Fielder has been somewhat deceived with regard to me. She thinks me capable of a guilt, of which, vicious as I am, I am yet incapable. Nay, she imagines I have actually committed a crime, of which I am wholly innocent.

What think you, madam (taking her hand, and eying her with stedfastness) she thinks me at once so artful and so wicked that I have made the wife unfaithful to the husband: I have persuaded Mrs. Talbot to forget what was due to herself, her fame, and to trample on her marriage vow.

This opinion is not a vague conjecture or suspicion. It is founded in what seems to be the most infallible of all evidence: the written confession of her daughter. The paper appears to be a letter which was addressed to the seducer soon after the guilty interview. This paper came indirectly into Mrs. Fielder's hands. To justify her charge, against us, she has shewn it to us. Now madam, the guilt imputed to us, is a stranger to our hearts. The crime which this letter confesses, never was committed, and the letter which contains the confession, never was written by Jane. It is a forgery.

Mrs. Fielder's misapprehension, so far as it relates to me, is of very little moment. I can hope for nothing from the removal of this error while so many instances of real misconduct continue to plead against me, but her daughter's happiness is materially affected by it, and for her sake I am anxious to vindicate her fame from this reproach.

No doubt, Miss Jessup, you have often asked me in your

347

heart since I began to speak, Why I have stated this transaction to you. What interest have you in our concerns?
What proofs of affection or esteem have you received from
us, that should make you zealous in our behalf? Or, what
relation has your interest in any respect to *our* weal or woe.
Why should you be called upon as a counsellor or umpire,
in the little family dissentions of Mrs. Talbot and
her mother?

And do indeed these questions rise in your heart, Miss
Jessup? Does not memory enable you to account for conduct which, to the distant and casual observer, to those who
know not what *you* know, would appear strange and absurd.

Recollect yourself. I will give you a moment to recall
the past. Think over all that has occurred since your original
acquaintance with Mrs. Talbot or her husband, and tell
me solemnly and truly whether you discern not the cause
of his mistake. Tell me whether you know not the unhappy
person, whom some delusive prospect of advantage, some
fatal passion has tempted to belie the innocent.

I am no reader of faces, my friend. I drew no inferences
from the confusion sufficiently visible in Miss Jessup. She
made no attempt to interrupt me, but quickly withdrew
her eye from my gaze; hung her head upon her bosom:
an hectic flush now and then shot across her cheek. But
these would have been produced by a similar address delivered with much solemnity and emphasis, in any one however innocent.

I believe there was no anger in my looks. Supposing her
to have been the author of this stratagem, it awakened in
me not resentment but pity. I paused: but she made no
answer to my expostulation. At length, I resumed with augmented earnestness, grasping her hand.

Tell me, I conjure you what you know. Be not deterred by
any self regard — but, indeed, how can your interest be affected by clearing up a mistake so fatal to the happiness of
one for whom you have always possessed a friendly regard.

Will your own integrity or reputation be brought into
question. In order to exculpate your friend, will it be

necessary to accuse yourself. Have you been guilty in withholding the discovery. Have you been guilty in contriving the fraud? Did your own hand pen the fatal letter which is now brought in evidence against my friend. Were you, yourself, guilty of counterfeiting hands, in order to drive the husband into a belief of his wife's perfidy?

A deadly paleness overspread her countenance at these words. I pitied her distress and confusion, and waited not for an answer which she was unable to give.

Yes, Miss Jessup, I well know your concern in this transaction. I mean not to distress you: I mean not to put you to unnecessary shame: I have no indignation or enmity against you. I come hither not to injure or disgrace you, but to confer on you a great and real benefit: to enable you to repair the evil which your infatuation has occasioned. I want to relieve your conscience from the sense of having wronged one that never wronged you.

Do not imagine that in all this, I am aiming at my own selfish advantage. This is not the mother's only objection to me, or only proof of that frailty she justly ascribes to me. To prove me innocent of this charge, will not reconcile her to her daughter's marriage. It will only remove one insuperable impediment to her reconciliation with her daughter.

Mrs. Fielder is, at this moment, not many steps from this spot. Permit me to attend you to her. I will introduce the subject. I will tell her that you come to clear her daughter from an unmerited charge, to confess that the unfinished letter was taken by you, and that, by additions in a feigned hand, you succeeded in making that an avowal of abandoned wickedness, which was originally innocent, at least, though, perhaps, indiscreet.

All this was uttered in a very rapid, but solemn accent. I gave her no time to recollect herself: no leisure for denial or evasion. I talked as if her agency was already ascertained and the feelings she betrayed at this abrupt and unaware attack, confirmed my suspicions.

After a long pause, and a struggle, as it were, for utterance, she faultered out — Mr. Colden — you see, I am very sick — this conduct has been very strange — nothing — I know nothing of what you have been saying. I wonder at your talking to me in this manner — you might as well address yourself, in this style, to one you never saw. What grounds can you have for suspecting me of any concern in this transaction?

Ah! madam! replied I, I see you have not strength of mind to confess a fault. Why will you compel me to produce the proof that you have taken an unauthorised part in Mrs. Talbot's concerns. Do you imagine that the love you bore her husband: even after his marriage: the efforts you used to gain his favour; his contemptuous rejection of your advances; — Can you imagine that these things are not known?

Why you should endeavour to defraud the wife of her husband's esteem, is a question which your own heart only can answer. Why you should watch Mrs. Talbot's conduct, and communicate your discoveries in anonymous letters and a hand disguised, to her mother, I pretend not to say. I came not to inveigh against the folly or malignity of such conduct. I come not even to censure it. I am not entitled to sit in judgment over you. My regard for mother and daughter makes me anxious to rectify an error fatal to their peace. There is but one way of doing this effectually, with the least injury to your character. I would not be driven to the necessity of employing *public* means to convince the mother that the charge is false, and that you were the calumniator: means that will humble and disgrace you infinitely more than a secret interview and frank confession from your own lips.

To deny and to prevaricate in a case like this is to be expected from one capable of acting as you have acted, but it will avail you nothing. It will merely compel me to have recourse to means less favourable to you. My reluctance to employ them arises from regard to you, for I repeat that I have no enmity for you, and propose, in reality, not only Mrs. Talbot's advantage, but your own.

I cannot paint the alarm and embarrassment which these

words occasioned. Tears afforded her some relief, but shame had deprived her of all utterance.

Let me conjure you, resumed I, to go with me this moment to Mrs. Fielder. In ten minutes all may be over. I will save you the pain of speaking. Only be present, while I explain the matter. Your silent acquiescence will be all that I shall demand.

Impossible! she exclaimed, in a kind of agony, I am already sick to death. I cannot move a step to such a purpose. I don't know Mrs. Fielder, and can never look her in the face.

A letter, then, replied I, will do, perhaps, as well. Here are pen and paper. Send to her, by me, a few lines. Defer all circumstance and comment, and merely inform her who the author of this forgery was. Here, continued I, producing the letter which Talbot had shewn to Mrs. Fielder, here is the letter in which my friend's hand is counterfeited, and she is made to confess a guilt to the very thought of which she has ever been a stranger. Inclose it in a paper, acknowledging the stratagem to be yours. It is done in a few words, and in half a minute.

My impetuosity overpowered all opposition and remonstrance. The paper was before her; the pen in her reluctant fingers; but that was all.

There may never be a future opportunity of repairing your misconduct. You are sick, you say, and indeed your countenance bespeaks some deeply rooted malady. You cannot be certain but that this is the last opportunity you may ever enjoy. When sunk upon the bed of death, and unable to articulate your sentiments, you may unavailingly regret the delay of this confession. You may die with the excruciating thought of having blasted the fame of an innocent woman, and of having sown eternal discord between mother and child.

I said a good deal more in this strain, by which she was deeply affected, but she demanded time to reflect. She would do nothing then; she would do all I wished by

351

tomorrow. She was too unwell to see any body, to hold a pen, at present.

All I want, said I, are but few words. You cannot be at a loss for these. I will hold: I will guide your hand: I will write what you dictate. Will you put your hand to something which I will write this moment in your presence, and subject to your revision.

I did not stay for her consent, but seizing the pen, put down hastily these words.

"Madam; the inclosed letter has led you into mistake. It has persuaded you that your daughter was unfaithful to her vows: but know, madam, that the concluding paragraph was written by me. I found the letter unfinished on Mrs. Talbot's desk. I took it thence without her knowledge, and added the concluding paragraph, in an hand as much resembling hers as possible, and conveyed it to the hands of her husband."

This hasty scribble I read to her, and urged her by every consideration my invention could suggest, to sign it. But no; she did not deny the truth of the statement it contained, but she must have time to recollect herself. Her head was rent to pieces by pain. She was in too much confusion to allow her to do any thing just now deliberately.

I now produced the letter I received from Hannah Secker, and said, I see madam you will compel me to preserve no measures with you. *There* is a letter which you wrote to Mrs. Fielder. Its contents were so important that you would not at first trust a servant with the delivery of it at the office. This however you were finally compelled to do. A fellow servant however stole it from your messenger, and instead of being delivered according to its address it has lately come into my hands.

No doubt (shewing the superscription, but not permitting her to see that the seal was unbroken) no doubt you recognize the hand; the hand of that anonymous detractor who had previously taken so much pains to convince the husband that his wife was an adultress and a prostitute.

Had I foreseen the effect which this disclosure would have

352

had, I should have hesitated. After a few convulsive breathings, she fainted. I was greatly alarmed and calling in a female servant, I staid till she revived. I thought it but mercy to leave her alone, and giving directions to the servant where I might be found, and requesting her to tell her mistress that I would call again early in the morning, I left the house.

I returned hither, and am once more shut up in my solitary chamber. I am in want of sleep, but my thoughts must be less tumultuous before that blessing can be hoped for. All is still in the house and in the city, and the "cloudy morning" of the watchman tells me that midnight is past. I have already written much, but must write on.

What my friend, can this letter contain? the belief that the contents are known and the true writer discovered, produced strange effects. I am afraid there was some duplicity in my conduct. But the concealment of the unbroken seal, was little more than chance. Had she enquired whether the letter was opened I should not have deceived her.

Perhaps however, I ascribe too much to this discovery. Miss Jessup was evidently very ill. The previous conversation had put her fortitude to a severe test. The tide was already so high, that the smallest increase sufficed to overwhelm her. Methinks I might have gained my purpose with less injury to her.

But what purpose have I gained? I have effected nothing, I am as far, perhaps farther than ever from vanquishing her reluctance. A night's reflection may fortify her pride, may furnish some expedient for eluding my request. Nay, she may refuse to see me, when I call on the morrow, and I cannot force myself into her presence.

If all this should happen, what will be left for me to do? *That* deserves some consideration. This letter of Miss Jessup's may possibly contain the remedy for many evils. What use shall I make of it? How shall I get at its contents?

There is but one way. I must carry it to Mrs. Fielder, and deliver it to her, to whom it is addressed. Carry it myself? Venture into her presence, by whom I am so much

353

detested? She will tremble with mingled indignation and terror, at the sight of me. I cannot hope a patient audience. And can I, in such circumstances, rely on my own equanimity? How can I endure the looks of one to whom I am a viper; a demon; who, not content with hating me for that which really merits hatred, imputes to me a thousand imaginary crimes.

Such is the lot of one that has forfeited his reputation. Having once been guilty, the returning path to rectitude is forever barred against him. His conduct will almost always be liable to a double construction; and who will suppose the influence of good motives, when experience has proved the influence, in former cases, of evil ones?

Jane Talbot is young, lovely, and the heiress, provided she retain the favor of her adopted mother, of a splendid fortune. I am poor, indolent, devoted, not to sensual, but to visionary and to costly luxuries. How shall such a man escape the imputation of sordid and selfish motives?

How shall he prove that he counterfeits no passion; employs no clandestine or illicit means to retain the affections of such a woman. Will his averments of disinterested motives be believed? Why should they be believed? How easily are assertions made, and how silly to credit declarations contradicted by the tenor of a man's whole conduct.

But can I truly aver that my motives are disinterested. Does not my character make a plentiful and independent provision, of more value to me, more necessary to my happiness than to that of most other men? Can I place my hand upon my heart, and affirm that her fortune has *no part* in the zeal with which I have cultivated Jane's affections. There are few tenants of this globe, to whom wealth is wholly undesirable, and very few whose actual poverty, whose indolent habits, and whose relish for expensive pleasure, make it *more* desirable than to me.

Mrs. Fielder is averse to her daughter's wishes. While this aversion endures, marriage, instead of enriching me, will merely reduce my wife to my own destitute condition. How are impartial observers, how is Mrs. Fielder to

354

construe my endeavors to subdue this aversion, and my declining marriage till this obstacle is overcome? Will they ascribe it merely to reluctance to bereave the object of my love, of that affluence and those comforts without which, in my opinion, *she* would not be happy. Yet this is true. My own experience has taught me in what degree a luxurious education endears to us the means of an easy and elegant subsistence. Shall I be deaf to this lesson? Shall I rather listen to the splendid visions of my friend, who thinks my love will sufficiently compensate her for every suffering: Who seems to hold these enjoyments in contempt, and describes an humble and industrious life, as teeming with happiness and dignity.

These are charming visions. My heart is frequently credulous, and is almost raised by her bewitching eloquence, to the belief that, by bereaving her of friends and property, I confer on her a benefit. I place her in a sphere where all the resources of her fortitude and ingenuity will be brought into use.

But this, with me, is only a momentary elevation. More sober views are sure to succeed. Yet why have I deliberately exhorted Jane to become mine? Because I trust to the tenderness of her mother. That tenderness will not allow her wholly to abandon her beloved child, who has hitherto had no rival, and is likely to have no successor in her love. The evil, she will think, cannot be repaired; but some of its consequences may be obviated or lightened. Intercession and submission shall not be wanting. Jane will never suffer her heart to be estranged from her mother. Reverence and gratitude will always maintain their place. And yet — confidence is sometimes shaken; doubts insinuate themselves. Is not Mrs. Fielder's temper ardent and inflexible? Will her anger be so easily appeased? In a contest like this, will she allow herself to be vanquished? And shall I, indeed, sever hearts so excellent? Shall I be the author of such exquisite and lasting misery to a woman like Mrs. Fielder; and shall I find that misery compensated by the happiness of her daughter? What pure and unmingled joy will the daughter taste, while conscious of having destroyed the peace, and perhaps hastened the end of one, who, with regard to her, has always deserved and always possessed a gratitude and veneration without bounds. And for whom is the tranquillity and affection of the mother to be sacrificed? For *me,* a poor unworthy wretch; deservedly despised by every strenuous and upright mind; a fickle, inconsiderate, frail mortal, whose perverse habits no magic can dissolve.

No. My whole heart implores Jane to forget and abandon *me;* to adhere to her mother; Since no earthly power and no length of time will change Mrs. Fielder's feelings with regard to me: since I shall never obtain, as I shall never deserve, her regard, and since her mother's happiness is, and ought to be dearer to Jane than her own personal and exclusive gratification. God grant that she may be able to perform and cheerfully perform her duty.

But how often my friend, have I harped on this string — Yet I must write, and I must put down my present thoughts, and these are the sentiments eternally present.

LETTER XLIV

TO HENRY COLDEN

Philadelphia, Dec. 1.

I SAID I would not write to you again: I would encourage, I would allow of no intercourse between us. This was my solemn resolution and my voluntary and no less solemn promise, yet I sit down to abjure this vow, to break this promise.

What a wretch am I! Feeble and selfish beyond all example among women; Why, why was I born, or why received I breath in a world and at a period, with whose inhabitants I can have no sympathy, whose notions of rectitude and decency, find no answering chord in my heart?

Never was creature so bereft of all dignity; all steadfastness. The slave of every impulse: blown about by the predominant gale: a scene of eternal fluctuation.

Yesterday my mother pleaded. Her tears dropped fast into my bosom, and I vowed to be all she wished: not merely to discard you from my presence, but to banish even your image from my thoughts. To act agreeably to her wishes was not sufficient. I must *feel* as she would have me feel. My actions must flow, not merely from a sense of duty, but from fervent inclination.

I promised every thing. My whole soul was in the promise. I retired to pen a last letter to you, and to say something to your father. My heart was firm: My hand steady. My mother read and approved — Dearest Jane! Now, indeed, are you my child. After this I will not doubt your constancy. Make me happy, by finding happiness in this resolution.

O, thought I, as I paced my chamber alone, what an

357

ample recompense for every self denial: for every sacrifice are thy smiles, my maternal friend. I will live smilingly for thy sake, while *thou* livest. I will live only to close thy eyes, and then, as every earthly good has been sacrificed at thy bidding, will I take the pillow that sustained thee when dead, and quickly breathe out upon it my last sigh.

My thoughts were all lightsome and serene. I had laid down methought, no life, no joy but my own. My mother's peace, and your peace for the safety of either of whom, I would cheerfully die, had been purchased by the same act.

How did I delight to view you restored to your father's house. I was still your friend, though invisible. I watched over you, in quality of guardian angel. I etherialized myself from all corporeal passions. I even set spiritual ministers to work to find out one worthy of succeeding me, in the sacred task of making you happy. I was determined to raise you to affluence, by employing, in a way unseen and unsuspected by you, those superfluities which a blind and erring destiny had heaped upon me.

And whither have these visions flown? Am I once more sunk to a level with my former self? Once I thought that religion was a substance with me: not a shadow, to flit, to mock and to vanish when its succour was most needed! yet now does my heart sink.

O comfort me, my friend! plead against yourself: against me. Be my mother's advocate. Fly away from those arms that clasp you, and escape from me, even if your flight be my death. Think not of me but of my mother, and secure to her the consolation of following my unwedded corse to the grave, by disclaiming, by hating, by forgetting the unfortunate

Jane.

LETTER XLV

TO HENRY COLDEN

Dec. 4.

A H! my friend! In what school have you acquired such fatal skill in tearing the heart of an offender? Why under an appearance of self reproach, do you convey the bitterest maledictions. Why with looks of idolatry, and accents of compassion, do you aim the deadliest contempts, and hurl the keenest censures against me.

"You acquit me of all shadow of blame." What! in proving me fickle; inconsistent; insensible to all your merit; ungrateful for your generosity; your love. How have I rewarded your reluctance to give me pain: your readiness to sacrifice every personal good for my sake? By reproaching you with dissimulation: By violating all those vows, which no legal ceremony could make more solemn or binding, and which the highest, earliest, and most sacred voice of heaven has ordained shall supersede all other bonds: By dooming you to feel "an anguish next to despair." Thus have I requited your unsullied truth; your unlimited devotion to me!

By what degrading standard do you measure my enjoyments! "In my mother's tenderness and gratitude: in the affluence and honour which her regard will secure to me" am I to find consolation for unfaithfulness to my engagements: for every evil that may befall you. *You* whom every hallowed obligation; every principle of human nature has placed *next* to myself: whom it has become, not a fickle inclination, but a sacred duty, to prefer to *all* others: whose

359

happiness ought to be my first and chief care, and from whose side I cannot sever myself without a guilt inexpiable.

Ah, cruel friend! You ascribe my resolution to a disinterested regard to your good. You wish me to find happiness in that persuasion. Yet you leave me not that phantom for a comforter. You convict me, in every line of your letter, of selfishness and folly. The only consideration that had irresistible weight with me, the restoration of your father's kindness, you prove to be a mere delusion, and destroy it without mercy!

Can you forgive me, Henry? Best of men! Will you be soothed by my penitence for one more rash and inconsiderate act? — But alas! My penitence is rapid and sincere, but where is the merit of compunction that affords no security against the repetition of the fault. And where is *my* safety?

Fly to me. Save me from my mother's irresistible expostulations. I cannot — *cannot* withstand her tears. Let me find in your arms, a refuge from them. Let me no more trust a resolution which is sure to fail. By making the tie between us such as even she will allow to be irrevocable: by depriving me of the power of compliance, only can I be safe.

Fly to me, therefore. Be at the front door at *ten* this night. My Molly will be my only companion. Be the necessary measures previously taken, that no delay or disappointment may occur. One half hour and the solemn rite may be performed. My absence will not be missed, as I return immediately. Then will there be an end to fluctuation for repentance cannot *undo*. Already in the sight of heaven, at the tribunal of my own conscience, am I *thy wife,* but somewhat more is requisite to make the compact universally acknowledged. This is *now* my resolve. I shall keep it secret from the rest of the world. Nothing but the compulsion of persuasion, can make me waver, and concealment will save me from that, and *to-morrow* remonstrance and entreaty will avail nothing.

My girl has told me of her interview with you: and where

360

you are to be found. The dawn is not far distant, and at sun rise she carries you this. I shall expect an immediate, and (need I add, when I recollect the invariable counsel you have given me?) a compliant answer.

And shall I? — Let me, while the sun lingers, still pour out my soul on this paper — Let me indulge a *pleasing, dreadful thought* — Shall I, ere circling time bring back *this* hour, become thy —

And shall my heart, after its dreadful langours, its excruciating agonies, know once more, a rapturous emotion? So lately sunk into despondency: so lately pondering on obstacles that rose before me like Alps, and menaced eternal opposition to my darling projects: so lately the prey of the deepest anguish, what spell diffuses through my frame this ravishing tranquillity?

Tranquillity, said I? *That* my throbbing heart gainsays. You cannot see me just now, but the palpitating heart infects my fingers and the unsteady pen will speak to you eloquently.

I wonder how far sympathy possesses you. No doubt — let me see — *ten minutes after four* — No doubt you are sound asleep. Care has fled away to some other head. Those invisible communicants; those aerial heralds whose existence, benignity and seasonable succour are parts, thou knowest, of *my* creed, are busy in the weaving of some beatific dream. At their bidding, the world of thy fancy is circumscribed by four white walls, a Turkey-carpeted floor, and a stuckoed cieling. Didst ever see such before? was't ever, in thy wakeful season, in the same apartment? never. And what is more, and which I desire thee to note well, thou art not hereafter to enter it except in dreams.

A poor taper burns upon the toilet: just bright enough to give the cognizance of something in woman's shape, and in negligent attire scribbling near it. Thou needst not tap her on the shoulder; she need not look up and smile a welcome to the friendly vision. She knows that thou art *here*, for is not thy hand already in her's, and is not thy cheek already wet with her tears? for thy poor girl's eyes are as sure to overflow with joy, as with sorrow.

And will it be always thus, my dear friend? will thy love screen me forever from remorse? will my mother's reproaches never intrude amidst the raptures of fondness and poison my tranquillity?

What will she say when she discovers the truth? my conscience will not allow me to dissemble. It will not disavow the name, or withhold the duties of a wife. Too well do I conceive what she will say; *how* she will act.

I need not apprehend expulsion from her house. Exile will be a voluntary act. — You shall eat, drink, lodge, and dress as well as ever. I will not sever husband from wife, and I find no pleasure in seeing those whom I most hate, perishing with want. I threatened to abandon you, merely because I would employ *every* means of preventing your destruction, but my revenge is not so sordid as to multiply unnecessary evils on your head. I shall take from you nothing but my esteem: my affection: my society. I shall never see you but with agony: I shall never think of you without pain. I part with you forever, and prepare myself for that grave which your folly and ingratitude have dug for me.

You have said, Jane, that having lost my favour, you will never live upon my bounty. That will be an act of needless and perverse cruelty in you. It will be wantonly adding to that weight with which you have already sunk me to the grave. Besides, I will not leave you an option. While I live, my watchful care shall screen you from penury in spite of yourself. When I die, my testament shall make you my sole successor. What I have shall be yours, at least, while *you* live.

I have deeply regretted the folly of threatening you with loss of property. I should have known you better than to think that a romantic head like yours would find any thing formidable in such deprivations. If other considerations were feeble, this would be chimerical.

Fare you well, Jane, and when you become a mother, may your tenderness never be requited by the folly and

362

ingratitude which it has been my lot to meet with, in the child of my affections.

Something like this has my mother already said to me, in the course of an affecting conversation, in which I ventured to plead for you. And have I then resolved to trample on such goodness.

Whither, my friend, shall I fly from a scene like this? into thy arms? and shall I find comfort *there?* can I endure life, with the burthen of remorse, which generosity like this will lay upon me?

But I tell you, Henry, I am resolved. I have nothing but evil to chuse. There is but one calamity greater than my mother's anger. I cannot mangle my own vitals. I cannot put an impious and violent end to my own life. Will it be mercy to make *her* witness my death, and can I live without you? if I must be an ingrate, be her and not you the victim. If I must requite benevolence with malice, and tenderness with hatred, be it *her* benevolence and tenderness, and not *yours* that are thus requited.

Once more, then, note well. The hour of *ten;* the station near the door: a duly qualified officiator previously engaged; — and my destiny in this life fixed beyond the power of recall — the bearer of this will bring back your answer. Farewell; *remember.*

J. Talbot.

LETTER XLVI

TO JAMES MONTFORD
December 9.

ONCE more, after a night of painful musing or troubled repose, I am at the pen. I am plunged into greater difficulties and embarrassments than ever.

It was scarcely daylight, when a slumber, into which I had just fallen, was interrupted by a servant of the Inn. A girl was below, who wanted to see me. The description quickly proved it to be Molly. I rose and directed her to be admitted.

She brought two letters from her mistress, and was told to wait for an answer. Jane, traversed her room, half distracted and sleepless during most of the night. Towards morning she sat down to her desk, and finished a letter, which, together with one written a couple of days before, were dispatched to me.

My heart throbbed — I was going to say with transport; but I am at a loss to say whether anguish or delight was uppermost, on reading these letters. She recalls every promise of eternal separation: she consents to immediate marriage as the only wise expedient: proposes ten o'clock *this night,* to join our hands; will conceal her purpose from her mother, and resigns to me the providing of suitable means.

I was overwhelmed with surprise, and — shall I not say? — delight at this unexpected concession. An immediate and *consenting* answer was required. I hurried to give this answer, but my tumultuous feelings would not let me write coherently. I was obliged to lay down the pen, and take a turn across the room, to calm my tremors. This gave me time to reflect.

What, thought I, am I going to do? To take advantage of a momentary impulse in my favor. To violate my promises to Mrs. Fielder — my letter to her may be construed into promises not to seek another interview with Jane, and to leave the country forever. And shall I betray this impetuous woman into an irrevocable act, which her whole future life may be unavailingly consumed in repenting. Some delay, some deliberation cannot be injurious.

And yet this has always been my advice. Shall I reject the hand that is now offered me? How will she regard these new-born scruples, this drawing back, when the door spontaneously opens and solicits my entrance?

Is it in my power to make Jane Talbot *mine? my wife?* And shall I hesitate? Ah! would to Heaven it were a destiny as fortunate for her as for me; that no tears, no repinings, no compunctions would follow. Should I not curse the hour of our union when I heard her sighs, and instead of affording consolation under the distress produced by her mother's displeasure, should I not need that consolation as much as she?

These reflections had no other effect than to make me irresolute. I could not return my assent to her scheme. I could not reject so bewitching an offer. This offer was the child of a passionate, a desperate moment. Whither, indeed, should she fly for refuge from a scene like that which she describes?

Molly urged me to come to some determination, as her mistress would impatiently wait her return. Finding it indispensible to say something, I at length wrote: —

"I have detected the author of the forgery which has given us so much disquiet. I propose to visit your mother this morning, when I shall claim admission to you. In that interview may our future destiny be discussed and settled. — Meanwhile, still regard me as ever ready to purchase your true happiness by every sacrifice."

With this billet Molly hastened away. What cold,

repulsive terms were these! My conscience smote me as she shut the door. But what could I do?

I had but half determined to seek an interview with Mrs. Fielder. What purpose would it answer while the truth, respecting the counterfeit letter, still remained imperfectly discovered? And why should I seek an interview with Jane? Would her mother permit it; and should I employ my influence to win her from her mother's side or rivet her more closely to it?

What, my friend, shall I do? You are too far off to answer me, and you leave me to my own destiny. You hear not, and will not seasonably hear what I say. To day will surely settle all difficulties, one way or another. This night, if I will, I may be the husband of this angel, or I may raise obstacles insuperable between us. Our interests and persons may be united forever, or we may start out into separate paths, and never meet again.

Another messenger! with a letter for me! Miss Jessup's servant — it is, perhaps — but let me read it.

LETTER XLVII

TO M. COLDEN

December 8.

Sir,

INCLOSED is a letter which you may, if you think proper, deliver to Mrs. Fielder. I am very ill. Don't attempt to see me again. I cannot be seen. Let the inclosed satisfy you. It is enough. Never should I have said so much, if I thought I were long for this world.

Let me not have a useless enemy in you. I hope the fatal effects of my rashness have not gone further than Mrs. Talbot's family. Let the mischief be repaired, as far as it can be; but do not injure me unnecessarily. I hope I am understood.

Let me know what use you have made of the letter you shewed me, and, I beseech you, return it to me by the bearer.

M. Jessup.

LETTER XLVIII

TO MRS. FIELDER

Madam,

December 8.

THIS comes from a very unfortunate and culpable hand. A hand that hardly knows how to sign its own condemnation, and which sickness no less than irresolution, almost deprives of the power to hold the pen.

Yet I call Heaven to witness, that I expected not the evil from my infatuation which, it seems, has followed it. I meant to influence none but Mr. Talbot's belief. I had the misfortune to see and to love him long before his engagement with your daughter. I overstepped the limits of my sex, and met with no return to my generous offers, and my weak entreaties, but sternness and contempt.

You, Madam, are perhaps raised above the weakness of a heart like mine. You will not comprehend how an unrequited passion can ever give place to rage and revenge, and how the merits of the object preferred to me, should only embitter that revenge.

Jane Talbot never loved the man, whom I would have made happy. Her ingenuous temper easily disclosed her indifference, and she married not to please herself, but to please others. Her husband's infatuation in marrying on such terms, could be exceeded by nothing but his folly in refusing one who would have lived for no other end than to please him.

I observed the progress of the intimacy between Mr. Colden and her, in Talbot's absence, and can you not conceive madam that my heart was disposed to exult in every event that verified my own predictions, and would convince Talbot of the folly of his choice? Hence I was a jealous observer. The worst construction was put upon your daughter's conduct. That open, impetuous temper of hers, confident of innocence, and fearless of ungenerous or malignant constructions, easily put her into my power. Unrequited love made me *her* enemy as well as that of her husband, and I even saw, in her unguarded deportment and in the reputed licentiousness of Mr. Colden's principles, some reason, some probability in my surmises.

Several anonymous letters were written to you. I thank heaven that I was seldom guilty of direct falshoods in these letters. I told you little more than what a jealous eye and a prying disposition easily discovered; and I never saw any thing in their intercourse that argued more than a temper thoughtless and indiscreet. To distinguish minutely between truths and exaggerations in the letters which I sent you, would be a painful, and I trust, a needless task, since I now solemnly declare that, on an impartial review of all that I ever witnessed in the conduct of your daughter, I remember nothing that can justify the imputation of guilt. I believe her conduct to Colden was not always limited by a due regard to appearances; that she trusted her fame too much to her consciousness of innocence, and set too lightly by the malignity of those who would be glad to find her in fault, and the ignorance of others who naturally judged of her by themselves. And this, I now solemnly take Heaven to witness, is the only charge that can truly be brought against her.

There is still another confession to make — If suffering and penitence can atone for any offence, surely my offence has been atoned for! But it still remains that I should, as far as my power goes, repair the mischief.

It is no adequate apology, I well know, that the consequences of my crime were more extensive and durable than I expected; but is it not justice to myself to say, that this confession would have been made earlier, if I had earlier known the extent of the evil? I never suspected but that the belief of his wife's infidelity, was buried with Talbot.

Alas! wicked and malignant as I was, I meant not to persuade the mother of her child's profligacy. Why should I have aimed at this? I had no reason to disesteem or hate you. I was always impressed with reverence for your character. In the letters sent directly to you, I aimed at nothing but to procure your interference, and make maternal authority declare itself against that intercourse which was essential to your daughter's happiness. It was not you, but her, that I wished to vex and distress.

I called at Mrs. Talbot's at a time when visitants are least expected. Nobody saw me enter. Her parlour was deserted; her writing-desk was open; an unfinished letter caught my eye. A sentiment half inquisitive and half mischievous, made me snatch it up, and withdraw as abruptly as I entered.

On reading this billet, it was easy to guess for whom it was designed. It was frank and affectionate; consistent with her conjugal duty, but not such as a very circumspect and wary temper would have allowed itself to write.

How shall I describe the suggestions that led me to make a most nefarious use of this paper? Circumstances most unhappily concurred to make my artifice easy and plausible. I discovered that Colden had spent most of the preceding night with your daughter. It is true a most heavy storm had raged during the evening, and the moment it remitted, which was not till three o'clock, he was seen to come out. His detention, therefore, candor would ascribe to the storm; but this letter, with such a conclusion as was too easily made, might fix a construction on it that no time could remove, and innocence could never confute.

I had not resolved in what way I should employ this letter, as I had eked it out, before Mr. Talbot's return. When that event took place, my old infatuation revived. I again sought his company, and the indifference, and even contempt with which I was treated, filled me anew with resentment. To persuade him of his wife's guilt was, I thought, an effectual way of destroying whatever remained of matrimonial happiness: and the means were fully in my power.

Here I was again favored by accident. Fortune seemed determined to accomplish my ruin. My own ingenuity in vain attempted to fall on a *safe* mode of putting this letter in Talbot's way, and this had never been done if chance had not surprizingly befriended my purpose.

One evening I dropped familiarly in upon your daughter. Nobody was there but Mr. Talbot and she. She was writing at her desk as usual, for she seemed never at ease but with a pen in her fingers; and Mr. Talbot seemed thoughtful and uneasy. At my entrance the desk was hastily closed and locked. But first she took out some papers, and mentioning her design of going up stairs to put them away, she tripped to the door. Looking back, however, she perceived she had dropped one. This she took up, in some hurry, and withdrew.

Instead of conversing with me, Talbot walked about the room in a peevish and gloomy humor. A thought just then rushed into my mind. While Talbot had his back towards me, and was at a distance, I dropped the *counterfeit,* at the spot where Jane had just before dropped her paper, and with little ceremony took my leave. Jane had excused her absence to me, and promised to return within *five minutes.* It was not possible, I thought, that Talbot's eye, as he walked backward and forward during that interval, could miss the paper, which would not fail to appear as if dropped by his wife.

My timidity and conscious guilt hindered me from attempting to discover by any direct means, the effects of my artifice. I was mortified extremely in finding no remarkable difference in their deportment to each other. Sometimes I feared I had betrayed myself; but no alteration ever afterwards appeared in their behaviour to me.

I know how little I deserve to be forgiven. Nothing can palliate the baseness of this action. I acknowledge it with the deepest remorse, and nothing, especially since the death of Mr. Talbot, has lessened my grief; but the hope that some unknown cause prevented the full effect of this forgery on his peace, and that the secret, carefully locked up in his own breast, expired with him. All my enmities and restless jealousy found their repose in the same grave.

You have come to the knowledge of this letter, and I now find that the fraud was attended with even more success than I wished it to have. Let me now, though late, put an end to the illusion, and again assure you, Madam, that the concluding paragraphs were *written by me,* and that those parts of it which truly belong to your daughter, are perfectly innocent.

If it were possible for you to forgive my misconduct — and to suffer this confession to go no farther than the evil has gone — you will confer as great a comfort as can now be conferred on the unhappy

H. Jessup.

LETTER XLIX

TO JAMES MONTFORD
Philadelphia, Dec. 9.

I WILL imagine, my friend, that you have read the letter* which I have hastily transcribed. I will not stop to tell you my reflections upon it, but shall hasten with this letter to Mrs. Fielder. I might send it; but I have grown desperate. A final effort must be made for my own happiness and that of Jane. From their own lips will I know my destiny. I have conversed too long at a distance, with this austere lady. I will mark with my own eyes, the effect of this discovery. Perhaps the moment may prove a yielding one. Finding me innocent in one respect, in which her persuasion of my guilt was most strong; may she not remit or soften her sentence on inferior faults? And what may be the influence of Jane's deportment, when she touches my hand in a last adieu?

I have complied with Miss Jessup's wish in one particular. I have sent her the letter which I got from Hannah, unopened; unread; accompanied with a few words, to this effect —

"If you ever injured Mr. Talbot, your motives for doing so, entitle you to nothing but compassion, while your present conduct lays claim, not only to forgiveness, but to gratitude. The letter you entrust to me, shall be applied to no purpose but that which you proposed by writing it. Inclosed, is the paper you request, the seal unbroken and

*The preceding one.

373

its contents unread. In this, as in all cases, I have no stronger wish than to act as

Your True Friend.''

And now my friend, lay I down the pen, for a few hours; Hours the most important, perhaps, in my eventful life. Surely this interview with Mrs. Fielder will decide my destiny. After it, I shall have nothing to hope.

I prepare for it with awe and trembling. The more nearly it approaches, the more my heart faulters. I summon up in vain a tranquil and stedfast spirit: but perhaps, a walk in the clear air will be more conducive to this end, than a day's ruminations in my chamber.

I will take a walk —

* * *

And am I then — but I will not anticipate. Let me lead you to the present state of things without confusion.

With what different emotions did I use to approach this house! It still contains, thought I, as my wavering steps brought me in sight of it, all that I love, but I enter not unceremoniously now. I find her not on the accustomed sofa, eager to welcome my coming with smiling affability and arms outstretched. No longer is it *home* to me, nor she, assiduous to please: familiarly tender and anxiously fond: already assuming the conjugal privilege of studying my domestic ease.

I knocked, somewhat timorously at the door: a ceremony which I had long been in the habit of omitting — but times are changed. I was afraid the melancholy which was fast overshadowing me, would still more unfit me for what was coming, but, instead of dispelling it, this very apprehension deepened my gloom.

Molly came to the door. She silently led me into a parlour. The poor girl was in tears. My questions as to the cause of her distress drew from her a very indistinct and sobbing confession that Mrs. Fielder had been made uneasy by Molly's going out so early in the morning; Had taken her daughter to task; and by employing entreaties and remonstrances in turn, had drawn from her the contents of her letter to me and of my answer.

A strange affecting scene had followed; indignation and grief on the mother's part; obstinacy; irresolution; sorrowful, reluctant, penitence and acquiescence on the side of the daughter: a determination, tacitly concurred in by Jane, of leaving the city immediately. Orders were already issued for that purpose.

Is Mrs. Fielder at home?

Yes.

Tell her, a gentleman would see her.

She will ask, perhaps — Shall I tell her, *who?*

No — Yes: Tell her, *I* wish to see her.

The poor girl looked very mournfully — She has seen your answer which talks of your intention to visit her. She vows she will not see you, if you come.

Go, then to Jane, and tell her I would see her for five minutes — Tell her openly; before her mother.

This message, as I expected, brought down Mrs. Fielder alone. I never saw this lady before. There was a struggle in her countenance between anger and patience: an awful and severe solemnity: a slight and tacit notice of me as she entered. We both took chairs without speaking. After a moment's pause —

Mr. Colden, I presume.

Yes, madam.

You wish to see my daughter?

I was anxious, madam, to see you. My business here chiefly lies with *you*, not *her.*

With me, sir? And pray, what have you to propose to me.

I have nothing to solicit madam, but your patient attention. (I saw the rising vehemence could scarcely be restrained.) I dare not hope for your favourable ear: All I ask is an audience from you of a few minutes.

This preface, sir, (her motions less and less controulable) is needless. I have very few minutes to spare at present. This roof is hateful to me while you are under it. Say what you will, sir, and briefly as possible.

375

No, madam. *Thus* received, I have not fortitude enough to say what I came to say. I merely intreat you to peruse this letter.

'Tis well Sir, (taking it, with some reluctance, and after eying the direction, putting it aside). And this is all your business?

Let me intreat you, madam, to read it in my presence. Its contents nearly concern your happiness, and will not leave mine unaffected.

She did not seem, at first, disposed to compliance, but at length opened and read. What noble features has this lady! I watched them as she read, with great solicitude, but discovered in them nothing that could cherish my hope. All was stern and inflexible. No wonder at the ascendency this spirit possesses over the tender and flexible Jane!

She read with visible eagerness. The varying emotion played with augmented rapidity over her face. Its expression became less severe, and some degree of softness, I thought mixed itself with those glances which reflexion sometimes diverted from the letter. These tokens somewhat revived my languishing courage.

After having gone through it she returned: read again and pondered over particular passages. At length, after some pause, she spoke, but her indignant eye scarcely condescended to point the address to me.

As a mother and a woman I cannot but rejoice at this discovery. To find my daughter *less* guilty, than appearances led me to believe, cannot but console me under the conviction of her numerous errors. Would to heaven she would stop here, in her career of folly and imprudence.

I cannot but regard *you*, sir, as the author of much misery. Still it is in your power to act, as this deluded woman, Miss Jessup, has acted. You may disist from any future persecution. Your letter to me gave me no reason to expect the honor of this visit, and contained something like a promise to shun any farther intercourse with Mrs. Talbot.

I hope, madam, the contents of *this* letter will justify me, in bringing it to you. —

Perhaps it has, but that commission is performed. That,

I hope, is all you proposed by coming hither, and, you will pardon me, if I plead an engagement for not detaining you longer in this house.

I had no apology for prolonging my stay, yet I was irresolute. She seemed impatient at my lingering: again urged her engagements: I rose: took my hat: moved a few steps towards the door: hesitated.

At length, I stammered out — Since it is the last — the last interview — if I were allowed — but one moment.

No, no, no — what but needless torment to herself and to you can follow? What do you expect from an interview?

I would see, for a moment, the face of one, whom — whatever be *my* faults, and whatever be *hers*, I *love.*

Yes. You would profit, no doubt, by your power over this infatuated girl. I know what a rash proposal she has made you, and you seek her presence to insure her adherence to it.

Her vehemence tended more to bereave me of courage than of temper, but I could not forbear (mildly however) reminding her that if I had sought to take advantage of her daughter's offer, the easiest and most obvious method was different from that which I had taken.

True, (said she, her eyes flashing fire,) a secret marriage would have given you the *destitute* and *portionless* girl, but your views are far more solid and substantial. You know your power over her: and aim at extorting from compassion for my child what — but why do I exchange a word with you? Mrs. Talbot knows not that you are here. She has just given me the strongest proof of compunction for *every* past folly and especially the *last.* She has bound herself to go along with me. If your professions of regard for her be sincere, you will not increase her difficulties. I command you, I implore you to leave the house.

I should not have resisted these entreaties on my own account. Yet to desert her — to be thought by her to have coldly and inhumanly rejected her offers!

In your presence, madam — I ask not privacy — let her own lips confirm the sentence — be renunciation her own act — for the sake of her peace of mind —

God give me patience, said the exasperated lady. How

God give me patience, said the exasperated lady. How securely do you build on her infatuation. But you shall not see her. If she consents to see you, I never will forgive her. If she once more relapses, she is undone. She shall write her mind to you — let that serve — I will permit her — I will urge her to write to you — let that serve.

I went to this house with a confused perception that this visit would terminate my suspense. One more interview with Jane, thought I, and no more fluctuations or uncertainty. Yet I was now far as ever from certainty. Expostulation was vain. She would not hear me. All my courage, even my words were overwhelmed by her vehemence.

After much hesitation, and several efforts to gain even an hearing to my pleas, I yielded to the tide. With a drooping heart, I consented to withdraw, with my dearest hope unaccomplished.

My steps involuntarily brought me back to my lodgings. Here am I again at my pen. Never were my spirits lower, my prospects more obscure, my hopes nearer to extinction.

I am afraid to allow you too near a view of my heart — at this moment of despondency. My present feelings are new even to myself. They terrify me. I must not trust myself longer alone. I must shake off or try to shake off this excruciating — this direful melancholy. Heavy: heavy is my soul: comfortless and friendless my condition. Nothing is sweet but the prospect of oblivion.

But, again I say, these thoughts must not lead me. Dreadful and downward is the course to which they point. I must relinquish the pen. I must sally forth into the fields. Naked and bleak is the face of nature at this inclement season — but what of that? dark and desolate will ever be *my* world — but I will not write another word —

* * *

So, my friend, I have returned from my walk with a mind more a stranger to tranquillity than when I sallied forth. On my table lay the letter, which, ere I seal this, I will enclose to you. Read it here.

LETTER L

TO MR. COLDEN

December 11.

HEREAFTER I shall be astonished at nothing but that credulity which could give even momentary credit to your assertions.

Most fortunately, my belief lasted only till you left the house. Then my scruples, which slept for a moment, revived, and I determined to clear up my doubts by immediately calling on Miss Jessup.

If any thing can exceed your depravity, Sir, it is your folly. But I will not debase myself — my indignation at being made the subject, and, for some minutes, the dupe of so gross and so profligate an artifice, carries me beyond all bounds. What Sir! — But I will restrain myself.

I would not leave the city without apprising you of this detection of your schemes. If Miss Jessup were wise she would seek a just revenge for so atrocious a slander.

I need not tell you that I have seen her; laid the letter before her which you delivered to me; nor do I need to tell *you* what her anger and amazement were on finding her name thus abused.

I pity you, Sir; I grieve for you; you have talents of a certain kind, but your habits, wretchedly and flagitiously perverse, have made you act on most occasions like an idiot. Their iniquity was not sufficient to deter you from impostures which — but I scorn to chide you.

My daughter is a monument of the success of your schemes. But their success shall never be complete. While

379

I live she shall never join her interests with yours. That is a vow which, I thank God I am able to accomplish; *and shall.*

H. Fielder.

LETTER LI

TO JAMES MONTFORD
December 13.

IS not this strange, my friend! Miss Jessup, it seems, has denied her own letter. Surely there was no mistake — no mystery. Let me look again at the words in the cover.

Let me awake! Let me disabuse my senses! Yes. It is plain. Miss Jessup repented her of her confession. Something in that unopened letter — Believing the contents of *that* known, there were inducements to sincerity which the recovery of that letter, and the finding it unopened, perhaps annihilated. Pride resumed its power. Before so partial a judge as Mrs. Fielder, and concerning a wretch so worthy of discredit as I, how easy, how obvious to deny — and to impute to me the imposture charged on herself?

Well, and what is now to be done? I will once more return to Miss Jessup. I will force myself into her presence, and then — but I have not a moment to lose —

* * *

And this was the night, this was the hour that was to see my Jane's hand wedded to mine. That event providence, or fate, or fortune stepped in to forbid. And must it then pass away like any vulgar hour?

It deserves to be signalized, to be made memorable. What forbids but sordid, despicable cowardice! Not virtue; not the love of universal happiness; not piety; not sense of duty to my God or my fellow creatures. These sentiments, alas! burn feebly or not at all within my bosom.

It is not hope that restrains my hand. For what is my

hope? Independence, dignity, a life of activity and usefulness, are not within my reach — And why not? What
obstacles arise in the way.

Have I not youth, health, knowledge, talents? Twenty
professional roads are open before me, and solicit me to
enter them — but no. I shall never enter any of them. Be
all earthly powers combined to force me into the right path
— the path of duty, honor and interest — they strive in vain.

And whence this incurable folly? This rooted incapacity
of acting as every motive, generous and selfish, combine
to recommend? Constitution; habit; insanity; the dominion
of some evil spirit, who insinuates his baneful power between the *will* and the *act*.

And this more congenial good; this feminine excellence;
this secondary and more valuable self; this woman who has
appropriated to herself every desire, every emotion of my
soul — what hope remains with regard to her? Shall I live
for her sake?

No. Her happiness requires me to be blotted out of existence. Let me unfold myself *to* myself; Let me ask my
soul — Canst thou wish to be rejected, renounced, and
forgotten by Jane? Does it please thee that her happiness
should be placed upon a basis absolutely independant of
thy lot. Canst thou, with a true and fervent zeal, resign
her to her mother.

I can. I do.

* * *

I wish I had words, my friend — yet why do I wish for
them. Why sit I here, endeavouring to give form, substance
and duration to images, to which it is guilty and opprobrious to allow momentary place in my mind? Why do I thus
lay up for the few that love me, causes of affliction?

Yet perhaps I accuse myself too soon. The persuasion
that I have one friend, is sweet. I fancy myself talking to
one who is interested in my happiness, but this shall satisfy
me. If fate impell me to any rash and irretrievable act, I
will take care that no legacy of sorrow shall be left to my

survivors. My fate shall be buried in oblivion. No busy curiosity, no affectionate zeal shall trace the way that I have gone. No mourning footsteps shall haunt my grave.

I am, indeed, my friend — never, never before, spiritless, and even hopeless as I have sometimes been, have my thoughts been thus gloomy. Never felt I so enamoured of that which seems to be the cure-all.

Often have I wished to slide obscurely and quietly into the grave; but this wish, while it saddened my bosom, never raised my hand against my life. It made me willingly expose my safety to the blasts of pestilence: it made me court disease, but it never set my imagination in search after more certain and speedy means —

Yet I am wonderfully calm. I can still reason on the folly of despair. I know that a few days; perhaps, a few hours, will bring me some degree of comfort and courage; will make life with all its disappointments and vexations, endurable at least.

Would to heaven, I were not quite alone. Left thus to my greatest enemy, myself, I feel that I am capable of deeds which I fear to name.

A few minutes ago I was anxious to find Miss Jessup: to gain another interview with Mrs. Fielder. Both the one and the other have left the city. Jane's dwelling is deserted. Shortly after I left it, they set out upon their journey, and Miss Jessup, no doubt, to avoid another interview with me, has precipitately withdrawn into the country.

I shall not pursue their steps. Let things take their course. No doubt, a lasting and effectual remorse will sometime or other, reach the heart of Miss Jessup, and this fatal error will be rectified. I need not live, I need not exert myself, to hasten the discovery. I can do nothing.

LETTER LII

TO MRS. FIELDER
Philadelphia Dec. 16.

IT is not improbable that as soon as you recognize the hand that wrote this letter, you will throw it unread into the fire, yet it comes not to sooth resentment or to supplicate for mercy. It seeks not a favourable audience. It wishes not, because the wish would be chimerical, to have its assertions believed. It expects not even to be read. All I hope is that, though neglected, despised and discredited for the present, it may not be precipitately destroyed or utterly forgotten. The time will come, when it will be read with a different spirit.

You inform me that Miss Jessup has denied her letter, and imputes to me the wickedness of forging her name to a false confession. You are justly astonished at the iniquity and folly of what you deem my artifice. This astonishment, when you look back upon my past misconduct, is turned from me to yourself: from *my* folly to your own credulity, that was, for a moment, made the dupe of my contrivances.

I can say nothing that *will* or that *ought* — that is my peculiar misery; — that ought, considering the measure of my real guilt, to screen me from this charge. There is but one event that can shake your opinion. An event that is barely possible; that may not happen, if it happen at all, till the lapse of years; and from which, even if I were alive, I could not hope to derive advantage. Miss Jessup's conscience may awaken time enough to enable her to undeceive you, and to repent of her *second,* as well as her *first* fraud.

If that event ever takes place, perhaps this letter may

384

still exist to bear testimony to my rectitude. Thrown aside and long forgotten, or never read, chance may put it in your way, once more. Time, that soother of resentment as well as lessener of love, and the perseverance of your daughter in the way you prescribe, may soften your asperities even towards me. A generous heart like yours, will feel an emotion of joy that I have not been quite as guilty as you had reason to believe.

Give me leave, Madam, to anticipate that moment. The number of my consolations are few. Your enmity I rank among my chief misfortunes, and the more so because I deserve *much,* though not *all* your enmity. The persuasion that the time will come when you will acquit me of this charge, is, even now, a comforter. This is more desirable to me since it will relieve your daughter from *one* among the many evils in which she has been involved by the vices and infirmities of

H. Colden.

LETTER LIII

TO JAMES MONTFORD
Philadelphia, Dec. 17.

I SOUGHT relief a second time, to my drooping heart by a walk in the fields. Returning, I met Harriet Thomson in the street. The meeting was somewhat unexpected. Since we parted at Baltimore, I imagined she had returned to her old habitation in Jersey. I knew she was pretty much a stranger in this city. Night had already come on, and she was alone. She greeted me with visible satisfaction; and though I was very little fit for society, especially of those who loved me not, I thought common civility required me to attend her home.

I never saw this woman till I met her lately at her brother's bed-side. Her opinions of me were all derived from unfavorable sources, and I knew from good authority, that she regarded me as a dangerous and hateful character. I had even, accidentally, heard her opinion of the affair between Jane and me. Jane was severely censured for credulity and indiscretion, but some excuse was allowed to her on the score of the greater guilt that was placed to my account.

Her behaviour when we first met, was somewhat conformable to these impressions. A good deal of coldness and reserve in her deportment, which I was sometimes sorry for, as she seems an estimable creature; meek, affectionate, tender, passionately loving her brother; convinced from the hour of her first arrival, that his disease was an hopeless one, yet exerting a surprising command over her feelings, and performing every office of a nurse with skill and firmness.

386

Insensibly the distance between us grew less. A participation in the same calamity, and the counsel and aid which her situation demanded, forced her to lay aside some of her reserve. Still, however, it seemed but a submission to necessity; and all advances were made with an ill grace.

She was often present when her brother turned the discourse upon religious subjects. I have long since abjured the vanity of disputation. There is no road to truth, but by meditation; severe, intense, candid and dispassionate. — What others say on doubtful subjects, I shall henceforth lay up as materials for meditation.

I listened to my dying friend's arguments and admonitions, I think I may venture to say, with a suitable spirit. The arrogant or disputatious passion could not possibly find place in a scene like this. Even if I thought him in the wrong, what but brutal depravity could lead me to endeavor to shake his belief at a time when sickness had made his judgment infirm, and when his opinion supplied his sinking heart with confidence and joy?

But, in truth, I was far from thinking him in the wrong. At any time I should have allowed infinite plausibility and subtilty to his reasonings, and at this time, I confessed them to be weighty. Whether they were *most* weighty in the scale, could be only known by a more ample and deliberate view and comparison, than it was possible, with the spectacle of a dying friend before me, and with so many solicitudes and suspenses about me respecting Jane, to bestow on them. Meanwhile I treasured them up, and determined, as I told him, that his generous efforts for my good, should not be thrown away.

At first, his sister was very uneasy when her brother entered on the theme nearest to his friendly heart. She seemed apprehensive of dispute and contradiction. This apprehension was quickly removed, and she thenceforth encouraged the discourse. She listened with delight and eagerness, and her eye, frequently, when my friend's eloquence was most affecting, appealed to me. It sometimes conveyed a meaning far more powerful than her brother's lips, and expressed, at once, the strongest conviction of the truth of his words, and the most fervent desire that they might convince me. Her natural modesty, joined, no doubt, to her disesteem of my character, prevented her from mixing in discourse.

She greeted me at this meeting, with a frankness which I did not expect. A disposition to converse, and attentiveness to the few words that I had occasion to say, were very evident. I was just then in the most dejected and forlorn state imaginable. My heart panted for some friendly bosom, in which I might pour my cares. I had reason to esteem the purity, sweetness, and amiable qualities of this good girl. Her aversion to me naturally flowed from these qualities, while an abatement of that aversion was flattering to me, as the triumph of feeling over judgment.

I should have left her at the door of her lodgings, but she besought me to go in so earnestly that my facility, rather than my inclination, complied. She saw that I was absent and disturbed. I never read compassion and (shall I say) good will, in any eye more distinctly than in hers.

The conversation for a time was vague and trite. Insensibly, the scenes lately witnessed were recalled, not without many an half stifled sigh and ill disguised tear on her part. Some arrangements as to the letters and papers of her brother were suggested. I expressed a wish to have my letters restored to me: I alluded to those letters written in the sanguine insolence of youth and with the dogmatic rage upon me, that have done me so much mischief with Mrs. Fielder. I had not thought of them before, but now it occurred to me that they might as well be destroyed.

This insensibly led the conversation into more interesting topics. I could not suppress my regret that I had ever written some things in those letters, and informed her that my view in taking them back was to doom them to that oblivion from which it would have been happy for me if they never had been called.

After many tacit intimations; much reluctance and timidity to enquire and communicate, I was greatly surprised to discover that these letters had been seen by her; that Mrs. Fielder's character was not unknown to her; that she was no stranger to her brother's disclosures to that lady.

Without directly expressing her thoughts, it was easy to perceive that her mind was full of ideas produced by these letters; by her brother's discourse; and by curiosity as to my present opinions. Her modesty laid restraint on her lips. She was fearful, I supposed, of being tho't forward and impertinent.

I endeavoured to dissipate these apprehensions. All about this girl was, on this occasion, remarkably attractive. I loved her brother, and his features still survive in her. The only relation she has left is a distant one, on whose regard and protection she has therefore but slender claims. Her mind is rich in all the graces of ingenuousness and modesty. The curiosity she felt respecting me, made me grateful as for a token of regard. I was therefore not backward to unfold the true state of my mind.

Now and then she made seasonable and judicious comments on what I said. Was there any subject of enquiry more momentous than the truth of religion? If my doubts and heresies had involved me in difficulties, was not the remedy obvious and easy? why not enter on regular discussions, and having candidly and deliberately formed my creed, adhere to it frankly, firmly and consistently. A state of doubt and indecision was in every view, hurtful, criminal and ignominious. Conviction, if it were in favour of religion, would insure me every kind of happiness. It would forward even those schemes of temporal advantage on which I might be intent. It would reconcile those whose aversion arose from difference of opinion: and in cases where it failed to benefit my worldly views, it would console me for my disappointment.

If my enquiries should establish an irreligious conviction, still any form of certainty was better than doubt. The love of truth and the consciousness of that certainty would raise me above hatred and slander. I should then have some kind of principle by which to regulate my conduct; I should then know on what foundation to build. To fluctuate, to waver, to postpone enquiry, was more criminal than any kind of opinion, candidly investigated and firmly adopted; and would more effectually debar me from happiness. At my age, with my talents, and inducements it was sordid; it was ignoble; it was culpable to allow indifference or indolence to slacken my zeal.

These sentiments were coveyed in various broken hints, and modest interrogatories. While they mortified, they charmed me, they enlightened me while they perplexed. I came away with my soul roused by a new impulse. I have emerged from a dreary torpor, not indeed to tranquillity or happiness, but to something less fatal, less dreadful.

Would you think that a ray of hope has broken in upon me? am I not still, in some degree, the maker of my fortune? why mournfully ruminate on the past, instead of looking to the future? How wretched, how criminal, how infamous are my doubts!

Alas! and is this the first time that I have been visited by such thoughts? how often has this transient hope, this momentary zeal, started into being, hovered in my fancy, and vanished. Thus will it ever be.

Need I mention — but I will not look back. To what end? Shall I grieve or rejoice at that power of now and then escaping from the past? Could it operate to my amendment, memory should be ever busy, but I fear that it would only drive me to desperation or madness.

H. C.

LETTER LIV

TO THE SAME

Philadelphia, Dec. 19.

I HAVE just returned from a visit to my new friend. I begin to think that if I had time to cultivate her good opinion I should gain as much of it as I deserve. Her good will; her sympathy at least might be awakened in my favour.

We have had a long conversation. Her distance and reserve are much less than they were. She blames, yet pities me. I have been very communicative, and have offered her the perusal of all the letters that I have lately received from Mrs. Talbot as vouchers for my sincerity.

She listened favourably to my account of the unhappy misapprehension into which Mrs. Fielder had fallen. She was disposed to be more severe on Miss Jessup's imposture, than even my irritated passions had been.

She would not admit that Mrs. Fielder's antipathy to my alliance with her daughter, was without just grounds. She thought that everlasting separation was best for us both. A total change of my opinions on moral subjects, might, perhaps, in time subdue the mother's aversion to me, but this change must necessarily be slow and gradual. I was indeed already, from my own account, far from being principled against religion, but this was only a basis whereon to build the hope of future amendment. No present merit could be founded on my doubts.

I spared not myself in my account of former follies. The recital made her very solemn. I had — I had, indeed, been very faulty: My present embarrassments were the natural

391

and just consequences of my misconduct. I had not merited a different destiny. I was unworthy of the love of such a woman as Jane. I was not qualified to make her happy. I ought to submit to banishment, not only as to a punishment justly incurred, but in gratitude to one whose genuine happiness, taking into view her mother's character and the sacrifices to which her choice of me would subject her, would be most effectually consulted by my exile.

This was an irksome lesson. She had the candour not to expect my cordial concurrence in such sentiments, yet endeavoured in her artless manner to enforce them. She did not content herself with placing the matter in this light. She still continued to commend the design of a distant voyage, even should I intend one day to return. The scheme was likely to produce health and pleasure to me. It offered objects which a rational curiosity must hold dear. The interval might not pass away unpropitiously to me. Time might effect desirable changes in Mrs. Fielder's sentiments and views. A thousand accidents might occur to level those obstacles which were now insuperable. Pity and complacency might succeed to abhorrence and scorn. Gratitude and admiration for the patience, meekness and self-sacrifices of the daughter might gradually bring about the voluntary surrender of her enmities; besides that event must, one day come, which will place her above the influence of all mortal cares and passions.

These conversations have not been without their influence. Yes, my friend, my mind is less gloomy and tumultuous than it was. I look forward to this voyage with stronger hopes.

Methinks, I would hear once more from Jane. Could she be persuaded cheerfully to acquiesce in her mother's will: reserve herself for fortunate contingencies: confide in my fidelity: and find her content in the improvement of her time and fortune: in befriending the destitute: relieving, by her superfluities, the needy, and consoling the afflicted by her sympathy, advice, and succour — Would

392

she not derive happiness from these sources, though disappointed in the wish nearest her heart.

Might I not have expected a letter ere this? But she knows not where I am — probably imagines me at my father's house. Shall I not venture to write? A last and a long farewell? Yet have I not said already all that the occasion will justify? But, if I would write I know not how to address her. It seems, she has not gone to New-York. Her mother has a friend in Jersey, whither she prevailed on Jane to accompany her. I suppose it would be no arduous undertaking to trace her footsteps and gain an interview, and perhaps, I shall find the temptation irresistable.

Stephen has just now told me by letter that he sails in ten days. There will be time enough to comply with your friendly invitation. My sister and you may expect to see me by Saturday night. In the arms of my true friends, I will endeavour to forget the vexations that at present pray upon the peace of

Your
H.C.

LETTER LV

TO HENRY COLDEN

MY mother allows me and even requires me to write to you. My reluctance to do so is only overcome by the fear of her displeasure — Yet do not mistake me, my friend. Infer not from this reluctance that the resolution of being henceforward all that my mother wishes, can be altered by any efforts of yours.

Alas! How vainly do I boast my inflexibility. My safety lies only in filling my ears with my mother's remonstrances and shutting them against your persuasive accents. I have therefore resigned myself wholly to my mother's government. I have consented to be inaccessible to your visits or letters.

I have few claims on your gratitude or generosity, yet may I not rely on the humanity of your temper? To what frequent and severe tests has my caprice already subjected your affection, and has it not remained unshaken and undiminished? Let me hope that you will not withhold this last proof of your affection for me.

It would greatly console me to know that you are once more on filial and friendly terms with your father. Let me persuade you to return to him; to beseech his favour; I hope the way to reconcilement has already been paved by the letter jointly addressed to him by my mother and myself; that nothing is wanting but submissive and suitable deportment on your part to restore you to the station you possessed before you had any knowledge of me. Let me exact from you this proof of your regard for me. It is the highest proof which it will henceforth be in your power to offer, or that can ever be received by

J. Talbot.

394

LETTER LVI

TO MRS. MONTFORD
Philadelphia, Oct. 7.

Madam,

I T is with extreme reluctance that I venture to address you in this manner. I cannot find words to account for or apologise. But if you be, indeed, the sister of Henry Colden, you cannot be ignorant of me, and of former transactions between us; and especially, the circumstance that now compels me to write — you can be no stranger to his present situation.

Can you forgive this boldness? in an absolute stranger to your person, but not to your virtues. I have heard much of you, from one in whom I once had some little interest; Who honored me with his affection.

I know that you lately possessed a large share of that affection. I doubt not that you still retain it, and are able to tell me what has become of him.

I have, a long time, struggled with myself and my fears in silence. I know how unbecoming this address must appear to you, and yet, persuaded that my character and my relation to your brother are well known to you, I have been able to curb my anxieties no longer.

Do then, my dearest madam, gratify my curiosity, and tell me without delay, what has become of your brother.

J. Talbot.

LETTER LVII

TO JANE TALBOT

New-York, October 9.

My Dear Madam,

YOU judge truly when you imagine that your character and history are not unknown to me; and such is my opinion of you, that there is probably no person in the world more solicitous for your happiness, and more desirous to answer any enquiries in a manner agreeable to you.

Mr. Colden has made no secret to us of the relation in which he stood to you. We are well acquainted with the cause of your late separation. Will you excuse me for expressing the deep regret which that event gave me? That regret is the deeper, since the measures which he immediately adopted, has put it out of his power to profit by any change in your views.

My husband's brother being on the point of embarking in a voyage to the western coast of America and to China, Mr. Colden prevailed upon his friends to permit him to embark also, as a joint adventurer in the voyage. They have been gone already upwards of a year. We have not heard of them since their touching at Tobago and Brazil.

The voyage will be very tedious, but as it will open scenes of great novelty to the mind of our friend, and as it may not be unprofitable to him, we were the more easily disposed to acquiesce.

Permit me, Madam, to proffer you my warmest esteem and my kindest services. Your letter I regard as a flattering proof of your good opinion, which I shall be most happy to deserve and to improve, by answering every enquiry you may be pleased to make respecting one, for whom I have ever entertained the affection becoming a sister. I am, &c.

M. Montford.

P.S. Mr. Montford desires to join me in my offers of service, and in my good wishes.

LETTER LVIII

TO MRS. MONTFORD
Philadelphia, October 12.

Dear Madam,

HOW shall I thank you for the kind and delicate manner in which you have complied with my request. You will not be surprized, nor, I hope, offended, that I am emboldened to address you once more.

I see that I need not practice towards you a reserve, at all times foreign to my nature, and now more painful than at any other time, as my soul is torn with emotions, which I am at liberty to disclose to no other human creature. Will you be my friend? Will you permit me to claim your sympathy and consolation? As I told you before, I am thoroughly acquainted with your merits, and one of the felicities which I promised myself from a nearer alliance with Mr. Colden, was that of numbering myself among your friends.

You have deprived me of some hope, by the information you give; but you have at least put an end to a suspense more painful than the most dreadful certainty could be.

You say that you know all our concerns. In pity to my weakness, will you give me some particulars of my friend. I am extremely anxious to know many things in your power to communicate.

Perhaps you know the contents of my last letter to him, and of his answer. I know you condemn me. You think me inconsiderate and cruel in writing such a letter, and my heart does not deny the charge. Yet my motives were not utterly ungenerous. I could not bear to reduce the man I loved to poverty. I could not bear that he should incur the violence and curses of his father. I fondly thought *myself*

398

the only obstacle to reconcilement, and was willing, whatever it cost me, to remove that obstacle.

What will become of me, if my fears should now be realized, if the means which I used, with no other view than to reconcile him to his family, should have driven him away from them and from his country forever? I thank my God that I was capable of abandoning him on no selfish or personal account. The maledictions of my own mother; the scorn of the world; the loss of friends, reputation, and fortune, weighed nothing with me. Great as these evils were, I could have cheerfully sustained them for his sake. What I did, was in oblivion of self; was from a duteous regard to his genuine and lasting happiness. Alas! I have, perhaps, mistaken the means, and cruel will, I fear, be the penalty of my error.

Tell me, my dear friend, was not Colden reconciled to his father before he went? When does he mean to return? What said he, what thought he of my conduct? Did he call me ungrateful and capricious? Did he vow never to see or think of me more?

I have regarded the promise that I made to the elder Colden, and to my mother, as sacred. The decease of the latter has, in my own opinion, absolved me from any obligation except that of promoting my own happiness, and that of him whom I love. I shall not *now* reduce him to indigence, and that consequence being precluded, I cannot doubt of his father's acquiescence.

Ah! dear Madam! I should not have been so long patient, had I not, as it now appears, been lulled into a fatal mistake. I could not taste repose till I was, as I thought, certainly informed that he continued to reside in his father's house. This proof of reconciliation, and the silence which, though so near him, he maintained towards me, both before and subsequently to my mother's death, contributed to persuade me that his condition was not unhappy, and especially, that either his resentment or his prudence had made him dismiss me from his thoughts.

I have lately, to my utter astonishment, discovered that

Colden, immediately after his last letter to me, went upon some distant voyage, whence, though a twelve month has since passed, he has not yet returned. Hence the boldness of this address to you, whom I know only by rumour.

You will, I doubt not, easily imagine to yourself my feelings, and will be good enough to answer my enquiries, if you have any compassion for your

J. T.

LETTER LIX

TO JANE TALBOT
New-York, October 15.

I HASTEN, my dear madam, to reply to your letter. The part you have assigned me, I will most cheerfully perform to the utmost of my power; but very much regret that I have not more agreeable tidings to communicate.

Having said that all the transactions between you and my brother are known to me, I need not apologise for alluding to events, which I could not excuse myself for doing without being encouraged by the frankness and solicitude which your own pen has expressed.

Immediately after the determination of his fate, in regard to you, he came to this city. He favoured us with the perusal of your letters. We entirely agreed with him in applauding the motives which influenced your conduct. We had no right to accuse you of precipitation or inconsistency. That heart must, indeed, be selfish and cold which could not comprehend the horror which must have seized you, on hearing of his father's treatment. You acted in the first tumults of your feelings, as every woman would have acted. That you did not immediately perceive the little prospect there was that a breach of this nature would be repaired; or that Colden would make use of your undesired and un-saught for renunciation, as a means of reconcilement with his father, was no subject of surprise or of blame. These reflections could not occur to you but in consequence of some intimations from others.

Henry Colden was no indolent or mercenary creature.

No one more cordially detested the life of dependance than
he. He always thought that his father had discharged all
the duties of that relation, in nourishing his childhood and
giving him a good education. Whatever has been since bestowed, he considered as voluntary and unrequited bounty;
has received it with irksomeness and compunction, and
whatever you may think of the horrors of indigence, it was
impossible to have placed him in a more painful situation
than under his father's roof.

We could not but deeply regret the particular circumstances under which he left his father's house, but the mere
leaving it, and the necessity which thence arose of finding
employment and subsistence for himself, was not at all to
be regretted.

The consequences of your mother's letter to the father
produced no resentment in the son. He had refused what
he had a right to refuse, and what had been pressed upon
the giver, rather than saught by him. The mere separation was agreeable to Colden, and the rage that accompanied it, was excited by the young man's steadiness in
his fidelity to you.

You were not aware that this cause of anger could not
be removed by any thing done by you. Colden was not
sensible of any fault. There was nothing, therefore for which
he could crave pardon. Blows and revilings had been patiently endured, but he was actuated by no tame or servile
spirit. He never would expose himself to new insults.
Though always ready to accept apology and grant an oblivion of the past, he never would avow compunction which
he did not feel, or confess that he had deserved the treatment which he had received.

All this it was easy to suggest to your reflections, and
I endeavoured to persuade him to write a second letter;
but he would not. No, said he, she has made her election.
If no advantage is taken of her tenderness and pity she will
be happy in her new scheme. Shall I subject her to new
trials: new mortifications? can I flatter myself with being
able to reward her by my love for the loss of every other

comfort? no. Whatever she feels for me, *I* am not her supreme passion. Her mother is preferred to me. *That* her present resolution puts out of all doubt. All upbraiding and repining from me would be absurd. What can I say in favor of my attachment to her, which she may not, with equal reason, urge in favor of her attachment to her mother? the happiness of one or other must be forfeited. Shall I not rather offer, than demand the sacrifice? and what are my boasts of magnanimity if I do not strive to lessen the difficulties of her choice, and persuade her that in graifying her mother she inflicts no exquisite or lasting misery on me?

I am not so blind but that I can foresee the effects on my tranquillity of time and variety of objects. If I go this voyage, I may hope to acquire resignation much sooner than by staying at home. To leave these shores, is, in every view, best for me. I can do nothing while here, for my own profit, and every eye I meet humbles and distresses me. At present, I do not wish ever to return, but, I suppose the absence and adventures of a couple of years, may change my feelings in that respect. My condition too, by some chance, may be bettered. I may come back, and offer myself to her, without offering poverty and contempt at the same time. Time, or some good fortune, may remove the mother's prejudices. All this is possible, but, if it never takes place, if my condition never improves, I will never return home.

When we urged to him the propriety of apprizing you of his views, not only for your sake, but for his own — what need is there? has she not prohibited all intercourse between us? have I not written the last letter she will consent to receive? On my own account, I have nothing to hope. I have stated my return as a mere possibility. I do not believe I shall ever return. If I did expect it, I know Jane too well to have any fears of her fidelity. While I am living, or as long as my death is uncertain, her heart will be mine, and she will reserve herself for me.

I know you will excuse me, madam, for being thus particular. I thought it best to state the views of our friend in his own words. From these your judgment will enable you to form the truest conclusions.

The event that has since happened has probably removed the only obstacle to your mutual happiness: Nor am I without the hope of seeing him one day return to be made happy by your favor. As several passages were expected to be made between China and Nootka, that desirable event cannot be expected to be very near.

M.M.

LETTER LX

TO MRS. MONTFORD

Philadelphia, Oct. 20.

AH! dear madam! how much has your letter afflicted: how much has it consoled me.

You have then some hope of his return: but, you say, 'twill be a long time first. He has gone where I cannot follow him: To the end of the world: Where even a letter cannot find him: Into unwholesome climates; through dangerous elements; among savages —

Alas! I have no hope. Among so many perils it cannot be expected that he should escape. And did he not say that he meant not to return?

Yet one thing consoles me. He left not his curses or reproaches on my head. Kindly, generously, and justly didst thou judge of my fidelity, Henry. While thou livest, and as long as I live, will I cherish thy image.

I am coming to pass the winter in your city. I adopt this scheme merely because it will give me your company. I feel as if you were the only friend I have in the world. Do not think me forward or capricious. I will not deny that you owe your place in my affections *chiefly* to your relation to the wanderer: but no matter whence my attachment proceeds. I feel that it is strong: merely selfish perhaps: the child of a distracted fancy: the prop on which a sinking heart relies in its uttermost extremity.

Reflection stings me to the quick, but it does not deny me some consolation. The memory of my mother calls forth tears, but they are not tears of bitterness. To her, at least, I have not been deficient in dutiful observance. I have sacrificed my friend and myself but it was to her peace. The melancholy of her dying scene will ever be cheered in my remembrance, by her gratitude and blessing. Her last words were these;

Thou hast done much for me, my child. I begin to fear that I have exacted too much. Your sweetness, your patience have wrung my heart with compunction.

I have wronged thee, Jane. I have wronged the absent. I greatly fear, I have. Forgive me. If you ever meet, intreat *him* to forgive me, and recompence yourself and him, for all your mutual sufferings.

I hope, all, tho' sorrowful, has been for the best. I hope that angelic sweetness, which I have witnessed, will continue when I am gone. That belief only can make my grave peaceful.

I leave you affluence and honour at least. I leave you the means of repairing *my* injury. *That* is my comfort: but forgive me, Jane. Say my child, you forgive me for what has past —

She stretched her hand to me, which I bathed with my tears — But this subject afflicts me too much.

Give my affectionate compliments to Mr. Montford and tell me that you wish to see your

Jane.

LETTER LXI

TO MRS. TALBOT

New-York, Oct. 22.

YOU tell me, my dear Jane, that you are coming to reside in this city, but you have not gratified my impatience by saying how soon. Tell me when you propose to come. Is there not something in which I can be of service to you? Some preparations to be made?

Tell me the day when you expect to arrive among us, that I may wait on you as soon as possible.

I shall embrace my sister, with a delight which I cannot express. I will not part with the delightful hope of one day calling you truly such —

Accept the fraternal regards of Mr. Montford.

M.M.

LETTER LXII

TO MRS. MONTFORD
Banks of Delaware, Sept. 5.

BE not anxious for me, Mary. I hope to experience very speedy relief from the wholesome airs that perpetually fan this spot. Your apprehension from the influence of these scenes on my fancy are groundless. They breathe nothing over my soul but delicious melancholy. I have done expecting and repining, you know. Four years have passed since I was here: since I met your brother, under these shades.

I have already visited every spot which has been consecrated by our interviews. I have found the very rail which, as I well remember, we disposed into a bench, at the skirt of a wood, bordering a stubble field. The same pathway through the thicket, where I have often walked with him, I now traverse morning and night.

Be not uneasy, I repeat, on my account. My present situation is happier than the rest of the world can afford. I tell you, I have done repining. I have done sending forth my views into an earthly futurity. Anxiety, I hope, is now at an end with me.

What do you think I design to do? I assure you it is no new scheme. Ever since my mother's death, I have thought of it at times. It has been my chief consolation. I never mentioned it to you because I knew you would not approve it. It is this.

To purchase this farm, and take up my abode upon it for the rest of my life. I need not become farmer, you know. I can lett the ground to some industrious person, upon easy terms. I can add all the furniture and appendages to this mansion, which my convenience requires. Luckily Sandford has for some time, entertained thoughts of parting with it, and I believe he could not find a more favourable purchaser.

You will tell me that the fields are sterile; the barn small: the stable crazy; the woods scanty. These would be powerful objections to a mere tiller of the earth, but they are none to me.

'Tis true, it is washed by a tide-water. The bank is low and the surrounding country sandy and flat, and you may think I ought rather to prefer the beautiful variety of hill and dale, luxuriant groves, and fertile pastures which abound in other parts of the country. But you know, my friend, the mere arrangement of inanimate objects, wood, grass, and rock, is nothing. It owes its power of bewitching us to the memory, the fancy and the heart. No spot of earth can possibly team with as many affecting images as this; for here it was —

But my eyes already overflow. In the midst of these scenes, remembrance is too vivid to allow me thus to descant on them. At a distance I could talk of them without that painful emotion, and now it would be useless repetition. Have I not, more than once, related to you every dialogue; described every interview?

God bless you, dear Mary, and continue to you all your present happiness.

Don't forget to write to me. Perhaps some tidings may reach you — down! thou flattering hope! thou throbbing heart, peace! He is gone. These eyes will never see him more. Had an angel whispered the fatal news in my wakeful ear, I should not more firmly believe it.

And yet — but I must not heap up disappointments for myself. Would to heaven there was no room for the least doubt: that, one way or the other, his destiny was ascertained.

How agreeable is your intelligence, that Mr. Cartwright has embarked after taking cheerful leave of you. It grieves me, my friend, that you do not entirely approve of my conduct towards that man. I never formally attempted to justify myself. 'Twas a subject on which I could not give utterance to my thoughts. How irksome is blame from those we love! there is instantly suspicion that blame is merited. A new process of self-defence is to be gone over, and ten to one, but that after all our efforts, there are some dregs at the bottom of the cup.

I was half willing to found my excuse on the hope of the wanderer's return; but I am too honest to urge a false plea. Beside, I know that certainty, in that respect, would make no difference, and would it not be fostering in him a hope, that my mind might be changed in consequence of being truly informed respecting your brother's fate?

I persuade myself that a man of Cartwright's integrity and generosity cannot be made lastingly unhappy by me. I know but of one human being more excellent. Though his sensibility be keen, I trust to his fortitude.

It is true, Mary, what you have heard. Cartwright was my school-fellow. When we grew to an age, that made it proper to frequent separate schools, he did not forget me. The schools adjoined each other, and he used to resist all the enticements of prison-base and cricket, for the sake of waiting at the door of our school, till it broke up, and then accompanying me home.

These little gallant offices made him quite singular among his compeers, and drew on him and on me, a good deal of ridicule. But he did not mind it. I thought him, and every body else thought him, a most amiable and engaging youth, though only twelve or thirteen years old.

'Tis impossible to say what might have happened, had he not gone with his mother to Europe; or rather, it is likely, I think, that our fates, had he staid among us, would in time have been united. But he went away when I was scarcely fourteen. At parting, I remember, we shed a great many tears and exchanged a great many kisses; and promises *not to forget*. And that promise never was broken by me. He was always dear to my remembrance.

410

Time has only improved all the graces of the boy. I will not conceal from *you,* Mary, that nothing but a preoccupied heart has been an obstacle to his wishes. If that impediment had not existed, my reverence for his worth, my gratitude for his tenderness would have made me comply. I will even go further; I will say *to you,* though my regard to his happiness will never suffer me to say it to him, that if three years more pass away, and I am fully assured that your brother's absence will be perpetual, and Cartwright's happiness is still in my hands — that then — I possibly may —— but I am sure that, before that time, his hand and his heart will be otherwise disposed of. Most sincerely shall I rejoice at the last event.

All are well here. My friend is as good natured and affectionate as ever; and sings as delightfully and plays as adroitly. She humours me with all my favorite airs, twice a day. We have no strangers; no impertinents to intermeddle in our conversations and mar our enjoyments.

You know what turn my studies have taken, and what books I have brought with me. 'Tis remarkable what unlooked for harvests arise from small and insignificant germs. My affections have been the stimulants to my curiosity. What was it induced me to procure maps and charts, and explore the course of the voyager over seas and round capes? there was a time when these objects were wholly frivolous and unmeaning in my eyes, but now they gain my whole attention.

When I found that my happiness was embarked with your brother in a tedious and perilous voyage, was it possible to forbear collecting all the information attainable respecting his route, and the incidents likely to attend it? I got maps and charts and books of voyages, and found a melancholy enjoyment in connecting the incidents and objects which they presented, with the destiny of my friend. The pursuit of this chief and most interesting object, has brought within view, and prompted me to examine a thousand others, on which, without this original inducement, I should never have bestowed a thought.

411

The map of the world exists in my fancy in a most vivid and accurate manner. Repeated meditation on displays of Shoal, Sand-bank and Water, has created a sort of attachment to Geography for its own sake. I have often reflected on the innumerable links in the chain of my ideas between my first eager examination of the route by sea between New-York and Tobago and yesterday's employment, when I was closely engaged in measuring the Marches of Frederic across the mountains of Bohemia.

How freakish and perverse are the rovings of human curiosity! The surprise which Miss Betterton betrayed, when, in answer to her inquiries, as to what study and what book I prized the most, you told her that I thought of little else than of the art of moving from shore to shore across the water, and that I pored over Cook's voyages so much that I had gotten the best part of them by rote, was very natural. She must have been puzzled to conjecture what charms one of my sex could find in the study of maps and voyages. *Once* I should have been just as much puzzled myself. Adieu.

J. T.

LETTER LXIII

TO MRS. TALBOT

New-York, Oct. 1.

BE not angry with me, my dear Jane. Yet I am sure when you know my offence, you will feel a great deal of indignation. You cannot be more angry with me than I am with myself. I do not know how to disclose the very rash thing I have done. If you knew my compunction you would pity me.

Cartwright embarked on the day I mentioned, but remained for some days wind-bound, at the Hook. Yesterday he unexpectedly made his appearance in our appartment, at the very moment when I was perusing your last letter. I was really delighted to see him, and the images connected with him, which your letter had just suggested, threw me off my guard. Finding by whom the letter was written, he solicited with the utmost eagerness the sight of it.

Can you forgive me? My heart overflowed with pity for the excellent man. I knew the transport one part of your letter would afford him. I thought that no injury but rather happiness, would redound to yourself.

I now see that I was guilty of a most culpable breach of confidence, in shewing him your delicate confession: but I was bewitched, I think.

I can write of nothing else just now. Much as I dread your displeasure, I could not rest till I had acknowledged my fault and craved your pardon. Forgive, I beseech you, your

M. Montford.

LETTER LXIV

TO MRS. TALBOT

New-York, Oct. 2.

I CANNOT leave this shore without thanking the mistress of my destiny for all her goodness. Yet I should not have ventured thus to address you, had I not seen a letter — Dearest creature! blame not your friend, for betraying you. Think it not a rash or injurious confession, that you have made.

And is it possible that you have not totally forgotten the sweet scenes of our childhood; that absence has not degraded me in your opinion; and that my devotion, if it continue as fervent as now, may look, in a few years, for its reward?

Could you prevail on yourself to hide these generous emotions from me? To suffer me to leave my country in the dreary belief that all former incidents were held in contempt, and that so far from being high in your esteem, my presence was troublesome, my existence was irksome to you?

But your motive was beneficent and generous. You were content to be thought unfeeling and ungrateful for the sake of my happiness. I rejoice inexpressibly in that event which has removed the veil from your true sentiments. Nothing but pure felicity to me, can flow from it. Nothing but gratitude and honor can redound from it to yourself.

I go: but not with anguish and despondency for my companions. I am buoyed up by the light wings of hope. The prospect of gaining your love is not the only source of my present happiness. If it were, I should be a criminal and selfish being. No. My chief delight is, that happiness is yet in store for you; that should heaven have denied you your first hope, there still lives one whose claim to make you happy will not be rejected.

G. Cartwright.

LETTER LXV

TO G. CARTWRIGHT

Banks of Delaware, Oct. 5.

My Brother,

IT would avail me nothing to deny the confessions to which you allude. Neither will I conceal from you that I am much grieved at the discovery. Far am I from deeming your good opinion of little value; but in this case, I was more anxious to deserve it, than possess it.

Little, indeed, did you know me, when you imagined me insensible to your merit and forgetful of the happy days of our childhood; the recollection of which has a thousand times made my tears flow. I thank heaven that the evils which I have suffered, have had no tendency to deaden my affections; to narrow my heart.

The joy which I felt for your departure was far from being unmixed. The persuasion that my friend and brother was going where he was likely to find that tranquillity of which his stay here would bereave him, but imperfectly soothed the pangs of a long and perhaps an eternal separation.

Farewell: my fervent and disinterested blessings go with you. Return speedily to your country, but bring with you a heart devoted to another, and only glowing with a brotherly affection for

J. T.

LETTER LXVI

TO MRS. TALBOT
New-York, Nov. 15.

THE fear that what I have to communicate may be imparted more abruptly and with false or exaggerated circumstances, induces me to write to you. Yesterday week, a ship arrived in this port from Batavia, in which my husband's brother Stephen Montford came passenger.

You will be terrified at these words; but calm your apprehensions. Harry does *not* accompany him, it is true, nor are we acquainted with his present situation.

The story of their unfortunate voyage cannot be minutely related now. Suffice it to say that a wicked and turbulent wretch, whom they shipped in the West Indies as mate, the former dying on the voyage thither, gave rise, by his intreagues among the crew, to a mutiny.

After a prosperous navigation and some stay at Nootka, they prepared to cross the ocean to Asia. They pursued the usual route of former traders, and after touching at the Sandwich Islands, they made the land of Japan.

At this period the mutiny which had long been hatching, broke out. The whole crew including the mate, joined the conspiracy. Montford and my brother were the objects of this conspiracy.

The original design was to murder them both and throw their bodies into the sea, but this cruel proposal was thwarted both by compassion and by policy, and it was resolved to set my brother ashore on the first inhospitable land they should meet, and retain Montford to assist them in the navigation of the vessel, designing to destroy him when his services should no longer be necessary.

This scheme was executed as soon as they came in sight of an out lying isle or dry sand back, on the eastern coast of Japan. Here they seized the two unsuspecting youths, at day break, while asleep in their *births,* and immediately putting out their boat landed my brother on the shore, without cloathing or provisions of any kind. Montford petitioned to share the fate of his friend, but they would not listen to it.

Six days, afterwards, they lighted on a Spanish ship bound to Manilla, who was in want of water. A party of the Spaniards came on board in search of some supply of that necessary article.

On their coming, Montford was driven below and disabled from giving by his cries any alarm. The centinel who guarded him, had received orders to keep him in that situation till the visitants had departed. From some impulse of humanity, or mistake of orders, the centinel freed him from restraint a few minutes earlier than had been intended, and he got on deck before the departing strangers had gone to any considerable distance from the ship. He immediately leapt into the sea and made for the boat, to which, being a very vigorous swimmer, he arrived in safety.

The mutineers, finding their victim had escaped, endeavoured to make the best of their way, but were soon overtaken by the Spanish vessel, to whose officers Montford made haste to explain the true state of affairs. They were carried to Manilla, where Montford sold his vessel and cargo on very advantageous terms. From thence, after many delays, he got to Batavia and from thence returned home.

I have thus given you, my friend, an imperfect account of their misfortunes. I need not add that no tidings has been received, or can reasonably be hoped ever to be received of my brother.

I could not write on such a subject sooner. For some days I had thoughts of being wholly silent on this news. Indeed my emotions would not immediately permit me to use the pen, but I have concluded, and it is my husband's earnest advice, to tell you the whole truth.

Be not too much distressed, my sister, my friend. Fain would I give you that consolation which I myself want. I entreat you, let me hear from you soon, and tell me that you are not very much afflicted. Yet could I not believe you if you did. Write to me speedily, however.

LETTER LXVII

TO MRS. TALBOT

New-York, Nov. 23.

YOU do not write to me, my dear Jane. Why are
you silent? Surely you cannot be indifferent to my
happiness. You must know how painful, at a
moment like this your silence must prove.

I have waited from day to day in expectation of a letter,
but more than a week has past, and none has come. Let
me hear from you, immediately, I intreat you.

I am afraid you are ill, or perhaps, you are displeased
with me. Unconsciously I may have given you offence.

But, indeed, I can easily suspect the cause of your silence.
I trembled with terror when I sent you tidings of our calamity. I know the impetuosity of your feelings, and the effects
of your present solitude. Would to heaven you were any
where but where you are. Would to heaven you were once
more with us.

Let me beseech you to return to us immediately. Mr. M.
is anxious to go for you. He wanted to set out immediately, on his brother's arrival, and to be the bearer
of my letter, but I prevailed on him to forbear until I heard
from you.

Do not, if you have any regard for me, delay answering
me a moment longer.

M. M.

LETTER LXVIII

TO MRS. MONTFORD
Banks of Delaware, Nov. 26.

I BESEECH you, dear Mrs. Montford, take some measures for drawing our dear Jane from this place. There is no remedy but absence from this spot, cheerful company and amusing engagements, for the sullen grief which has seized her. Ever since the arrival of your letter giving us the fatal tidings of your brother's misfortune, she has been — in a strange way — I am almost afraid to tell you; I know how much you love her: but indeed, indeed, unless somebody with more spirit and skill than I possess, will undertake to console and divert her, I am fearful we shall lose her forever.

I can do nothing for her relief. You know what a poor creature I am. Instead of summoning up courage to assist another in distress, the sight of it confuses and frightens me. Never, I believe was there such another helpless good-for-nothing creature in existence. Poor Jane's affecting ways only make me miserable, and instead of my being of any use to her, her presence deprives me of all power to attend to my family and friends. I endeavour to avoid her, though, indeed, that requires but little pains to effect, since she will not be seen but when she cannot choose, for whenever she looks at me steadily, there is such expression in her features, something so woeful, so wild, that I am struck with terror. It never fails to make me cry heartily.

Come hither yourself, or send somebody immediately. If you do not, I dread the consequence.

421

LETTER LXIX

TO MR. MONTFORD
New-Haven, February 10.

My dear friend,

THIS letter is written in extreme pain; yet no pain that I ever felt, no external pain possible for me to feel, is equal to the torment I derive from suspense. Good heaven! what an untoward accident! to be forcibly immured in a tavern chamber; when the distance is so small between me and that certainty after which my soul pants!

I ought not thus to alarm my beloved friends, but I know not what I write — my head is in confusion; my heart in tumults; a delirium more the effect of a mind stretched upon the rack of impatience, than of limbs shattered and broken, whirls me out of myself.

Not a moment of undisturbed repose have I enjoyed for the last two months. If awake, omens and conjectures, menacing fears, and half-formed hopes have haunted and harrassed me. If asleep, dreams of agonizing forms and ever varying hues, have thronged my fancy and driven away peace.

In less than an hour after landing at Boston, I placed myself in the swiftest stage and have travelled night and day, till within a mile of this town, when the carriage was overturned and my left arm terribly shattered. I was drawn with difficulty hither, and my only hope of being once more well is founded on my continuance, for I know not how long, in one spot and one posture.

By this time, the well known hand has told you who it is

422

that writes this — the exile; the fugitive; whom four long years of absence and silence have not, I hope, erased from your remembrance, banished from your love, or even totally excluded from the hope of being seen again.

Yet that hope, surely, must have been long ago dismissed. Acquainted as you are with some part of my destiny; of my being left on the desert shore of Japan; on the borders of a new world; a world, civilized, indeed, and peopled by men, but existing in almost total separation from the other families of mankind; with language, manners and policy almost incompatible with the existence of a stranger among them: all entrance, or egress from which, being commonly supposed to be prohibited by iron laws and inflexible despotism: that I, a stranger; naked; forlorn; cast upon a sandy beach; frequented, but at rare intervals, and by savage fishermen, should find my way into the heart of this wonderful empire, and finally explore my way back to my native shore, are surely most strange and incredible achievements — yet all this, my friend, has been endured and performed by your Colden.

Finding it impossible to move immediately from this place, and this day's post having gone out before my arrival, I employed a man to carry you these assurances of my existence and return, and to bring me back intelligence of your welfare; and some news concerning — may I perish if I can, at this moment, write her name. Every moment, every mile that has brought me nearer to *her,* or rather nearer to certainty of her life or death, her happiness or misery, has increased my trepidation: added new tremors to my heart.

I have some time to spare. In spite of my impatience, my messenger cannot start within a few hours. I am little fitted, in my present state of pain and suspense, to write intelligibly. Yet what else can I do but write, and will you not, in your turn, be impatient to know by what means I have once more set my foot in my native land.

I will fill up the interval, till my messenger is ready, by writing. I will give you some hints of my adventures. All particulars must be deferred till I see you. Heaven grant that I may once more see you and my sister. Four months ago you were well, but that interval is large enough to breed ten thousand disasters. Expect not a distinct or regular story. That, I repeat, must be deferred till we meet. Many a long day would be consumed in the telling, and that which was hazard or hardship in the encounter and the sufferance, will be pleasant to remembrance, and delightful in narration.

You know by what accident, and in what remote and inhospitable region, Stephen and I were separated. How did I know, you will, perhaps, ask, the extent of *your* knowledge? By strange and unexpected means; but have patience, and, in due time, I will tell you.

What a scene did I pass through! what uncouth forms, strange accents, and ferocious demeanour presented themselves in the fishermen that found me, half famished, on a sand bank! My fate, whether death or servitude, depended on the momentary impulse of untutored hearts: perhaps, on some adroitness and dexterity in myself.

They carried me from the solitary shore, into the heart of a cultivated island. Rumour became instantly busy, and at length reached the ears of a sort of feudal or territorial lord. By his orders, I was brought into his rustic palace. I found humanity and curiosity in this man. I passed several months in his house, acquiring gradually a smattering of the language, and some insight into the policy and manners of the people.

I endeavoured to better my condition, and gain respect to my person by the display of all the accomplishments of which I was master. These, alas, were but few: yet some of them were not altogether useless; and the humane temper of one whom I may call my patron, secured me gentle and even respectful treatment.

After some months this lord, whose name was Tekehatsin, left his island, and set out on a journey to the metropolis. He left me with promises of the continuance of his favor and protection, and urged his regard for my safety as a reason for not taking me along with him. I heard nothing of him for six weeks after his departure. Then a messenger arrived, with orders to bring me up to his master.

The incidents of this journey; the aspects of the country; of the cities, of the villages thro' which I passed, will afford an inexhaustible theme for future conversations — I reached, at length, the residence of Tekehatsin, in the chief city of the kingdom, the name of which is *Jedho*. Shortly after I was introduced to one in whom I recognized a native of Europe; and therefore, in some respects, a countryman.

This person's name was Holtz. He was the agent of the Dutch East-India company in Japan. He was then at court in a sort of diplomatic character. He was likewise a physician and man of science. He had even been in America, and found no difficulty in conversing with me in my native language.

You will easily imagine the surprise and pleasure which such a meeting afforded me. It likewise opened a door to my return to Europe, as a large trade is regularly maintained between Java and Japan.

Many obstacles, however, in the views which Tekehatsin had formed, of profit and amusement, from my remaining in his service; and in the personal interests and wishes of my friend Holtz, opposed this design, nor was I able to accomplish it, but on condition of returning.

I confess to you, my friend my heart was not extremely averse to this condition.

I left America with very faint hopes, and no expectation of ever returning. The longer I resided among this race of men, the melancholy and forlornness of my feelings declined. Prospects of satisfaction from the novelty and grandeur of the scene into which I had entered, began to open upon me: Sentiments of affection and gratitude for Holtz, and even for the Japanese lord, took root in my heart. Still however happiness was bound to scenes and to persons very distant from my new country, and a restlessness forever haunted me, which nothing could appease but some direct intelligence from you and from Jane Talbot. By returning to Europe I could likewise be of essential service to Holtz, whose family were Saxons, and whose commercial interests required the presence of a trusty agent for a few months at Hamburg.

Let me carry you, in few words through the difficulties of my embarkation: and the incidents of a short stay at Batavia and a long voyage over half the world to Hamburg.

Shortly after my return to Hamburg, from an excursion into Saxony to see Holtz's friends, I met with Mr. Cartwright, an American. After much fluctuation I had previously resolved to content myself with writing to you of whom I received such verbal information from several of our countrymen, as removed my anxiety on your account. A very plausible tale, told me by some one that pretended to know, of Mrs. Talbot's marriage with a Mr. Cartwright, extinguished every new-born wish to revisit my native land, and I expected to set sail on my return to India, before it could be possible to hear from you.

I was on the eve of my departure, when the name of Cartwright, an American, then at Hamburg, reached my ears. The similarity of his name to that of the happy man who had supplanted the poor wanderer in the affections of Jane, and a suspicion that they might possibly be a kin, and consequently, that *this,* might afford me some information, as to the character or merits of *that* Cartwright, made me throw myself in his way.

You may easily imagine, what I shall defer relating, the steps which led us to a knowledge of each other, and by which I discovered that this Cartwright was the one mentioned to me, and that, instead of being already the husband of my Jane, his hopes of her favour depended on the certain proof of my death.

Cartwright's behaviour was, in the highest degree, disinterested. He might easily have left me in my original error, and a very few days would have sent me on a voyage, which would have been equivalent to my death. On the contrary his voluntary information and a letter which he shewed me, written in Jane's hand, created a new soul in my breast. Every foreign object vanished, and every ancient sentiment, connected with our unfortunate loves, was instantly revived. Ineffable tenderness, and an impatience, next to rage, to see her, reigned in my heart.

Yet, my friend, with all my confidence of a favourable reception from Jane; her conduct now exempt from the irresistible controul of her mother and her tenderness for me as fervent as ever; yet, since so excellent a man as Cartwright existed; since his claims were, in truth antecedent to mine; since my death or everlasting absence would finally insure success to these claims; since his character were blemished by none of those momentous errors with which mine was loaded; since that harmony of opinions on religious subjects, without which marriage can never be a source of happiness to hearts touched by a true and immortal passion, was perfect in *his* case; never should mere passion have seduced me to her feet. If my reflections and experience had not changed my character; if all *her* views, as to the final destiny and present obligations of human beings, had not become *mine,* I should have deliberately ratified the act of my eternal banishment —

Yes, my friend; this weather-beaten form and sunburnt face, are not more unlike what you once knew, than my habits and opinions now and formerly. The incidents of a long voyage, the vicissitudes through which I have passed have given strength to my frame, while the opportunities and occasions for wisdom which these have afforded me, have made *my mind whole.* I have awakened from my dreams of doubt and misery, not to the cold and vague belief, but to the living and delightful consciousness of every tie that can bind man to his divine parent and judge.

Again I must refer you to our future interviews. A broken and obscure tale it would be, which I could now relate. I am hurried, by my fears and suspenses — Yet it would give you pleasure to know every thing as soon as possible — sometime likewise must elapse — *You* and my sister have

427

always been wise. The lessons of true piety it is the business of your lives to exemplify and to teach. Henceforth, if that principle, which has been my stay and my comfort in all the slippery paths and unlooked for perils from which I have just been delivered, desert not my future steps, I hope to be no mean example and no feeble teacher of the same lessons. Indefatigable zeal and strenuous efforts are indeed incumbent on me in proportion to the extent of my past misconduct, the depth of my former degeneracy.

By what process of reflection I became thus, you shall speedily know: Yet can you be at a loss to imagine it? *You,* who have passed thro' somewhat similar changes; who always made allowances for the temerity of youth; the fascinations of novelty: Who always predicted that a few more years; the events of my peculiar destiny; the leisure of my long voyage; and that goodness of intention to which you were ever kind enough to admit my claims, would ultimately provide the remedy for all errors and evils, and make me worthy of the undivided love of all good men; — You, who have had this experience, and who have always regarded me in this light, will not wonder that reflection has, at length, raised me to the tranquil and stedfast height of simple and true piety.

Such my friend, were my inducements to return: but first, it was necessary to explain, by letter, to Holtz — but my messenger is at the door: eager to be gone. Take this my friend. Bring yourself or send back by the same messenger, without a moments delay, tidings of her, and of your safety. As to me, be not much concerned on my account. I am solemnly assured by my Surgeon, that nothing but time, and a tranquil mind are necessary to restore me to health. The last boon no hand but yours can confer on your

H. Colden.

LETTER LXX

TO HENRY COLDEN
New-York, Feb. 12.

AND are you then alive? Are you then returned? Still do you remember, still love the ungrateful and capricious Jane? Have you indeed come back to soothe her almost broken heart; to rescue her from the grave: to cheer her with the prospect of peaceful and bright days yet to come?

O my full heart! Sorrow has not hitherto been able quite to burst this frail tenement. I almost fear that joy — so strange to me *is* joy, and so far, so *very* far, beyond my notions of possibility was your return — I almost fear that joy will do what sorrow was unable to do —

Can it be that Colden — that self-same, dear, pensive face; those eyes, benignly and sweetly mild; and that heart dissolving voice, have escaped so many storms: so many dangers? Was it love for me that led you from the extremity of the world, and have you indeed, brought back with you an heart full of "ineffable tenderness" for *me?*

Unspeakably unworthy am I of your love. Time and grief, dear Hal, have bereft me of the glossy hues, the laughing graces which your doating judgment once ascribed to me — but what will not the joy of your return effect? I already feel lightsome and buoyant as a bird. My head is giddy — But, alas! you are not well; Yet, you assure us, not dangerously sick. Nothing, did you not say, but time and repose necessary to heal you? Will not my presence, my nursing hasten thy restoration? Tuesday evening — they say it can't possibly be sooner — I am with you. No

429

supporters shall you have but my arms: no pillow but my breast. Every holy rite, shall instantly be called in to make us one: And when once united, nothing but death shall ever part us again. What did I say? Death itself, at least *thy* death, shall never dissever that bond:

Your brother will take this. Your sister — she is the most excellent of women, and worthy to be your sister — She and I will follow him to morrow. He will tell you much, which my hurried spirits will not allow me to tell you in this letter. He knows every thing. He has been, since my mother's death — She is dead, Henry. She died in my arms; And will it not give you pleasure to know, that her dying lips blessed me, and expressed the hope that you would one day return to find, in my authorised love, some recompense for all the evils to which her antipathies subjected you? She hoped, indeed, that observation and experience would detect the falacy of your former tenets: that you would become wise, not in speculation only, but in practice, and be in every respect, deserving of the happiness and honour which would attend the gift of her daughter's hand and heart.

My words cannot utter but thy own heart perhaps can conceive the rapture which thy confession of a change in thy opinions has afforded me. *All* my prayers, Henry have not been *merely* for your return. Indeed, whatever might have been the dictates, however absolute the dominion of passion, union with you would have been *very* far from compleating my felicity, unless our hopes and opinions, as well as our persons and hearts were united. Now can I look up with confidence and exultation to the shade of my revered and beloved mother. Now can I safely invoke her presence and her blessing to a union, which death will have no power to dissolve. O what sweet peace, what serene transport is there in the persuasion that the selected soul will continue forever to commune with *my* soul, mingle with mine its adoration of the same divine parent, and partake with me in every thought, in every emotion, both *here* and *hereafter!*

Never, my friend, without *this* persuasion, *never* should

I have known one moment of true happiness. Marriage, indeed, instead of losing its attractions, in consequence of your errors, drew thence only new recommendations. Since with a zeal, a tenderness and a faith like mine, my efforts to restore such an heart and such a reason as yours, could not fail of success, but *till* that restoration were accomplished, never, I repeat, should I have tasted repose, even in *your* arms.

Poor Miss Jessup! She is dead, Henry; Yet not before she did thee and me, poor justice. Her death-bed confession removed my mother's fatal suspicions. This confession, and the perusal of all thy letters, and thy exile, which I afterwards discovered was known to her very early, tho' unsuspected by me till after her decease, brought her to regard thee with some compassion and some respect.

I can write no more; but must not conclude till I have offered thee the tenderest, most fervent vows of an heart that ever was and always will be *thine own*. Witness

Jane Talbot.

THE END

HISTORICAL ESSAY

I

The inception of *Clara Howard* and *Jane Talbot* can be dated as early as April 1800, when Charles Brockden Brown responded to a letter from his brother James, who had apparently objected to "the gloominess and out-of-nature incidents of" *Edgar Huntly*. Though Brown did not believe his brother's criticism was entirely just, he knew that most readers were likely to agree with it. That alone, he wrote, was "sufficient reason for dropping the doleful tone and assuming a cheerful one, or, at least substituting moral causes and daily incidents in place of the prodigious or the singular. I shall not fall hereafter into that strain." Brown's decision was a purely practical one, based on the realities he faced as an American writer trying to support himself by his pen. He needed an audience to succeed, and both he and Hocquet Caritat, the New York bookseller, sought means for increasing its size. Caritat took to England, Brown informed his brother, "a considerable number of Wieland, Ormond and Mervyn," in the hope that their popularity abroad would increase the sales at home,[1] and Brown himself determined to produce a kind of fiction that would appeal to a wider audience.

The change at first glance seems radical. Brown turned away from precisely those elements in his fiction that have

[1]William Dunlap, *The Life of Charles Brockden Brown* (Philadelphia: James P. Parke, 1815), II, 100.

433

become identified with his name: strange phenomena, like spontaneous combustion, ventriloquism, and sleepwalking; mysterious villains, like Ormond and Ludloe, who belong to a secret society and seem to possess preternatural powers; realistic descriptions, like the absorbing accounts of the yellow fever in *Ormond* and *Arthur Mervyn;* frontier warfare, like that in *Edgar Huntly;* and effective Gothic devices, like those that give *Wieland* and *Edgar Huntly* their characteristic tone. In their place he substituted the sentimental mode with focus on a heroine who is most deeply concerned with affairs of the heart and who concentrates on questions of proper social behavior. Both *Clara Howard* and *Jane Talbot* revolve around the conflict of love and duty that both heroines face and the effect its resolution will have on their marriage and subsequent happiness. The latter book, in particular, develops a typical theme of sentimental fiction, the lovers thwarted by parental objections that place great obstacles in their path.[2] Brown's last two novels are thus in important ways quite different from his earlier ones, and critics have generally lamented the choice he made to write in this mode.

Examined more closely, however, the change seems to be less striking. Brown had, after all, used many of the devices of sentimental fiction in his already published works. As long ago as 1926, Fred Lewis Pattee discussed the strong influence of Samuel Richardson on *Wieland,* which, on one level at least, is a sentimental tale of seduction, and he noted that Clara Wieland resembles the heroines of such fiction in her constant analysis of her emotions.[3] *Ormond,* too, bears a strong relation to this kind of fiction. The heroine, Constantia Dudley, is a virtuous young lady who triumphs over her undeserved misfortunes, supports herself by her needle, is threatened twice with rape, but emerges unscathed from her ordeal. Ormond plays the role

---

[2]For a discussion of this theme, see Henri Petter, *The Early American Novel* (Columbus: Ohio State Univ. Press, 1971), pp. 192–196.

[3]Fred Lewis Pattee, Introduction to *Wieland* (New York: Harcourt, Brace, 1926), pp. xxxvi–xxxviii.

of the unprincipled seducer who would woo the girl from
her virtue, and who is eventually struck down by her pen-
knife when he attempts to force himself upon her.[4] To view
both *Wieland* and *Ormond* in these terms is to see at once
that Brown was no stranger to sentimental fiction; his use
of the mode in *Clara Howard* and *Jane Talbot* is not so sharp
a departure from his usual practice as might be supposed.

Neither can it be said that Brown abandoned the intellectual content that had characterized his first four novels.
Both *Clara Howard* and *Jane Talbot* develop themes that
resemble some in his earlier fiction. The rise of Edward
Hartley in *Clara Howard* from simple apprentice to man
of wealth through his association with an older benefactor
and his marriage to Clara bears an unmistakable resemblance to the progress of Arthur Mervyn, who attains success by much the same means. In a similar fashion, the
conflict between religious faith and Godwinian rationalism
in *Jane Talbot,* though presented in a less sensational manner, is a variation upon the theme that Brown had developed in *Ormond.* The characters in these two late books
live in a more domestic world, but they are as actively involved in discussing the motives and consequences of their
behavior as are those in the earlier novels, and if they do
not have such strange and frightening experiences as do
their counterparts in the other books, they are no less
interested in ideas nor less concerned with how they should
act in the everyday world in which they find themselves.

It will not do, therefore, to posit a radical break in
Brown's career in 1800, or to treat *Clara Howard* and *Jane
Talbot* as if they marked a complete—and unfortunate—
departure from his fictional practice. The change is not
quite so dramatic. Brown did indeed put aside the prodigious and the singular, and he substituted "moral causes
and daily incidents" for the "out-of-nature" events that
James Brown had objected to, but he did not totally alter

[4]Cf. Donald A. Ringe, "Charles Brockden Brown," *Major Writers
of Early American Literature,* ed. Everett Emerson (Madison: Univ. of
Wisconsin Press, 1972), p. 277.

his fictional practice. The sentimental mode was as much a part of his fictional style as was the Gothic, and it provided an effective—if to the modern taste less attractive—vehicle for the exploration of ideas. *Clara Howard* and *Jane Talbot* may not appeal so strongly to the modern reader as do *Wieland, Ormond, Arthur Mervyn,* and *Edgar Huntly,* but their relation to at least three of these works is unmistakable. They are written in a fictional mode that had played an important role in Brown's first two published novels, and they carry forward at least some of the intellectual themes that Brown had been developing throughout his short career as a writer of fiction.

II

Clara Howard and *Jane Talbot* were probably not yet planned when Brown wrote his brother in April 1800. He had still to arrange the publication of the second part of *Arthur Mervyn*—it would not appear till summer—and seeing it through the press and editing the *Monthly Magazine* must have taken up much of his time. Brown was apparently also planning a novel based on the international theme, the story of an American girl who goes to Europe and lives in both England and Italy before she returns to New York to marry in January 1800. If, as has been suggested, this novel was planned in the spring of that year, it may have been what Brown had in mind in his letter to James.[5] He did not complete it, however, and after the second part of *Arthur Mervyn* appeared, Brown turned his attention to *Clara Howard.* When he began the book is uncertain, but if William Dunlap's statement is correct—this ''was the last of the novels written by Mr. Brown during his residence in New York'' (Dunlap, *Life,* II, 47)—he

[5]Charles E. Bennett, ''Charles Brockden Brown and the International Novel,'' *Studies in the Novel,* 12 (Spring 1980), 62–64. Bennett also believes that the fragment ''Jessica'' was written at this time. See ''The Charles Brockden Brown Canon,'' Diss. University of North Carolina 1974, p. 223.

must have been at work on it in the fall of 1800, for Brown moved permanently to Philadelphia late in that year.[6]

The book derives from a real incident in the life of one of Brown's friends, who became involved in a triangle much like that of Mary Wilmot, Edward Hartley, and Clara Howard in the novel. The episode appears in the volume of Brown's biography written by Paul Allen, but turned over to Dunlap, who revised it as Volume I of the life of Brown he published in 1815. In the course of his revision, Dunlap excised the passage, and the incident was not made public until the recent discovery and publication of the bound proof sheets of Allen's volume.[7] According to Daniel E. Kennedy, who devoted a lifetime to the study of Brown and left a massive manuscript biography of him, Dunlap "rigidly suppressed" the material because the persons

---

[6]Harry R. Warfel, *Charles Brockden Brown: American Gothic Novelist* (Gainesville: Univ. of Florida Press, 1949), p. 189. Although Warfel states here that Brown moved to Philadelphia "early in 1801," the footnotes to his biography (put together in "dittoed" form in 1953 and privately distributed), cite an entry in Thomas Pym Cope's manuscript diary, 31 November 1800, that Brown had "concluded to remain permanently in Philadelphia," as the source for a correction of the text to read "late in 1800" (p. 10). It should also be noted that Brown seems to have moved back and forth between New York and Philadelphia during the late summer and fall of 1800. He was certainly in Philadelphia on 1 September 1800 (Dunlap, *Life,* II, 100), and he met Elizabeth Linn in Philadelphia in November of that year (David Lee Clark, *Charles Brockden Brown: Pioneer Voice of America* [Durham, N.C.: Duke Univ. Press, 1952], p. 197). Clark also states, however, that "Brown returned to New York by the middle of September and remained there until he had edited the last issue of the *Monthly Magazine*" for December 1800 (p. 196). Thus, although Dunlap seems to suggest that *Clara Howard* was written—that is, completed—in New York, it may well be that Brown only began the book in the fall of 1800 and continued to work on it in Philadelphia in 1801.

[7]Two editions have been published, the texts of which, facsimiles of the Allen volume, are identical. Thus, either may be used for reference. They are Allen, *Life,* ed. Charles E. Bennett (Delmar, N.Y.: Scholars' Facsimiles & Reprints, 1975), and Allen, *Life,* ed. Robert E. Hemenway and Joseph Katz (Columbia, S.C.: J. Faust, 1976). The passage may be found on pp. 44–48. For convenience sake, the book, in either edition, is hereafter referred to as *Life.*

involved—though given the fictitious names of Emilius, Arabella, and Ophelia—were readily identifiable by a contemporary audience. Kennedy himself thought that Emilius was Brown's close friend and fellow law student, William W. Wilkins, perhaps because the passage occurs in a long account of Brown's friendship and correspondence with him. Kennedy even tried to identify, though without much success, the two women involved.[8]

Charles E. Bennett believes, on the other hand, that Emilius was "a pseudonym for John Davidson,"[9] another of Brown's friends who helped to found the Belles Lettres Club to which Brown and Wilkins belonged. The evidence seems convincing. The name Emilius appears in a second context in Allen's biography. Well before he presents the episode that provided the source for *Clara Howard,* Allen describes the correspondence between Brown and Emilius in such a way as to suggest his identity with Davidson (*Life,* pp. 13–14, 17–21), and Dunlap himself gives tacit corroboration because in his revision, he strikes all mention of Emilius and inserts Davidson's name where Allen would have used the pseudonym (Dunlap, *Life,* I, 18; cf. *Life,* p. 17). The matter is perhaps of no great importance to *Clara Howard* except insofar as the identification of Emilius helps in dating the incident. In either case the date is approximately the same. Since Wilkins died early in 1795, Kennedy dates the episode as before that year and "possibly as early as 1790" (Kennedy, p. 1414). Bennett, on his part, dates the letter of Brown to Emilius as sometime between 1788 and 1792 (Bennett, "Letters," pp. 167–168). Brown, in other words, reached back as far as a decade or more to find material for his fifth published novel.

In Allen's account, Emilius, Charles's friend, describes

[8]Daniel Edwards Kennedy, "Charles Brockden Brown: Life and Works," pp. 1407A–1409. Kennedy's unpublished MS biography is in the Kent State University Brown collection. It is referred to hereafter as Kennedy.

[9]Charles E. Bennett, "The Letters of Charles Brockden Brown: An Annotated Census," *Resources for American Literary Study,* 6 (Autumn 1976), 168.

the situation in which he finds himself with two young women, and he asks Brown his opinion on how he should act toward them. He is beloved of Arabella, a lady he esteems but does not love. His treatment of her, he believes, has been honorable. He has not encouraged her in any way, nor has he led her to believe that he would be anything but her friend. "In short whatever motives she might have to persevere in her addresses, he had supplied her with none; and the blame if any must be attributed to the indulgence of an unfortunate passion, equally ardent and hopeless." Though Emilius resists the blandishments of Arabella, he falls in love with Ophelia, a girl who possesses "every quality to ensure happiness to a lover" (*Life,* pp. 44–45). Ophelia, however, behaves as honorably toward him as he had toward Arabella. She gives him no grounds to believe that she is anything more than a friend, yet he, like Arabella, persists in his passion. The three are caught in an impasse, a situation Brown approximates in *Clara Howard.* Arabella is the prototype of Mary Wilmot, Emilius of Edward Hartley, and Ophelia of Clara Howard.

In turning the incident into fiction, Brown altered the case in a number of important ways. Unlike Emilius, who does not encourage Arabella, Edward is already engaged to Mary when he falls in love with Clara, and unlike Ophelia, Clara returns her admirer's love. Because of his previous commitment, moreover, Clara insists that he fulfill his promise to Mary if she will have him, for Clara refuses to wed him as long as Mary is unmarried and unhappy. What Brown has done is to take the basic facts of his friend's experience and change them in such a way as to increase the complications and place the focus sharply on the character of Clara, through whom he examines some of the questions raised by the real incident: the extent to which Emilius is obligated to Arabella and what his attitude and behavior toward both the young women ought to be. The answer Brown gave—that his first duty was to the girl who loved him—is similar to the view that Clara maintains in the novel, so that Clara Howard assumes, in effect, the intellectual position that Brown had argued in his answer to his friend.

Though the major elements in *Clara Howard* derive from a true experience, some parts of the book were simply lifted from Brown's already published fiction. Edward Hartley and his sisters, who depend on an uncle for support, fear they will lose their livelihood when he dies because his son hates and will dispossess them—precisely the situation of Edgar Huntly and his sisters in the earlier book. Hartley and Mary Wilmot can afford to marry only after her brother dies leaving a large sum of money that they are reluctant to spend because they know that he, a poor school-teacher, could not have accumulated such wealth—an exact parallel to the experience of Huntly and Mary Waldegrave. They discover that her murdered brother, who taught in a Negro school, also left a large sum at his death. And the appearance of Morton, in *Clara Howard,* to claim the $5,000 he says he sent Wilmot for safekeeping is like the arrival of Weymouth, in *Edgar Huntly,* seeking the $7,500 he claims to have sent Waldegrave. The sums are different, of course, and in *Clara Howard* the money turns out to be legitimately Mary's, but otherwise the incidents are much the same.

Echoes of other novels also appear in *Clara Howard.* Like Arthur Mervyn, Edward Hartley is a poor country lad, who, moving to the city, becomes the protégé of a wealthy man and attaches himself to more mature women, all of whom can advance his career. Though Hartley does not seem to be so much of an opportunist as Arthur Mervyn, he speaks, in his introduction to the book, with a voice that sounds like that of the earlier character. And like Stephen Calvert, in the unfinished novel of that name, Hartley decides at one point to withdraw from civilization and go west, not like Calvert to the shores of Lake Michigan, but across the Mississippi to the Pacific coast. Too much, of course, must not be made of such similarities. Brown left many works unfinished and was always willing to borrow from both them and his completed novels to provide materials for the book on which he was currently working. Despite the echoes of *Edgar Huntly, Arthur Mervyn,* and "Memoirs of Stephen Calvert," *Clara Howard* is drawn from an identifiable incident in real life, develops a theme that derives from that incident, and actually bears little relation to the works that are partially reflected in it.

If Brown did indeed begin *Clara Howard* in the late summer or fall of 1800, he may still have been at work on it the following spring, for it is not until 25 April 1801 that we start to hear news of its publication. On that date, the *Port Folio,* a literary weekly published by Joseph Dennie, announced as "Literary Intelligence": "Mr. Asbury Dickins is preparing for the press, a new novel, of the epistolary class, from the pen of a well-known and popular writer."[10] One is ordinarily reluctant to take such a squib too seriously, for publishers would sometimes announce a book as in the press long before it was actually under way. In this case, however, the information seems to have been accurate, as indeed it should have been since Dennie, Dickins, and Brown were closely associated in Philadelphia. Two weeks later (8 May 1801), Brown himself wrote to John E. Hall, an aspiring young writer from Baltimore, on the status of his new novel: "The printer has made considerable progress in the publication which I believe I mentioned to you in my last, as having been begun. It will be, typographically considered, a very beautiful book."[11]

Within a month the work was finished. According to the records of Hugh Maxwell, the Philadelphia printer, an edition of 500 copies had been completed by 6 June at a cost of $114.00 for the composition and $27.60 for the presswork. Four days later, 10 June, Maxwell charged the publisher an additional $2.00 for printing "500 labels for C. Howard."[12] Once the book was printed, Asbury Dickins moved quickly to secure the copyright, for on 13 June, he "deposited . . . the title" with the clerk of the court in the

[10] *Port Folio,* 1 (25 April 1801), 133.

[11] *The Library of American Biography,* ed. Jared Sparks (Boston: Hilliard, Gray, and Co., 1834), I, facing p. 117. See also Bennett, "Letters," p. 186.

[12] Maxwell's "Day Book," MS Historical Society of Pennsylvania.

District of Pennsylvania.[13] By late June, copies were apparently ready for sale. The *American Review, and Literary Journal,* in its issue for "April, May and June 1801," announced "A *new novel* . . . entitled *Clara Howard,* in a series of letters; elegantly printed in one vol."[14] Since this issue is dated 1 July 1801, it has sometimes been said that the book appeared near this date (see Warfel, *Brown,* p. 191).

It is much more likely, however, that *Clara Howard* was published about a week or ten days earlier. On 22 June 1801, the Philadelphia *Gazette of the United States, and Daily Advertiser* printed an ad bearing the same date and stating that *Clara Howard* was "this day Published." Though one cannot be certain that the book was in fact issued on that specific day, it was heavily advertised for the next three weeks, somewhat more spottily presented in late July, and heavily advertised again during the first two weeks of August. In all, the ad was published thirty-two times between 22 June and 25 August 1801.[15] Such concentrated advertising over a two-month period surely indicates that the book was available for sale. We can conclude with some confidence, therefore, that *Clara Howard* was published on 22 June 1801 or within a day or two of that date.

Only one American edition of *Clara Howard,* printed by Hugh Maxwell and published in Philadelphia by Asbury Dickins, appeared during Brown's lifetime, and it was not until 1807 that a British edition was published, printed at the Minerva Press, that source of so much popular literature in England, for Lane, Newman and Company. This edition contains some important changes from the first American one. The novel appeared in Philadelphia as *Clara Howard; in a Series of Letters* with a hero named Edward Hartley. The British edition changed the hero's name to Philip Stanley and retitled the book *Philip Stanley; or, The*

[13]MS Library of Congress.

[14]1 (April, May, and June 1801), 263.

[15]The ad appeared in the *Gazette* on the following dates: 22, 23, 25, 26, 27, 30 June; 1, 2, 3, 7, 8, 9, 10, 11, 17, 18, 22, 28, 29 July; 3, 4, 5, 6, 7, 8, 11, 12, 13, 14, 22, 24, 25 August 1801.

Enthusiasm of Love. No one knows why the change was made, but one may speculate. The English editor may simply have wanted a man's name for the title, and, as Petter has suggested, "Edward Hartley may have been rejected" as too close to Edgar Huntly (*Early American Novel,* p. 184). Be that as it may, subsequent American editions, beginning in 1827, retain Philip Stanley as hero, but give the book the hybrid title, *Clara Howard; or, The Enthusiasm of Love.* In this form, the book was reissued in 1857, 1859, 1887, and, of course, in modern reprints of the 1887 collected edition in 1963 and 1970.

III

Not much is known about the composition of *Jane Talbot.* The few firm references that have survived are tantalizingly vague, and scholars have interpreted them in radically different ways. The crucial piece of evidence is a passage in John Davis's *Travels,* which, though not as precise in detail as one might wish, is central to the history of *Jane Talbot* and must be examined with some care. As he was about to leave New York on a journey to Washington, Davis writes, he stopped at the post office, where he found a long letter, the last part of which is dated 23 June 1801, from a friend on Long Island. After quoting the letter, he simply states that he left New York for Philadelphia, where he must have arrived several days after that date. There he found Charles Brockden Brown at work on a book. "He was ingratiating himself into the favour of the ladies by writing a new novel, and rivalling *Lopez de Vega* by the multitude of his works." Davis mentions the other people he met, among them Asbury Dickins and Joseph Dennie. Then he observes: "Mr. *Brown* said little, but seemed lost in meditation; his creative fancy was, perhaps, conjuring up scenes to spin out the thread of his new novel."[16]

[16]John Davis, *Travels of Four Years and a Half in the United States of America; During 1798, 1799, 1800, 1801, and 1802* (London: T. Ostell and T. Hurst, 1803), pp. 203–204.

Davis, unfortunately, does not name the book, and scholars have, at one time or another, identified it as both *Clara Howard* and *Jane Talbot*. Harry R. Warfel believed that it was the former. He quotes the passage from Davis in his biography of Brown and concludes that the "new novel was *Clara Howard*," a view that Charles E. Bennett calls "very probably right."[17] This conclusion has always been open to question, mainly because the publication dates suggested for *Clara Howard* seemed to indicate that the book was too close to publication in June for Davis to have seen Brown still at work on it near the end of the month. The newly discovered printing history of *Clara Howard* now makes it certain that Warfel's and Bennett's identification cannot be correct. *Clara Howard* was already printed by 6 June, long before Davis left New York. Thus, the novel he found Brown working on when he arrived in Philadelphia sometime after the twenty-third could not have been *Clara Howard*. It must have been *Jane Talbot*.

Because they had misidentified the book Davis mentions, Warfel and Bennett could not write satisfactory accounts of the writing and publication of *Jane Talbot*. Warfel has nothing to say about the book's composition. He merely states that *Jane Talbot* was published "late in 1801" (*Brown*, pp. 197–201). Bennett, on the other hand, argues that *Jane Talbot* may have been written as early as the fall of 1800, citing a passage that Brown wrote in a letter to Elizabeth Linn dated 10 March 1801: "I mean not to publish 'Jane Talbot.' My reasons for a change of plan, I will tell you, when I have all your ear" (Clark, *Brown*, p. 203). On the basis of this statement and his misinterpretation of the Davis incident, Bennett suggests "that *Jane Talbot* was finished or nearly finished in early March," and that only then did Brown turn to *Clara Howard*, on which he was still at work when Davis saw him in June ("Brown Canon," pp. 224–226).

[17]Warfel, *Brown*, p. 191; Charles E. Bennett, "The Charles Brockden Brown Canon," p. 225.

Though he does not mention Brown's letter to Elizabeth Linn of 10 March 1801, Daniel E. Kennedy is more accurate in his reconstruction of the events. He accepts 22 June as the publication date for *Clara Howard* and believes that the book Davis mentions is *Jane Talbot*. But misreading the date of the incident, he places Davis in Philadelphia on 23 June, and he writes that Brown hastily began his new novel the day after *Clara Howard* was published! (pp. 1440–1441). Kennedy cites a passage from Dunlap, moreover, that reveals yet another fact about the composition of *Jane Talbot*. A week or so after the Davis incident, Brown left on a trip up the Hudson River during which he kept a journal. In the entry for 10 July, he records a tale told by the vessel's mate. "A very crude and brief tale it was," Brown writes, "but acceptable and pleasing to me. A voyage round the globe is a very trivial adventure, now-a-days. This man has been twice to Nootka, thence to Canton, and thence to Europe and home" (Dunlap, *Life*, II, 53–54). Since Brown used this material for Henry Colden's travels near the end of *Jane Talbot*, he had not yet finished the book in July 1801.

Sketchy though the facts may be, taken together and rightly understood they provide the basis for a hypothetical history of the book's composition that is probably close to the truth. Brown must have begun *Jane Talbot* by early 1801, perhaps while he was still at work on *Clara Howard*. We know that *Jane Talbot* was at least planned by early March, and since Brown speaks of its publication in his letter to Elizabeth Linn, he had probably begun the writing and may even have carried it well forward. Though he gave up the book for a while, he must have returned to it during the spring while *Clara Howard* was going through the press, for by late June, when Davis was in Philadelphia, Brown was still at work on it. Soon thereafter, he took his trip up the Hudson, learned of the sailor's voyage to Nootka and around the world, and traveled through Massachusetts and Connecticut. He returned to Philadelphia no sooner than late July—he was still in New Haven on the twentieth of the month (ibid., II, 56)—and sometime during the summer or fall, he completed his book, incorporating into it the information he derived from the sailor's story.

Although the sailor's account of his travels is the only material in *Jane Talbot* that can be traced to an actual incident, there are echoes from other of Brown's novels and fragments. Henry Colden seems to be related to the Coldens who appear in Brown's unfinished works. In "Jessica," for example, printed in both Allen's and Dunlap's biographies, Colden is a well-educated young man, recently come from Europe, who keeps completely to himself and appears to have some deep mystery in his background. His countenance seems to reveal a mind and soul ill at ease. Jessica's brother becomes acquainted with him and arranges to have him board with his mother and sister. Fascinated by their new boarder, Jessica promptly falls in love with him, but when she tries to strike up an intellectual conversation, she asks a question that greatly disturbs him. She had seen him reading in Mosheim's history about the Hussite movement in Bohemia, and she asks him to tell her what harm there is "in leaving the Romish religion and turning Protestant, that people must be burnt alive for doing so." At Jessica's question, Colden starts, casts her "a dreadful look," and hurries from the room (ibid., I, 165–166). Though the mystery is never explained, this Colden, like the one in *Jane Talbot,* has a disturbing past connected in some manner with questions of religion.

Another Colden appears in "Harry Wallace," a summary plan for a novel that Allen printed in his biography, but which Dunlap excised from his. This Colden is an Englishman who travels to America on some business for his father in 1768. He becomes acquainted with Hobart, a Quaker merchant connected with Colden's firm, and seduces his fifteen-year-old daughter Mary, who secretly bears Colden's son. The couple manage to conceal the child's parentage, and Colden arranges to have him taken in by a family named Wallace. He even contrives to become the boy's protector and to give him his name. This young Harry Colden, born in 1770, grows up to be a virtuous man who cares for those who come under his charge. Since the Henry Colden of *Jane Talbot* is said to have badly treated a "Woodbury girl,"[18] he bears some resemblance to the elder Colden in "Harry Wallace," but because the action of *Jane Talbot* seems to take place between 1797 and 1801, he is certainly much younger than the seducer would have been at that time, and there is nothing in the book to suggest that he has ever been that much of a villain. His sins in *Jane Talbot*—his youthful espousal of radical views, as well as his mistreatment of the girl—are treated much more lightly.

The Colden in Brown's last novel seems, therefore, to be perhaps the final development of a character that Brown had used in his unpublished fiction. All three Coldens, moreover, resemble the character of Ormond in the 1799 novel of that name. Like Ormond, the Colden of "Jessica" has a mysterious past, and like him, too, the Colden of "Harry Wallace" is a seducer of women. Even more to the point, the Colden of *Jane Talbot* has shared the radical ideas espoused by Ormond and, it is suggested, has treated at least one girl badly. Significant too is the Colden–Jane Talbot relationship, which seems to be a reworking of that between Ormond and Constantia Dudley. Jane is like Constantia in that she is unprepared to argue intellectual matters with a man "of superior subtlety and knowledge,"[19] but she possesses a resource that Constantia lacks: she has religion to support her. Colden, too, is different from Ormond in that he has long since passed through his radical phase before the book begins, and he makes no attempt to batter down Jane's defenses or to seduce her to his will. He wishes, instead, to marry her.

Minor elements in *Jane Talbot* are also related to some in Brown's other fiction. Jane's cousin, named Risberg, whom she was supposed to marry, bears the name of several characters—a Swiss merchant, his wife, daughter, and

[18]See Letter XXXVII, p. 318 of this edition.
[19]See Letter XXXIV, p. 305 of this edition.

nephew—in "Harry Wallace," but there seems to be no specific connection between them. More important is the series of letters Henry Colden wrote to Thomson before the action of *Jane Talbot* begins, letters in which he argued the radical ideas he had adopted. These resemble the letters Waldegrave wrote to Edgar Huntly, in which he attempted to convert his friend to similarly irreligious views. Both Colden and Waldegrave commit their radical ideas to paper, and though Colden, unlike Waldegrave after his reconversion, does not attempt to destroy the letters lest they influence others, he is himself hurt by them when Mrs. Fielder, Jane's foster mother, learns what they contain, and he too eventually renounces his radical opinions. As he had done before, Brown transferred both characters and incidents from other works to the one he was currently writing. The echoes, however, are rather minor ones, and *Jane Talbot*, like *Clara Howard*, is a very different book from those by Brown that treat similar material.

Although Brown could not have finished *Jane Talbot* until after his trip up the Hudson in July 1801, we do not know how much work remained to be done nor when he returned to the writing. Because Colden's voyage is mentioned first at the beginning of Letter XL, a third of the book was perhaps still to be written, and Brown may not have returned to it at once. Daniel E. Kennedy writes that Brown began a riding trip west with his brother James on 19 August, basing his belief on a journal, which he attributes to Brown, printed in the December 1803 and January 1804 issues of the *Literary Magazine* as "Memorandums Made on a Journey through Part of Pennsylvania."[20] The attribution, though plausible, is by no means certain, however, and since the journal breaks off at the end of the second installment and was never continued, we do not know how long the trip took. If Brown did indeed make this journey, he could have finished *Jane Talbot* before he left in August,

[20]Kennedy, pp. 1380–1398. The journal may be found in the *Literary Magazine, and American Register,* 1 (December 1803), 167–173, and (January 1804), 250–255.

or he might have laid it aside until after his return and picked it up again in the late summer or fall.

The only known facts suggest the latter. On 21 August 1801, *Jane Talbot* was advertised as "in the press" in the Philadelphia *Aurora General Advertiser,*[21] indicating, perhaps, that part of the manuscript at least was ready to print. If so, publication was long delayed, for the book did not appear until very late in the year. Though no one knows the reason for the delay, a possible explanation is that Brown was still at work on the book and writing against the press. Be that as it may, we do not hear of *Jane Talbot* again until December. In the Baltimore *Telegraph and Daily Advertiser* for 19 December 1801, it was advertised as "just received" under the date of 12 December (ibid.); and beginning on 8 January 1802, it was advertised for about a month in the *Alexandria Advertiser and Commercial Intelligencer.*[22] In light of this evidence, it seems reasonable to conclude that *Jane Talbot* appeared in early December 1801. Printed by John Bioren, the book was published as Volume IV of Conrad's Select Novels and was embellished with two engraved illustrations.[23] The title page bears the imprint of three related firms: John Conrad, and Co. of Philadelphia, M. and J. Conrad, and Co. of Baltimore, and Rapin, Conrad, and Co. of Washington City.

Although little is known about Conrad's Select Novels, the series is of some importance for what it can tell us about

[21]Jacob N. Blanck, ed., *Bibliography of American Literature* (New Haven: Yale Univ. Press, 1955), I, 305.

[22]See the *Alexandria Advertiser and Commercial Intelligencer,* 8 January to 3 February 1802. Since some issues are missing, the record is not complete. In the surviving issues the ad appears on the following dates: 8, 12, 13, 19, 23, 26, 29 January; 3 February 1802.

[23]Although Daniel E. Kennedy claims that *Jane Talbot* was published both independently and as Volume IV of Conrad's Select Novels, it is impossible to tell from extant copies whether this was indeed the case. Since the half title page and the illustrations that identify the series are not integral to the gatherings in which they appear, their absence does not necessarily imply independent publication. They may simply have been removed from the copy. Kennedy quotes a catalog description of the series, dated 15 October 1804. See Kennedy, p. 1439.

the context in which Brown's last novel was published. The first two titles, comprising Volumes I to III, were Agnes Maria Bennett's *De Valcourt* and Regina Maria Roche's *The Nocturnal Visit*. These books were announced in the *Port Folio* for 25 April and 2 May 1801[24] and were noticed as published in the "July, August and September" issue of the *American Review, and Literary Journal* that appeared on 1 October.[25] *Jane Talbot* followed toward the end of the year, and the next two books, Roche's *Clermont* and Charlotte Smith's *Emmeline,* were published in 1802. What is especially important to note is that *Jane Talbot* is the only original, American novel to appear among a group of reprints of widely read British books, and that the authors of these works were very well known. Roche was especially famous for her *Children of the Abbey,* which went through multiple editions in the United States, and Smith, a respectable writer by any standard, was the author of *The Old Manor House,* a book much read both here and abroad. From the point of view of contemporary readers, *Jane Talbot* was in excellent company.

It also had the distinction of being the only first edition of Brown's novels to be illustrated. Two scenes from the book were selected: Jane's visit to the watchmaker's shop in Letter VI and the meeting between Colden and Jane's brother Frank in Letter XXXII. Both were designed by John James Barralet (c. 1747–1815), a native of Ireland who settled in Philadelphia around 1796, "painted portraits and landscapes in water-colors and designed work for the engravers." For a time he was associated with Alexander Lawson (1773–1846), who engraved the second of these illustrations. A native of Scotland, Lawson grew to maturity in Liverpool and Manchester, and, because he could not sail directly from England, he came to the United States in 1794 intending to continue his journey to Revolutionary France. Attracted by "the social and political conditions"

[24]*Port Folio,* 1 (25 April 1801), 133; (2 May 1801), 143.
[25]1 (July, August, and September 1801), 374.

he found here, however, Lawson changed his plans and eventually settled in Philadelphia, where he found employment as an engraver. He later produced "the best plates in [Alexander] Wilson's famous 'Ornithology.' " The first illustration in Brown's novel was engraved by Joseph H. Seymour (fl. 1791–1822), who had worked for Isaiah Thomas in Worcester before moving to Philadelphia.[26] Both illustrations bear the caption "Jane Talbot" and are headed "Conrad & Cos. Edition of Select Novels."

Though *Jane Talbot* appeared in a series of books by popular writers, the first edition was apparently not well known. Even William Dunlap, who, as a long-standing friend, should have been familiar with all of Brown's works, was not aware of it. In his 1815 biography, Dunlap writes: "In the year 1804, Mr. Brown published in England his last novel 'Jane Talbot.' "[27] Since Dunlap makes no other mention of the book, he clearly implies that the British edition was its first publication, an error perpetuated by William Hickling Prescott in the essay on Brown he wrote for Jared Sparks's *Library of American Biography* in 1834,[28] and by other critics in both England and America until at least as late as 1912.[29] *Jane Talbot* was indeed published in England in 1804, printed at the Minerva Press for Lane, Newman, and Co., but this was simply a reprint of the first American edition of 1801. The book was reprinted again for the 1827

[26]Material on all three artists is derived from David M. Stauffer, *American Engravers upon Copper and Steel* (New York: Grolier Club, 1907), I, 17–18, 156–158, 244.

[27]Dunlap, *Life*, II, 67. See also Dunlap's 1836 article on Brown, where he compounds the error: "in 1804, his last novel, 'Jane Talbot,' was published, first in London by his brother James, and immediately reprinted in America." See *The National Portrait Gallery of Distinguished Americans,* ed. James Herring and James B. Longacre (New York: Herman Bancroft, 1836), III, 5.

[28]I, 162; repeated in his "Memoir of Charles Brockden Brown, the American Novelist," *Biographical and Critical Miscellanies* (New York: Harper and Brothers, 1845), p. 40.

[29]See George B. Smith, "Brockden Brown," *Fortnightly Review,* NS 24 (September 1878), 407; W. P. Trent and John Erskine, *Great American Writers* (New York: Henry Holt, 1912), pp. 19–20.

collected edition of Brown's novels and was included in the sets of 1857, 1859, and 1887. It appears as well in the modern reprints of the 1887 collected edition, published in 1963 and 1970.

IV

The first editions of *Clara Howard* and *Jane Talbot* seem to have elicited no critical response in American magazines when they appeared in 1801, nor was *Clara Howard* reviewed when it was reprinted in England as *Philip Stanley* in 1807. *Jane Talbot,* however, did receive two reviews when the first British edition was published in 1804. The May issue of the *Literary Journal* contained a brief notice of the book in which the anonymous reviewer, who had apparently read *Arthur Mervyn* and *Edgar Huntly,* dismissed the new novel as a "silly publication," so far inferior to the earlier works by Brown as to suggest that he was not in fact the author. It has something of "his style and manner," the reviewer writes, but it lacks his "nervous language and vigour of imagination."[30] The November issue of the *Imperial Review* was more favorable in its estimate of the book. The critic knew all four of Brown's major novels, and though he thought *Jane Talbot* "far inferior to Wieland," he preferred it to the other three. He includes the usual summary and long excerpts from the book, rejoices at the conversion of Colden, and concludes by pointing out some "inconsistencies and errors" in style.[31]

These were the only reviews of either book. Critical discussion of *Clara Howard* and further treatment of *Jane Talbot* had to wait for articles reviewing Brown's fiction as a whole, and in Great Britain these were long in coming. In December 1820, an anonymous critic in the *New Monthly Magazine and Universal Register* tried to account for the fact

[30]*Literary Journal: A Review of Literature, Science, Manners, Politics,* 3 (1 May 1804), 492.
[31]*Imperial Review; or London and Dublin Literary Journal,* 3 (November 1804), 392–401.

that Brown's novels were so little known or valued in England when most of them had been available in British circulating libraries for seventeen years. The books, he concludes, had unfortunately been introduced to the British public through "one of the common reservoirs of sentimental trash" (the Minerva Press), and they were thought "to share in the general contempt attached to those poor productions." He had recently discovered, however, several of Brown's novels, and on the basis of this reading, he concludes that Brown had not received the attention he deserved. Because, as he adds in a footnote, he had not read *Clara Howard*—he uses the American title—nor *Jane Talbot*, his critical remarks do not refer to those books.[32] Nonetheless, the article is important for what it implies about their reception. Brown had to be recognized for his four major novels before his final ones, so different in subject and tone, could attract attention at all.[33]

In the two important estimates of Brown's fiction that soon followed, *Clara Howard* and *Jane Talbot* got mixed reviews. John Neal, an American living in England and writing for *Blackwood's Edinburgh Magazine*, dismissed them both in 1824 as "mere newspaper novels; sleepy, dull common-sense—very absolute prose—nothing more."[34] In 1826, however, a reviewer in the *British Critic* seriously tried to estimate their virtues and faults. *Philip Stanley*, he writes, is relatively weak. Though the "struggle between love and duty . . . is skillfully worked up throughout," the novel borrows too much of its plot from *Edgar Huntly* and, in "style and matter," nowhere "rises above that ordinary and matter-of-fact level which soon becomes tedious without

[32] "On the Writings of Charles Brown, the American Novelist," *New Monthly Magazine and Universal Register*, 14 (December 1820), 609.

[33] Brown's reputation in England was undoubtedly enhanced by the publication in London of Dunlap's biography and selections from his uncollected writings: *Memoirs of Charles Brockden Brown, the American Novelist* (London: Henry Colburn, 1822) and *Carwin, the Biloquist, and Other American Tales and Pieces* (London: Henry Colburn, 1822).

[34] [John Neal], "American Writers, No. II," *Blackwood's Edinburgh Magazine*, 16 (October 1824), 424.

humour or incident to enliven it." *Jane Talbot,* he goes on to say, is "written in the same level style" and, like *Philip Stanley,* is "more full of love and argument than of adventure." There is, nonetheless, much to be said for the book. It is "composed with great ability and knowledge of human nature; and whether the characters be or be not intended to be held up to our admiration, there is a truth and individuality about them which impress their features strongly on the recollection."[35]

In general, however, Brown's last two novels were not well received in England, even by those who knew and admired the major fiction. Thomas Love Peacock, for example, on whose authority we know that Percy Bysshe Shelley was fond of Brown's four best-known novels, observes that in *Philip Stanley* and *Jane Talbot,* Brown abandoned his usual practice "and confined himself to the common business of life. They had little comparative success."[36] Mary Shelley had no use for them at all. In her journal for 30 November 1814, she records her reading of *Philip Stanley* with the succinct "very stupid." Two weeks later, 15 December, she notes that she was reading *Jane Talbot* and writes a somewhat longer but no more favorable comment: "very stupid book; some letters so-so; but the old woman in it is so abominable, the young woman so weak, and the young man (the only sensible one in the whole) the author of course contrives to bring to idiotcy at the end."[37] Mary Shelley's reaction may, of course, have been influenced by the book's rejection of Godwinian philosophy, but her judgments are not inconsistent with those of other critics in early nineteenth-century England.

The American reception of *Clara Howard* begins with the biography by Paul Allen that was revised and completed by William Dunlap in 1815. Allen discovered the apparent

[35]*British Critic,* 3rd ser., 2 (April 1826), 60–61.

[36]*Peacock's Memoirs of Shelley,* ed. H. F. B. Brett-Smith (London: Henry Frowde, 1909), p. 36.

[37]*Mary Shelley's Journal,* ed. Frederick L. Jones (Norman: Univ. of Oklahoma Press, 1947), pp. 27, 29.

origin of the book's main plot in Brown's correspondence, and he saw in that discovery a basis for criticizing the novel. *Clara Howard,* he wrote, had been "censured on the ground that the characters were not to be found in nature," yet it turns out "that with a little embellishment the incidents were actually taken from real life." Nonetheless, he goes on to say, the criticism is just, for it is no defense of the characters to state that they really existed. "If one such example is only to be found, it proves not what nature is, but what nature is not. If the anomalies and eccentricities of the human character are to be regarded as furnishing precedents for an author; it will be impossible to outrage human nature by any species of extravagance. This is not that nature by which the merits of an author must be tried, for fancy herself may be defied to furnish such strange and wild combinations as real life occasionally exhibits." *Clara Howard,* in Allen's judgment, contains just such "anomalies and eccentricities" (*Life,* p. 47).

When Dunlap excised this passage from Allen's book, he opened the way for his own discussion of the novel in Volume II of his work. Dunlap makes no mention of the book's origin, nor does he criticize the characters for being "out of nature." Instead, he provides a long summary of the book with some incidental judgments. He points out the novel's relation to *Edgar Huntly,* and he quotes with approval a passage in which Edward Hartley notes the pernicious influence of foreign books that instill in the American mind concepts that are inimical to American principles and which are false to American experience, a nationalistic idea to be expected in the early years of the century. In his general discussion, moreover, Dunlap presents the book in a rather favorable light. Though different, of course, from the works that Brown had previously written, it is not by any means, he implies, inferior to them. "It has a regular plan. It is satisfactorily concluded. Its incidents are more within the scope of probability. Its difficulties arise from the conflicting passions of persons eminently moral and delicate. It has no passages so highly

455

wrought and eloquent, neither has it those glaring defects, which I have lamented as appertaining to the former works'' (Dunlap, *Life*, II, 42).

Brief as their comments are, Allen's and Dunlap's critiques of *Clara Howard* are as full and as serious a commentary as the book was to receive for nearly a century. *Jane Talbot* did not fare so well at their hands. Allen did not mention it at all. He had treated *Clara Howard* out of order in his discussion of Brown's early correspondence, and since he never wrote the second volume, where *Jane Talbot* would presumably have been treated, we do not know his opinion of that novel. Dunlap does include the book in his second volume of the *Life*. But he mistakes the date and place of first publication, and he describes it in such vague terms as to make one wonder if he had actually read it. *Jane Talbot,* he writes, ''has little of the excellence of his previous romances. It is deficient in interest. The author it is true is seen in it, and it is therefore worthy of perusal, but I shall decline entering into an analysis of it, after having gone so largely into the merits of his previous romances'' (ibid., II, 67). This, of course, says nothing. It is the kind of thing one might write when required to express an opinion about a matter on which he has no specific knowledge.

After the publication of Dunlap's biography, critics paid little attention to *Clara Howard* and *Jane Talbot*. In his review of Dunlap's book, E. T. Channing dismissed them in a sentence: ''Clara Howard and Jane Talbot . . . are so very inferior to and unlike the others, that they require no particular notice.''[38] The books fared little better in Richard Henry Dana's review of the first collected edition of Brown's novels in 1827. Dana believed that the set should have included ''Memoirs of Carwin, the Biloquist'' and ''Memoirs of Stephen Calvert,'' and he suggested that, ''had any sacrifice been necessary, which we very much doubt, 'Clara Howard' should have been omitted, for it has all Brown's defects, with little or none of his power.'' In his discussion of Brown's women, moreover, Dana also reveals his un-

[38]*North American Review,* 9 (June 1819), 63.

favorable opinion of *Jane Talbot*. He restricts himself to a comment on the impropriety of the heroine's actions and the improbability of her remaining virtuous when she puts herself so often into temptation with the man she loves. Dana concludes, however, that Brown—''one of the purest of men''—was so intellectual as to be unaware of the strength of temptation in others.[39]

An anonymous critic in the *Western Monthly Review*, a journal published in Cincinnati, also recognized that Jane Talbot's actions were open to censure, but he nonetheless defends Brown's handling of the character. ''The lady will, perhaps, be thought by some too frank and unrestrained in her expressions of affection, for the climate, in which she wrote. But we are clearly of the opinion, that more interest is excited in the mind of the reader of writings of this class by the spirit, which is infused into them, by the open expression of the overflowings of the heart, than there is harm done, by trenching upon the bounds of an unnatural, freezing, and heartless self-called decorum.'' But if freer western manners are reflected in this judgment, western pride was piqued by an error in geography that the critic notes in *Clara Howard*. Edward Hartley travels in his imagination along the Ohio River to the Mississippi and then floats passively *down* that stream to the mouth of the Missouri—an error, the critic writes, that evinces ''the ignorance, which existed at the time, these volumes were written, with regard to the Western Country.''[40] He has little else to say about either book.

A third review of the collected edition, however, is ambivalent in its treatment of Brown's last two novels. Because his ''article [had] already extended beyond the bounds [he] had prescribed for it,'' the critic writes, he could not dwell longer on *Ormond*, the novel he was discussing, nor devote any space to a consideration of *Clara Howard* and *Jane Talbot*. ''Nor do they require it,'' he goes on to say. ''They are

[39] *United States Review and Literary Gazette*, 2 (August 1827), 322, 327–328.

[40] *Western Monthly Review*, 1 (December 1827), 491, 493.

both inferior to either of those on which we have commented.'' Yet the critic, who clearly admired Brown, was unable to let the matter end there. He immediately qualifies the judgment: "Still they are works of merit, displaying in their composition the ability of a deep thinker as well as of a practised writer. They could not, indeed, be otherwise, for Brown is their author; and nothing could proceed from the mint of his rich intellect, without having upon it the stamp of genius and high literary merit.''[41] Like many another critic of Brown, the reviewer was able to see in *Clara Howard* and *Jane Talbot*, inferior though they may be to his four major novels, clear signs of that intellectual strength that is a major element in all of Brown's fiction.

Critical opinion in later years sometimes varied widely. In his biographical sketch of Brown, written for Jared Sparks in 1834, William Hickling Prescott simply noted that *Clara Howard* and *Jane Talbot* were "composed in a more subdued tone, discarding those startling preternatural incidents of which he had made such free use in his former fictions,'' and, after quoting Brown's well-known letter to James on *Edgar Huntly*, he dismissed them in a sentence. "The two last novels of our author, . . . although purified from the more glaring defects of the preceding, were so inferior in their general power and originality of conception, that they never rose to the same level in public favour'' (Prescott, ''Memoir,'' pp. 40–41). An anonymous critic of *Jane Talbot*, however, thought highly of that book. In a brief review in *Graham's Illustrated Magazine*, generated, apparently, by the 1857 edition of Brown's collected novels, he wrote: "This is a curious and deeply interesting work, written in the epistolary form, but all the better on that account in these days when letter-writing is becoming one

---

[41]*American Quarterly Review*, 8 (December 1830), 337. In other reviews of the period, *Clara Howard* and *Jane Talbot* are simply dismissed as inferior. See *New-York Mirror, and Ladies' Literary Gazette*, 4 (2 June 1827), 359, and [Richard Penn Smith], ''Progress of Literature in Pennsylvania, No. V,'' *Philadelphia Monthly Magazine*, NS 1 (July 1829), 602.

of the lost arts. It has a thrilling plot—is written in English of singular purity and strength—and involves a deep moral. We commend it to all."[42]

Other critics were not so enthusiastic. In the few discussions of the novels written toward the end of the century, *Clara Howard* and *Jane Talbot* are generally dismissed as inferior. Writing in the *Fortnightly Review* in 1878, George Barnett Smith considered *Jane Talbot* "the least meritorious" of Brown's novels, and though he had a somewhat higher opinion of *Clara Howard,* he stressed its limitations: "Told in the form of letters, the history of Clara Howard is related with a method and perspicuity absent from Brown's other works; but what he gains in straightforward narrative and orderly plan, he loses in passion, force, intensity, genius" ("Brockden Brown," pp. 407, 419). E. L. Philips and Martin S. Vilas were even more negative in their judgments. Philips, in 1890, dismissed the books as works of "little merit," and Vilas, in a book written in 1899 but published in 1904, found them to be deficient in characterization and method of presentation. He disliked the "sickly sentimentalism" he discerned in *Clara Howard* and the "gush and unhealthy sentiment" of *Jane Talbot,* in his opinion, Brown's poorest novel.[43] As the nineteenth century closed, the verdict seemed to be in. *Clara Howard* and *Jane Talbot* were hardly considered worthy of serious critical attention.

V

The twentieth century brought a major change. Growing interest in American literature as a field of study necessarily focused attention on Brown as a significant early

---

[42]*Graham's Illustrated Magazine,* 51 (July 1857), 86.

[43]E. L. Philips, "The Earliest American Novelist," *Cornell Magazine,* 2 (1890), 203; Martin S. Vilas, *Charles Brockden Brown: A Study of Early American Fiction* (Burlington, Vt.: Free Press Association, 1904), pp. 40–46.

writer, all of whose works had to be considered if his accomplishment was to be understood. In the studies of
American literature that followed, Brown was accorded a
due proportion of space, and by mid-century, two major
biographies had appeared. The ensuing thirty years have
produced a relatively large number of studies based on one
or another of the critical systems that have flourished during the period, in which the various critics reflect the
diversity—or, if you will, confusion—that has characterized
literary study for at least a generation. Most attention has,
of course, been focused on the major novels, but *Clara
Howard* and *Jane Talbot* have become the subjects of a small
but increasingly important body of substantial criticism.
Not all of it is positive. Some, indeed, is as negative as the
opinions expressed in the nineteenth century. The best of
it, however, helps us to see what Brown hoped to accomplish in his last two novels and makes us better able to
evaluate his success.

The earliest critics of Brown in this century concentrated
on the subject matter of the books. In *The Early American
Novel* (1907), Lillie Deming Loshe followed a feminist line
in placing *Clara Howard* and *Jane Talbot* in the context of
Alcuin and seeing both heroines as the same kind of independent woman that Brown had created in Constantia Dudley
in *Ormond.* She praises Clara Howard as a strong spirit and
obviously approves of her role as "the resolute and reasonable woman directing the gentle and irresolute boy."
Jane Talbot, in Loshe's view, is also a woman of the "newer
type" who speaks, acts, and loves for herself, and who relies
"not on the conventions of society, or on the divinely inspired wisdom of a father or husband," but on her "own
judgment." Views like these have echoed down the century. W. P. Trent and John Erskine, in 1912, see in Clara
Howard "a concrete sort of modern woman," and David
Lee Clark, in 1952, considers her "Brown's ideal woman."
Though Trent and Erskine have little to say about Jane
Talbot, Clark sees in her a "new confidence," a "new

460

assertion of self'' that gives the character ''an unmistakable air of modernity.'' She is a person of independent mind.[44]

The focus on feminist themes among early critics had the important result of calling attention to a major aspect of the novels that foreshadows a great deal of later fiction. As early as 1932, Grant Knight called attention to the importance of *Clara Howard* and *Jane Talbot* as ''prophetic of the psychological school of George Eliot and Henry James,'' while Alexander Cowie, in 1948, wrote that ''*Clara Howard* was a pioneer novel which, in however rudimentary fashion, adumbrates the love casuistry of the domestic novelists of the sixties and seventies and even of Henry James.'' The idea has not died. As recently as 1970, Kenneth Bernard has pointed out that Brown's last novels are ''not without interest,'' and that ''*Jane Talbot* in particular is far better than most critics have claimed, Brown there portraying a woman of intellect, wit, and charm who was not to be duplicated in American literature until James.''[45] These are highly suggestive statements. If the critics are right, the precise relation of *Clara Howard* and *Jane Talbot* to later social fiction needs to be determined. Such a study might well reveal a neglected area of American literary history.

Yet another early critic, approaching the book from the point of view of its philosophy, found forward-looking elements in *Jane Talbot*. In his important essay on Brown and

[44]Lillie Deming Loshe, *The Early American Novel* (New York: Columbia Univ. Press, 1907), pp. 45–49; Trent and Erskine, *Great American Writers,* pp. 19–20; Clark, *Brown,* pp. 182–184. Though Clark's book is dated 1952, the opinions expressed may date from his 1923 dissertation. It should also be noted, perhaps, that four of these scholars were associated with Columbia University at around the same time and may be reflecting one another's opinions.

[45]Grant Knight, *American Literature and Culture* (New York: R. Long and R. R. Smith, 1932), p. 102; Alexander Cowie, *The Rise of the American Novel* (New York: American Book Co., 1948), p. 88; Kenneth Bernard, ''Charles Brockden Brown,'' *Minor American Novelists,* ed. Charles A. Hoyt (Carbondale: Southern Illinois Univ. Press, 1970), p. 8.

the novel published in 1910, W. B. Blake stressed the influence of William Godwin on Brown's intellectual development and showed that, after he had passed through that phase in his thinking, he had turned it to good account in his final novel. Other critics, before and since, have, of course, commented upon the relation. It is a major element in the book and must be taken into account in any interpretation of the novel. But Blake saw in Brown's handling of the material an opportunity for a new development in his career that unfortunately came to nothing. Blake especially admired the book's central focus. He could recall no earlier novel "where the conflict lies so uniquely in ideas; where it is a question of faith and practise, of love and abstract duty." In writing this novel of religious doubt, "Brown all but opened up a new field" and might have established "himself in a new reputation," one "sounder than his first." All he did, however, was to throw out a hint. He did not bring it to fruition.[46]

Concerned as they were with literary history, the early critics were more interested in placing the books in an appropriate historical context than they were in critical evaluation. By the 1940s, however, literary scholars turned their attention to close study of individual texts in an attempt to determine their fundamental meaning and establish their literary value—an approach that yielded important results, but which also opened the way for diverse and even contradictory interpretations. What the critic sometimes forgot is that his view of the work was strongly influenced by the ideas he brought to it, that the interpretation he made was as much a reflection of his own mind as a description of the text he was studying. Norman S. Grabo's recent book on Brown is a case in point. Though Grabo proposes to make New Critical examinations of the texts he interprets, his own predisposition to psychological criticism leads him to read them mainly in psychological terms.[47] His inter-

[46]W. B. Blake, "Brockden Brown and the Novel," *Sewanee Review*, 18 (October 1910), 440.

[47]Norman S. Grabo, *The Coincidental Art of Charles Brockden Brown* (Chapel Hill: Univ. of North Carolina Press, 1981), p. xi.

pretive readings are, without question, provocative, but one is not always sure whether he is discovering the ideas in the books or placing them there. Other close readings of the texts by different scholars yield, predictably, quite other meanings, and the reader is thus faced with critical studies that present him with different conclusions.

Clara Howard and *Jane Talbot* have not fared well with the psychological critics. Leslie A. Fiedler, in 1960, discussed them in terms of Samuel Richardson's influence on American fiction. According to Fiedler, Brown "submitted to Richardson as enthusiastically as any of his female contemporaries," and he cites a passage in one of the unfinished novels as an example of Brown's sentiments in favor of the English writer. In his final books, moreover, Fiedler goes on to say, "Brown made a valiant attempt to redeem Richardson from his genteel imitators, to create, by casting aside the seduction theme, a Richardsonian novel of sentimental analysis in a domestic setting, stripped of tragic and melodramatic elements alike." But Brown did not succeed: "aiming at modesty, he created dullness; and avoiding the spectacular, he fell into the inane." Fiedler discusses the books at some little length, always in terms of his psychological theories, and he dismisses them both as failing to fulfill the archetypal patterns which his theories lead him to expect. *Clara Howard* and *Jane Talbot* were, Fiedler believes, attempts to win "the great female audience" and represent, on Brown's part, a movement "toward silence" as a writer of fiction.[48]

Norman Grabo comes to similarly negative conclusions. He makes too much of the few similarities in plot between *Edgar Huntly* and *Clara Howard* and then dismisses the latter book because it fails to exhibit the qualities he admires in the former. He considers *Jane Talbot* a failure largely because "the correlation between ideas or principles and characters" in that book "is entirely different from those correlations in the major romances." And he sees both books as deficient because, as epistolary novels, they are

[48]*Love and Death in the American Novel* (New York: Criterion Books, 1960), pp. 73-76, 138-139.

not structured about the central point of view that Brown apparently needed to write successful books.[49] In statements like these, Grabo seems to imply that the only kind of fiction Brown could write effectively was the type he produced in the major romances. Though there is truth in this opinion, he seems to suggest as well that any novel which deviated from the pattern established in his four most famous ones must for that reason be considered a failure—an unlikely position for a critic to assume who uses the technique of New Critical close analysis, a system predicated on the assumption that each work will be judged on its own terms.

Grabo's book is a good example, too, of the problem faced by critics who write broad overviews of Brown's career. By taking the books in the order of publication, they approach the last two novels with vivid memories of Brown's best-known fiction, and the change they perceive in both *Clara Howard* and *Jane Talbot* is interpreted as an artistic decline. Thus, Harry Warfel writes: "In *Clara Howard*, Brown tossed aside his most distinctive and his most attractive substance.... Horror and terror, not love and romance, were Brown's proper precinct. By withdrawing from the areas of terror, he became merely another purveyor of romantic narrative." Warfel echoes the point in his discussion of *Jane Talbot:* though the novel "has its moments," it too "lacks high passions and monsterlike characters." It is difficult not to concur. I reached the same conclusion in my own study of Brown, pointing out that in *Clara Howard* and *Jane Talbot*, "Brown ... turned his back upon the kind of fiction in which he had achieved his greatest success." Though Warfel and I tried to be fair to both books and made a particular case for the intellectual vitality of *Jane Talbot*, we could not avoid comparing them to their more absorbing predecessors.[50]

[49]Grabo, *Coincidental Art*, pp. 129–143. Grabo also speculates, though there is no hard evidence for the opinion, that *Clara Howard* was written before *Edgar Huntly* (pp. 131, 142).

[50]Warfel, *Brown*, pp. 191–194, 197–201; Donald A. Ringe, *Charles Brockden Brown* (New York: Twayne Publishers, 1966), pp. 112–128.

Even an inferior book, however, may have its value. The problem is to see those aspects of the work that render it worthy of serious consideration. For Robert E. Hemenway and Joseph Katz, that quality in *Clara Howard* and *Jane Talbot,* as well as the fragments that resemble them most closely, is what they reveal about Brown's social and moral thought. *Clara Howard* and *Jane Talbot* affirm a world of moral and social order where individual desires are made to conform to prevenient social values, a world that stands in sharp contrast to the "chaos and uncertainty" of the earlier books where "the moral and social orders are under violent pressur [*sic*] from the attempts of individuals to define them for themselves." What the contrast between the two groups of novels reveals, therefore, is a bifurcation in Brown's view of the world. He was always "torn between a drive for social responsibility and an imagination that persistently envisioned alternate behaviors." Though Hemenway and Katz conclude, with most other critics, that "Brown was at his best in fiction when his imagination freed him from the fetters that bind his domestic romances,"[51] they recognize the importance of his final novels in providing evidence for the proper understanding of his social and moral vision.

How good those novels are as works of fiction is, however, another question, one that scholars have tried to answer through a variety of means. In his *Early American Novel* (1971), Henri Petter takes a genre approach. He places the books in the context of contemporary sentimental novels that develop similar subjects. Thus, *Clara Howard* is included among novels that deal with "self-denial," *Jane Talbot* with those that treat "cruel parents," and Petter draws his conclusions about the relative success or limitations of each by viewing it in relation to a group of novels that contain the same element (pp. 174–177, 192–196, 201). The conclusions that one can draw from such a comparison, however, are at best limited and at worst highly suspect. To conclude

[51]Robert E. Hemenway and Joseph Katz, Introduction to Allen, *Life,* pp. li–lv.

that Brown's books are better than some admittedly bad ones does not advance the critical discussion very far. Worse, to treat the books in terms of such cliches as ''self-denial'' and ''cruel parents'' does them a serious disservice. It tends to reduce them to the lowest level of popular fiction and blind the critic to those unique qualities which, if properly understood, would set them apart from the run-of-the-mill novels among which they appear.

In the only articles focused exclusively on *Clara Howard* and *Jane Talbot,* two critics have attempted to discover just those qualities. Paul Witherington examines the books from several perspectives and concludes that they are ''Brown's most mature novels.'' Seen from the point of view of his whole career, they reveal ''the continuity of Brown's narrative forms, ideas, and tone.'' Thus, although *Clara Howard* and *Jane Talbot* seem to differ from their predecessors in that they ''show the victories of social normalcy over individuality and of order over eccentricity and indecisiveness,'' all of Brown's novels, in Witherington's view, exhibit ''a similar pattern: the rebellious individual chastened and reunited with society,'' so that the difference between the two groups of books ''is only in degree.'' Because their themes, moreover, are developed in a more orderly manner—the endings implicit in the beginnings—one may also say that *Clara Howard* and *Jane Talbot* represent ''the logical end of Brown's quest for form.'' The themes he has consistently developed find in the social mode of these two books their proper means of expression. As Witherington sees it, therefore, Brown's career as a novelist has a unity and completeness that is fully revealed only in his last two books: ''the early novels develop toward *Clara Howard* and *Jane Talbot,* theme finally coming to rest in its most appropriate form.''[52]

Nor is this all. Witherington believes that Brown's final novels are worthy of consideration on two additional

[52]Paul Witherington, ''Brockden Brown's Other Novels: *Clara Howard* and *Jane Talbot,*'' *Nineteenth-Century Fiction,* 29 (December 1974), 257–263.

grounds. *Clara Howard* and *Jane Talbot* "model Brown's view of the artist and of his own artistry," an idea he develops by showing how "Brown's belief in eighteenth-century values of benevolence" led him to mistrust the premises of art "as he came to understand its ways." It "always works by indirection, by suspense rather than by immediate disclosure, thus by the very opposites of benevolence." The development of Brown's career from *Wieland* and *Ormond* to *Clara Howard* and *Jane Talbot* shows, therefore, "the victory of benevolence over the constricted Gothic ego," and a movement "away from the shifting perspectives of art" to the letter form, in which people speak artlessly from the heart. A similar movement is apparent in Brown's treatment of the relation of the artist to his benefactor: in the early novels, "ambiguous and morally deficient" males perform that role; in the final ones, "females close to the heart of society, morally impeccable, but emotional stranglers." The experience of Colden in *Jane Talbot,* the poet who is brought to social conformity, thus recapitulates and brings to a close the whole movement of Brown's career as a novelist (ibid., pp. 258, 263–267).

Yet quite apart from their significance in the development of Brown's career, *Clara Howard* and *Jane Talbot* also "deserve recognition on their own terms for the excellence of structure, point of view, and characterization." Witherington is warm in his praise: "the form of *Clara Howard* and *Jane Talbot* is remarkably tight, the subplots well integrated, and the point of view consistent." The epistolary form is handled with considerable subtlety. In both books, the "setting . . . is used in a thematic way" with *Jane Talbot* having the more complex geography, and if "the technique of letter juxtaposition is better in *Clara Howard, " Jane Talbot* "presents the letters as a whole more realistically" and includes "significant differences in style. Colden's reserved, heavily qualified letters are quite different from Jane's direct, passionate ones." Though the characters "in *Clara Howard* are somewhat stereotyped," those in *Jane Talbot*— especially Frank, Jane's brother, and Jane herself—are well drawn. Frank "is perhaps Brown's most believable villain" and Jane, "a thinking romantic" who "is sometimes splendidly unpredictable," "is a triumph of Brown's art" (ibid., pp. 258, 267–272). Not everyone, of course, will agree with Witherington's views, but his article is a challenge to any critic reluctant to accord the books sufficiently close attention.

A different approach is taken by Sydney J. Krause, who argues that *Clara Howard* and *Jane Talbot* have not been properly evaluated because they have not been understood. Critics have failed to perceive Brown's intention in these books: to put "on trial the moral and social ideals of the one writer [William Godwin] who had the most pervasive influence on the intellectual content of his novels over all."[53] In turning to the sentimental tradition for the form of his books, however, Brown also drew heavily on the works of Samuel Richardson and Jean Jacques Rousseau, whose influence is apparent in both of Brown's last novels. Krause points out many parallels between *Clara Howard* and *Jane Talbot,* on the one hand, and both *Clarissa* and *Julie, ou la Nouvelle Héloïse,* novels Brown certainly knew on the other. The voice of feeling is heard at times in *Clara Howard,* especially when Clara reacts to Edward's illness, and in *Jane Talbot,* especially in the title character (ibid., pp. 188–191, 195–196). The sentimental code, implicit in both books, is played off against the Godwinian ideas that Brown, true to form as a novelist, puts to the test through the actions of his characters.

The Godwin that Brown investigates is not, however, the anti-social radical who, as Mrs. Fielder's attitude clearly suggests, had come to represent all kinds of enormities to the popular imagination. It is, rather, the Godwin of *Political Justice,* the philosopher whose views, Krause argues, "heavily weighted toward an individualistic (as opposed to statist) conservatism," are quite unlike the radical

[53]Sydney J. Krause, "*Clara Howard* and *Jane Talbot:* Godwin on Trial," in *Critical Essays on Charles Brockden Brown,* ed. Bernard Rosenthal (Boston: G. K. Hall, 1981), p. 186.

thought of the time. Brown examines the ''characteristic premises'' of *Political Justice* and shows, through the actions of his characters, the practical effects they would have if people attempted to live by them in the world. In *Clara Howard,* for example, Clara herself is a thoroughgoing Godwinian whose attempt to apply the principle of benevolent disinterest to everyday life produces the moral conflict that lies at the heart of the book. Ideas that look good in the abstract involve the characters in contradictions from which they cannot extricate themselves. The conflict, as Krause describes it, becomes exceedingly complex. The characters become involved in paradox, they even change positions, and variations are played on variations. But though Clara may sometimes waver, she does not relent, and the book ends with Clara still in control, but with her intellectual position thoroughly devastated (ibid., pp. 196–202).

Jane Talbot carries the argument further in that it considers alternatives to the Godwinian position. In Krause's analysis, Mrs. Fielder, the voice of authority in the book, ''is made the servant of hardened conventionalism,'' and the lovers assume a middle ground between her position and that of Clara Howard. Jane and Colden try to live by the ''Godwinian ethic that happiness is achieved through sacrificing one's own interests for the benefit of others,'' but the action demonstrates that, ''in the volatile arena of the 'affections,''' it simply will not work. As in the previous book, the characters become involved in paradox, and in the process, ''the crux of the problem with the Godwinian ethic'' is revealed. ''Its means do not bring about the end that is proposed.'' The characters must try another direction, one that ''goes from Reason to Faith.'' Both Jane and Colden rethink their positions: she through her association with him, he through his intense meditation on his four-year voyage. Their final reward ''is not just marriage, but the firmest basis for it, a whole-hearted concurrence of minds—or exactly the sort of harmony which Godwin, in his diatribe against matrimony, felt it was impossible to expect and inadvisable to strive for'' (ibid., pp. 202–207).

Seen in these terms, *Clara Howard* and *Jane Talbot* occupy an important position in Brown's intellectual and artistic career. He was in effect "going back to unfinished business"—to re-examine the philosophies that had influenced him during the 1790s, not only the Godwinian that he had tested in "Carwin," *Ormond,* and *Arthur Mervyn,* but also the Rousseauistic that had preceded it in his thinking. These ideas come together in *Clara Howard* and *Jane Talbot,* which, "far from representing a deviation in form, both confirm and consummate the tendency of the earlier novels." If Krause is right, Brown's final books are intellectually a brilliant virtuoso performance in which he effectively dismissed the philosophical positions that had so strongly attracted him just before he began his career as a novelist. In *Clara Howard* and *Jane Talbot,* Krause concludes, Brown "gave Godwinian morality the ultimate trial of proving its effectiveness at achieving its own ends, and found it wanting. To put Brown's findings in their simplest terms, the experience of his characters with Godwin seems to suggest that his moral philosophy was as easy to believe as it was impossible to live by" (ibid., pp. 188, 186, 208).

In these two long and well argued essays, Paul Witherington and Sydney Krause have taken the study of *Clara Howard* and *Jane Talbot* a long way forward. Though other critics have pointed out matters of interest in both, only they have accorded the books the kind of critical attention most often reserved for Brown's other novels. Their strong, positive conclusions may—or may not—be accepted in detail, but the fundamental nature of their accomplishment is clear. By reading the books in and for themselves, they have taken them out of competition with Brown's better-known novels, a practice that allows us to see them more clearly than has heretofore been possible. Yet such an examination has led to a somewhat paradoxical result. To split the books off in this way has revealed to both Witherington and Krause that Brown's career is a unit, that *Clara Howard* and *Jane Talbot* represent no falling off in skill, but rather serve as an appropriate culmination to his career as a novelist. These are important conclusions that must be taken into account not only by future critics of Brown but by all serious students of early American fiction.

VI

Though critical opinion on *Clara Howard* and *Jane Talbot* has been diverse and at times contradictory, it provides a good basis for further evaluation of the novels. Even the most negative critics can contribute to the process, not because their conclusions are right, but because they sometimes direct our attention to matters that must be examined if we are to arrive at a just appreciation of the books. Fiedler is certainly correct in observing, for example, that Brown cast aside the Richardsonian theme of seduction, but it does not necessarily follow that the novels are for that reason failures. Another critic may see the rejection as a successful attempt by Brown to escape the constrictions of the run-of-the-mill sentimental romance and open the genre to the intense examination of ideas that Krause finds in the books. Grabo is also correct in noting that Brown abandoned the central point of view that served him so well in his earlier novels to adopt the epistolary form, yet one need not agree that the choice contributed to the weakness of his last two books. It is possible, after all, that Brown knew precisely what he was about and adopted the form for sound artistic reasons.

It is time, therefore, to abandon the view that *Clara Howard* and *Jane Talbot* are merely sentimental tales written by Brown in a retreat from the kind of fiction that has won him an important place in the history of American literature. No one wants to deny, of course, that both books draw heavily on the sentimental tradition, but Brown always adapted whatever he borrowed. Just as he turned the Gothic romance to his own artistic purposes in *Wieland, Ormond,* and *Edgar Huntly,*[54] so too did he transform the

[54]See Donald A. Ringe, *American Gothic: Imagination and Reason in Nineteenth-Century Fiction* (Lexington: Univ. Press of Kentucky, 1982), pp. 36–57.

sentimental tale when he wrote *Clara Howard* and *Jane Talbot*. He eschewed such typical subjects as the seduction of the naive girl or the sufferings of persecuted innocence, and he made no attempt to moralize as sentimental writers so often did. He turned his attention instead to questions of meaning and used the books as vehicles for the exploration of ideas. That he was successful in his thematic purpose has been amply demonstrated by Krause. What remains to be examined is whether or not the form he selected is an appropriate one for the expression of his meaning. This question may best be answered by addressing the way he handles point of view.

Brown's four most famous novels are presented for the most part through the technique of a first person point of view. Though other voices are occasionally heard, each book is narrated by a character—Clara Wieland, Sophia Westwyn Courtland, Arthur Mervyn, or Edgar Huntly— whose perceptions and attitudes shape the material through which the story is presented and the theme expressed. The epistolary technique Brown adopted in *Clara Howard* and *Jane Talbot,* on the other hand, permits each character to speak as his background, attitudes, and predilections dictate, allows conflicts to develop among the views expressed, and forces the characters to consider and adjust to the opinions of others, sometimes changing their own in the process. From the intellectual drama that develops as the characters present their positions and react to those of their correspondents, Brown was able to suggest thematic meanings that do not derive from the views of any one character but emerge only from the interplay of all. Far from being an artistic lapse on Brown's part, his selection of the epistolary method for his final books allowed him to examine ideas in a new and effective way.

The function of the epistolary method in *Clara Howard* is somewhat obscured by the dominant role played by the heroine, who asserts her Godwinian ideas and forces Edward Hartley to do as she directs. Yet Clara does not go unchallenged. Another voice is heard in Letter XXIV when Hartley, believing that Clara is lost to him, writes her the truth: that her judgment has been misguided and her application of principle faulty. By this means, Brown provides a corrective to the opinions expressed in Clara's letters. But this is not all. He raises as well an important question about the young man's motives. If Hartley so clearly perceives Clara's intellectual errors, why does he submit to her at the end? Other letters by Hartley suggest an answer, letters in which he is much concerned with dignity, position, and wealth, all of which he acquires when Clara marries him. Brown does not labor the point. He merely includes in Hartley's letters elements that suggest more subtlety of motivation in the young man's character than appears on the surface and more complexity of meaning in the conclusion of the book than Clara's apparent triumph might seem to indicate.

In *Jane Talbot,* on the other hand, the function of the epistolary method is more obvious. There is no character like Clara Howard to dominate the others with her philosophic theories. We find instead three persons in conflict who differ markedly in attitude and opinion and who reveal through their letters their personal limitations. The religious Jane is too emotional, too pliant, too volatile; the skeptical Colden too cool, too rational; the strict Mrs. Fielder too stern and inflexible in her judgments on them. Through the many letters they write, the characters explain their positions, respond to the others' statements, and react to their replies. In the course of time all are forced to alter their opinions. For Mrs. Fielder the change is sudden. She eventually discovers that she has wronged Jane and Colden and begs forgiveness. For the lovers, however, the change is more gradual. Jane becomes aware that her association with Colden has given her piety a rational basis, and Colden is awakened to a living religious faith by a long process that culminates during his voyage to the Pacific. Through the letters they exchange, Brown is able to suggest how their positions have gradually come together.

How effective Brown was in his use of the technique may,

473

of course, be questioned. Petter has observed, for example, that in *Clara Howard* the letters are "stylistically uniform," and "Brown's handling of the epistolary device is stiff and ungainly" (*Early American Novel,* p. 177). One may also note that *Jane Talbot* is a rather static book largely because, as I have written elsewhere, so much of the change in Jane and Colden "has already taken place before the novel opens" (Ringe, *Brown,* pp. 127–128). Such failures in execution, however, are not unusual in Brown. All of his books are flawed. But if we have learned to look beyond the aesthetic failings of his first four novels to understand and appreciate his fundamental artistic achievement, we should we willing to do the same for his last two books. The themes Brown developed in them are no less important than those he had previously explored, and the form and technique he adopted were suited to their expression. *Clara Howard* and *Jane Talbot* will never rank among Brown's most important novels, but they must not be dismissed, as they have so often been, as inconsequential failures. Though lacking the fascination of his more famous books, they are substantial works of fiction well worth our critical attention.

D.A.R.

Textual Essay

Although they appeared in the same year and were similar in content, literary form, and physical format, Charles Brockden Brown's *Clara Howard* and *Jane Talbot* have had different publishing histories. Both the printer and the publisher of the first edition of *Clara Howard* were tradesmen well known to Brown who had been involved with previous publications of his; for *Jane Talbot* they were replaced by men equally if not more prominent in the trade, but involved with Brown for the first time. The first edition of *Clara Howard* proved to be unusually free of error and textual problems, that of *Jane Talbot* unusually complicated by them. Although both novels were published in England by the Minerva Press in Brown's lifetime, *Clara Howard* followed *Jane Talbot* by three years, and when it finally appeared did so under the new title *Philip Stanley*. It is best to consider these novels' histories and the textual problems they present individually.

CLARA HOWARD

On or about the twenty-second of June 1801, *Clara Howard; In a Series of Letters* appeared in Philadelphia in a single volume. Two experienced members of the book trade in that city, Asbury Dickins and Hugh Maxwell, collaborated on this first edition. As its publisher, Dickins "deposited . . . the title" with the court of the District of Pennsylvania on 13 June. How long before that date Maxwell had begun printing the book is unclear, but in a letter to John E. Hall on the eighth of May Brown reported that Maxwell had made "considerable progress" on it, and by the sixth of June he had completed printing the 500 copies.[1] Neither the manuscript which served as Maxwell's copy nor any other manuscript which Brown may have created during the some six months he worked on the novel has survived.

The first edition (A) is a duodecimo in half-sheets, a relatively common format for novels of the day. It collates as follows: $12°$: π^2 A–Y^6 ($1, 3 signed, $3 [first leaf of insert] as 2); 134 leaves, pp. i–iii iv 5 6–268. The first leaf ($\pi1$) contains the title and, on its verso, the copyright notice; the second leaf ($\pi2$) comprises the two pages of the 'Introduction'. The first letter begins on the third leaf (A1, p. 5), and all subsequent letters also begin on rectos (or right-hand pages), with the result that many versos have only partially filled pages and eight of them are entirely blank. Preceding each letter is a heading that includes not only the number of the letter, the name of the recipient, the place of origin, and the date of composition, but also a repetition of the head-title 'Clara Howard'; consequently, the entire heading for a given letter occupies about half a page. What moved Dickins to agree to such a design, hardly an economical one, can only be guessed, but the fact is that the first edition is a very thin volume textually, if not in other ways, though Brown himself regarded it as "typographically considered, a very beautiful book."[2]

---

[1] *The Library of American Biography,* I, facing page 117; see the Historical Essay, pp. 441–442. *Note:* references to works already cited in the Historical Essay appear in short form here.

[2] *The Library of American Biography,* I, facing page 117. Maxwell's records surviving at the Historical Society of Pennsylvania give us the details of the printing: the 500 copies printed from twenty-three formes cost $27.60 for presswork (46 tokens at 60 cents per token) and $114.00 for composition.

It is, too, a stark contrast to Maxwell's other first editions of Brown in its freedom from textual tangles. Now and again a defective type or improperly locked-up forme produces a typographical error or a variant amongst copies, but such phenomena are infrequent in A.[3] The most blatant blunder, the misnumbering of the last few letters resulting from repetition of XXVII, is less likely to be owing to a compositor's mistranscription than to Brown's decision to let his printer assign numbers as he proceeded; if, as apparently in *Jane Talbot* (see p. 488), he omitted such numbers from his manuscript, it would be no wonder that the compositor lost track after having set the long letter that precedes the mistake. Elsewhere there is relatively little positive evidence of compositorial error in this first edition, whereas in his earlier editions of *Arthur Mervyn, First Part* and *Edgar Huntly,* Maxwell quite clearly committed errors of substitution and of omission and produced frequent "literals" as well as numerous alterations of spelling, punctuation, and word-division.[4] It is a matter of conjecture whether the relative accuracy of A is ascribable more to a change in Maxwell's practices than to Brown's greater care in preparing the manuscript copy and in reading proofs, but the sparse evidence suggests that Brown himself made some of the difference in this case.

From the imprint on A's title page it is clear that by 1801 Maxwell had again changed his shop's quarters, the third time at least in as many years. That he had moved to Columbia-House from 25 North Second Street, where he had occupied quarters along with Asbury Dickins, might suggest greater prosperity for his business as a whole. Perhaps of even greater importance would have been his regular employment as the printer, for Joseph Dennie and Dickins, of the *Port Folio,* recently begun with the new year. Such

[3]See 'changos', 'relations he', and the omission of 'it' from some copies (12.7, 96.28–29, 58.19).
[4]See the Textual Essay, in *Edgar Huntly; or, Memoirs of A Sleep-Walker,* ed. Sydney J. Krause and S. W. Reid (Kent, Ohio: Kent State Univ. Press, 1984), pp. 430–432.

improving prospects, it could be speculated, might have been translated into more competent workmanship and more professional operations, including the employment of a proofreader—an office not earlier filled in Maxwell's shop (according to Brown) because of his "indigence."[5] However reasonable they may seem, such inferences are largely speculative, and the fact is that Maxwell's printing of "Carwin" in the *Literary Magazine* two years later exhibits the same kinds of errors manifest in the earlier *Arthur Mervyn, First Part* and *Edgar Huntly* and therefore does not support the inference that he had made steady improvements as a printer. Although the quality of his work may have improved temporarily in 1801, we cannot with any conviction credit Maxwell alone with the accuracy exhibited in *Clara Howard.*

Moreover, there does seem to be reason to believe that Brown was responsible, at least in part, for the relative accuracy of the first edition. Whereas it is the shortest of his completed novels, *Clara Howard* occupied him for a surprisingly long period. So far as we can tell, he wrote *Ormond* and *Edgar Huntly,* for instance, in stints of about two or three months, but he devoted about six to *Clara Howard.* Although he had other projects in hand, chiefly the editing of the *Monthly Magazine* during some of these months, the period given over to this rather thin series of letters is unusually long. Furthermore, it seems almost certain that, unlike his first three published novels, *Clara Howard* was not written against the press. There is, then, some reason to believe that Brown labored rather carefully over the manuscript for his penultimate novel, and the fairness of the printer's copy may help explain the relative accuracy of the first edition.

What seems even more certain from the sparse evidence is that Brown gave some attention to proofreading this edition. When Maxwell had printed *Arthur Mervyn, First Part* and *Edgar Huntly,* Brown had been in New York, and the proofreading apparently had been entrusted to his brother

[5]Dunlap, *Life,* II, 99.

James and to Maxwell himself, with regrettable results. But by the time *Clara Howard* went to press, Brown had moved back to Philadelphia, and his letter to Hall about the first edition and its status in the press suggests closer supervision on Brown's part than we find in his other novels. Certainly A's relatively clean text indicates that it was proofread with some effectiveness, and it seems reasonable to conclude that Brown himself participated in the process, with good results.

The first edition remained the only one of *Clara Howard* until 1807, when the novel appeared as two volumes in London with a new title and the imprint of the Minerva Press. Edward Hartley's rechristening as Philip Stanley is the most obvious alteration in the English edition (E), but it also begins a new sequence of letter numbers with the second volume (starting with Letter XV), and contains additions of signatures to unsigned letters, expansions of abbreviated signatures (e.g., 'C. H.', or 'C. Howard.'), additions of complimentary closings (especially 'Yours'), some changes in the wording of the letters themselves, and many changes in punctuation, especially terminal. These changes increase in frequency at the end of the first volume and the beginning of the second and are like those a publisher might make extemporaneously before sending copy to his printer. That they are not authorial is virtually certain. They exhibit the usual attempt of Brown's English publishers to smooth out and clean up his prose. Besides being concentrated in the opening and closing pages of the two volumes—a division Brown would not have anticipated had he revised—the editor's alterations exhibit misconstruction of Brown's sense, as when 'my' becomes 'its' and 'consistent' becomes 'not consistent' in complicated passages (24.12, 81.36). Although the number of E's changes is smaller than in other English editions of Brown, their editorial nature is the same.

As the first American edition of 1801 is the only one with authority, it serves as copy-text for the present edition. Because A's text is a generally accurate one, relatively few emendations have proven to be necessary. Aside from the corrections made (without further notice) in the numbering of the last five letters, fewer than ten substantive emendations are scattered across the novel, and about half of these involve the singular possessive and A's lack of the apostrophe. There are as well a few corrections of genuine spelling errors, a handful of changes in punctuation, and some mending of typographical errors. By far the single largest group of emendations concerns A's failure to capitalize 'miss' when it serves as a title. If not simple mental or manual errors of the compositor, the twenty-odd instances of 'miss' probably represent a kind of graphic error, for Brown's majuscule M often differs only in size from the miniscule and could fairly easily be mistaken for it. Since contemporary sources indicate that the capitalized title was the well-established standard usage of Brown's time, this edition corrects all such instances without further notice.[6]

Probably the single most difficult feature of A's usage for the modern reader is its variable punctuation after questions. Like many first editions of Brown, A closes interrogative statements not only with the standard question mark but with the period and, more rarely, with the exclamation point. The imprecision in this stylistic matter so typical of Brown's work is in A compounded by the frequency of rhetorical questions posed by the correspondents, chiefly to themselves. Even in discourse it is not always clear whether a statement is interrogative or declarative (see, for example, 130.1-2), and sometimes a clause represents not an inquiry actually stated so much as the sort of leading question that might have been raised in a given situation (104.21-22). It is difficult not to conclude that A's general system, if that is not too honorific a term for it, reflects that of Brown's manuscript. To draw that conclusion is not, of course, to argue that A reproduces the pointing of

<hr/>

[6]These emendations occur on the following pages, in the following lines: 46.34, 48.35, 49.35, 57.16, 67.19, 69.7, 69.17, 70.24, 71.6, 71.16, 72.27, 72.33, 72.36, 73.4, 74.17, 80.32, 81.4, 82.1, 98.9, 112.36, 113.22, 127.22, 128.28, 129.34. Another kind of graphic error occurred at 29.10.

Brown's manuscript in every particular case, for it seems clear that the compositors attempted to normalize the manuscript's usage and in the attempt sometimes erred. But since A's punctuation after questions is not unlike that found in other first editions of Brown, thoroughly overhauling it to conform to modern usage would be inconsistent with the general principles of this edition, if not impossible practically. Consequently, this edition follows A's general system but emends its pointing in a few instances where it seems to have misrepresented Brown's intentions or genuinely obscured the sense.

A's system of setting off discourse with commas, successive dots, periods, and other punctuation also resembles that of other first editions of the author. Again, in general, it would appear that A's system reflects Brown's. Once or twice quotation marks appear around actual direct discourse (51.10 ff., 91.15–17), but these represent lapses from A's usual practice of restricting such marks to proverbial phrases, inscriptions, and the like (e.g., 10.31, 42.17). Whether these few lapses are authorial or compositorial it is impossible to demonstrate, but other first editions of Brown—including Maxwell's—suggest that some compositors momentarily yielded to an almost instinctive tendency to supply quotation marks where Brown had none. In accord with its policies, this edition adopts A's general system of representing direct and indirect discourse, retaining its quotation marks around proverbial phrases and in other such specific situations, while emending the remarkably few instances in which such marks surround actual discourse.

Successive dots appear in A not only to introduce or merely conclude discourse but also to interrupt a speech, to mark a shift in thought (whether dramatic or subtle), to set off a parenthetical phrase, to stand for an omitted word, and most often to represent a rhetorical pause—in short, to perform the various functions usually reserved for the modern-day dash. Only once does A use a dash for one of these purposes, at the end of the penultimate letter

481

(147.22). There is every reason to believe that A's dots reflect the usage of its manuscript copy. Indeed, they suggest a printer trying with moderate success to reproduce a feature which is commonly found in Brown's extant manuscripts. In these manuscripts Brown, like many other writers, frequently uses quick successive strokes of the pen to represent pauses and shifts; the strokes look as much like dots as dashes, though they cannot be imitated exactly by either of these two printer's sorts. Throughout A the number of dots ranges from three to nine, the norm being four both at the ends of sentences and within them, and there is no real distinction between the use of these devices to set off discourse and to represent pauses or shifts. Certainly the number appears to have no rhetorical or syntactical significance. Because nothing but distraction would be achieved by slavishly reproducing the typography of the dots, even were that possible, this edition (without further notice) regularizes them in accordance with the first edition's prevailing norm, setting all the dots as three spaced ones while retaining the additional periods at the ends of sentences. There are two exceptions to this rule: we substitute long dashes to represent omitted words (3.1, 36.28, 56.17), and we make one emendation of dots which seem to reflect compositorial error (54.38). However, we have declined to regularize A's single dash to dots and instead have reproduced it.

JANE TALBOT

Late in 1801, probably in early December, *Jane Talbot* made its appearance as the fourth volume in the series of "Select Novels" published by John Conrad, who reissued *Edgar Huntly* at about the same time. It was sold not only by Conrad in Philadelphia but by other members of the Conrad syndicate in Baltimore and Washington and by other booksellers throughout the States who had been organized to distribute the series. Brown apparently had been working on the novel for six months or so before it went to press in late August, but no manuscripts or other pre-printing documents from that period have survived.[7]

The printer of the first American edition (A) was John Bioren, a reputable member of the trade whose shop was just down Chestnut Street from Conrad's own.[8] With its disjunct series title, the duodecimo volume collates as follows: π1 A–2F^6 ($1, 3 signed, –A1, $3 [first leaf of insert] as 2); 175 leaves, pp. *i–ii 1–3 4–346 347–348*. The series title, identifying the novel as 'Volume IV', occupies π1; A1 contains the title, and its verso the copyright statement. The first letter begins on A2 beneath the head-title, and the ensuing letters, beginning on rectos and versos, fill the succeeding leaves to the very bottom of 2F5^V. The last leaf is blank and is wanting in some copies, and many lack the disjunct series title as well.

The lack of the series title raises the question whether there were two issues of the book, one in the series and one as a separate.[9] It is impossible to demonstrate that this was not the case, but it seems unlikely that it was. What Conrad could have gained by such a procedure is unclear. If he had had more copies of the book printed than he had hoped to sell as part of his series of "Select Novels," an independent issue might have made some sense, but it is improbable that the print order for *Jane Talbot* would have exceeded those for books by Charlotte Smith and Regina Maria Roche, whose popularity was well established (see pp. 449–450). Moreover, in the interest of the series as a whole, having the series title before the eyes of the public as much as possible must have seemed a desirable end in itself. Had the series title been printed as part of the last sheet (π1 = 2F6), a perfectly normal procedure that Bioren could have adopted in the interest of economy, the like-

[7]See the Historical Essay, pp. 443–449. See also the Textual Essay, in *Edgar Huntly,* pp. 1–2.

[8]See Marion S. Carson and Marshall W. S. Swan, "John Bioren: Printer to Philadelphia Publishers,"*PBSA,* 43 (1949), 321–334.

[9]See the Historical Essay, p. 449, n. 23.

lihood that some copies were issued without the series title would have been reduced to a minimum, for to Conrad's mind wasting the leaf could have served no useful purpose. But because some copies survive with 2F6 intact, we must conclude that Conrad had a special forme made up to print the series title, rather than having it imposed as part of the last forme of the work (that is, $\pi 1$ does not equal 2F6). It follows that issuing a certain number of copies of the book without the series title would have involved no real trouble and no waste. Nevertheless, the other considerations already mentioned make the likelihood greater that there was only one issue—with the series title—and that the extant copies lacking the first leaf are defective.

Certainty about a more important question, the source of A's numerous errors and inadvertencies, is still more difficult to obtain. Even in its simplest mechanical features A's text is defective. Its numbering of the letters exhibits two breaks in sequence: V is omitted and XXXI is repeated. According to A's numeration, the cross-reference to 'XXX' in XXXII (294.27) should be to the first letter numbered XXXI, though it is ultimately accurate when the double numeration error is corrected. The recipient of one letter (LIV) is not identified. Four letters are misdated: Cartwright's of early October as 'Dec. 12', Jane's second in succession to Mrs. Fielder as 'October 15' instead of the seventeenth, and two of her earlier ones to Colden by one day (VII and VIII). Numerous other mechanical blunders occur. As Daniel Edwards Kennedy noted, there is a similar inconsistency regarding the date of Colden's departure with Stephen Montford in letters XL (325.13-15), LIV (393.13-14), and LVIII (400.2-3). Kennedy also deplored further faults. "In letter XIX [XVIII] Molly is to be sent home to her mother and Tom retained as a servant, but later, for no reason at all, Molly is the one kept and Tom is sent off; in letter XXVII [XXVI] Colden says he was offered four or five thousand dollars to go to Europe, in letter XVIII [XVII] the amount offered was three hundred pounds sterling; in letter XXVIII [XXVII] Colden speaks of his sister Sue, whereas her name is afterward given as Mary; . . . the name of Miss Jessup is one time Polly another time Hetty; Clarges' name is said to be remembered as part of the conversation overheard in the watchmaker's shop but as the conversation was given it was not included . . . ; the very letter in which Jane complains that Frank's letter is unsigned is likewise lacking in that respect'' (pp. 1446–1448). Such inconsistencies and oversights are not unlike those found in Brown's other works, but anyone will admit that this first edition has more than its share.

In addition to a smattering of press-variants which seem to reflect press-run accidents,[10] the first edition has a system of punctuation that not only bemuses the modern reader but probably presented some difficulties for Brown's contemporaries. In kind, A's usage resembles that in the first edition of *Clara Howard,* but the problems of A are much more severe. The most striking instance is its representation of questions. It has a seemingly endless confusion of the question mark with the exclamation point and the simple period. The first two of these points frequently occur mid-sentence, often in a series of questions (see, for example, the paragraph beginning at 390.16). Occasionally they do not appear but are implied (e.g., 208.30). A's general mode of representing questions, especially of distinguishing them from declarative statements and exclamations, amounts to chaos. Indeed, it is not always possible to distinguish a rhetorical question in A from a straightforward statement or an emotional outburst. Although its use of uppercase and lowercase in a series of questions is generally satisfactory, in some instances capitalization is needed to signal the end of a question and the beginning of a declaration but is missing (e.g., 403.31).

Beyond this major matter of punctuation associated with questions or possible questions, there are some less widespread problems with A's pointing, which is nothing if not

[10]Some copies have '[]ate' for 'fate' (188.8), 'apprehensi[]ns' for 'apprehensions' (225.22), 'paison' for 'poison' (229.9), 'grieve[]' for 'grieved' (321.18), or '[]f' for 'of' (337.28).

erratic. For instance, it is fairly obvious that Bioren's men, like other compositors, often confused Brown's comma and period. Less frequently A omits the apostrophe in possessives. Once it supplies it unnecessarily (280.18). In a few other cases A includes punctuation that is not needed (154.5, 190.8, 358.22). And throughout the letters it uses quotation marks with a variety and inconsistency calculated to bewilder its readers, whether of Brown's day or our own.

Responsibility for this state of affairs is not easy to fix, but it is likely that the chaos has two sources rather than one. Brown's manuscript was probably defective in many respects, especially in its punctuation of questions. At one time he frankly admitted, even somewhat defensively, that his method of writing produced "slighter inaccuracies of grammar, orthography, and punctuation,"[11] and if indeed he had begun the novel by March 1801 and resumed it after his trip north in July, the discontinuity of composition may have aggravated the problem. Moreover, the kinds of problems found in the first edition of *Jane Talbot* are also found, to a lesser degree, in most of his other first editions. In *Jane Talbot,* however, Brown's chronic inattention to such matters is compounded by the rhetorical, meditative, and sentimental nature of the letters, and the principals' penchant for stringing together a series of questions further aggravates the situation. It seems fairly clear from A's rather frequent practice of ending declarations and exclamations with the question mark and questions with the exclamation point that Bioren's compositors took it upon themselves to style Brown's manuscript in an attempt to reduce its punctuation to some semblance of order. In many cases, however, they misinterpreted the nature of a statement and supplied an inappropriate point (e.g., at 207.4,

[11]Brown to Bringhurst, 20 May 1792, quoted in Herbert R. Brown, "Charles Brockden Brown's 'The Story of Julius'; Rousseau and Richardson 'Improved'," in *Essays Mostly on Periodical Publishing in America,* ed. James Woodress (Durham, N.C.: Duke Univ. Press, 1973), p. 40.

231.21). In a still larger number of cases, they simply failed to use the question mark and set the period, which presumably reproduces the pointing of Brown's manuscript often enough but is unsatisfactory to the modern reader and may have been so to the more enlightened of Brown's contemporaries.

We have no firm knowledge about Brown's composition of the novel, except that it was apparently under way by early March and was resumed after he had returned from his trip north in late July (see pp. 445–449), and we have even less knowledge about the nature of the manuscript copy he submitted for printing, except what can be inferred from these facts and the text of A itself. It may well be that he began a riding trip west with his brother James on 19 August, but the inference that he did so is based on the attribution to him of "Memorandums Made on a Journey through Part of Pennsylvania,"[12] and the attribution is uncertain, though reasonable (see p. 448). If Brown returned to Philadelphia in late July having gleaned the hint for Colden's trip from his own travels, he must have had more than one-third of the novel yet to write at that time (see 325.3–4). Given the rate at which he wrote *Ormond* and finished off *Arthur Mervyn, First Part,* it is possible that he completed *Jane Talbot* before his departure on 19 August, a date which coincides closely with the advertisement of the novel on the twenty-first in the *Aurora General Advertiser.*[13] On the other hand, the printers of these earlier novels and of *Wieland* had begun production before receiving a complete manuscript, thereby forcing Brown to write his con-

---

[12]*Literary Magazine,* 1 (1803–1804), 167–173, 250–255. Kennedy, pp. 1380–1398, argues persuasively for Brown's authorship; Charles E. Bennett, "The Charles Brockden Brown Canon," is, however, silent on the question.

[13]See the Historical Essay, p. 449; also Russel B. Nye, Historical Essay, in *Ormond or The Secret Witness,* ed. Sydney J. Krause et al. (Kent, Ohio: Kent State Univ. Press, 1982), pp. 307–309; Norman S. Grabo, Historical Essay, in *Arthur Mervyn or Memoirs of the Year 1793: First and Second Parts,* ed. Sydney J. Krause et al. (1980), pp. 453–456.

clusions against the press, and there is no reason to believe that Brown could not have adopted such a procedure once again and completed *Jane Talbot* after returning from the August trip and after printing had begun. In either case, there would have been considerable discontinuity in the writing of the manuscript, and the last third in particular would have been produced in genuine haste.

Some of the effects of this process have already been mentioned. Responsibility for the larger inconsistencies must generally be laid at Brown's own feet. Certainly the confusion over the first names of Miss Jessup and Colden's sister is authorial, as it has parallels in other novels.[14] It is also difficult to see how the printers could have created the variable dating of Colden's trip and the similarly mismanaged details of the plot which so troubled Kennedy. However, Bioren's men probably are responsible for at least one of the erroneous datings of a letter ('Dec. 12' for 'Oct. 2', 414.2), though perhaps not for the others. Furthermore, they may have had a hand in the confusion over the numbering of the letters. The footnote in letter XXXII which refers the reader to letter XXX is actually correct, and so is the number of the letter itself—for the first time since V was omitted. The righting of the sequence at this precise point is too much to attribute to coincidence. Brown himself must have written the footnote and hence must have calculated the number of the letters to this point. If he had supplied the number 'XXXII' in his manuscript but left to the printer the actual numbering of the previous letters, the result would have been that the compositors would have followed their own error in the fifth letter until they came upon Brown's 'XXXII', which would have prompted them to set the duplicate 'XXXI' deliberately in the same sheet. This measure, of course, would have been their only recourse for correcting the sequence up to that point, because previous formes would already have been wrought off when the problem was discovered.

[14]See the Textual Essay, in *Arthur Mervyn,* p.483; also the Textual Essay, in *Edgar Huntly,* p. 439.

That this long-standing sequence of errors survives in
A is clear evidence—if further evidence were needed—
that the proofreading of the volume was far from satisfactory. We can only conjecture why it was unsatisfactory.
Bioren was a reputable and prosperous printer who produced about one dozen other books during 1801, including
several sumptuous volumes, and one might have expected
fewer errors in his first edition of Brown than have survived. Yet it must be granted that, aside from the mistakes
in numeration and the few instances of press-variation, the
errors in this first edition of Brown are not unprecedented
in number or in nature, and of course there is no way of
knowing how many were in the type set up from the
manuscript before putative press-correction.

In fact, some of A's most startling faults are the kind
that a printer might well have relied on an author to correct. Why Brown appears to have read proof for *Jane Talbot*
much less carefully than for *Clara Howard* is a matter of
mere speculation. We might conjecture that, having finished *Jane Talbot* and closed his career as a novelist, Brown
was simply inattentive to the printing of his last novel, but
the evidence for that argument is largely internal and incon-
clusive. On the other hand, if he was in fact writing against
the press, his preoccupation with completing the novel
would account for his failure to give the proofs close attention. Yet, as already noted, the course of the composition
is uncertain. Still more uncertain are the nature and extent
of his other occupations during late 1801. His letter to
Anthony Bleeker at the end of October mentions an aborted
trip "southward" and a possible "week's jaunt" to New
York in the winter, but it indicates that for all practical purposes Brown expected to continue in Philadelphia for the
rest of the year.[15] There is considerable uncertainty and
scholarly disagreement about his activities during this time
and indeed during all of 1801. How much time and attention his participation in his brothers' mercantile business

[15]Brown to Anthony Bleeker, 31 October 1801, printed in Dunlap,
Life, II, 104.

and his related legal studies consumed is not at all clear, nor is it even agreed precisely when during the year Brown entered the business.[16] About his involvement in the *American Review* (the successor to the *Monthly Magazine* which he edited in New York in 1799 and 1800), in the *Ladies' Monitor,* and in editorial work for the Conrad syndicate there is equal uncertainty and disagreement.[17] In short, the external evidence that might help account for Brown's failure to proofread A effectively is either wanting or ambiguous. The only conclusion we can draw is that, for whatever reason, he did so fail, for the evidence of his failure—and perhaps of Bioren's as well—survives in the first edition.

This edition was succeeded in 1804 by a second edition published in London over the imprint of the Minerva Press, the only other edition of the novel that appeared in Brown's lifetime. The English edition (E) is in two volumes and renumbers the letters for the second, beginning with XXIX. It thus circumvents the problem of the duplicated 'XXXI', but it fails to correct A's omission of V, which it numbers 'IV' without altering the succeeding numbers. Like other English editions of Brown, E exhibits a number of editorial alterations as well as spontaneous compositorial errors. Some of the alterations are corrections, but there is no reason to believe that they derive from Brown. Rather, they seem to be of a piece with the other changes, which are clearly editorial and result in errors, such as misreadings of the context, alterations of Brown's distinctive idioms or those of his characters, and other miscues that reveal a mind

[16]For discussion of this matter, see Clark, *Brown,* pp. 183, 197; Warfel, pp. 189, 191; Charles E. Bennett, "Charles Brockden Brown: Man of Letters," in *Critical Essays on Charles Brockden Brown,* ed. Bernard Rosenthal (Boston: G. K. Hall, 1981), p. 212.

[17]See Bennett, "Man of Letters," p. 212; Warfel, p. 188; Bennett, "Canon," pp. 95–97; Kennedy, pp. 1500–1503, 1510–1515; Warfel, p. 201. See also Frank Luther Mott, *A History of American Magazines 1741–1850* (1930; rpt. Cambridge: Harvard Univ. Press, 1970), pp. 218–222.

and hand alien to the authorial.[18] Well into the second volume, after letter LIV (p. 394), the editorial hand virtually disappears. But there is no reason to think that anywhere in E we have revised readings or corrections derived from Brown.

Since E lacks authority, the only authoritative document for *Jane Talbot* that has come down to us is the first edition. Derived directly from Brown's manuscript, so far as we know, A serves as copy-text for the present edition.

Where A is press-variant (see p. 485, n. 10), the present edition adopts the correct readings on the premise that they have precedence, and no further record of these variants appears. Aside from correcting the errors in the numbering of the letters (without further report) and the four misdatings already discussed, this edition makes about two dozen other substantive emendations. About half of these involve possessives. There are also eight emendations of 'miss' as a title,[19] a dozen of graphic errors in total, and three dozen of literals. However, on the theory (developed above) that many of A's inconsistencies and inadvertencies are Brown's own, this edition allows to stand a number of readings that may seem wrong to modern readers. These include the double names for Miss Jessup and Colden's sister already mentioned, many instances of authorial ellipsis, inconsistencies of number and tense, grammatical faults, and variant spellings which apparently represent alternatives still legitimate in Brown's day (e.g., 'irresistable' and 'irresistible').

The most difficult editorial problem which A presents is its punctuation, as earlier discussion has suggested. From that discussion it should be plain that there is really no satisfactory way to bring genuine order out of A's virtual chaos without imposing a rigorous modern system that

[18]See the variants in the Historical List at 210.33, 219.19, 219.20, for examples.

[19]These emendations occur on the following pages, in the following lines: 334.6, 334.37, 335.4, 335.8, 336.35, 337.2, 340.15, 344.1. On the probable source of these errors, see above, p. 480.

would be alien not only to A's text but probably to Brown's manuscript. Even if such emendation were undertaken, it would be impossible to distinguish exclamatory, declarative, and interrogative statements from each other throughout the novel.[20] The only viable policy, then, is to accept A's general texture, its general fluidity in this respect, and to correct readings that can be identified as positive error on A's own terms.

Hence this edition emends A's text when its compositors seem to have erred in styling Brown's manuscript by misinterpreting and mispointing declarative or exclamatory statements as interrogative or interrogative as exclamatory. It also changes such punctuation when it genuinely obscures or obstructs Brown's sense and constitutes, in effect, an isolated error within A's general system. Otherwise, this edition retains A's pointing not only in the frequent rhetorical questions but also in the numerous instances in which A's period would normally have been expected to be a question mark or an exclamation point and in cases where a question is posed in indirect discourse (e.g., 164.7) or mid-sentence (e.g., 208.30, 395.11). It is of course impossible to be sure in every case, especially where two alternative corrections exist, that an emendation restores the text of Brown's manuscript, but by and large this policy brings us nearer to that text than would indiscriminate emendation or wholesale retention of A's pointing.

The first edition's other punctuation raises problems that are less widespread but only a little less difficult. The present edition treats these problems individually rather than as a group. For instance, it is fairly obvious that Bioren's men, like earlier compositors of Brown's first editions, often confused his manuscript's comma and period, which frequently would have been virtually indistinguishable if the copy was in his small hand; simple corrections of this con-

[20]Three examples in Colden's long letter to James Montford suggest something of the nature of the problem: the sentence at 348.37–38, which is complicated by ellipsis, and those at 355.22–23 and 355.38–356.4.

fusion eliminate a fair amount of nonsense in A. On the other hand, there is no convincing evidence that the compositors frequently interchanged the comma and the semicolon; the semicolons in series, after long introductory phrases, and in other positions where the modern reader would expect to see a comma are not anomalies in the larger system of A's pointing and cannot be emended as actual errors. Likewise, the use of capitalized words after the semicolon is certainly part of A's style, if not surely of Brown's, and should be retained. The similar alternation between uppercase and lowercase in a series of questions also appears to be part of A's generally freewheeling system and may well reflect Brown's manuscript; in this edition A's usage is generally retained, though in a few cases a word is capitalized when it marks the end of a question and the beginning of a declarative statement. A few other instances of odd pointing in A seem to be genuine errors and anomalies beyond the pale of its generally erratic system, but by and large what seem to us moderns to be defects—like the sometimes incomplete pointing around parenthetical phrases or the vocative (e.g., 153.4, 162.15, 181.29)—stand in this edition as representing the usage of the copy-text and as perhaps reflecting the author's usage as well.

One final matter requires comment. The conventions adopted for representing discourse and other quotations are usually problematic in first editions of Brown. The first edition of *Jane Talbot* follows the freewheeling system found in most others in its use of the comma, the dash, the semicolon, the colon, the period, the paragraph, and other such devices to signal the beginning and the end of both direct and indirect discourse, although there are a few instances in which quotations set off such discourse. But in keeping with its generally erratic punctuation and capitalization, this first edition is even more unpredictable than others in its use of quotations. Its erratic style, compounded by the frequent occurrence in the novel of maxims, letters within letters, quotations or paraphrases from earlier letters, remarks that are typical of a speaker though not actually voiced, and similar passages make for a very complicated but loose set of conventions for quoting matter. In accord with its general policy, the present edition adopts A's dominant system of representing quotations, whether direct, indirect, or simply hypothesized (e.g., 183.3–4, 183.8, 303.20–304.2), including the use of lowercase to open some of them (e.g., 162.3–4, 164.10, 165.31). However, emendations occur in the relatively small number of instances in which discourse appears within quotation marks and in the fewer instances in which such marks surround imagined speeches, which are not always easy to distinguish from actual ones. Furthermore, quotation marks are retained for written matter—letters within letters, passages from earlier letters, Jane's signature (194.15)—and for maxims, titles, proverbial phrases, and the like.

Both *Clara Howard* and *Jane Talbot* appeared in the unauthoritative nineteenth-century American collected editions of Brown that began with the 1827 series published by S. G. Goodrich, but neither has appeared in a new twentieth-century edition. To present the texts of these two novels in modern print, the present editors have been obliged to make a number of inconsequential silent changes of the original documents' typography. By and large these have involved regularizing the spacing and the typefaces of the headings, signatures, and postscripts. Additionally, two features of eighteenth-century printers' style have been altered: the periods terminating the headings that state the letter number and the recipient have been removed, and the asterisks which fill a type-line within a few letters have been reduced to three.

The appendixes that follow contain reports on the variants from each of the copy-texts in the present edition, on the substantive variants in the editions of each work examined for the present one, and on similar matters concerning the editing of each of the texts. A statement of the general textual principles of the edition, as well as of the handling of "silent" changes and of other matters connected with the apparatus, appears in the first volume of the series.

S.W.R.

APPENDIXES

Textual Notes
CLARA HOWARD

NOTE: In these discussions of readings adopted by this edition, either by emendation of the copy-text or retention of its reading when emendation is possible, citations of passages in other works by Brown refer to earlier volumes of the Bicentennial Edition. Those not preceded by an abbreviation are to the present volume. The following sigla identify the editions discussed.

A: the copy-text: *Clara Howard; In A Series of Letters.* (Philadelphia, 1801), the first edition
E: *Philip Stanley; or, The Enthusiasm of Love. A Novel.* (London, 1807), without authority

5.16 in melancholy] Although we might expect the indefinite article here, A's omission of it is no doubt an example of Brown's typical ellipsis.

6.14–18 This ... visits.] This sentence fragment elaborates the previous sentence; emendations might be invented to make that relationship clearer, but A's pointing and capitalization almost certainly reflect Brown's.

16.13 It] The referent for this word—marriage—cannot be found in the previous sentences except by implication (e.g., 'I cannot be yours'), but the construction is almost certainly Brown's.

59.3 chair] Brown is being a little imprecise here: what he has in mind, apparently, is a small chaise, not a sedan, and A's reading must stand.

69.20 me] It is difficult to construct a defense for A's 'us'; E's 'me' seems the inevitable correction.

80.12 feel] A's 'feel' should, strictly, be 'felt', but Brown's lax attitude towards tenses suggests he wrote 'feel'.

81.36 consistent] The particular innuendo here seems to be that Mary has become Sedley's mistress, whereas E's 'not consistent' incorrectly assumes that Sedley is in fact married.

86.24 but who] This is an example of Brown's ellipsis, the earlier 'one' (86.23) being understood.

100.33 had come] Although Brown's imprecision in tenses is evidenced throughout his work, A's 'had came' is beyond the pale, can be shown to be wrong by contemporary standards, and probably represents a simple graphic error. See *EH,* 100.13 and textual note; also Robert Lowth's *Short Introduction to English Grammar* (1765; rpt. Menston, England: Scolar Press, 1967), p. 80.

105.10 her children to at least∧] A's syntax is garbled: the comma after 'at least' coupled with the lack of the comma before the phrase creates an ambiguity presumably unintentional on Brown's part. Whether 'at least' is meant to modify 'her children' or 'a part' is debatable, but the entire construction of the sentence suggests the latter, and we have accordingly deleted A's comma, which may represent compositorial styling.

List of Emendations

CLARA HOWARD

NOTE: This list contains all instances of alterations of the copy-text, except for those already noted in the Textual Essay (pp. 480, 482) and the silent changes specified in the note on the Bicentennial texts in Volume I of this edition. (See the Textual Essay for the treatment of the copy-text's press-variants.) Each note gives the reading of the Bicentennial text before the bracket, followed by a siglum identifying its earliest source (either the English edition, or the present editors) and then by the variant reading(s) in the copy-text and in the English edition. This information is provided for both substantives and accidentals; for a complete history of substantive variants among the editions examined, see the Historical List. An asterisk (*) before the lemma indicates that the Textual Notes discuss the emendation. A wavy dash (~) represents the same word appearing before the bracket and occurs only in the recording of variants in punctuation or other accidentals associated with that word, when the word itself is not the variant being noted; the inferior caret (∧) shows that punctuation is absent. Three dots (. . .) mean that the note omits one or more words in a series, and a vertical stroke (|) marks the break between lines. "B" following the bracket identifies readings adopted for the first time in the Bicentennial Edition (that is, readings not appearing in the editions examined). Preceding the list are the sigla which identify the editions examined and cited in the list.

A: the copy-text: *Clara Howard; In A Series of Letters.* (Philadelphia, 1801), the first edition
E: *Philip Stanley; or, The Enthusiasm of Love. A Novel.* (London, 1807), without authority

19.19	Valentine] B; Vallentine A-E
21.11	My act] E; Myact A
24.14	demand self-denial] E; demandself-denial A
29.10	opinion, it] E; ~. It A
30.10	delirium] E; dilerium A
33.6	Edward] B; Edgar A; Philip E
40.14	he] E; be A
42.5	degrees] E; degress A
42.13	sister's] E; sisters A
48.29–30	efforts] E; effosts A
50.8	regret] E; reget A
51.10	∧My dear Ned,∧] E; "~ ~ ~," A
51.11–35	∧I ... but∧] B; "~ ... ~" A-E
51.24	∧My] B; "~ A-E
51.37–52.14	∧her ... journey.∧] B; "~ ... ~." A-E
54.38	respect, which] E; ~ .... ~ A
60.19	another's] E; anothers A
* 69.20	me] E; us A
73.32	lovelier] E; lovlier A
80.36	know.] E; ~? A
84.2	result.] E; ~? A
91.15–17	∧Clara ... moment.∧] B; "~ ... ~." A-E
93.18–19	circumstances,] E; ~; A
96.28–29	relation she] E; relations he A
* 100.33	come] E; came A
103.27	compassion,] E; ~; A
* 105.10	least∧] E; least, A
107.29	another's] E; anothers A
121.37	these] E; there A
122.35	friend's] E; friends A
130.27	Mrs.] E; Mrs∧ A
140.3	you?] E; ~! A
144.6	ruin!] E; ~? A
146.17	land!] E; ~? A
147.10	prerogatives] E; perogatives A

END-OF-LINE WORD-DIVISION
CLARA HOWARD

NOTE: The two following lists provide information on the word-division of divisible compounds that are hyphenated at the ends of lines in the copy-text or in the Bicentennial Edition. List A contains, in the form of the established text, such compounds which are hyphenated and divided at the break between lines in the copy-text. A double dagger (‡) precedes the notation if the word happens to be similarly hyphenated in the Bicentennial Edition (see List B for more information on such words). List B contains all examples of possible compounds hyphenated at the break between lines in this edition which are meant to be hyphenated in the established text; the absence of such compounds hyphenated in this edition shows that they are meant to be unhyphenated in the established text. A dagger (†) precedes the notation if the word is an emendation (see the List of Emendations for further information) and a double dagger (‡) precedes it if the word happens to be similarly hyphenated in the copy-text (see List A of this appendix on such words). Both lists omit words that have hyphens between capitalized elements (e.g., North-|American) and those that are clearly mere compositorial syllabication (including syllabication of compound words falling elsewhere than at the point of word-division).

A.   *Word-Division in the Copy-Text*

8.3	to-morrow	28.19	afterwards
21.24	sometimes	29.38	reappearance
23.19	southward	38.12	somewhat
26.24	headlong	39.36	whatever

41.5	*Brandywine*	102.15	himself
48.22	favourable	108.24	herself
48.28	overlook	109.1	withdrew
53.8	awe-creating	112.13	yourself
53.9	likewise	117.10	hand-writing
53.31	elsewhere	122.19	myself
57.36	cannot	126.6	themselves
62.7	undertaking	126.30	yourself
‡71.31-32	herself	128.7	mankind
83.24	withholding	134.15	myself
86.22	something	138.21	day-dawn
94.4	afterwards	140.13	helpless
95.23	likewise	146.14	somewhat

B. *Word-Division in the Bicentennial Edition*

18.29-19.1	after-repentance	64.7-8	half-whisper
35.5-6	self-condemnation	72.37-73.1	self-denial
51.2-3	farmer-boy	90.25-26	earth-worm
56.27-28	New-York		

HISTORICAL LIST OF
SUBSTANTIVE VARIANTS
CLARA HOWARD

NOTE: This appendix lists only substantive variants from the Bicentennial text in the editions examined. Accidentals— including accidentals variants of the readings—are not, as such, listed; thus the report that two texts agree in having one of two readings (e.g., 'apprized' as against 'surprised') implies only that they both have the same word (e.g., perhaps in the spellings *apprized* and *apprised*) and not necessarily the identical form. Also not listed are variants in letter headings (see the Textual Essay), the English edition's change of names (see the note at the end of the main list), and such features as are silently emended throughout the Bicentennial Edition (see "The Bicentennial Texts: A Note," p. xxiii, in Volume I of this series). By the same token, as the purpose of this report is to list the genuinely substantive variants which constitute the evidence for decisions on genealogy and authority ("The Bicentennial Texts," p. xxiv), this list does not report as variants impossible readings created by pulled types or other merely typographical faults. Nor does it record a second time examples of foul-case, mechanical transposition of letters, or other similar "literals" which appear in the copy-text and are correct in another edition. Reports on such readings appear in the Textual Essay (when they involve press-variation) or in the List of Emendations. Throughout the list, each note gives the reading of the Bicentennial text before the bracket, followed by the variant reading(s) and then the sigla for the editions having that variant. A wavy dash (~) represents the same word appearing before the bracket and occurs when variation involves punctuation associated with that word but the word itself is not the variant being noted; the inferior caret ($\wedge$) shows that punctuation is absent. In each entry, the editions are cited only when they vary substantively from the reading of the Bicentennial text given in the lemma (i.e., omission of sigla implies agreement). The following sigla identify the editions cited.

A: the copy-text: *Clara Howard; In A Series of Letters.* (Philadelphia, 1801), the first edition

E: *Philip Stanley; or, The Enthusiasm of Love. A Novel.* (London, 1807), without authority

head-title	CLARA HOWARD]	38.17	artless] ardent E
	PHILIP STANLEY E	39.27	with] from E
6.3	her] your E	41.5	an] a E
12.27	this] he E	42.13	sister's] sisters A
15.32–33	most lovely and] most E	44.26	in] in the E
		45.12	as] so E
19.34	conceptions] conception E	47.4	an] a E
		47.8	an] a E
23.16	an] a E	51.2	that the] the E
24.12	my] its E	52.2	of her] her E
24.30	should] would E	53.36	an] a E
27.6	acrimoniously] hastily E	54.15	wakeful] waking E
		56.18	niece] daughter E
32.5	possible] impossible E	56.22	Howard] Yours, E. Howard E
32.28	be.]$\sim$ $\wedge$ for the wretched E	57.3	whereabout] whereabouts E
33.6	Edward] Edgar A; Philip E	57.8	advice] my advice E
33.25	E. Howard] Yours, very sincerely, E. Howard E	58.14	lodging] lodgings E
		59.12	napkins and sheets] sheets E
34.22	years] tears E	60.19	another's] anothers A
35.8	union] an union E	61.22	within] within my E
35.13	Adieu.] Adieu. Yours, E	69.20	me] us A
		70.17–18	embarassment] embarassments E
36.26	Adieu.] Adieu. Yours, E	71.7	disappearance and silence] silence and disappearance E
37.21	beginnings] beginning E		

78.9	she is, for] for E	115.15	preparation]
78.20	your fond, your] your		preparations E
	E	115.23	indulged] indulged in
80.5	unaware] unawares E		E
80.12	feel] felt E	116.2	of] of the E
81.36	consistent] not	116.26	an] a E
	consistent E	121.17	misfortune]
87.31	that] the E		misfortunes E
88.16	not] no E	121.37	these] there A
89.11	inclination and ability]	122.15	this] the E
	inclination E	122.35	friend's] friends A
90.20	reward that] reward E	125.18	an] a E
93.3	girl] Clara E	125.33	acquisitions]
96.13	twenty-four] twenty E		acquisition E
96.17	with those with] with E	128.23	not you] you not E
96.28–29	relation she] relations	132.7	an] a E
	he A	133.25	an] a E
98.22	employer] employers	134.29	an] a E
	E	135.35	and yet] and E
98.36	his engagement]	136.26	motives in] motives for
	engagement E		E
99.7	lay] lays E	137.12	an] a E
99.30	soon and] soon E	137.38	to me] of me E
100.33	come] came A	138.18	the] the next E
103.27	abated] blunted E	140.5–6	of your] of E
105.4	this] his E	144.9	open on] open to E
107.29	another's] anothers A	146.9	an] a E
108.12	cursory] a cursory E	146.14	an] a E
113.15	to oppose] oppose E	147.22	fire-side!—] fire-side!
114.13	an] a E		Clara Howard E
115.11	denied to] denied E	148.7–8	settles] settle E

[NOTE: E changes A's 'Edward Hartley' to 'Philip Stanley' (12.1, 63.34, 119.18, 120.8) and 'Edward' to 'Philip' (11.5, 12.16, 17.3, 25.21, 32.4, 34.7, 52.1, 77.14, 83.9, 84.1, 91.18, 91.28, 104.23, 106.20, 109.11, 136.5, 137.22); E expands A's 'E.H.' to 'Philip Stanley' (19.37, 23.21, 31.8, 76.6, 82.4, 95.38, 113.37, 114.16, 118.8, 145.26) and expands 'E. Hartley' to 'Philip Stanley' (20.1, 24.1, 26.1, 32.1, 34.1, 77.1, 83.1, 87.39, 91.1, 96.1, 107.1, 146.1). In E 'Ned' becomes 'Philip' (49.26, 51.10, 80.17, 96.19); 'Neddy' becomes 'Philip' (80.11, 80.19, 80.34). E expands 'Hartley' to 'Philip Stanley' (90.27), and changes 'Hartley' to 'Stanley' (124.16, 124.25, 124.31, 124.34,

127.6, 127.20, 128.23, 128.30, 129.15, 129.24, 130.15, 130.26, 130.33, 131.1, 131.6, 131.19, 131.22, 131.26, 131.34, 132.3), while 'Hartley' becomes 'Philip' in E (139.8). Likewise, 'C.H.' is expanded to 'Clara Howard' (21.35, 25.39, 27.32, 32.29, 84.3, 109.28, 141.30), and 'Clara' to 'Clara Howard' (78.21, 92.23, 148.23); 'Mary' is expanded to 'Mary Wilmot' (139.8, 143.28), as is 'M.W.' (132.11). 'Mary Wilmot' is once shortened to 'Mary' (77.28).]

TEXTUAL NOTES

JANE TALBOT

NOTE: In these discussions of readings adopted by this edition, either by emendation of the copy-text or retention of its reading when emendation is possible, citations of passages in "Carwin" refer to the first volume of the Bicentennial Edition, while citations of *Alcuin* refer to the first edition (New York, 1798). Those not preceded by an abbreviation are to the present volume. The following sigla identify the editions discussed.

A: the copy-text: *Jane Talbot, A Novel.* (Philadelphia, 1801), the first edition

E: *Jane Talbot. A Novel.* (London, 1804), without authority

153.16 making it] The referent for Brown's 'it' here and later (153.18) is not simply 'the retrospect' (153.14–15) but the account or 'the story' (153.10–11), and it seems likely that A has rendered Brown's construction faithfully.

160.9 evil,] It is possible that A has omitted Brown's 'since' under the misapprehension that 'as' serves the same function, but the greater likelihood is simply that A's comma stands where we would have expected a semi-colon.

160.12 was waste] The construction invites 'a', it would seem, but probably the ellipsis is Brown's, who often omits articles. Cf. *Alcuin*, 21.14.

161.4 enter] A's 'inter' is apparently not Brown's pun, although given his attitudes toward the legal profession, it might well have been.

161.6 extravagant; or] Brown means that the stipend was neither extravagant nor more than sufficient; A may have replaced his 'nor'

509

with 'or', but the greater likelihood is that the ambiguity here arises from the use of the semi-colon after 'extravagant' where we might have expected a comma.

161.7–8 the temple] Brown apparently has in mind one of the London Inns of Court, either the Middle or the Inner Temple, but A's lower-case spelling of the word is probably authorial.

163.22 complaint] Despite A's pronoun 'them' later in the sentence (163.23), the singular 'complaint' probably represents what Brown wrote, as his frequent lack of agreement elsewhere suggests.

165.4 lenient] A's 'lenitent' is an error, but whether for 'lenient' or 'lenitive' is not obvious. As both words would mean essentially the same thing in the context, there are no grounds on which to choose between them other than decorum and the probable source of A's error, which is more likely to have arisen from the simple insertion of the 't' than the misreading of 'tive' as 'tent'. It is unlikely Jane's father would have used, or even known, the less familiar word.

165.7 is] A's omission of the word at a line-break is probably a simple error, rather than an egregious case of Brown's ellipsis. Whether the full word or a contraction (i.e., 'income's') was in Brown's manuscript it is impossible to tell, but the context suggests that 'is' was probably there.

170.35 interest] E's 'interests' is certainly more logical, but Brown's usual sloppiness in matters of number makes it likely that A here reproduces his manuscript.

181.24–25 fall on] Frank's love of colloquialism (see 181.11–12) suggests that A has accurately reproduced what Brown wrote, presumably as a rough equivalent to "make use of" (*OED,* 64.d). The phrase got by E's editor, and the temptation to emend A's unusual phrase to the more predictable 'follow' should be resisted.

186.14 till] From all that has been said repeatedly about the borrowing of money, it seems clear that Frank wants 'this trifiling sum' immediately, not 'to-morrow evening'. E's 'till' seems to be the correct amendment of A's probable eyeskip.

197.2 shewn] The absence of the predictable verb 'was' here is quite in character with the clipped indirect discourse which summarizes Frank's appeal. Although the first edition may have dropped a word here, A's text probably reflects Brown's manuscript.

TEXTUAL NOTES

212.29 knew] A simple emendation would reconcile the tenses, of course, but Brown's inattention to such consistency elsewhere makes emendation here a doubtful proposition.

223.14 thy] A's 'the' is surely a possible reading, but the tone of Mrs. Fielder's letter calls for the correction of the simple error.

225.37-38 disposed of] Although A's lack of 'of' might be an egregious example of Brown's ellipsis, it is really of a different character; the fact that 'or' follows immediately suggests eyeskip on the part of A's compositor, rather than substitution (as for E's 'disputed').

248.2 thee] There is really no way to construe A's 'the' as what Brown wrote: Colden is making no claim to a knowledge of "the good," but simply to an intimate knowledge of Jane's character.

255.35 leader] Jane's precise meaning here is not quite clear, but she seems to mean something vaguely like the general direction her letter has taken her, as her remarks earlier in the letter and her reference to 'this scribble' later in this sentence suggest. That she has in mind something as precise as 'leader' in the sense of "leading article" seems doubtful.

273.27 specious] Although 'spacious' would also fit the context, A's reading is quite clearly correct, as speciousness is frequently alluded to in the novel (cf., e.g., 302.23, 306.30, 307.28-29). Brown seems to use the word in its original and neutral sense as simply beautiful, rather than with its later and narrower connotation of beautiful but false.

279.2 was wont] This does not appear to be an ellipsis on Brown's part, but an eyeskip on the compositor's.

281.32 the dear Lord] A's phrase 'the dear knows' appears to be defective, not an ellipsis meant to suggest a colloquialism or to refer to 'my good woman' (281.29-30). A's slightly larger than ordinary space after 'dear' may have been intended to represent the lacuna, or it might have resulted from the removal of a typeset word after proofreading, but in any case we seem to have here an example of omission that is easily amended. Cf. 174.38-175.1

283.38-284.1 not mind] A's reading seems at first blush to create the wrong meaning, but what the poor dear is saying is that she would not take pains 'to be hard with such a one', and Brown seems to have gotten the colloquial expression right.

312.13-14 scruple the less] Although a bit awkward, and indeed capable of being misread to mean "will not the less be thought to scruple,'' A's construction is probably Brown's, who means simply to create a parallel with 'will commit the greater crime'.

339.11 laid] The confusion here is probably Brown's, rather than that of A's compositor, particularly since a similar reading appears in "Carwin," 259.34. Fox's *Instructions for Right Spelling* (p. 89) confuses 'lain' and 'laid' and Brown may have suffered from a similar confusion, although Johnson (sig. b4), Lowth (p. 76), and Webster's *Dictionary* (pp. 173, 176) argue for a usage more consistent with the modern.

367.1 M. Colden] It is tempting to change this to 'H.' to stand for Colden's first name. But to do so requires an identical change at the end of the letter to represent Miss Jessup's name (see 372.16) and additionally the hypothesis of two identical errors within a short space. Probably 'M.' is meant in these two cases simply to stand for 'Mr.' and 'Miss', respectively.

403.14 go this] Although A may have omitted the predictable 'on', this is probably an example of Brown's ellipsis, if not a colloquialism.

414.2 Oct. 2] A's 'Dec. 12' must be an error, as the ensuing letter of October 5 is a response to this one and as Colden's narration of his meeting with Cartwright suggests an earlier departure for Europe than mid-December (see 426.21–427.6). The October 5 date of Jane's letter combines with the date of Mary Montford's to indicate that Cartwright wrote Jane almost immediately upon having seen her letter (413.17–20). But his letter apparently did not precede Mary's, so we are left with a date of either October 1st or 2nd; the likelihood of graphic error supports the latter, though the choice between them is largely a matter of conjecture. Cf. 216.2

424.35–36 Tekehatsin] This appears to be another one of Brown's phonetic spellings, in this case somewhat anglicized perhaps. The Japanese name, which might be rendered ''wooden bridge'' with the suffix for ''dear'' (''-san''), accords with the reference to *'Jedho'* (425.9), a legitimate spelling for Yedo, or Tokyo. Since the compositor probably copied this name letter for letter, there is no call to emend the spelling here or later (425.8), though the still later transposition (425.23) requires changing.

List of Emendations
JANE TALBOT

NOTE: This list contains all instances of alterations of the copy-text, except for those already noted in the Textual Essay (p. 491, n.19) and the silent changes specified in the note on the Bicentennial texts in Volume I of this edition. (See the Textual Essay for the treatment of the copy-text's press-variants.) Each note gives the reading of the Bicentennial text before the bracket, followed by a siglum identifying its earliest source (either the English edition, or the present editors) and then by the variant reading(s) in the copy-text and in the English edition. This information is provided for both substantives and accidentals; for a complete history of substantive variants among the editions examined, see the Historical List. An asterisk (*) before the lemma indicates that the Textual Notes discuss the emendation. A wavy dash (~) represents the same word appearing before the bracket and occurs only in the recording of variants in punctuation or other accidentals associated with that word, when the word itself is not the variant being noted; the inferior caret (∧) shows that punctuation is absent. Three dots (. . .) mean that the note omits one or more words in a series, and a vertical stroke (|) marks the break between lines. Successive square brackets ([ ]) mark a space where a letter or letters within a word do not print. "B" following the bracket identifies readings adopted for the first time in the Bicentennial Edition (that is, readings not appearing in the editions examined). Preceding the list are the sigla which identify the editions examined and cited in the list.

CHARLES BROCKDEN BROWN

A: the copy-text: *Jane Talbot, A Novel.* (Philadelphia, 1801), the first edition
E: *Jane Talbot. A Novel.* (London, 1804), without authority

153.19	with] E; wish A
154.5	recall∧] E; ~ , A
155.24	mother's] E; mothers A
156.14	lived] E; livid A
*161.4	enter] E; inter A
161.11	deal.] B; ~ , A; ~ ; E
161.37	conference] E; coference A
162.11	support.] E; ~ , A
162.38	His] B; his A-E
163.14-15	∧I ... interference.∧] B; "~ ... ~ ." A-E
163.15	me.] B; ~ , A; ~ ; E
163.15	interference] E; interferance A
163.19	deference] E; deferance A
163.21-26	∧Dear ... him.∧] B; "~ ... ~ ." A-E
*165.4	lenient] E; lenitent A
*165.7	income is] B; income A-E
165.10	Risberg's] E; Risbergs' A
166.8	adventurous] E; adventrous A
166.27	him,] E; ~ . A
166.28	about∧] E; ~ , A
167.24	from] E; frem A
168.4	interference] E; interferance A
168.37	me,] B; ~ ; A-E
169.11	truth!] B; ~ ? A-E
172.15	permanent] E; permament A
172.23	precarious] E; precarius A
174.36-7	success] E; sucess A
176.7	plausible!] B; ~ ? A; ~ . E
178.32	it.] E; ~ ∧ A
179.4	pr'ythee] B; pr'y thee A; pri'thee E
180.12	eyes.] B; ~ , A; ~ ; E
181.11	freak] E; friek A
183.3-4	∧dear ... you.∧] B; "~ ... ~ ." A-E
183.8	∧dear ... me,∧] B; "~ ... ~ ," A-E
183.16	∧a ... old?∧] B; "~ ... ~ ?" A-E
*186.14	sum till] E; sum A
190.8	how∧] E; ~ , A
193.5	calumny,] B; ~ ∧ A; ~ . E
195.·8	day's] E; days A

514

200.21	others.] E; ∼ ∧ A
200.34	age:] B; age. A; age— E
204.2	8] B; 9 A-E
204.26	preference] E; preferance A
204.29	Were] E; Where A
205.8	rheumatism] E; rhumatism A
207.2	10] B; 11 A-E
207.4	I!] E; ∼? A
208.11	heightened] E; heigtened A
209.7	European] E; Eropean A
210.17	Henry.] B; ∼, A-E
216.2	17] B; 15 A-E
*223.14	thy] B; the A-E
223.21	every] E; evey A
*225.37–38	disposed of] B; disposed A; disputed E
228.2	fascinating] E; facinating A
228.37	Godwin's] E; Godwins A
229.14	whether] E; whither A
229.14	destroying] E; desroying A
229.31	sacrifice] E; sacrafice A
230.14	unavoidable] E; unavoiable A
231.21	profligate!] B; ∼? A-E
231.22	letter.] E; ∼ ∧ A
234.20	Hal] E; Hall A
234.25–235.5	∧I ... grace.∧] B; "∼ ... ∼." A-E
236.4	power.] E; ∼, A
240.15	Jane.] E; ∼, A
241.16	prejudice?] B; ∼. A-E
241.19	thee?] B; ∼. A-E
245.26	atrocious] E; attrocious A
245.34	ill-fated] E; illfated A
*248.2	thee] E; the A
252.13	or] E; []r A
255.21	myself!] E; ∼? A
258.7	callousness] E; calousness A
263.1	Mrs.] E; ∼ ∧ A
271.30	thou'lt] B; thoul't A-E
275.13	are!] E; ∼? A
*279.2	was wont] E; wont A
280.18	Hennings] B; Hennings' A-E
281.3	wishes,] E; ∼. A
*281.32	dear Lord] B; dear A-E
284.3	it.∧] E; ∼." A
285.8	thou?] E; ∼ ∧ A
286.12	motion.] B; ∼? A-E

286.25   Do'st] B; Dos't A-E
287.1   One] B; one A-E
287.2   *thyself!*] B; ~? A-E
288.11   ∧A ... waiting.∧] B; "~ ... ~." A-E
291.10   obvious,] E; ~. A
291.11   It] E; it A
299.13-14   porringers] B; poringers A-E
299.17   delectable] E; dilectable A
299.29   repairing] E; reparing A
303.20   ∧Ah ... Jane!∧] B; "~ ... ~!" A-E
303.20   ∧rash] B; "~ A-E
303.28   ∧Subtle wretch!∧] B; "~ ~!" A-E
303.28-304.2 ∧accomplished ... faculties.∧] B; "~ ... ~." A-E
307.19   knowledge] E; knowldege A
308.8   delicately] E; delcately A
309.3   truly] E; Truly A
310.32   drawest!] B; ~? A-E ˙
318.17   acquiescence] E; acquiescene A
318.37   principles;] B; ~∧ A; ~— E
323.10   parent's] E; parents A
326.2   friend's] E; friends A
330.17   revisit] E; re visit A
331.1   sacrifice?] E; ~! A
335.30   unsought] E; unsaught A
336.1   neighbour's] E; neighbours A
338.11   mother's] E; mothers A
339.28   Jessup's] E; Jessups A
343.35   effect] E; affect A
344.4   unappeasable] E; unappeasible A
344.28   mother!] E; ~? A
344.32   bestow,] E; ~. A
344.32   would] E; Would A
346.22   trepidation] E; trepedation A
347.21   or] B; on A-E
348.19   innocent.∧] B; ~." A-E
348.33-349.6 ∧Tell ... perfidy?∧] B; "~ ... ~?" A-E
349.10-31   ∧Yes ... indiscreet.∧] B; "~ ... ~." A-E
350.6   transaction?] E; ~! A
351.25-34   ∧There ... child.∧] B; "~ ... ~." A-E
352.4   these.] E; ~∧ A
352.23   deliberately.] E; ~∧ A
357.26   ∧Dearest] B; "~ A-E
358.22   shadow,] B; ~; A-E
358.23   needed!] B; ~? A; ~.— E
361.9-10   excrutiating] B; excruiating A-E

362.12-363.2 ∧You ... affections.∧] B; " ~ ... ~." A-E
368.24   husband's] E; husbands A
374.20   unceremoniously] E; uncerimoniously A
374.35   Fielder] E; Feilder A
375.24   moment's] E; moments A
376.1   madam.] E; ~, A
376.1   received,] E; ~. A
381.2   December] E; Decembnr A
390.11   mortified,] E; ~. A
390.11   they] E; They A
390.19   How] E; how A
390.20   doubts!] E; ~? A
391.1-2   TO THE SAME | Philadelphia] E; Philadelphia A
394.11   mother's] E; mothers A
397.2   becoming] E; be coming A
403.28-36   ∧what ... me.∧] B; " ~ ... ~." A-E
403.31   On] E; on A
406.5-19   ∧Thou ... past∧] B; " ~ ... ~." A-E
412.9   across] E; acros A
*414.2   Oct. 2] B; Dec. 12 A-E
416.25   T.] E; ~∧ A
417.2   New-York,] E; ~. A
418.33   imperfect] E; imper-|[ ]ct A
421.5   absence] E; absense A
423.22   day's] E; days A
425.23   Tekehatsin] E; Tekehastin A
430.36   adoration] E; adoratian A

517

End-of-Line Word-Division

Jane Talbot

NOTE: The two following lists provide information on the word-division of divisible compounds that are hyphenated at the ends of lines in the copy-text or in the Bicentennial Edition. List A contains, in the form of the established text, such compounds which are hyphenated and divided at the break between lines in the copy-text. A double dagger (‡) precedes the notation if the word happens to be similarly hyphenated in the Bicentennial Edition (see List B for more information on such words). List B contains all examples of possible compounds hyphenated at the break between lines in this edition which are meant to be hyphenated in the established text; the absence of such compounds hyphenated in this edition shows that they are meant to be unhyphenated in the established text. A double dagger (‡) precedes the notation if the word happens to be similarly hyphenated in the copy-text (see List A of this appendix on such words). Both lists omit words that have hyphens between capitalized elements (e.g., North-|American) and those that are clearly mere compositorial syllabication (including syllabication of compound words falling elsewhere than at the point of word-division).

A. *Word-Division in the Copy-Text*

153.23	nothing	165.3	without
154.6	recalling	169.30	Somebody
156.14	childhood	170.34	elsewhere
161.25	downcast	176.16	useless

178.35	baby-things	302.20	without
183.15	careless	302.21	useless
188.16	Nevertheless	302.36	without
196.26	overwhelm	305.23	ourselves
198.25	Farewell	307.25	myself
200.14	Frenchman	312.25	midnight
205.35	however	315.35	cannot
219.4	shortsighted	317.24	herself
231.5	within	325.4	Northwest
232.35	without	328.15	herself
234.23	*nobody*	332.10	myself
237.8	well-wisher	332.14	mankind
239.10	nevertheless	336.17	shop-keeper
244.37	mankind	338.38	afterwards
246.4	re-echoed	339.32	myself
246.10	henceforth	340.38	cannot
253.4	themselves	352.30	however
263.29	yourself	353.12	midnight
264.2	recall	355.4	without
‡268.4–5	self-denial	360.18	withstand
271.3	betake	360.31	somewhat
273.14	Whatever	362.9	withhold
273.19	household	367.5	cannot
274.6	nothing	374.17	without
274.11	Three-fourths	379.3	nothing
284.31	herself	379.14	myself
285.9	wholesome	382.16	herself
285.32	somewhat	383.5	sometimes
288.6	without	386.22	somewhat
288.8	somebody	391.19	everlasting
292.17	forthwith	422.25	overturned
292.19	Newport	425.20	likewise
294.10	something	429.26	Nothing

B. *Word-Division in the Bicentennial Edition*

163.35–36	To-morrow	‡268.4–5	self-denial
192.3–4	cotton-weaving	286.34–35	shame-confessing
205.10–11	forty-five	339.18–19	New-York
208.1–2	self-upbraidings	392.22–23	self-sacrifices
221.16–17	all-seeing		

519

HISTORICAL LIST OF
SUBSTANTIVE VARIANTS

JANE TALBOT

NOTE: This appendix lists only substantive variants from the Bicentennial text in the editions examined. Accidentals—including accidentals variants of the readings—are not, as such, listed; thus the report that two texts agree in having one of two readings (e.g., 'apprized' as against 'surprised') implies only that they both have the same word (e.g., perhaps in the spellings *apprized* and *apprised*) and not necessarily the identical form. Also not listed are variants in letter headings (see the Textual Essay) and such features as are silently emended throughout the Bicentennial Edition (see ''The Bicentennial Texts: A Note,'' p. xxiii, in Volume I of this series). By the same token, as the purpose of this report is to list the genuinely substantive variants which constitute the evidence for decisions on genealogy and authority (''The Bicentennial Texts,'' p. xxiv), this list does not report as variants impossible readings created by pulled types or other merely typographical faults. Nor does it record a second time examples of foul-case, mechanical transposition of letters, or other similar ''literals'' which appear in the copy-text and are correct in another edition. Reports on such readings appear in the Textual Essay (when they involve press-variation) or in the List of Emendations. Throughout the list, each note gives the reading of the Bicentennial text before the bracket, followed by the variant reading(s) and then the sigla for the editions having that variant. A wavy dash ($\sim$) represents the same word appearing before the bracket and occurs when variation involves punctuation associated with that word but the word itself is not the variant being noted; the inferior caret ($\wedge$) shows that punctuation is absent. In each entry, the editions are cited only when

520

they vary substantively from the reading of the Bicentennial text given in the lemma (i.e., omission of sigla implies agreement). The following sigla identify the editions cited.

A: the copy-text: *Jane Talbot, A Novel* (Philadelphia, 1801), the first edition

E: *Jane Talbot. A Novel.* (London, 1804), without authority

151.23	not to] not E	213.31	of my] in my E
153.19	with] wish A	216.2	17] 15 A-E
153.20	and] and I E	219.19	that] that moment E
155.24	mother's] mothers A	219.20	power] power so E
156.14	lived] livid A	220.10	it] them E
156.20	the] that the E	221.22	hope] hopes E
159.7–8	plodding] plotting E	223.14	thy] the A-E
161.4	enter] inter A	225.28	not] not so E
165.4	lenient] lenitent A	225.37–38	disposed of] disposed
165.7	income is] income A-E		A; disputed E
165.10	Risberg's] Risbergs' A	228.37	Godwin's] Godwins A
170.35	interest] interests E	229.14	whether] whither A
174.36	be so] be E	232.4	as] as your E
177.7–8	farther] further E	236.28	to attempt to] to E
186.14	sum till] sum A	241.10	as of] as E
186.26	What,] ~ ∧ E	241.14	thou] you E
190.2	cheek] cheeks E	241.14	hast] have E
190.12	my] all my E	244.11–12	hitherto] merely E
191.5–6	found that] found E	244.12	merely] hitherto E
191.34	from] from the E	244.15–16	and I] I E
192.17	am really] really am E	247.17	simple truth] truth E
195.18	day's] days A	248.2	thee] the A
200.30	goal] gaol E	248.20	owe to] owe E
201.6	know] I know E	249.11	their] the E
202.12	purpose] purposes E	250.27	not] no E
203.14–15	a reason] reason E	254.1–2	TO HENRY
204.2	8] 9 A-E		COLDEN|
204.29	Were] Where A		Philadelphia]
206.12	has] is E		Philadelphia E
207.2	10] 11 A-E	254.18	occupies] occupy E
210.32	wash-woman]	254.29	with] at E
	washer-woman E	260.22	forbear to] forbear the
210.33	imputation]		E
	temptation E	261.16	than] and E

521

263.21	involved her] involved E	336.1	neighbour's] neighbours A
265.14	never] not E	338.11	mother's] mothers A
265.31	then] than E	339.28	Jessup's] Jessups A
266.14	humiliation] humiliations E	343.35	effect] affect A
268.16	would never] never would E	346.36	objections] objection E
		347.21	or] on A-E
268.18	run] ran E	349.20	she] she so E
269.3	Colden] Henry Colden E	349.28	by] to E
		352.3	few] a few E
272.1	THE SAME] Mrs. Talbot E	352.15	an] a E
		352.22	too] two E
279.2	was wont] wont A	354.9	to] of E
280.18	Hennings] Hennings' A-E	354.28	to that] that E
		354.34	pleasure] pleasures E
281.32	dear Lord] dear A-E	356.17	perform] to perform E
282.21	her,] ~ ∧ E	356.18	on] upon E
286.9	is] it E	356.20	present.] present. Colden E
290.2	introduced,] ~ ∧ E	357.19	agreeably] agreeable E
292.3	come] to come E	357.24	and to] to E
293.18	was] were E	358.22	flit] flirt E
294.8	a] the E	360.9	be] me E
295.9	that my] my E	365.9	repenting] repenting of E
295.26	who] why E		
309.11	crush] grasp E	368.24	husband's] husbands A
311.12	the] my E		
314.13	an] a E	370.17	I] I had E
314.15	life] her life E	370.35	my old] my E
316.18	wish] wished E	375.24	moment's] moments A
316.19	J.] Jane E	377.5	at] of E
323.10	parent's] parents A	378.37	here.] here. H. Colden E
326.2	friend's] friends A		
326.3	had lingered] lingered E	380.4	H.] M. E
		381.4	letter] letters E
326.18	vain] in vain E	383.33	[omitted]] H. Colden E
329.8–9	now beg leave] beg leave now E		
		384.29	takes] take E
333.8	washwomen] washer-woman E	394.12	mother's] mothers A
		397.2	becoming] be coming A
334.28	Hannah Secker's] Secker's E		
		405.21	affections] affection E
335.22	and the] and E	406.2	ever be] be ever E
335.31	to] too E	408.25	it to] to E
		414.2	Oct. 2] Dec. 12 A-E

421.9	—in] in— E	428.28	moments] moment's E
423.22	day's] days A	431.5	a reason] reason E
426.26–27	information] consolation E		

RECORD OF COLLATIONS
AND COPIES CONSULTED

Clara Howard; In A Series of Letters.
(Philadelphia, 1801), first edition: A
Copies unique to the following libraries have been examined and
collated (by different operators) at least twice by machine: NBu,
NNSL; also NN—*KL.

Philip Stanley; or, The Enthusiasm of Love. A Novel.
(London, 1807): E
This rare edition has been collated (by different operators) against
A four times by hand; the collation was based on the Kimball
copy at NNHi.

Jane Talbot, A Novel.
(Philadelphia, 1801), first edition: A
Copies unique to the following libraries have been examined and
collated (by different operators) at least twice by machine: ICN,
OU; two other copies were so collated once: DLC, MB.

Jane Talbot. A Novel
(London, 1804): E
This rare edition has been collated (by different operators) against
A four times by hand; the collation was based on the Sadleir-
Black copy at ViU.

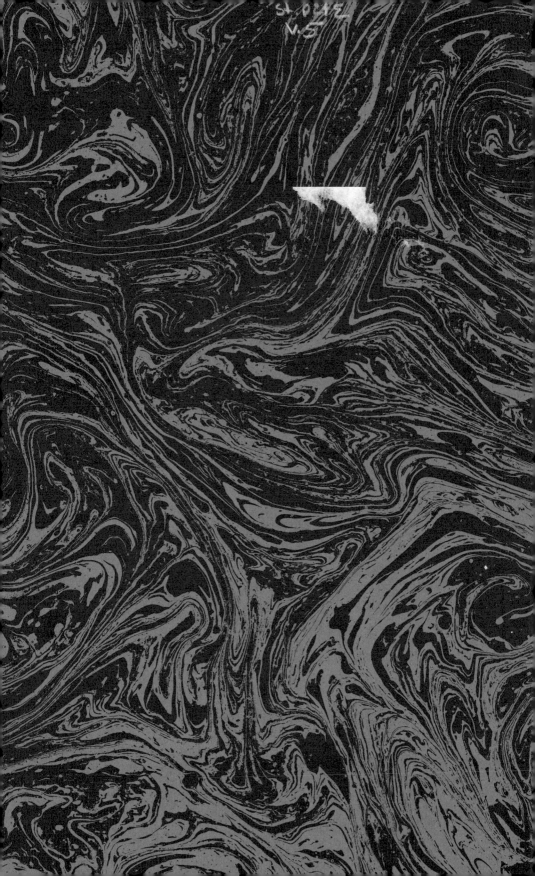